CHARISMATIC CHAOS

D0973801

CHARISMATIC
CHAOS

John F. MacArthur, Jr.

ZONDERVAN®

CHARISMATIC CHAOS
Copyright © 1992 by John F. MacArthur, Jr.

Requests for information should be addressed to:
Zondervan, 3900 Sparks Dr. SE, Grand Rapids, Michigan 49546

International Trade Paper Edition ISBN 0-310-57570-2

Library of Congress Cataloging-in-Publication Data

MacArthur, John, 1939-
    Charismatic chaos / John F. MacArthur, Jr.
      p.   cm.
    Includes bibliographical references and index.
    ISBN 0-310-57572-9
    1. Pentecostalism—Controversial literature. I. Title.
BR1644.M269 1992
234'.13—dc20   91-37794
                                         CIP

All Scripture quotations in this book, except those noted otherwise, are from the New American Standard Bible. Copyright © 1960, 1962, 1963, 1968, 1971, 1972, 1973, 1975, and 1977 by The Lockman Foundation, and are used by permission.

Material from Charisma magazine excerpted with permission from Charisma magazine 600 Rinehart Road, Lake Mary, Florida 32746. Copyright © 1991, Strang Communications Company.

All rights reserved. No part of this publication may be reproduced, stored in a retrieval system, or transmitted in any form or by any means—electronic, mechanical, photocopy, recording, or any other—except for brief quotations in printed reviews, without the prior permission of the publisher.

Edited by Leonard G. Goss

Printed in the United States of America

23 /BVGM/ 30 29 28 27

To my friend Jacob Kusmich Dukhonchenko—defender of the truth, man of God, faithful pastor, leader of the church in the Ukraine, who endured a half century of communist oppression, a decade of imprisonment, all the while standing firm for our Christ—and who may now be fighting his greatest battle in a free USSR to preserve sound doctrine and the purity of the church. The wall of communism kept the church confined but also protected it from heresy. Now the wall is down and he is set for the challenge of building a new wall of protection against the influx of false teaching.

Be filled with the Spirit, speaking to one another in psalms and hymns and spiritual songs, singing and making melody with your heart to the Lord; always giving thanks for all things in the name of our Lord Jesus Christ to God, even the Father; and be subject to one another in the fear of Christ.

Ephesians 5:18–21

The fruit of the Spirit is love, joy, peace, patience, kindness, goodness, faithfulness, gentleness, self-control; against such things there is no law.

Galatians 5:22–23

Contents

Acknowledgments

I am grateful to the staff at "Grace to You" for their support throughout this project. Dave Enos did much of the preliminary editing, suggesting the chapter divisions and copy editing the 1978 version of *The Charismatics* to prepare it for this edition. Allacin Morimizu read the manuscript in several stages and prepared the indexes. Phil Johnson spent several hours editing the final manuscript, blending the new material with the 1978 version.

I also want to thank Len Goss, Stan Gundry, and the editorial staff at Zondervan for their extreme patience and flexibility on deadlines. In the end, they assumed the challenging task of preparing this book for publication in only a few weeks' time.

Introduction

When the original edition of this book[1] was first published in 1978, I was unprepared for the widespread and varied responses it would generate. I was, of course, braced for some reaction. Practically every book ever published on the subject has evoked disagreement. The issues involved seem to stir people's deepest emotions. Perhaps it is not possible to take any position on the charismatic movement without upsetting *someone*.

Curiously, however, the expressions of *agreement* I received were what most caught me off guard. Literally thousands of people have written to thank me for attempting a biblical and doctrinal treatment of the charismatic question. Among them were countless pastors and other Christian leaders who were grateful for a biblical treatment of an issue they were afraid to touch. I was astonished to realize how many Christians think that the charismatic movement lacks biblical support, but are reluctant to say so aloud.

In the years since the book's initial release, I've gained a new understanding of why there is so much confusion about the charismatic gifts in the church. A powerful intimidation factor works against those who want to deal with the issues biblically. To critique charismatic doctrine or practice is commonly viewed as inherently divisive or unkind. Charismatic extremists can promote almost any idea they fancy on Christian television and radio, but those who attempt to examine such teaching critically, in light of Scripture, are muzzled.

I speak from firsthand knowledge. Our radio broadcast, "Grace to You," is heard daily on a network of more than two hundred stations. Nearly all of them share our doctrinal perspective and commitment to the absolute sufficiency of Scripture. Yet most of them balk at broadcasting series that deal with 1 Corinthians 12–14, Acts 2, Romans 12, or other passages that confront charismatic imbalances. Many espouse ministry philosophies explicitly prohibiting any teaching that might challenge the beliefs of their charismatic constituents.

One network executive wrote this to me: "Please reconsider your policy of dealing with the charismatic movement and other controversial topics on your radio broadcasts. Though we share your convictions on these issues, many of our listeners do not. These people are dear brothers and sisters in Christ, and we do not feel it is helpful to the cause of Christ to attack what they believe. We are committed to keeping peace among brethren and unity in the body of Christ. Thank you for being sensitive to these concerns."

That kind of thinking sacrifices truth for the sake of a superficial peace. Such an attitude pervades the contemporary church. In effect it has given charismatic extremists the freedom to propound fantastic views while imposing a code of silence on those who object. Those who do speak out inevitably are branded divisive, strident, or unloving.[2] The legacy of such a position is *not* unity and peace, but confusion and turmoil. Proof of that can be seen in the hundreds of churches, missions boards, schools, and other Christian organizations that have allowed charismatic influence to seep in and go unanswered. They ultimately must either sacrifice their non-charismatic position altogether or suffer the devastating effects of a split.

And so charismatic chaos spreads because the voices promulgating eccentric teachings drown out the feeble whispers of those who challenge Christians to examine the Scriptures to see whether these things are so (cf. Acts 17:11).

It is *not* unkind to analyze doctrinal differences in the light of Scripture. It is not necessarily factious to voice disagreement with someone else's teaching. In fact, we have a moral imperative to examine what is proclaimed in Jesus' name, and to expose and condemn false teaching and unbiblical behavior. The apostle Paul felt it necessary at times to rebuke people by name in epistles meant to be read publicly (Phil. 4:2–3; 1 Tim. 1:20; 2 Tim. 2:17). John, the apostle of love, wrote a scorching condemnation of Diotrephes, a church leader who was ignoring the apostles' teaching (3 John 9–10). As his second epistle shows, John's view of real love was inextricably bound with truth. In fact, love apart from truth is nothing more than hypocritical sentimentality. That sentimentality is running rampant in evangelicalism today.

The biblical challenge is not to avoid truth that is controversial, but to speak the truth in love (Eph. 4:15). I have endeavored to do that. I have many charismatic friends who sincerely love the Lord, and though we disagree on some fundamental issues, I count them as precious brethren. It pains me that some of them believe my criticism of the charismatic movement is hurtful. But Scripture is the rule against which we must measure all teaching, and my only desire is to turn the light of God's Word on a movement that has taken the contemporary church by storm.

Although some reviewers imagined ridicule or sarcasm in some of my comments in this book's first edition, I assure you my design was not then and is not now to mock. A number of charismatics felt I misrepresented their movement by choosing the most grotesque and outlandish illustrations of charismatic silliness. The first edition, for example, included this:

> Recently on television I saw a lady tell about how her flat tire was healed. Not long ago I got a letter from somebody in Florida who had heard a wonderful testimony by a woman

who had taught her dog to praise the Lord in an unknown bark.

Granted, both of these examples are bizarre. Perhaps it is unfair to characterize the Charismatic movement with illustrations like these. I wish that were true. I wish those two examples were rare, but they are not. And the reason they are not is that in the Charismatic ranks no experience has to stand the test of Scripture.[3]

I believe the past decade or so has confirmed that appraisal. Preposterous examples of charismatic recklessness grow more and more numerous as the fringes of the movement spin out of control. If anything, radical charismatics have increased in influence and visibility, with no end in sight.

Item: Jan Crouch, who with her husband, Paul, leads Trinity Broadcasting Network (TBN), told a live audience in Costa Rica that "God answered the prayers of two little twelve-year-old girls to raise our pet Chicken from the dead!"[4] Mrs. Crouch has recounted that same tale on TBN broadcasts that air coast to coast and around the world.

Item: Charisma magazine, the movement's flagship periodical, runs full-page ads and two-page spreads for Rapha Ranch, a charismatic healing center that treats cancer patients with "Subliminal Scripture Tapes." "You Don't Have to Die" is the title of a videotape you can buy from Rapha for $29.95. A blurb describes the ranch as a place where cancer patients can "come and be healed." The ad heralds the healing powers of Rapha's subliminal "Word Therapy" tapes:

Healing, salvation, deliverance reports by the hundreds! In our Word Therapy Tape series, the Word of God is read aloud so that it is not only heard by your conscious ear but penetrates your subconscious mind as tens of thousands of subliminal scriptures are heard in just one hour. The reading of the Word is accompanied by beautifully anointed music that creates an atmosphere of faith with which [sic] you may receive from God. Every day astounding reports come into our ministry acknowledging healing, changed lives, salvation and miracles as their minds are renewed to the Word of God.[5]

Item: Evangelist Robert Tilton mailed a "miracle coin" (actually a worthless token) to hundreds of thousands of people, promising a "financial miracle" to those who follow his instructions and send him "a check for the best possible gift that you can give!" An ominous reminder, "Only you and God know what your best gift is," was printed in handwritten script at the bottom of the flyer. A secular newspaper calls "Success-N-Life," Tilton's television program, "The fastest growing empire in Christian television."[6]

Item: A close associate of mine attended a charismatic businessmen's meeting in Chicago where a Catholic priest testified that Mary had given him the gift of tongues while he was saying the rosary. Then the charismatic pastor leading the meeting got up and said, "What an amazing testimony! Aren't you glad God isn't bound by our ideas of what's doctrinally acceptable? Some people would try to dismiss this brother's testimony just because it doesn't jibe with their doctrinal system. But how you get filled with the Holy Ghost doesn't matter, as long as you know you've got the baptism!" The audience, numbering in the hundreds, broke into wild, sustained applause. No one seemed to question whether that man's testimony, so obviously in conflict with biblical truth, might be spurious.

That incident epitomizes the charismatic tendency to test doctrine by experience instead of the reverse. The most visible and influential charismatic celebrities barely even give lip service to biblical authority. Charismatic leaders concerned with biblical truth—and I'm convinced there are many—should be the loudest voices crying out against these abuses by those they identify with. Unfortunately, few have. Those who *have* denounced error have rendered an invaluable service,[7] but they have been viciously attacked by other charismatics. In effect, they have been shouted down by people who quote 1 Chronicles 16:22 ("Do not touch My anointed ones, and do My prophets no harm")[8] as if that verse silenced all doctrinal discussion—and as if we were supposed to assume that everyone who *claims* an anointing from God is speaking the truth. As a result, charismatics as a whole have failed to expose and reject the most obvious unbiblical and even anti-Christian influences in the movement.

Instead, most charismatics fall back on the all-too-easy defense that virtually every critique of their movement is unfair and unkind. Non-charismatics, intimidated by that accusation, are effectively silenced. Is it any wonder so many people in the pews are confused?

As non-charismatics grow more and more fearful of questioning charismatic claims, charismatic influence spreads virtually unchecked. Through modern communication media—especially television—the charismatic movement has swept the globe and is expanding at a rapid pace. Charismatic teaching has now reached beyond the United States and Europe to the remotest parts of South America, the Orient, Africa, India, the South Pacific, Eastern Europe, and the Soviet Union—nearly everywhere the name of Christ is known. Literally millions worldwide believe God is giving people signs, wonders, and miracles on a scale unprecedented since biblical times. These claims continue to multiply at a rate so prolific that they can hardly be cataloged, let alone verified.

Fantastic encounters with Jesus Christ and the Holy Spirit are reported as commonplace. Personal messages from God are supposedly routine. Healings of all kinds are claimed. It is not unusual to hear striking testimonies about how God, in response to faith, has corrected spinal injuries, lengthened legs, and removed cancerous tissue. Seemingly omniscient Christian talk-show hosts discern that miracles and healings of various types are happening during their broadcasts. They urge viewers to call in and "claim" healings.

Some of the miracles seem almost bizarre: one-dollar bills turn into twenties, washing machines and other appliances are "healed," empty fuel tanks fill up supernaturally, and demons are exorcised from vending machines. People are "slain" (knocked flat) in the Spirit; others claim to have been to heaven and back. Several even claim to have been to hell and back!

Amazing experiences seem to be the order of the day as God, in an apparent hyperkinetic outburst, puts on a supernatural performance rivaled only by the six days of Creation and the Egyptian plagues!

Some even go so far as to deny the effectiveness of evangelism without such miracles. They argue that the gospel message is weakened or nullified if not accompanied by great signs and wonders. They believe some people *need* to see signs and wonders before they will believe. That notion has spawned a whole new movement, grandiosely tagged "the Third Wave of the Holy Spirit," also known as the Signs and Wonders movement (see chapter 6). This recent variation on the old charismatic theme is attracting many evangelicals and others from mainline denominations who were formerly wary of Pentecostal and charismatic influences.

Charismatics and non-charismatics alike desperately need to take a clear look at the biblical issues at stake.

Some argue that those outside the charismatic movement have no right to evaluate it. Charismatic Baptist Howard Ervin wrote:

> The attempt to interpret the Charismatic manifestations of the Holy Spirit without a Charismatic experience is as fatuous as the application of the "Christian ethic" apart from a regenerate dynamic. . . . Understanding of spiritual truth is predicated on spiritual experience. The Holy Spirit does not reveal spiritual secrets to the uncommitted, and quite frankly, the Pentecostal experience is one of total commitment.[9]

J. Rodman Williams reflects the same view:

> Against the background of sharing in the Holy Spirit and
> the consequent gifts of the Holy Spirit, information,
> instruction, and teaching concerning them becomes rele-
> vant. A fundamental thesis may here be set forth: *Any vital
> information concerning the gifts of the Spirit, the pneumatic
> charismata, presupposes a participation in them.* Without such a
> participation, whatever is said about the gifts may only
> result in confusion and error.[10]

Experience, however, is not the test of biblical truth;
rather, biblical truth stands in final judgment on experience.
That more than any other single issue is what this book is
about. It is also the key point to be made in answering the
claims of the charismatic movement. Frederick Dale Bruner
has stated it clearly: "The test of anything calling itself
Christian is not its significance or its success or its power,
though these make the test more imperative. The test is
truth."[11]

It has become practically impossible to define the
charismatic movement in doctrinal terms. In the years since
the first edition of this book appeared, the movement has
broadened dramatically. In effect, it is accomplishing what
the ecumenical movement has been ineffectual in achieving—an external unity that is generally indifferent to any
doctrinal concerns. The charismatic movement has opened its
doors to practically every denomination and sect that embraces some manifestation of the charismatic gifts.

Also known as "neo-pentecostalism," the charismatic
movement is heir to Pentecostalism, which began around
1900. Until 1959 Pentecostalism was contained in denominations such as Assemblies of God, Foursquare Gospel
Churches, and the United Pentecostal Church. But in 1959
Pentecostalism spilled over denominational lines when Dennis Bennett, rector at St. Mark's Episcopal Church in Van
Nuys, California, experienced what he believes was the

baptism of the Holy Spirit and the gift of tongues.[12] After that, as John Sherrill put it, the walls came tumbling down.[13] The charismatic movement spread to the Episcopalian, Methodist, Presbyterian, Baptist, and Lutheran denominations. From there it has swollen to encompass Catholics, theological liberals, and even several pseudo-Christian fringe groups.

It is therefore difficult if not impossible to define the charismatic movement by some doctrine or teaching that all members of the movement advocate. Rather, what charismatics hold in common is an *experience*—which they believe is the baptism of the Holy Spirit. Most charismatics define Spirit baptism as a post-salvation, second-blessing experience that adds something vital to what Christians receive at salvation. Spirit baptism, they believe, is usually accompanied by the evidence of speaking in tongues, or perhaps other charismatic gifts. Such an experience is considered essential for any Christian who wants to know the fullness of divine and miraculous power in his or her life.

If you are a Christian who has not experienced some supernatural charismatic phenomenon, perhaps you are feeling left out. You may be wondering whether God views you as a second-class Christian. If he honestly cares about you, why haven't you had a special miracle or manifested some spectacular gift? Why haven't you ascended to a higher level of spiritual bliss? Why haven't you heard Jesus speak to you in an audible voice? Why hasn't he appeared physically to you? Do our charismatic friends really have a closer walk with God, a deeper sense of the Holy Spirit's power, a fuller experience of praise, a stronger motivation to witness, and a greater devotion to the Lord Jesus Christ? Could it be that we noncharismatics just do not measure up?

As I talk with Christians who have not had charismatic experiences, I often sense feelings of apprehension, dismay, and even alarm. It seems that the charismatic movement has separated the Christian community into the spiritual "haves" and "have-nots."

Although I have devoted my life to preaching sound biblical doctrine that centers on the work of the Holy Spirit in every believer's life, I must confess that by the charismatics' definition, I am among the "have-nots." And I admit to having asked myself, *Are all those people who are supposedly having all those amazing experiences for real? Could it be that I'm missing out on what God is doing? Are my charismatic brothers and sisters reaching a higher level in their walk with Christ?*

I suspect a similar anxiety reaches right into the ranks of the charismatics themselves. Could it be that some who attend these fellowships are tempted to exaggerate, dramatize, or even fabricate some miracle or special experience because of their need to keep up with the brethren who appear to be more spiritual?

I am certain that is the case. I see it happening daily on Christian television, as charismatic claims become more and more fantastic. Occasionally, some chicanery is exposed. One nationally-known television evangelist was discovered using a hidden receiver in his ear through which his wife was broadcasting information supposedly being revealed to him by the Holy Spirit. Another lesser-known faith healer was discredited when it was shown that he planted healthy people in his audience with crutches and wheel chairs to receive supposed "healings."

Worse, appalling sex scandals among ostensibly "Spirit-filled" charismatic leaders have become epidemic in the past decade. These have been catastrophic to the cause of Christ worldwide, undermining the corporate testimony of all Christians in the eyes of the world. Such scandals are the legacy of a movement that touts spectacular signs and wonders as the only irrefutable verification of true spirituality. To authenticate their claims, some charismatic leaders resort to fraudulent or simulated "miracles." Spirituality is viewed as an external issue; godly character is nonessential to those who believe supernatural phenomena validate their claims to speak for God. Such a system breeds duplicity, trickery, charlatanism, and fraud.

Please understand that I am not saying all charismatic leaders are corrupt. I know that is not the case. Many of my charismatic friends are genuinely committed to Christ and are examples of true godliness. Nor am I saying that their movement is the only one that produces hypocrites. But I am convinced that the fundamental teachings of the charismatic movement create an extreme emphasis on external evidences and thereby encourage bogus claims, false prophets, and other forms of spiritual humbug.[14] Where such things flourish, there is bound to be scandal—and the charismatic movement in the past decade has certainly been marked by more than the normal amount of scandal.

I thank God for the many charismatics who sincerely love our Lord and want to obey Him. Paul wrote, "In every way, whether in pretense or in truth, Christ is proclaimed. . . . In this I rejoice, yes, and I will rejoice" (Phil. 1:18). I rejoice that in many charismatic ministries, Christ is preached, and people are won to Him. But that should not exempt the charismatic movement or charismatic teachings from careful biblical scrutiny. Scripture admonishes us to "examine everything carefully; hold fast to that which is good" (1 Thess. 5:21).

At first glance this book may appear to be somewhat academic because of the number of endnotes. Please don't be put off by that. I trust you won't find the book dry or abstract. But I felt it was important wherever possible to present the charismatics' teachings in their own words, and to be precise in documenting all quotations.

In nearly every instance, I have quoted from *published* material rather than personal conversations, letters, and other informal sources. Only in chapter 12, which deals with the Word Faith movement, have I drawn heavily from teaching tapes and television broadcasts. In doing so I recognize that some whose tapes I have cited may claim I have not quoted them at their best. But having researched the movement, I assure you that what I have quoted *does* accurately—and, to the best of my ability, fairly—represent what the Word Faith preachers are actually teaching.

My prayer is that God will use this book to remind all Christians, charismatic and non-charismatic, of our responsibility to examine everything carefully in light of Scripture, to let God's Word be the test of our experience and not vice versa, and to hold fast *only* to that which is good.

— 1 —

Is Experience a Valid Test of Truth?

A woman wrote to me, seething. "You resort to Greek translations and fancy words to explain away what the Holy Spirit is doing in the church today. Let me give you a piece of advice that might just save you from the wrath of almighty God: *put away your Bible* and your *books* and *stop studying.* Ask the Holy Ghost to come upon you and give you the gift of tongues. You have no right to question something you have never experienced."

A radio listener, after hearing my teaching on 1 Corinthians 12–14, wrote, "You people, and especially ministers of the Gospel, who claim that speaking in tongues is not for today are, in my opinion and all those who do, grieving the Holy Spirit and missing a blessing from God. To me—it is as ridiculous as if an unsaved person tried to persuade you that you absolutely cannot be sure that you will enter heaven. . . . If you haven't experienced it—you can NOT tell someone who HAS that it doesn't exist."

Both of those letters reflect the tendency to gauge truth by personal experience rather than Scripture. There is little doubt that most charismatics, if they are honest with themselves, would have to acknowledge that personal experience—and not Scripture—is the foundation of their belief system. As much as some charismatics might want to give the Bible a high place of authority in their lives, the Scriptures too often rank second to experience in defining what they believe. As one writer puts it, "Experiences with God provide a basis for their faith."[1]

That is exactly backward from how it should be. Our faith should provide a basis for our experiences. A true spiritual experience will be the result of the quickening of truth in the Christian's mind—it does not occur in a mystical vacuum.

Non-charismatics are often accused of opposing emotion and experience. Let me state as clearly as possible that I believe both emotion and experience are essential outgrowths of genuine faith. Many of my own spiritual experiences have been profound, overwhelming, life-changing events. Please do not think for a moment that I would defend a cold, inanimate religion based on a barren creed or some empty ritual.

In an authentic spiritual experience, emotion, feelings, and the senses often become intense, transcending the normal. These may include strong feelings of remorse over sin, a mighty sense of trust that surpasses the pain of a traumatic situation, an overpowering peace in the midst of trouble, the overwhelming sense of joy related to confidence and hope in God, intense sorrow over the lost, the exhilarating praise in understanding the glory of God, or a heightened zeal for ministry. Spiritual experience by definition is an internal awareness that involves strong emotion in response to the truth of God's Word, amplified by the Holy Spirit and applied by him to us personally.

Charismatics err because they tend to build their teachings on experience, rather than understanding that authentic experience happens in *response* to truth. Too many charismatic experiences are utterly detached from—and in some cases contrary to—the revealed plan and operation of God indicated in Scripture. When these become the basis for one's beliefs, there is almost no limit to the kinds of false teaching that can emerge.

We see this in many charismatic books and television programs. Visions, dreams, prophecies, "words of knowledge," private messages from God, and other personal experiences determine what is taught. Scripture—when used at all—is typically employed for proof texts or twisted to fit some novel opinion. Often passages of Scripture are so mauled that they are made to mean the antithesis of what they actually teach. Kenneth Copeland, for example, claims he gets many of his novel interpretations by direct revelation. Teaching on the account of the rich young ruler in Mark 10, Copeland was clearly seeking support for his own notion that God wants his people materially wealthy. Jesus' words in verse 21 seem clear enough: "One thing you lack: go and sell all you possess, and give it to the poor, and you shall have treasure in heaven; and come, follow Me." Copeland, however, claims God revealed to him that this verse actually promises earthly, monetary dividends. Copeland says, "This was the biggest financial deal that young man had ever been offered, but he walked away from it because he didn't know God's system of finance."[2]

Sometimes a self-styled prophet develops a whole new set of teachings based wholly on experience—or pure whimsy. Dr. Percy Collett, for example, a charismatic medical missionary, devised an extensive series of detailed messages on heaven, all drawn from his extraordinary personal experience. Collett claims that in 1982 he was transported to heaven for five-and-a-half days. He says he saw Jesus, who is supervising the building of mansions there, and he claims he was able to speak face-to-face with the Holy Spirit.

A newsletter rhapsodically detailing Dr. Collett's journey to heaven began, incredibly, with these words:

While Christianity abounds with accounts of glimpses of the "other" dimension from those who've had "out of body" experiences, Dr. Collett's is unlike these. Obviously he was "caught up in the third heaven" even as Paul was. The difference being, Paul was not allowed to utter the things he saw and heard, while Dr. Collett, almost 2000 years later, was commanded to do so.[3]

Collett offers videotapes detailing his sojourn in heaven, and his accounts are peculiar indeed: "Everything God created upon the earth is in heaven—horses, cats, dogs. Everything that He created upon earth is in heaven—in the way of animals, only these are perfect. For example, the dogs do not bark. . . . You don't need plumbing. You can go to the Banqueting House and eat all you want and no plumbing is needed."[4]

Collett describes "the Pity Department, the place [where] the souls of aborted babies go, and also some severely retarded babies, and it is here that these little souls are trained for a period of time before they go before the Throne of God."[5] He claims he also saw the Record Room, "an immense area where all the 'idle' words spoken by Christians are being retained until after Christians give an account of them, or are judged, at which time these will be emptied into the Sea of Forgetfulness."[6] Collett describes a "Garment Room," where angels are sewing our robes, mansions under construction, a "Holy Ghost elevator," and many other astonishing sights.[7] He adds one macabre detail: "When I was traveling back to earth, I saw two girls, one brunette and one a red-head. We stopped to talk to them—their soul bodies—on the way back. We asked them what had happened to them. They indicated they had gotten killed in a car accident on a California highway. Their bodies (physical) were in a funeral home. They said their mother was weeping over them, so would I please tell her."[8]

Dr. Collett feels he has conclusive proof to verify that

tale: "About a year later I went to that area where the mother lived, and was giving this testimony. A mother jumped up in the congregation and said, that's a description of my daughters. I told her she shouldn't fret, that her daughters are in that wonderful place. She said that she would never cry again."[9]

After Dr. Collett lectured on heaven to his third straight standing-room-only audience in Montgomery, Alabama, he offered to take questions from the floor. The first question was something I admit I had never contemplated: "I am a cowboy. Are there rodeos in heaven?"

But Dr. Collett was ready with an answer. "There are horses in heaven, beautiful horses. These are all praising God. There is no foolishness in heaven. I am not saying that a rodeo is foolish, but there is no Will Rogers style acting up there."[10]

Charismatics have no way to judge or stop testimonies like that because in their system *experience validates itself*. Instead of checking such experiences against the Bible for validity, typically charismatics try to get the Bible to fit the experience or, failing that, they just ignore the Bible. How many charismatics, taught to believe that God is giving them or their leaders fresh revelation, simply put their Bibles permanently on the shelf?[11]

It All Starts with the Baptism of the Spirit

One reason experience is the touchstone for charismatics is their undue emphasis on the baptism of the Holy Spirit as a post-salvation experience (see chapter 8). Charismatics generally believe that after someone becomes a Christian, he or she must seek diligently for the baptism of the Spirit. Those who get this baptism also experience various phenomena, such as speaking in tongues, feelings of euphoria, visions, and emotional outbursts of various kinds. Those who have not experienced the baptism and its accompanying phenomena are not considered Spirit-filled; that is, they are immature, carnal, disobedient, or otherwise incomplete Christians.

That kind of teaching opens the floodgates for believing that vital Christianity is one sensational experience after another. It sets in motion a contest to see who can have the most vivid or spectacular experience. And, of course, those with the most awesome testimonies are held in highest esteem spiritually. Incredible claims are made, and they almost always go unchallenged.

For example, the following advertisement ran in several 1977 issues of *The National Courier*, a charismatic newspaper:

> A genuine photograph of our Lord. Yes, I believe I have one recorded on film. In mid-summer I awoke at 3:30 A.M. to a strong voice-thought impression, "Go and photograph my sunrise." Beside the river I set up my camera and waited for the sun. In that predawn, I felt so very close to God, perfect peace. On one negative is the perfect shape of a figure, arms raised in blessing as reflected in the water exactly opposite to every other shadow. I believe God gave me an image of Himself to share.

That item is signed "Dudley Danielson, photographer." Dudley gave his address and also stated that 8 x 10 copies in perfect natural color are available for $9.95 prepaid (larger sizes available on request). He indicated that the portrait would bless whoever receives it.

It does not seem to bother Dudley that the Bible says, "No man has seen God at any time" (John 1:18). Nor does it appear to matter to him that the Bible says, "God is spirit" (John 4:24) and "no man can see Me and live!" (Ex. 33:20). Evidently what Scripture says is not as weighty an issue to him as "a voice-thought impression" and a feeling of peace and closeness to God. Dudley believes he has a photograph of God, and for $9.95 he is willing to share it.

The Ultimate Trip

Percy Collett is not the only charismatic who believes he has seen heaven and returned to tell about it. During the summer of 1976, on "The 700 Club," Marvin Ford told about his experience of dying, going to heaven, and then returning. Ford claims the necktie he was wearing that day retained the aroma of heaven. He kept it so that whenever he wants to refresh his memory of that experience, he simply sniffs the tie.

One up-and-coming young charismatic leader is Roberts Liardon. He says he took an extensive tour of heaven as an eight-year-old, supposedly with Jesus as his personal tour guide. He recalls,

> Many people have asked me what Jesus looks like. He's 5 feet 11 to 6 feet tall, and He's got sandy brown hair. It's not too long and it's not too short. He is a perfect man. Whatever you picture as a perfect man, that's what Jesus is. He's perfect in everything—the way He looks, talks—everything. That's the way I remember Him.
>
>   . . . .
>
> We walked a little farther—and *this is the most important part of my story.* I saw three storage houses 500 to 600 yards from the Throne Room of God. They're very long and very wide. . . . We walked into the first. As Jesus shut the front door behind us, I looked around the interior in shock!
>
> On one side of the building were arms, fingers, and other exterior parts of the body. Legs hung from the wall, but the scene looked natural, not weird. On the other side of the building were shelves filled with neat little packages of eyes: green ones, brown ones, blue ones, etc.
>
> *This building contained all the parts of the human body that people on earth need,* but they haven't realized these blessings are waiting for them in heaven. . . . And they're for saints and sinners alike.
>
> Jesus said to me, "*These are the unclaimed blessings. This building should not be full. It should be emptied every single day.*

> *You should come in here with faith and get the needed parts for*
> *you and the people you'll come in contact with that day.* "[12]

Liardon describes many other incredible sights he witnessed in
heaven: the River of Life; a stadium full of people who he says
were the "cloud of witnesses" spoken of in Hebrews 12:1; and
a medicine cabinet with pill bottles labeled "PEACE" and
"OVERDOSE OF THE HOLY GHOST."[13]

Here is Liardon's extraordinary description of what took
place at the River of Life:

> Jesus and I visited a branch of the River of Life. This branch
> was knee-deep and crystal clear. We took off our shoes and
> got in. And do you know the first thing Jesus did to me? He
> dunked me! I got back up and splashed Him, and we had a
> water fight. We splashed each other and laughed. . . .
>
> That meant something to me for the King of Glory, the
> Son of God, to take time out for little 8-year-old Roberts
> and dunk him in the River of Life!
>
> When I get back to heaven, I'm going to put up a
> historical marker on that spot. It's going to say, "This is the
> spot where Jesus Christ became not only my Lord and
> Saviour, but my friend." Yes, He became my Friend. Now
> we walk and talk together. When I hear a good joke, I can
> run to Jesus and listen to Him laugh at it. And when He gets
> a good one, He tells me.[14]

Liardon also claims that while in heaven, he was
ordained to the ministry by Jesus himself. "We walked a while
and were quiet. Then Jesus turned around and took both my
hands in one of His. He placed His other hand on top of my
head and said, 'Roberts, I am calling you to a great work. You
will have to run like no one else, preach like no one else, be
different from everyone else. . . . Go, go, go like no one else
has gone. Go and do as I have done.' "[15]

Liardon's trip to heaven supposedly happened in 1973.
He says he didn't tell anyone about it for eight years, though.
He says Jesus appeared twice more to him. The second time,

Liardon says was too sacred; he can't talk about it. The third time, however, was a bit more mundane:

> The third time I saw Jesus was when I was about 11 years old. Jesus walked in through the front door of my home while I was watching "Laverne & Shirley" on television. He came over and sat down beside me on the couch, kind of glanced at the TV, and everything in this natural world clicked off. I couldn't hear the telephone or television set—all I heard was Jesus and all I saw was His glory.
>
> He looked at me and said, "Roberts, I want you to study the lives of my generals in my great army throughout time. Know them like the back of your hand. Know why they were a success. Know why they failed. And you'll want nothing in that area."
>
> He got up, walked back out through the door, the TV clicked back on, and I resumed watching "Laverne & Shirley."[16]

Liardon has now reached adulthood and is prominently featured on the charismatic speaking circuit. Large advertisements for his ministry appear nearly every month in *Charisma* magazine. Nonetheless, Liardon's accounts of heaven are bizarre to the point of silliness. It is inconceivable that someone who saw Jesus face-to-face could go back to watching an episode of "Laverne & Shirley."

Most Christians will immediately write off Liardon's stories as fanciful and absurd if not outright blasphemous. But in the charismatic world such tales are not lightly dismissed. Multitudes listen to accounts like that and long for similar experiences. As a result, excursions to heaven and back have become almost chic—the "ultimate experience" for those who want something unusual—and many say they have made the trip.[17] On April 11, 1977, a charismatic television network based in the Los Angeles area carried an interview with Dr. Richard Eby, who claimed to have died, gone to heaven, and come back again.

According to Dr. Eby, he fell off a balcony, struck his head, and was supposedly dead. He reports that he experienced "paradise." His formerly weak eyes needed no glasses; now he could see for a hundred miles. His body took on a wonderful quality—he could move anywhere at will; he was visible yet transparent.

Dr. Eby said that he found some flowers, broke them off, and noticed they had no water in their stems because "Jesus is the living water."

The aroma of heaven was especially overwhelming with the sweet savor of sacrifices, Dr. Eby said. He said the human brain has twelve cranial nerves and then added that those twelve nerves represent the twelve tribes of Israel. Further, he explained that the primary nerve in God's cranium is the sense of smell. Eby said he learned that the whole purpose of sacrifices was to send a sweet aroma up to heaven to satisfy God's main cranial nerve.

As Dr. Eby went on, the talk-show host kept saying, "Marvelous! Wonderful! Oh, this is meaty."

Meaty? Nothing in Scripture indicates Dr. Eby or anyone else in heaven gets a transparent body that floats in midair. The resurrected Christ did not have such a body. In fact, according to Scripture believers will not have bodies in heaven until after the resurrection of our bodies at the return of Christ.[18]

As for the sweet aroma of sacrifices, Dr. Eby betrayed a complete misunderstanding of the biblical sacrificial system. The major feature of sacrifices was the death of the animal, not the smell of the burning flesh (cf. Heb. 9:22).

In regard to the twelve cranial nerves representing the twelve tribes of Israel, it would be just about as reasonable to say that because you have two eyes, they represent the two witnesses of Revelation 11. I checked with a medical doctor on the twelve cranial nerves and found that actually there are twelve pairs, which make twenty-four. Perhaps, then, it would be better to say they correspond to the twenty-four elders mentioned in Revelation 4!

Such careless adulteration of God's Word should grieve the heart of every Christian. But was Dr. Eby challenged during the broadcast on biblical grounds? No! He was told that his information was "meaty"—meaning substantially deeper truth of some kind. Deeper than what? Scripture? Certainly not. Dr. Eby had an experience, and because the charismatic approach is to let the experience validate itself, no one questioned his claims. Dr. Eby's ideas were heard in thousands, if not millions, of homes as representative of "the wonderful things God is doing today."

Two Basic Approaches to Christianity

Granted, Percy Collett, Dudley Danielson, Marvin Ford, Roberts Liardon, Aline Baxley, and Richard Eby are all outrageous examples, but they are *not* uncommon. Their testimonies are representative of what one hears all too often among our charismatic brethren. As experience after experience is reported in the press and on religious radio and television, a subtle but sinister pattern is developing. Instead of responding to a proper interpretation of God's Word, Christianity is collecting fantastic and preposterous experiences. The Bible is either mangled to fit those experiences or simply ignored altogether. The result is pseudo-Christian mysticism.

Mysticism is a system of belief that attempts to perceive spiritual reality apart from objective, verifiable facts. It seeks truth through feelings, intuition, and other internal senses. Objective data is usually discounted, so mysticism derives its authority from within. Spontaneous feeling becomes more significant than objective fact. Intuition outweighs reason. An internal awareness supersedes external reality. As we shall see shortly, mysticism is at the heart of modern existentialism, humanism, and even many forms of paganism—most notably Hinduism and its close ally, New Age philosophy.

Irrational mysticism is also at the heart of the charismatic experience. It has subverted biblical authority within the movement and replaced it with a new standard: personal experience. And make no mistake—the practical effect of charismatic teaching is to set one's experience on a higher plane than a proper understanding of Scripture. That is precisely why the woman I quoted at the outset of this chapter advised, *"Put away your Bible* and your *books* and *stop studying."* Her private "revelations" and personal feelings mean more to her than the eternal truth of God's inspired Word.

There are only two basic approaches to biblical truth. One is the historical, objective approach, which emphasizes God's action toward men and women as taught in Scripture. The other is the personal, subjective approach, which emphasizes the human experience of God. How should we build our theology? Should we go to the Bible—or to the experiences of thousands of people? If we go to the people, we will have as many views as there are individuals. And that is exactly what is happening throughout the charismatic movement today.

Objective, historic theology is Reformation theology. It is historical evangelicalism. It is historical orthodoxy. We begin with Scripture. Our thoughts, ideas, or experiences are validated or invalidated on the basis of how they compare with the Word.

On the other hand, the subjective view is the methodology of historic Roman Catholicism. Intuition, experience, and mysticism have always played a central role in Catholic theology.[19] The subjective view has also been at the heart of liberalism and neoorthodoxy (see my comments on this in chapter 3). Truth in those systems is determined by intuition and feeling. Truth is what happens to you.

The subjective view is also the methodology of historic

Pentecostalism, which began at the turn of the century. Charismatic historians trace the movement's modern origins to a small Bible college in Topeka, Kansas, run by Charles Fox Parham. Parham was a member of the Holiness movement, which teaches that entire sanctification—a spiritual state amounting to sinless perfection in this life—is obtainable by Christians through a "second blessing," a dramatic post-salvation experience of transformation. Parham was an enthusiastic advocate of faith healing. After an experience in which he says he was healed of "heart disease in its worst form," he discarded all his medicine, canceled his insurance, and refused every form of medical treatment for the rest of his life.[20]

Parham founded the College of Bethel in 1900, and the school went out of business a year later. But what happened at Bethel on January 1, 1901 was to have ramifications throughout Christianity for the rest of the twentieth century.

Bethel College's approach to Bible classes was peculiar, employing "the 'chain reference' idea, which was popular at the time. Major topics would be studied by following consecutive readings on the subject as they appeared in Scripture."[21] In other words, topics were studied by using a concordance to trace key terms. Never was a book of the Bible studied as a unit. Thus, no verse would ever have been considered as part of a larger context. Whole doctrines were studied by examining an index of Scriptures, strung together and isolated from their proper contexts. Sound hermeneutics and careful exegesis were therefore impossible. But Parham had a clear agenda: "When the school opened, the students began by studying the major tenets of the Holiness movement."[22]

Charismatic historian Vinson Synan records,

For some years, Parham had been especially interested in the differing views on the question of receiving the baptism in the Holy Spirit. By the 1890s, most Holiness people were equating the baptism in the Holy Spirit with the reception of the sanctification experience. The fire of the Holy Ghost, it was taught, cleansed the heart from inbred sin and empowered the recipient to witness to others and live an overcoming life. Yet from the days of John Wesley, who had first emphasized the second blessing, there had been no commonly accepted evidence of receiving such a blessing.

In presenting this problem to the students, Parham explained that Holiness people differed in their teachings on evidences of receiving the baptism. "Some," he noted for example, "claim blessings or demonstrations, such as shouting or jumping." At the same time, Parham had for years been impressed with the possibility that glossolalia [speaking in tongues] might be restored in the form of foreign language facility granted to missionaries who would no longer have to take the time for normal language studies.[23]

Parham's interest in these issues determined his classroom curriculum. He enlisted his students and their concordances to help him solve the riddle.

During the last days of December 1900 . . . Parham gave his students an unusual homework assignment. Since he was scheduled to preach in a church in Kansas City over the weekend, he instructed his class:

"The gifts are in the Holy Spirit, and with the baptism of the Holy Spirit, the gifts, as well as the graces, should be manifested. Now, students, while I am gone, see if there is not some evidence given of the baptism so there may be no doubt on the subject."

When he returned on December 30, Parham found that the verdict was unanimous. The report was "while there were different things [that] occurred when the Pentecostal blessing fell . . . the indisputable proof on each occasion was, that they spake with other tongues." In the light of this conclusion, the entire school agreed to seek for a restoration of Pentecostal power with the evidence of speaking in tongues.[24]

And so it was that the first person of modern times who sought the baptism of the Holy Spirit with evidence of tongues and supposedly received it was a student of Parham's. New Year's Day 1901 was chosen as the day the student body would seek the baptism. Early in the morning on the first day of this century, a small group of students in Topeka commenced their prayer meeting. For hours nothing unusual happened. Then—

> Later during the day, a 30-year-old student by the name of Agnes Ozman came to Parham and requested the laying on of hands so that she might receive the Holy Spirit with the apostolic sign of speaking in tongues. She testified: "As he prayed and layed [sic] hands [upon] my head, I began to speak in tongues, glorifying God. I talked several languages, for it was manifested when a [dialect] was spoken. Glory to God!"[25]

After that, others reported receiving the baptism. Most testified that they could not help speaking in tongues; when they tried to speak English, other languages would come out. All who were there believed they were uttering recognizable earthly languages. In fact, Agnes Ozman claimed she tried to record her experience on paper, but found herself writing in Chinese, although she had never studied the language.[26]

Were these experiences thoroughly examined in the total context of Scripture? Was careful exegesis of the biblical passages about tongues used to interpret any of the students' experiences? Was any consideration given to the fact that these might have been demonic phenomena? On the contrary, Synan records, "This experience confirmed Parham's testimony and teaching that tongues were indeed the initial evidence of the baptism in the Holy Spirit."[27] No further Bible study on the matter was deemed necessary. And thus Pentecostalism was born.

Sixty years later, the charismatic movement was launched with the experience of Dennis Bennett, rector at St.

Mark's Episcopal Church in Van Nuys, California.[28] Both the Pentecostal and charismatic movements of today are based on experience, emotion, phenomena, and feelings. As Frederick Dale Bruner has written:

> Pentecostalism wishes, in brief, to be understood as experiential Christianity, with its experience culminating in the baptism of the believer in the Holy Spirit. . . .
>
> It is important to notice that it is not the *doctrine*, it is the *experience* of the Holy Spirit which Pentecostals repeatedly assert that they wish to stress.[29]

Was Peter a Charismatic?

It is interesting to speculate on whether Peter would be a charismatic if he were living today. After all, he spoke in tongues, healed people, and prophesied. He also had some fantastic experiences. He was, for example, an eyewitness to Christ's transfiguration, which he recalled in 2 Peter 1:16–18.

That experience left him stunned and muttering something about building three tabernacles on the spot—one for Jesus, one for Elijah, and one for Moses—because it was good for all of them to have been there (Matt. 17:1–4). He was so overwhelmed by the experience that, as usual, he said the wrong thing.

Still, it was an incredible experience. Jesus pulled aside the veil of his flesh and revealed his glory, the glory he will manifest at his second coming. Peter, James, and John all got a glimpse of that second-coming glory. That was the "majesty" Peter talked about in 2 Peter 1:16.

But did Peter build his theology on experiences like that? Read on in 2 Peter 1:19–21:

> We have the prophetic word made more sure, to which you do well to pay attention as to a lamp shining in a dark place, until the day dawns and the morning star arises in your

hearts. But know this first of all, that no prophecy of Scripture is a matter of one's own interpretation, for no prophecy was ever made by an act of human will, but men moved by the Holy Spirit spoke from God.

A better rendering of the Greek text in verse 19 would be: "We have the even surer prophetic Word." The King James Version is especially clear: "We have also a more sure word of prophecy." More sure than what? Than experience. Peter was saying, in effect, that although the transfiguration was a wonderful experience, Scripture was a more trustworthy verification of his faith. Though he had seen no less than the Lord in his glory, Peter was certain that the Word of God recorded by holy men moved by the Holy Spirit was a more solid foundation for what he believed.

Peter's point was precisely the issue that so many charismatics fail to understand: *all experience must be tested by the more sure word of Scripture.* When we seek the truth about Christian life and doctrine, we cannot rely solely on someone's experience. We must base all our teaching on the revealed Word of God. The major flaw in the charismatic movement is that it calls on experience rather than the Word of God to dictate what is true.

Most charismatics believe progress in the Christian life is having something more, something better, some electrifying experience. An ex-charismatic in my congregation told me why he had grown frustrated in the charismatic movement: "You spend the rest of your life trying to find another experience." The Christian life becomes a pilgrimage from experience to experience, and if each one is not more spectacular than its predecessor, many people begin to wonder if something is wrong.

I heard one man on television say that as he was driving in his car, suddenly he looked and there was Jesus sitting right next to him in physical form. The man said, "It was wonderful. I drove along and just talked with Jesus, and He was sitting right beside me." And then he said, "If you have enough faith, you can talk with Jesus—he will appear to you!"

The Bible says about Christ, *"Though you have not seen Him, you love Him, and though you do not see Him now,* but believe in Him, you greatly rejoice with joy inexpressible and full of glory" (1 Peter 1:8, emphasis added). Obviously Peter did not believe it was possible for his first-century readers to see Jesus, nor did he feel such visions were necessary for faith, hope, love, or joy. But more than one charismatic has concluded that you can experience the physical presence of Jesus Christ if you have enough faith.

It is not just uninformed or immature charismatics who imagine such experiences. A few years ago I had lunch with a very well-known and influential charismatic pastor. He is also a widely read author and a national media figure. This man told me, "When I'm shaving in the mornings, Jesus comes into the bathroom and puts his arm around me, and we talk." He paused to measure my reaction, and then he said, "John, do you believe that?"

"No, I don't," I replied. "But what troubles me most is I think *you* believe it."

"Why?" he asked. "Why is it so hard for you to accept the idea that Jesus visits me in a personal way every morning?"

Does he keep shaving? I wondered. *Or does he collapse in utter fear and trembling in the presence of the holy, glorified Lord?* When Isaiah saw the Lord on His throne, he said, "Woe is me, for I am ruined!" (Isa. 6:5). Peter saw Him and fell on his face and said, "Depart from me, for I am a sinful man, O Lord!" (Luke 5:8). I don't believe anyone could keep shaving in the presence of the risen Lord!

The reason so many charismatics seem drawn to supposed visions of Jesus and tours of heaven is that they make the same error advanced by Henry Frost in his book *Miraculous Healing:*

It may confidently be anticipated, as the present apostasy increases, that Christ will manifest His deity and lordship in increasing measure through miracle-signs, including healings. We are not to say, therefore, that the word is sufficient.[30]

Not to say that Scripture is sufficient? God *Himself* says His Word is sufficient! (Ps. 19:7–14; 2 Tim. 3:15–17). Who is Henry Frost to claim that it is not?

Although most charismatics would not state their position as clearly as Frost, the truth is, at the core of their belief system is a denial of Scripture's sufficiency. They are guilty of the same kind of thinking as Philip in John 14:6–9. Jesus was with His disciples at the Last Supper and declared: "I am the way, and the truth, and the life; no one comes to the Father, but through Me. If you had known Me, you would have known My Father also; from now on you know Him, and have seen Him."

Jesus was saying something wonderful here. He had been telling his disciples that he was going to leave them. Now he consoled them by telling them not to worry; they had seen the Father in him, and they knew God through him. Everything was going to be okay.

But Philip was not satisfied. It wasn't enough for him to hear the words of Jesus. Apparently Philip had to have something more—a vision, miracle, sign, or something— because he said, "Lord, show us the Father, and it is enough for us" (John 14:8). In other words, "What you have done and said is not sufficient. Your promise is not enough. Prove it. Do one more thing for us—give us a vision of God; give us an experience."

Jesus was evidently grieved by Philip's request. He said sadly, "Have I been so long with you, and yet you have not come to know Me, Philip? He who has seen Me has seen the Father" (14:9). He was saying, "Philip, I'm not enough? You

have seen me, you have seen my works, you have heard my
words, and you still have to have more?"

What Philip said was an insult to God the Son. Sadly,
many people today are repeating the insult by seeking
something more. They are insulting God, who has sufficiently
revealed himself in Scripture.

No one should seek experiences in preference to the
Word of God. All experience must be qualified and validated
by the Scriptures. Any other kind of experience is a false one.
Remember the two lonely, broken-hearted disciples who
walked with the Lord on the road to Emmaus (Luke 24:13–
35)? As they went along, Jesus opened the Scriptures to them.
Beginning at Moses and the Prophets, he taught them the
things concerning himself. Later they said, "Were not our
hearts burning within us while He was speaking to us on the
road, while He was explaining the Scriptures to us?" (24:32).

Those disciples had an experience; their hearts burned
within them. But first the Lord opened the Scriptures to
them. Again and again the Scriptures talk about joy, blessing,
and experience (see Ps. 34:8; Mal. 3:10). But all such
experiences, if they have any soundness at all, conform wholly
to the plan God has revealed in Scripure, and come from
studying and obeying the Word of God, not by looking for
something beyond what God has revealed to us.

Did Paul Rely on Experience?

How about the apostle Paul? Like Peter, he was unusually
gifted. And he certainly had amazing experiences, such as his
sudden conversion on the road to Damascus. He saw a light so
bright it blinded him. He heard a voice. He was knocked to
the ground. He was instantly changed from a killer of
Christians into a slave of the Lord Jesus Christ (Acts 9).

But when Paul went on to preach and teach, did he make
his experience the heart of his message? Acts 17:2–3 states
clearly that Paul's appeal was from the Scriptures: "*According*

to Paul's custom, he went to them, and for three Sabbaths *reasoned with them from the Scriptures,* explaining and giving evidence that the Christ had to suffer and rise again from the dead, and saying, 'This Jesus whom I am proclaiming to you is the Christ'" (emphasis added).

Even after God took Paul to the third heaven (2 Cor. 12:1–4), he was not allowed to speak the things he saw. Obviously God did not feel that that experience gave any more impact or credibility to the gospel message than simply preaching its truth. That contrasts sharply with the approach of the contemporary Signs and Wonders movement (see chapter 6).

Right up to the end of his life, Paul kept reasoning out of God's Word. While he was a prisoner in Rome, "they came to him at his lodging in large numbers; and he was explaining to them by solemnly testifying about the kingdom of God, and trying to persuade them concerning Jesus, from both the Law of Moses and from the Prophets, from morning until evening" (Acts 28:23).

Regrettably, many charismatics do not follow in Paul's footsteps. Instead, they travel a road frequented by liberal and neoorthodox theologians, existentialists, humanists, and pagans. Unquestionably, most charismatics do it unwittingly. They would say, "We believe the Bible. We don't want to contradict the Scriptures; we want to uphold God's Word." But charismatics are caught in a terrible tension as they try to hold onto the Bible while at the same time making experience their real authority. The views of charismatic leaders and theologians show their struggle.

For example, Charles Farah tried to harmonize the tension between the Word of God and experience. Noting that there are two Greek words translated "word," he devised the theory that *logos* is the objective, historic Word and *rhema* is the personal, subjective Word. The problem with that idea is that neither the Greek meaning nor the New Testament usage make any such distinction. The *logos,* said Farah, becomes *rhema* when it speaks to you. The *logos* is forensic while the *rhema* is experiential. Farah wrote, "The *logos* doesn't always become the *rhema*, God's Word to you."[31] In other words, the *logos* becomes *rhema* when it speaks to you. The historic, objective *logos*, in Farah's system, has no transforming impact until it becomes *rhema*—your own personal word from God.

That sounds dangerously close to what neoorthodox theologians have been saying for years: that the Bible becomes God's Word only when it speaks to you. But God's Word is God's Word whether someone experiences its power or not. The Bible doesn't depend on the experience of its readers to become the inspired Word of God. Paul said the Bible was able in and of itself to give Timothy "the wisdom that leads to salvation" (2 Tim. 3:15). It did not need Timothy's experience to validate it.

Paul went on to say, "All scripture is inspired by God and profitable for teaching, for reproof, for correction, for training in righteousness" (3:16). Paul taught that the Scriptures *are already inspired* and profitable, not that they will become inspired or profitable, depending on the experience of the reader. Clearly, God's Word *is* altogether sufficient.

Keen but Clueless

For the most part, charismatics appear sincere. Many of them are like the Jews of whom Paul said, "I bear them witness that they have a zeal for God, but not in accordance with knowledge" (Rom. 10:2). Charismatics have zeal without knowledge; they have enthusiasm without enlightenment. As John Stott put it, "They are keen [eager] but clueless."[32]

When charismatics make experience the major criterion for truth, they reveal what Stott calls "avowed anti-intellectualism."[33] They are approaching the Christian life without their minds, without thinking, without using their understanding. Indeed, some charismatics claim God deliberately gives people unintelligible utterances in order to bypass, and thus humble, the proud human intellect.

But the notion that God wants to supplant or mortify our rational minds is patently unbiblical. God has said, "Come now, and let us reason together" (Isa. 1:18). And, "Be transformed by the renewing of your *mind*" (Rom. 12:2, emphasis added). God wants our minds renewed, not discarded. He has revealed himself in rational revelation that demands the use of reason and an understanding of historic, objective truth (cf. Eph. 3:18; 4:23; Phil. 4:8; Col. 3:10).

The whole of God's revelation is geared to perception, thought, knowledge, and understanding. That is Paul's main point in 1 Corinthians 14—a key passage on the charismatic question. He concludes that great chapter with these words: "In the church I desire to speak five words with my mind, that I may instruct others also, rather than ten thousand words in a tongue" (14:19). We who know Christ are to use our minds to apprehend God's truth. We are not instructed to rely on our emotions or try to extrapolate truth out of our experiences. As James Orr wrote, "A religion divorced from earnest and lofty thought has always, down the whole history of the Church, tended to become weak, jejune, and unwholesome."[34] Certainly, we *respond* to truth with our emotions, but we must first apprehend it with our understanding and submit to it with our will.

The Origins of Experiential Theology

Mysticism, or the idea that theology can grow out of personal experience, is not original with the charismatics. Several other key influences, all anti-Christian, have contributed to building the concept of experiential theology: existentialism, humanism, and paganism.

Existentialism is a philosophical view that says life is meaningless and absurd.[35] It teaches that we should be free to do our own thing just as long as we are willing to take responsibility for our choices. Existentialists are concerned primarily about how they feel. They answer to no authority; in fact, they become their own authority. Existentialists believe truth is whatever grabs you, whatever turns you on.

The experiential theology that we see in the charismatic movement is not the legacy of historic Christianity. It is the legacy of existentialism. Clark Pinnock has written the following:

> Experience alone is too flimsy a base on which to rest the Christian system. The mere fact that a psychological event has taken place in one's brain cannot establish the truthfulness of the gospel. . . . Religious sensation by itself can only prove itself. . . . However unique an experience may be, it is capable of a number of radically differing interpretations. It may be only an encounter with one's own subconscious. Those who place all their emphasis on a subjective validating process . . . eventually reduce the content of revelation and fit it to their taste. The central thing becomes that which comes across to *me*, rather than what God has done and spoken. The reason some theologians favor the use of drugs to heighten religious perception is patent. Whenever the existential cart is put before the historical horse, theology becomes a synthesis of human superstitions, and putting LSD into the communion wine is fair play![36]

LSD in the communion wine? Why not? If it is an experience we are after, why shouldn't we go for it in a big way?

Humanism is the philosophy that says humanity has unlimited potential.[37] Give people enough time and education, and they can solve any problem. A stepsister to existentialism, humanism urges everyone to self-authenticate, to *be* someone. In this computer age, where too many people feel like a number without a real name, humanism is very appealing. This is the day of the live phone-in listener forum, the talk show, and trivia by the hour. Everyone wants to have a say, and everyone gets an opportunity.

Like the existentialist, the humanist recognizes no final authority. All truth is relative. What is true matters little; the question is, "What do *you* think?" There are no absolutes, and everyone does what is right in his own eyes (cf. Judg. 21:25).[38]

Paganism is another illustration of experiential theology. Most pagan beliefs and practices find their roots in mystery religions spawned at Babel. By the time of Christ, people throughout the Greek and Roman world participated in mystery religions featuring multiple gods, sex orgies, idolatry, mutilation, and perhaps human sacrifice. Historians point out that people who took part in such pagan practices had experiences of peace, joy, happiness, and ecstasy.

Historian S. Angus wrote, "The pious could in ecstasy feel himself lifted above his ordinary limitations to behold the beatific vision [God], or in enthusiasm believe himself to be God-inspired or God-filled—phenomena in some respects akin to the experiences of the early Christians on the outpouring of the Spirit."[39]

According to Eugene H. Peterson, experiential theology was also the heart of Baal worship, the religion of the Canaanites:

> The emphasis of Baalism was on psychological relatedness and subjective experience. . . . The transcendence of the deity was overcome in the ecstasy of feeling. . . .
>
> Baalism is worship reduced to the spiritual stature of the worshiper. Its canons are that it should be interesting, relevant, and exciting. . . .
>
> Yahwism [Old Testament Judaism] established a form of worship which was centered in the proclamation of the word of the covenant God. The appeal was made to the will. Man's rational intelligence was roused to attention as he was called upon to respond as a person to the will of God. In

Yahwism something was said—words which called men to
serve, love, obey, act responsibly, decide. . . .

The distinction between the worship of Baal and the
worship of Yahweh is a distinction between approaching the
will of the covenant God which could be understood and
known and obeyed, and the blind life-force in nature which
could only be felt, absorbed, and imitated.[40]

Today, with their extreme emphasis on experience, many in
the charismatic movement are perilously close to a type of
neo-Baalism! Experience can be a dangerous weapon in the
hands of Satan. He delights in getting Christians to seek
experience and de-emphasize God's Word.

Christianity is in danger. We are being victimized by the
experiential spirit of the day. The legacy of mysticism, with its
philosophical and religious offspring—existentialism, humanism, and paganism—will overrun the church if we are not
vigilant. As Pinnock aptly put it, "The new theologian
abandons confidence in the intellectual and historical content
of the Christian message and places his trust in a subjective
man-centered experience which is indistinguishable from
gastric upset."[41] Experiences can be produced by psychological, physiological, or demonic phenomena. The only real test
for any experience is this: Does it square with the Word of
God?

The Battle for the Bible Rages On

Harold Lindsell's landmark book, *The Battle for the
Bible,*[42] was well named. The battle for the Bible has raged for
centuries, and it has become especially heated in the past
hundred years or so. At the turn of the century and into the
1920s, liberals and neoorthodox theologians mounted a
frontal attack on biblical authority, openly accusing the Bible
of error. Now a subtle second attack has come through the
back door, and those caught up in experiential Christianity

seem to be leading the charge, hammering away at the Bible by questioning its sufficiency. And that experientialism undermines the authority of God's revelation just as surely as liberalism has done for several decades.

An article by Robert K. Johnson in *Christianity Today* describes the recent shift in evangelical theology:

> Evangelicals are beginning to . . . explore the possibility of an experientially based theology. Influenced by those who stress either a charismatic approach to faith (e.g., Michael Harper, Robert Mumford, Dennis Bennett, David Wilkerson, Larry Christenson) or a relational approach (e.g., Bruce Larson, Keith Miller, Charlie Shedd, Wes Seeliger, Ralph Osborne), evangelicals are beginning to build their theologies around what it means for man to be in the presence of God [rather than around the objective truth of the Word of God].
>
> . . . What is being increasingly attempted today is a reversal of the [Reformers'] *approach* to the Christian faith. Evangelicals are suggesting that theology must travel from Spirit to Word, not from Word to Spirit, the pattern of their heritage.
>
> Influenced by the wider Christian world, evangelicals who have adopted either a relational ("incarnational") approach or a charismatic ("neo-pentecostal") approach to their theology are more and more challenging their fellow believers to rethink the Gospel from the standpoint of their own experience with it. Their claim is that traditional evangelical theology is largely irrelevant or inadequate.
>
> . . . .
>
> The prescription for health that is increasingly being sounded from within evangelicalism is this: if the church is ever again to set forth a relevant and adequate theology, it must begin not with reflection on the person of Christ but with reflection on our *experience* with him through the Holy Spirit.[43]

In other words, some evangelicals are now contending that relevant theology must begin with subjective experience, not objective revelation. Viewed that way, theology is merely an explanation of experience. Objective truth has no meaning until we experience it.

That kind of thinking is what led Larry Christenson, well-known Lutheran charismatic, to write, "There is a sound biblical theology for the baptism with the Holy Spirit. But the baptism with the Holy Spirit is not a theology to be discussed and analyzed. It is an experience one enters into."[44]

Admittedly, that way of looking at doctrine has some appeal. Lifeless, dry orthodoxy is the inevitable result of isolating objective truth from vibrant experience. But the answer to dead orthodoxy is not to build a theology on experience. Genuine experience must grow out of sound doctrine. We are not to base what we believe on what we have experienced. The reverse is true. Our experiences will grow out of what we believe. And we must continually examine and evaluate our experiences in light of the objective truth of God's precious Word. Any other approach leads inevitably to speculation and error. To build a theology on experience is to build on sand. But to build a theology on God's inspired, revealed Word is to build on rock (cf. Matt. 7:24–27).

It is all a question of authority. What is the authority in your life? Is it your experience or is it God's Word? Jesus said, "Sanctify them in the truth; Thy word is truth" (John 17:17). Maturity, sanctification, and all legitimate experiences depend on the truth of Scripture. True growth in grace cannot be obtained through an experience.

Still, the experiential wave rolls on, and doctrine and theology are being washed out the door. Indeed, the trend threatens the next generation. They may seek the truth only to find that the historical connection will not be there.

Charismatics tend to disagree. They view rational issues such as theology and biblical orthodoxy as an impediment to the church's testimony. Michael Harper has said, "The world awaits a fresh manifestation of Christ within His body, the Church. It is tired of . . . the airy-fairy doctrines of theologians."[45]

J. Rodman Williams argues that we should adapt our theology to experience, rather than insisting that experience be evaluated by theology: "What I have been attempting to stress is that the theological implications of this dynamic movement of the Spirit are of no little significance. At the critical center there is the knowledge that something has happened!"[46] That is the key—*something has happened.* Never mind if it fits "airy-fairy" doctrine or theology. Something has happened and we must assume the Holy Spirit did it. Williams even admits, "One has difficulty finding adequate theological language or ways of relating it to various doctrines of the Christian faith."[47]

I fear that the contemporary church is losing the battle for the Bible. Very few Christians today are like the Bereans, who "received the word with great eagerness, examining the Scriptures daily, to see whether these things were so" (Acts 17:11). We must commit ourselves to searching the Scriptures, and let our experience of the living Word come from that, not from inner feelings, supernatural phenomena, or other potentially counterfeit or untrustworthy evidences. Then our experience will bring the greatest, purest joy and blessing imaginable—because it is rooted and grounded in divine truth.

2

Does God Still Give Revelation?

"God told me . . . " has become the anthem of the charismatic movement. Strange private prophecies are proclaimed by all kinds of people who evidently believe God speaks to them. Surely the most infamous is Oral Roberts' preposterous death-threat prophecy. Roberts told his nationwide audience in 1987 that God had threatened to "call him home" if he couldn't raise eight million dollars by his creditors' deadline. Whether and how that threat might have been carried out, the world will never know; Roberts received a last-minute reprieve in the form of a large check from a Florida dog-track owner.

Even so, two years later, when Roberts was forced to close his multimillion-dollar Tulsa-based City of Faith medical center, he asked God why. Roberts maintains that God gave him an answer:

> God said in my spirit, "I had you build the City of Faith large enough to capture the imagination of the entire world about the merging of My healing streams of prayer and medicine. I did not want this revelation localized in Tulsa,

however. And the time has come when I want this concept of merging My healing streams to be known to all people and to go into all future generations."

As clearly in my spirit as I've ever heard Him, the Lord gave me an impression. "You and your partners have merged prayer and medicine for the entire world, for the church world and for all generations," He said. "It is done."

I then asked, "Is that why after eight years you're having us close the hospital and after eleven years the medical school?"

He said, "Yes, the mission has been accomplished in the same way that after the three years of public ministry My Son said on the cross, 'Father, it is finished.' "[1]

We may gasp at Oral Roberts' hubris, but he is not the only charismatic who thinks he is receiving private revelation from God. Most charismatics at one time or another feel that God speaks to them in some specific manner, either through an audible voice, an internal impression, a vision, or simply by using them as a vehicle to write a song, compose a poem, or utter a prophecy.

Linda Fehl, founder of Rapha Ranch, sells a tape with a song titled, "The Holy Ghost." She says the song was given to her by the Holy Spirit as she was being healed of cancer.[2] An editor for a Christian publisher once told me he receives submissions every week from charismatics who claim God inspired them to write their book, article, song, or poem.[3] My editor friend noted that the manuscripts are often poorly written, filled with bad grammar, marred by factual and logical errors, or full of poems that either mutilate the language or attempt to rhyme but just miss.

Lest you think cranks, obscure eccentrics, or naïve charismatic believers are the only ones who would make such claims, listen to Jack Hayford, internationally known author, media minister, and pastor of The Church on the Way in Van

Nuys, California. Hayford told the Pentecostal Fellowship of North America that God has told him a new era is coming:

> Hayford . . . related a vision in which he had seen Jesus seated on His throne at the right hand of the Father. In Hayford's vision, Jesus began to lean forward and rise from his seat. As the anointing caught in the folds of His garments, it began to splash out and fall over the church. Jesus said, "I am beginning to rise now in preparation for my second coming. Those who will rise with Me will share in this double portion of anointing."[4]

And Larry Lea, popular charismatic author and pastor, wrote,

> Recently, when I was in Chicago preparing to preach, the Lord's Spirit came upon me. He spoke in my heart: *"I'm going to tell you now the name of the strongman over this nation."*
>
> I listened intently.
>
> *"The spiritual strongman you are facing—the demonic strongman that has your nation under his control—is the strongman of greed."*
>
> We certainly don't have to look very long to find evidence to back up this Word of the Lord.[5]

Kenneth Hagin surely has the most unusual story of all. He says that when he was younger and still single, God led him to break off a relationship with a woman by revealing to him that she was morally unfit. How did that happen? In a most unconventional way. Hagin claims God miraculously transported him out of church one Sunday, right in the middle of the sermon. Worst of all, Hagin was the preacher delivering the sermon!

> Suddenly I was gone! Right in the middle of my sermon, I found myself standing along a street in a little town fifteen miles away—and I knew it was Saturday night. I was leaning against a building, and I saw this young lady come walking down the street. About the time she got to where I

was standing, a car came down the street. The driver pulled up to the curb, sounded the horn, and she got into his car. He backed out, turned the other direction, and started out of town—and suddenly I was sitting in the back seat!

They went out in the country and committed adultery. And I watched them. I was still in the cloud. Suddenly I heard the sound of my voice, and the cloud lifted. I was standing behind my pulpit. I didn't know what to say, because I didn't know what I had been saying, so I just said, "Everyone bow your head," and we prayed. I looked at my watch, and . . . I'd been gone about fifteen minutes in the cloud.

While I was shaking hands with people as they went out the door, this young lady came by. I said, "We missed you last night." She said, "Yes, I was over in _____" (and she named the little town). I said, "Yes, I know."[6]

On the basis of that questionable experience, Hagin determined that the woman was promiscuous and assumes to this day that she was guilty of adultery. He follows that report with a similar one, in which he was suddenly transported into a car where another young woman was supposedly engaged in moral compromise.[7] Ironically, immediately after telling those two tales, he writes, "You've got to realize, friends, that there is a fine line between fanaticism and reality. Many people get off into error seeking experiences."[8] Hagin has never drawn a truer application from his anecdotes.

Would God really transport Hagin miraculously into cars so he could witness acts of fornication? Did God talk to Oral Roberts? Did he write a song for Linda Fehl? Did Jack Hayford actually see Christ rise from his seat next to God? Was Larry Lea's prophecy really a "Word of the Lord"? Are Christians still receiving, by the inspiration of the Holy Spirit, direct revelation from God? Can people today—writing songs or books, preaching or teaching, or making decisions—legitimately claim that they are under divine inspiration?

Many charismatics answer a loud "Yes!" For example, J. Rodman Williams wrote:

> The Bible truly has become a fellow witness to God's present activity. . . . If someone today perhaps has a vision of God, of Christ, it is good to know that it has happened before; if one has a revelation from God, to know that for the early Christians revelation also occurred in the community; if one speaks a "Thus says the Lord," and dares to address the fellowship in the first person—even going beyond the words of Scripture—that this was happening long ago. How strange and remarkable it is! If one speaks in the fellowship of the Spirit the Word of truth, it is neither his own thoughts and reflections (e.g., on some topic of the day) nor simply some exposition of Scripture, for the Spirit transcends personal observations, however interesting or profound they may be. The Spirit as the living God moves through and beyond the records of past witness, however valuable such records are as a model for what happens today.[9]

What is Williams saying? He is alleging that the Bible is not our final source of God's revelation but simply a "witness" to additional revelation that God is giving today. Williams is declaring that Christians can add to the Bible—and that they can accept others' additions to Scripture as normal and conventional. He believes the Bible is a "model" for what the Holy Spirit is doing today to inspire believers.

That is a frighteningly relativistic view, but it is growing in popularity as the charismatic movement expands. Edward N. Gross, noting this deadly trend in the church today, observes:

> The age of models has come. A model takes the place of a law. Models are human perceptions of truth. They are tentative and thus subject to change as new data becomes available. These models are open and constantly tested. No scientist dares claim any longer that one model is the way to

explain all known phenomena for fear that some newly discovered data will prove that scientist to be a precipitous old fool. The world of science has progressed from the old approach (closed systems) to the new approach (open systems). . . .

If the Bible is a closed system of truth, with no new revelation being given through inspired prophets or apostles, then the "model approach" is an erroneous and dangerous tool in hermeneutics.

There should be no confusion in this area. The orthodox teaching of Christianity has always affirmed that God's special, saving revelation to mankind is restricted to the teachings of the Scriptures. . . .

This is the issue. If the Bible is complete, then it represents a closed system of truth. If it entails a fixed and absolute standard of truth, then the teachings of Scripture may be ascertained and dogmatically asserted. If God is still granting new revelation, then the truth of God is still being progressively revealed, and if this were the case, our duty would be to faithfully listen to today's prophets as they unravel God's truth in new and clearer representations than we find in Scripture. Few Christians really consider the subtleties of today's "prophets" as an improvement upon the sanctifying truths given in the Word. I certainly do not.[10]

Nor do I. Scripture *is* a closed system of truth, complete, sufficient, and not to be added to (Jude 3; Rev. 22:18–19). It contains all the spiritual truth God intended to reveal.

What Does Inspiration Mean?

Our word *inspired* comes from a Latin root meaning, "to breathe in." Unfortunately, that does not convey the true meaning of the Greek term for "inspired" that is used in Scripture. Actually the concept of breathing *in* is not found in 2 Timothy 3:16 ("All Scripture is inspired by God"). Reading this meaning in has misled many people about the true meaning of *inspiration*. They have assumed that God breathed some kind of divine life into the words of those who penned the original documents of Scripture. But the Greek term for inspiration is *theopneustos*, which means "God-breathed." Literally the verse says, "All Scripture is God-breathed"— that is, Scripture is not the words of men into which God puffed divine life. It is the very breath of God! Scripture is God Himself speaking.

That truth is one many people seem prone to misunderstand. Inspiration does not mean the Bible *contains* God's revelation. It does not mean gems of revealed truth are *concealed* in Scripture. It does not mean men wrote God's truth in their own words. It does not mean God merely assisted the writers. It means that the words of the Bible are the words of God Himself. Every word of Scripture was breathed *out* by God.

At the burning bush, God said to Moses, "Go, and I, even I will be with your mouth, and teach you what you are to say" (Ex. 4:12). Jeremiah, the weeping prophet of Judah, received this charge from God: "All that I command you, you shall speak. . . . Behold, I have put My words in your mouth" (Jer. 1:7, 9). And God said to Ezekiel, "Son of man, go to the house of Israel. . . . Take into your heart all my words which I shall speak to you, and listen closely . . . and speak to them" (Ezek. 3:4, 10–11).

A key verse describing how God speaks through Scripture is 2 Peter 1:21. Literally it says "No prophecy was ever made by an act of human will, but men moved by the Holy Spirit spoke from God." The most important word here is "moved," which speaks of being carried along by the Holy Spirit.

Theologian Thomas A. Thomas recalls that as a boy he would play in the little streams that ran down the mountainside near his home.

We boys liked to play what we called "boats." Our "boat" would be any little stick which was placed in the water, and then we would run along beside it and follow it as it was washed downstream. When the water would run rapidly over some rocks the little stick would move rapidly as well. . . . In other words, that little stick which served as my boyhood "boat" was carried along, borne along, under the complete control and direction of the water. It moved as the water moved it. So it is with reference to the writers of the Scriptures. They were carried along, borne along, under the control and direction of the Holy Spirit of God. They wrote as the Spirit directed them to write. They were borne along by Him so that what they wrote was exactly that which the Holy Spirit intended should be there. What they wrote was, in a very real sense, not their words; it was the very Word of God.[11]

Modern Views of Inspiration

What, then, is the contemporary approach to Scripture? Some modern theologians want to allow for continued inspiration or updated revelation. At least one, Dewey Beegle, believes that some of the classic anthems of the church are inspired in the same way as Scripture. He has written, "Some of the great hymns are practically on a par with the Psalms, and one can be sure that if Isaac Watts, Charles Wesley, Augustus Toplady, and Reginald Heber had lived in the time of David and Solomon, and been *no more inspired than they were in their own day*, some of their hymns of praise to God would have found their way into the Hebrew canon."[12]

Beegle refers in particular to the experience of George Matheson, a blind Scottish pastor who ministered in the nineteenth century and wrote "O Love That Wilt Not Let Me Go" during a time of great personal distress. On the evening of his younger sister's wedding, Matheson was reminded vividly of the agony he had suffered twenty years before when his fiancée had rejected him because she had learned he was going blind. Matheson wrote the hymn in just a few minutes, though he claimed he had no natural sense of rhythm. According to Matheson, he did no changing or correcting of "O Love That Wilt Not Let Me Go"; it came "like a dayspring from on high."

Beegle believes George Matheson's experience was

> . . . the kind of inspiration of which the Psalms were made. There is no difference in kind. If there is any difference, it was a matter of degree. When the Biblical writers served as channels of God's revelation they needed more divine help, but the inspiration was not distinct in kind from that given to all the messengers of God down through history. What distinguishes the Bible is its record of special revelation, not a distinctive kind of inspiration.[13]

Beegle believes the canon of Scripture has never been closed.[14] He has written, "The revelation and inspiration of God's Spirit continues. . . . For this reason there is no basis in considering all of the biblical writers and editors as qualitatively different from postcanonical interpreters."[15] He continues,

> If the church had a more dynamic sense of God's inspiration in the twentieth century, it would be more effective in its witness and outreach. It is well and good to protect the distinctiveness of the Bible, but to think only in terms of its inspiration as absolutely different in kind from inspiration in our time is too high a price to pay. Christians today need to have the same sense of being God-motivated and God-sent as did the biblical writers and interpreters. In a genuine sense, the difficulty of interpreting God's record of revelation to this complex age requires as much of God's inbreathing and wisdom as did the process of interpretation in the biblical periods.[16]

In effect, that is precisely what charismatics believe. The truth, however, is that there is no way to "protect the distinctiveness of the Bible" if God is inspiring new revelation today. If the canon is still open, and if God is still giving new prophecies, new songs, and new words of wisdom, we should be earnestly seeking to compile and study these most recent revelations along with Scripture—and maybe even more diligently, since they speak expressly to our time and culture.

Some charismatics actually reason that way.[17] But it is error of the worst kind. The canon is *not* still open. God's Word, made of the Old and New Testaments, is one unique miracle. It came together over a period of fifteen hundred years. More than forty men of God, prophets and apostles, wrote God's words—every jot and tittle—without error and in perfect harmony. No hymn is worthy to be compared to Scripture. No modern prophecy or word of wisdom is even in the same realm with God's eternal Word. Heaven and earth will pass away; God's Word will abide (Matt. 5:18).

Progressive Revelation?

Charismatics struggle to explain how the supposed revelation they receive through tongues, prophecies, and visions fits with Scripture. J. Rodman Williams, as we have seen, claims these charismatic phenomena are simply new manifestations of what was happening in biblical times: "It is good to know . . . if one speaks a 'Thus says the Lord,' and dares to address the fellowship in the first person—*even going beyond the words of Scripture*—that this was happening long ago."[18] His explanation of the spiritual gifts amounts to an argument for continuing revelation: "In the Spirit the present fellowship is as much the arena of God's vital presence as anything in the Biblical account. Indeed, in the light of what we may learn from this past witness, and take to heart, we may expect *new* things to occur in our day and days to come."[19] Williams went on to describe just how new revelation occurs. He put great emphasis on the "gift of prophecy":

> In prophecy God speaks. It is as simple, and profound, and startling as that! What happens in the fellowship is that the Word may suddenly be spoken by anyone present, and so, variously, a "Thus says the Lord" breaks forth in the fellowship. It is usually in the first person (though not always), such as "I am with you to bless you . . ." and has the directness of an "I—Thou" encounter. It comes not in a "heavenly language," but in the native tongue of the person speaking and with his accustomed inflections, cadences, and manners. Indeed, the speech may even be coarse and ungrammatical; it may be a mixture of "King James" and modern; it may falter as well as flow—such really does not matter. For in prophecy God uses what He finds, and through frail human instruments the Spirit speaks the Word of the Lord. . . .
>
> All of this—to repeat—is quite surprising and startling. Most of us of course were familiar with prophetic utterance as recorded in the Bible, and willing to accept it as the Word of God. Isaiah's or Jeremiah's "Thus says the Lord . . ." we were accustomed to, but to hear a Tom or a Mary today, in the twentieth century, speak the same way . . . ! Many of us also had convinced ourselves that prophecy ended with the New Testament period (despite all the New Testament evidence to the contrary), until suddenly through the dynamic thrust of the Holy Spirit prophecy comes alive again. Now we wonder how we could have misread the New Testament for so long![20]

That is tantamount to saying that current instances of charismatic prophecy are divine revelation equal to Scripture. Such a claim is disturbing because the possibilities of fraud and error by present-day "prophets" are obvious. Williams recognized that danger and wrote:

> Prophecy can by no means be taken casually. Since it is verily God's message to His people, there must be quite serious and careful consideration given to each word spoken, and application made within the life of the fellowship. Also because of the ever present danger of prophecy being abused—the pretense of having a word from God—there is need for spiritual discernment. [21]

Though Williams admits the risks, nowhere in his book does he spell out how "careful consideration" and "spiritual discernment" are to be employed to distinguish the false from the true.

Perhaps Williams later realized the problems he had raised, because he attempted to clarify his thinking in the *Logos Journal:*

> I do not intend in any way to place contemporary experience on the same level of authority as the Bible. Rather do I vigorously affirm the decisive authority of Scripture; hence, God does not speak just as authoritatively today as He spoke to the biblical authors. But *he does continue to speak* (he did not stop with the close of the New Testament canon); thus, he "moves through and beyond the records of past witness," for he is the living God who still speaks and acts among His people. [22]

That explanation fails to resolve the issue. The distinction between biblical authority and additional revelation seems to be artificial. How could some of God's words be less authoritative than others?

The fact is, Williams's view is indistinguishable from the neoorthodox position espoused by Dewey Beegle. If evangelicalism allows that view to gain a foothold, the uniqueness of Scripture will be sacrificed, and the basis for all we believe will be compromised. That is precisely what is happening today. Because of the growing influence of charismatic teaching, much of the church may mistakenly abandon its cornerstone:

Sola Scriptura, the principle that God's Word is the only basis for divine authority.

Once a congregation sees Scripture as less than the final, complete, infallible authority for faith and practice, it has opened the doors to theological chaos. Anyone can claim to be speaking God's revelation—and almost anything can be passed off as divinely revealed truth. Make no mistake, some of the best-known charismatic leaders have abused their people's trust by claiming they are receiving new truth from God, when what they really teach are lies and fabrications.

Perhaps the most brazen example of that is a widely publicized "prophecy" delivered by Kenneth Copeland. He claims Jesus gave him a message "during a three-day Victory Campaign held in Dallas, Texas."[23] Judge for yourself whether this could be a message from the Christ of Scripture:

> It's time for these things to happen, saith the Lord. It's time for spiritual activity to increase. Oh, yes, demonic activity will increase along at the same time. But don't let that disturb you.
>
> Don't be disturbed when people accuse you of thinking you're God. Don't be disturbed when people accuse you of a fanatical way of life. Don't be disturbed when people put you down and speak harshly and roughly of you. They spoke that way of Me, should they not speak that way of you?
>
> The more you get to be like Me, the more they're going to think that way of you. They crucified me for claiming that I was God. But I didn't claim I was God; I just claimed I walked with Him and that He was in Me. Hallelujah. That's what you're doing.[24]

Copeland's "prophecy" is clearly false. The real Jesus—the Jesus of the New Testament—*did* claim he was God; using the covenant name of God, he told the Jewish leaders, "Truly, truly, I say to you, before Abraham was, I am" (John 8:58). He made such claims repeatedly (Mark 14:61–64; John 5:16–

18; 10:30–33). The apostle John wrote an entire gospel to highlight and substantiate those claims (cf. John 1:1, 14).

Is Copeland genuinely a prophet, or is he one whom Peter spoke of when he warned, "False prophets also arose among the people, just as there will also be false teachers among you, who will secretly introduce destructive heresies, even denying the Master who bought them" (2 Peter 2:1)? The obvious answer to that question is clouded only to those who are not sure whether modern "prophecies" might supersede God's Word.

Not all charismatic prophecies and visions are so clearly in conflict with Scripture. Some are merely frivolous. Larry Lea wrote,

> Several years ago one of my dear pastor friends said, "Larry, when I was praying for you the other day, I had a vision. I saw you with great big 'Mickey Mouse' ears. Everything else about you looked normal except for those elephant-sized ears. When I asked the Lord to tell me what the vision meant, the Spirit of the Lord spoke back to me and said: 'Larry Lea has developed his hearing. He has developed his spiritual ears.' "[25]

Charismatics have abandoned the uniqueness of Scripture as the only Word of God, and the result is a spiritual free-for-all. A longing for something new and esoteric has replaced historic Christianity's settled confidence in the Word of God—and that is an invitation to Satan's counterfeit. Confusion, error, and even satanic deception are the inescapable results.

Melvin Hodges is a charismatic pastor who has admitted his strong reservations about "new" revelations:

> Today, some people tend to magnify the gifts of prophecy and revelation out of their proper proportion. Instances have occurred in which a church has allowed itself to be governed by gifts of inspiration. Deacons have been appointed and pastors removed or installed by prophecy.

Chaos has resulted. The cause is obvious. Prophecy was never intended to usurp the place of ministries of government or of a gift of a word of wisdom. Paul teaches us that the body is not made up of one member but of many, and if prophecy usurps the role of the word of wisdom or the word of knowledge, the whole body is dominated by one ministry, that is, prophecy. In other words, the whole body becomes ruled by the prophetic member. . . .

The idea that the voice of prophecy is infallible has confused many people. Some have felt that it is a sin to question what they consider to be the voice of the Spirit. However, in the ministry of all gifts there is a cooperation between the divine and the human. [26]

Note that Hodges speaks of "the gifts of prophecy and revelation." It is evident that he believes God is giving new revelation today. At the same time, he is obviously well aware that so-called prophetic utterances create problems in the church. Throughout, he assiduously avoids concluding that the charismatic "gift of prophecy" is in any way less authoritative than Scripture. Yet he still wants to warn charismatics against taking modern prophecies too seriously or placing too much emphasis on them. He is seeking a way to resolve the confusion, but there is no way. When "prophetic utterance" is equated in any degree with "divine revelation," the result is a hopeless muddle. Scripture loses its uniqueness, and all the damaging results Hodges describes are sure to occur.

Not all charismatics would agree that the problem of prophetic abuses is one of overemphasis. Some blame it on ignorant misuse of the gift. Their answer to the problem is to offer training. One group has started a "School of the Prophets." Their appeal for students says, in part,

Perhaps you feel that you have been called to be an oracle of the Lord and have had difficulty explaining your experiences or finding someone that you could relate to and learn from.

The School of the Prophets is designed to help bring grounding and clarity to the myriad of dreams and visions that are the hallmark of the prophet and seer ministries and to assist in the restoration of the prophetic ministry within the Body of Christ. There are many that have become disillusioned and disenchanted with the prophetic ministry because of abuses and ignorant usage of the gifting. Don't throw the baby out with the bath water, for if you've had the bitter experience of the counterfeit, know that there is a reality to discover. . . . Abuses and misrepresentations occur simply because of the abomination of ignorance. Come and be trained at the School of the Prophets so that you will be properly prepared to fulfill the destiny that God has chosen for you![27]

That strikes me as a peculiar approach to the problem of false prophecy. Can a school teach neophyte prophets how to use their "gift"? Can people be taught to give their dreams and visions "grounding and clarity"? Is the distinction between true and false prophecy simply a matter of education?

I think not. False prophecy is hardly a peccadillo. God told the Israelites, "My hand will be against the prophets who see false visions and utter lying divinations. They will have no place in the council of My people, nor will they be written down in the register of the house of Israel, nor will they enter the land of Israel, that you may know that I am the Lord God" (Ezek. 13:9).

The law prescribed a stern remedy for false prophets:

The prophet who shall speak a word presumptuously in My name which I have not commanded him to speak, or which he shall speak in the name of other gods, that prophet shall die. And you may say in your heart, "How shall we know the word which the Lord has not spoken?" When a prophet speaks in the name of the Lord, if the thing does not come about or come true, that is the thing which the Lord has not

spoken. The prophet has spoken it presumptuously; you
shall not be afraid of him (Deut. 18:20–22).

No second chance was offered. A false prophet—anyone who
prophesied something that did *not* come to pass—was to be
put to death. It is a serious matter to claim to speak for the
Lord.

Nevertheless, some charismatics believe *any* believer
who wants to can get revelation from God. The same issue of
Charisma that carried the above ad also featured one touting a
cassette tape album promising to teach believers "How you
can hear the voice of God." The ad asserts, "It is the
inheritance of every believer to hear God's voice for every
need and every situation." Jerry Hester, the speaker on the
tapes, features "Listening Seminars," which he claims "instruct you how to talk with God on an intimate conversation-
al level 24 hours a day!"[28]

Evidently, if you want to *declare* a private revelation from
God, you can go to the School of the Prophets; if you only
want to *receive* private revelation from God, you can go to a
Listening Seminar.

All of that has the unfortunate effect of pointing
Christians away from Scripture, which is trustworthy, and
teaching them to seek truth through subjective means—
private conversation with God, prophecies, dreams, and
visions. It depreciates God's eternal, inspired Word, and
causes people to look beyond the Bible for fresher, more
intimate forms of revelation from God. It is perhaps the
charismatic movement's most unwholesome and destructive
tendency, as René Pache has noted:

> The excessive preeminence given to the Holy Spirit in their
> devotions and their preoccupation with gifts, ecstacies, and
> "prophecies" has tended to neglect of the Scriptures. Why
> be tied to a Book out of the past when one can communicate
> every day with the living God? But this is exactly the danger
> point. Apart from the constant control of the written

revelation, we soon find ourselves engulfed in subjectivity; and the believer, even if he has the best intentions, can sink rapidly into deviations, illuminism or exaltation. Let each remind himself of the prohibition of taking anything away from Scripture or adding anything to it (Deut. 4:2; Rev. 22:18–19). Almost every heresy and sect has originated in a supposed revelation or a new experience on the part of its founder, something outside the strictly biblical framework.[29]

The Canon Is Closed

The truth is, there is no fresher or more intimate revelation than Scripture. God doesn't need to give us private revelation to help us in our walk with Him. "All Scripture is inspired by God and profitable for teaching, for reproof, for correction, for training in righteousness; that the man of God may be adequate, *equipped for every good work*" (2 Tim. 3:16–17, emphasis added). Scripture is sufficient. It offers all we need for every good work.

Christians on both sides of the charismatic fence must realize a vital truth: *God's revelation is complete for now.* The canon of Scripture is closed. As the apostle John penned the final words of the last book of the New Testament, he recorded this warning: "I testify to everyone who hears the words of the prophecy of this book: if anyone adds to them, God shall add to him the plagues which are written in this book; and if anyone takes away from the words of the book of this prophecy, God shall take away his part from the tree of life and from the holy city, which are written in this book" (Rev. 22:18–19). Then, the Holy Spirit added a doxology and closed the canon.

When the canon closed on the Old Testament after the time of Ezra and Nehemiah, there followed four hundred "silent years" when no prophet spoke God's revelation in any form.

That silence was broken by John the Baptist as God

spoke once more prior to the New Testament age. God then moved various men to record the books of the New Testament, and the last of these was Revelation. By the second century A.D., the complete canon exactly as we have it today was popularly recognized. Church councils in the fourth century verified and made official what the church has universally affirmed, that the sixty-six books in our Bibles are the only true Scripture inspired by God. The canon is complete.

Just as the close of the Old Testament canon was followed by silence, so the close of the New Testament has been followed by the utter absence of new revelation in any form. Since the book of Revelation was completed, no new written or verbal prophecy has ever been universally recognized by Christians as divine truth from God.

How the Biblical Canon Was Chosen and Closed

Jude 3 is a crucial passage on the completeness of our Bibles. This statement, penned by Jude before the New Testament was complete, nevertheless looked forward to the completion of the entire canon: "Beloved, while I was making every effort to write to you about our common salvation, I felt the necessity to write to you appealing that you contend earnestly for the faith which was once for all delivered to the saints" (Jude 3). In the Greek text the definite article preceding "faith" points to the one and only faith: "*the* faith." There is no other. Such passages as Galatians 1:23 ("He who once persecuted us is now preaching the faith") and 1 Timothy 4:1 ("In latter times some will fall away from the faith") indicate this objective use of the expression "the faith" was common in apostolic times. Greek scholar Henry Alford wrote that *the faith* is "objective here: the sum of that which Christians believe."[30]

Note also the crucial phrase "once for all" in Jude 3. The Greek word here is *hapax*, which refers to something done for all time, with lasting results, never needing repetition. Nothing needs to be added to *the faith* that has been delivered "once for all."

George Lawlor, who has written an excellent work on Jude, made the following comment:

> The Christian faith is unchangeable, which is not to say that men and women of every generation do not need to find it, experience it, and live it; but it does mean that every new doctrine that arises, even though its legitimacy may be plausibly asserted, is a false doctrine. All claims to convey some additional revelation to that which has been given by God in this body of truth are false claims and must be rejected.[31]

Also important in Jude 3 is the word "delivered." In the Greek it is an aorist passive participle, which in this context indicates an act completed in the past with no continuing element. In this instance the passive voice means the faith was not discovered by men, but *given to men by God*. How did He do that? Through His Word—the Bible.

And so through the Scriptures God has given us a body of teaching that is final and complete. Our Christian faith rests on historical, objective revelation. That rules out all inspired prophecies, seers, and other forms of new revelation until God speaks again at the return of Christ (cf. Acts 2:16–21; Rev. 11:1–13).

In the meantime, Scripture warns us to be wary of false prophets. Jesus said that in our age "false Christs and false prophets will arise and will show great signs and wonders, so as to mislead, if possible, even the elect" (Matt. 24:24). Signs and wonders alone are no proof that a person speaks for God. John wrote, "Beloved, do not believe every spirit, but test the spirits to see whether they are from God; because many false prophets have gone out into the world" (1 John 4:1).

Ultimately, Scripture is the test of everything; it is the Christian's standard. In fact, the word *canon* means "a rule, standard, or measuring rod." The canon of Scripture is the measuring rod of the Christian faith, and it is complete.

Of course throughout history, spurious books have been offered as genuine Scripture. For example, the Roman Catholic Bible includes the Apocrypha (writings that were produced at the same time some of the Old Testament and New Testament writings were produced, but which were left outside of canonical literature). The Roman Catholic Church accepts those books as Scripture, but it is clear that they are not.[32] They contain errors in history, geography, and theology.

Although Jerome (345–419) clearly was a spokesman for excluding from the canon the apocryphal books, some of the early church fathers (most notably Augustine) did accept them, though not necessarily on a par with the Hebrew Old Testament. Finally, in the sixteenth century, the Reformers affirmed *Sola Scriptura*, the truth that the Bible alone is authoritative revelation, and thus denied the Apocrypha a place among the inspired writings. The Roman church reacted against the Reformers in the Council of Trent (1545–63) by stating that all the Apocrypha was canonical. Protestants and Catholics have maintained the disparity to the present time.

The Old Testament canon was generally agreed upon by the people of God from the time the last Old Testament book was written. How did the Jewish people know which books were inspired? They chose the books written by those known as spokesmen for God. They studied those books carefully and found no errors in history, geography, or theology.

Christians in the early church applied similar tests to prove which New Testament books were authentic and which were not. A key test was *apostolic authorship*. Every New Testament book had to be written by an apostle or a close associate of the apostles. For example, Mark, who was not an apostle, was a companion of Peter. Luke, who was not an apostle, worked closely with the apostle Paul.

A second test used by the early church was *content*. Acts 2:42 tells us that the first time the church met, they gave themselves to prayer, fellowship, the breaking of bread, and the apostles' doctrine. Later, in considering which writings were to be revered as Scripture, they asked, "Does it agree with apostolic doctrine?" This test was very important because of all the heretics that tried to worm their way into the church. But their doctrinal errors were easily spotted because they contradicted the apostles' teaching.

A third test was *the response of the churches*. If God's people accepted it, used it for worship, and made it part of their lives, and if Christians were universally being taught and blessed by the book, that was another important stamp of approval.

By A.D. 404 the Latin Vulgate version of the Bible was complete. It was the earliest known translation of all sixty-six books of the Bible. They were the same books we still have in our modern English Bibles. God spoke once for all, and his Word has been preserved through the ages.[33]

From the time of the apostles until the present, the true church has always believed that the Bible is complete. God has given his revelation, and now Scripture is finished. God has spoken. What he gave is complete, efficacious, sufficient, inerrant, infallible, and authoritative. Attempts to add to the Bible, and claims of further revelation from God have always been characteristic of heretics and cultists, not the true people of God.

Although charismatics deny that they are trying to add to Scripture, their views on prophetic utterance, gifts of prophecy, and revelation really do just that. As they add—however unwittingly—to God's final revelation, they undermine the uniqueness and authority of the Bible. New revelation, dreams, and visions are considered as binding on the believer's conscience as the book of Romans or the gospel of John.

Some charismatics would say that people misunderstand what they mean by prophetic utterance and new revelation.

They would say that no effort is being made to change Scripture or even equal it. What is happening, they assume, is the clarifying of Scripture as it is applied or directed to a contemporary setting, such as the prophecy of Agabus in Acts 11:28.[34]

The line between clarifying Scripture and adding to it is indeed a thin one. But Scripture is not clarified by listening to someone who thinks he has the gift of prophecy. Scripture is clarified as it is carefully and diligently studied. (See the account of Philip and the Ethiopian eunuch in Acts 8:28–35.) There are no shortcuts to interpreting God's Word accurately (cf. Acts 17:11; 2 Tim. 2:15).

Christians must not play fast and loose with the issues of inspiration and revelation. An accurate understanding of those doctrines is essential for distinguishing between the voice of God and the human voice. As we have seen, men who professed to speak for God but spoke their own opinions were to be executed under the Old Testament law (Deut. 13:1–5). New Testament believers are also urged to test the spirits and judge all supposed prophecies, shunning false prophets and heretics (1 John 4:1; 1 Cor. 14:29).

It has always been important to be able to separate God's Word from that which is false. God worked through a historical process to establish the authenticity of the canon so that the whole church might have a clear standard. If we now throw out that historical standard and redefine inspiration and revelation, we undermine our own ability to receive God's truth. If we subvert the uniqueness of the Bible, we will have no way of distinguishing God's voice from man's. Eventually, anyone could say anything and claim it is God's Word, and no one would have the right to deny it. We are perilously close to that situation even now.

The Holy Spirit is working mightily in the church today, but not in the way most charismatics think. The Holy Spirit's role is to empower us as we preach, teach, write, talk, witness, think, serve, and live. He *does* lead us into God's truth and direct us into God's will for our lives. But He does it *through* God's Word, never apart from it. To refer to the Holy Spirit's leading and empowering ministry as inspiration or revelation is a mistake. To use phrases such as "God spoke to me," or "This wasn't my idea; the Lord gave it to me," or "These aren't my words, but a message I received from the Lord" confuses the issue of the Spirit's direction in believers' lives today.

Inviting that kind of confusion plays into the hands of the error that denies the uniqueness and absolute authority of Scripture. The terms and concepts of Ephesians 5:18–19 and 2 Peter 1:21 are not to be mixed. Being filled with the Spirit and speaking to one another in psalms and hymns is not the same as being moved by the Holy Spirit to write inspired Scripture.

___ 3 ___

Prophets, Fanatics,
or Heretics?

Perhaps the most disturbing aspect of the charismatic movement's thirst for new revelation is the reckless and indiscriminate way so many questionable prophecies are hailed as truth from God.

The Kansas City Prophets

One group of so-called prophets in Kansas City demonstrates how far the abuse of prophecy in the charismatic movement has gone. A recent book touting the group became an immediate international best-seller.[1] Hundreds—perhaps thousands—of churches worldwide are now patterning prophetic ministries after the "Kansas City Prophets."

These men, all associated with a single church—formerly Kansas City Fellowship, now called Metro Vineyard Fellowship—say they don't like being labeled "prophets." They prefer to call themselves "prophetically gifted." In other words, they don't believe they hold an office of authority like the Old Testament prophets. Nor do they claim infallibility.

On the contrary, all the Kansas City Prophets admit they have prophesied falsely.[2]

Nevertheless, the prophecies these men deliver are received by thousands as revealed truth from God. Metro Vineyard's pastor, Mike Bickle, actively encourages his flock to embrace modern prophecy as God's means of revealing fresh truth to the church.

One of the church's more colorful seers, Bob Jones, claims that God speaks to him annually on the Jewish Day of Atonement. In Jones's terminology, the Lord places him "under the Shepherd's Rod" and gives him a message that pertains to the whole church for the coming year.[3] In recent years, Bickle and Jones have delivered and explained the Shepherd's Rod prophecies before the congregation, encouraging people to act on the prophecies as if they were the Word of God.

Jones's 1989 Shepherd's Rod prophecy included a novel explanation about why so many modern prophecies go unfulfilled. Jones claimed:

> [God] said, "If I release the hundred-percent rhema right now, the accountability would be awesome and you'd have so much Ananias and Sapphiras going on that the people couldn't grow—they'd be too scared." But He said, "If it was on target, it would kill instead of scaring the people to repentance." . . . This is what He told me, so I figure if I hit two-thirds of it, I'm doing pretty good.[4]

Bickle added, "Now the two-thirds, you know when Bob first said it I said 'Two thirds?' He said, 'Well, that's better than it's ever been in this nation up to now, you know. That's the highest level it's ever been.' "[5]

In other words, these so-called prophets claim they have a word from the Lord, but the odds are one in three—at best—that it will be false! No wonder their prophecies throw so many Christians into hopeless confusion.

Despite their poor track record, the Kansas City Prophets

continue to garner global accolades. They often are featured speakers in John Wimber's international conference ministry (see chapter 6).[6]

In his foreword to *Some Said It Thundered*, Dr. John White notes:

> Battles about prophets have plagued the church from time to time. Early last century it was the Irvingite controversy in London, with the leading prophet having to confess after years that he had been deceived. Many of us have found that hearing from God is no easy thing. In fact, the Church has had so many bad experiences with prophets that now we react too rapidly and fearfully. We could be in danger of discarding a live baby in our horror over dirty bath water.[7]

But is there really a live baby in the murky water of modern prophetic revelation? That is a question many charismatics seem unwilling to consider.

White, for example, fiercely defends the Kansas City Prophets. Although he acknowledges that they have "made mistakes,"[8] he seems to believe that criticism of them is inherently satanic: "Satan fears those words that come fresh from God's lips. . . . Because Satan so dreads the fresh Word, he will arouse controversy wherever it comes forth miraculously through the lips of a real prophet or from the lips of an evangelist aflame with the Spirit."[9]

Curiously, White believes the controversy surrounding the Kansas City Prophets is strong evidence of their genuineness. In a section mistitled "Beware of False Prophets," White quotes Jesus' warnings about false prophets in Matthew 7:15, Matthew 24:11, and Mark 13:22, then says, "We are warned that it is to happen. Most scholars feel the words of Jesus apply particularly to the last days. They may be approaching us now. How are we to discern the false from the true? For one thing, *true prophets will be unpopular.*"[10]

Let me state as plainly as possible: that is about the *worst* imaginable starting point for a discussion of how to discern false prophets. Certainly those who speak truth are often unpopular, but notoriety is not a test of authenticity, or even of faithfulness. Both Jesus and John the Baptist went through stages in their ministries when they were enormously popular.

The only test of a true prophet is the truthfulness of his prophecies: " 'How shall we know the word which the Lord has not spoken?' When a prophet speaks in the name of the Lord, if the thing does not come about or come true, that is the thing which the Lord has not spoken. The prophet has spoken it presumptuously" (Deut. 18:21–22). What was the penalty under the law for such a prophecy? "The prophet who shall speak a word presumptuously in My name which I have not commanded him to speak . . . *that prophet shall die*" (18:20, emphasis added).

Astonishingly, in a five-page discussion of how to discern false prophets, *White never once speaks of accuracy or truthfulness as a test!* In fact, he explicitly states that he believes those are *not* valid tests of the prophet's credentials. He believes lying prophecies do not necessarily disqualify a person from speaking for God. He concludes his section on discerning false prophets with this: "Prophets are, of course, human beings. *As such, they can make mistakes and lie.* They need not cease to be prophets for their mistakes and failings."[11]

That statement betrays an appalling ignorance of what Scripture says about inspired prophecy. The New Testament prophetic gift (Rom. 12:6; 1 Cor. 12:10) primarily has to do with declaration, not revelation. The New Testament prophet "speaks to men for edification and exhortation and comfort" (1 Cor. 14:3). He is a preacher, not a source of ongoing revelation. His task is one of forth-telling, not foretelling. That is, he proclaims already revealed truth; he is not generally a conduit for new revelation.

In the early church, before the New Testament was complete, certain prophets were used by God on occasion to exhort the church with messages inspired as the prophet spoke. That was necessary to instruct the churches in matters that were not yet covered by Scripture. This revelatory aspect of prophecy was unique to the apostolic era.

The contemporary charismatic perspective that makes every prophet an instrument of divine revelation cheapens both Scripture *and* prophecy. By permitting these so-called prophets to mix error with messages supposedly "fresh from God's lips," charismatics have opened the floodgates to false teaching, confusion, error, fanaticism, and chaos.

How could a message genuinely inspired by God be tainted with error or lies? Inspired prophecy would have to be on a level with Scripture. It is the very Word of God. *Every* prophetic revelation contains a "Thus saith the Lord"—if not explicitly, then implicitly. Revelatory prophecy is not the prophet's opinion or speculation. It is not a mere impression in his mind. It is not a guess or a divination. It has nothing whatever to do with soothsaying. It is *a word from the Lord* (cf. 1 Sam. 3:1, Jer. 37:17). And since the prophet purports to speak for God, he is held to the highest standard of accountability—and judged with the utmost severity if he prophesies falsely (Deut. 13:1–5; 18:20–22).[12]

It stands to reason that since a prophet speaking revelation is a mouthpiece for God's own words, every authentic prophetic revelation will be as true, reliable, and inerrant as Scripture itself. Otherwise, either we make God a liar, or we must downgrade the meaning of revelation and in effect embrace a secondary level of inspiration. We would have to devise a theory in which God somehow enables contemporary prophets to deliver a message that is a true word from him, but not as authoritative as Scripture. That is precisely what some apologists for modern charismatic prophecy have attempted to do.

Bill Hamon, for example, heads a network of "prophetic ministries." He writes,

> Of course, prophetic ministry has not been given to the church in order to supersede the Bible. Any new "additions"

to Scripture given as prophetic messages and accepted as infallibly inspired would be counterfeits. Instead, prophetic ministry brings illumination and specifics about what has already been written, personalizing it for believers.[13]

Understand that when Hamon and other charismatics speak of prophecy, they are referring to new revelation from God. Hamon believes "all personal prophecies are conditional, whether or not any conditions are made explicit."[14] That is, prophecies "*can* be canceled, altered, reversed or diminished. For prophecy of this kind to come to pass requires the proper participation and cooperation of the one who receives the prophetic word."[15] So in Hamon's scheme, the fact that a prophecy goes unfulfilled is no proof it was false to begin with. If circumstances change, or if the prophet himself lacks faith, God may change the prophecy—or even cancel it.[16]

Hamon would undoubtedly deny that he puts modern prophetic revelation on the same level as Scripture. But in practice it becomes impossible to maintain any distinction. Later in the same article, Hamon writes,

> *Record, read and meditate on your personal prophecies.* The apostle Paul told Timothy: "Neglect not the gift that is in thee, which was given thee by prophecy, with the laying on of the hands of the presbytery. Meditate on these things; give thyself wholly to them; that thy profiting may appear to all" (1 Tim. 4:14–15).[17]

Wrenching a verse out of context, Hamon actually encourages people to give personal prophecies the kind of reverent study and reflection we are to reserve for Scripture (cf. Josh. 1:8; Ps. 1:2). This is precisely where charismatics who want to affirm the supremacy of Scripture, yet accept private revelation, run into trouble. Must I record and meditate on my prophecies? If I ignore them, is it sin? If so, I've canonized the revelation. If not, I've rendered it superfluous. Hamon has opted for canonizing it.

He compounds that error by advising people to ignore reason, logic, and the senses when attempting to "bear witness with a prophetic word's accuracy in spirit and content."[18] He writes,

> I have sometimes heard people say, "I did not witness with that prophecy." But after questioning them, I discovered that what they really meant was that the prophecy did not fit their theology, personal desires or goals, or their emotions reacted negatively to it. They failed to understand that we do not bear witness with the soul—the mind, emotions or will.
>
> Our reasoning is in the mind, not the spirit. So our traditions, beliefs and strong opinions are not true witnesses to prophetic truth. The spirit reaction originates deep within our being. Many Christians describe the physical location of its corresponding sensation as the upper abdominal area.
>
> A negative witness—with a message of "no," "be careful" or "something's not right"—usually manifests itself with a nervous, jumpy or uneasy feeling. There is a deep, almost unintelligible sensation that something is wrong. This sense can only be trusted when we are more in tune with our spirit than with our thoughts. If our thinking is causing these sensations, then it could be only a soulish reaction.
>
> On the other hand, when God's Spirit is bearing witness with our spirit that a prophetic word is right, is of God and is according to His will and purpose, then our spirit reacts with the fruit of the Holy Spirit. We have a deep, unexplainable peace and joy, a warm, loving feeling—or even a sense of our spirit jumping up and down with excitement. This sensation lets us know that the Holy Spirit is bearing witness with our spirit that everything is in order, even though we may not understand everything that is being said, or our soul may not be able to adjust immediately to all the thoughts being presented.[19]

In other words, ignore your mind, forget your beliefs, disregard your theology and common sense; the sensation in your upper abdominal area will let you know how much weight a "prophecy" really has.

That is all utter nonsense. You will not find any advice like it in Scripture. How your upper abdomen feels says nothing about whether a supposed prophecy is true or not. You may be suffering from indigestion! How many people following that kind of counsel hear some self-proclaimed oracle speak, and then move their church membership or donate their life savings to the prophet's ministry?

That kind of thinking permeates the charismatic movement. In the end, many prophecies are judged on nothing more than gut feeling. That is precisely why error and confusion run rampant in congregations led by those who call themselves prophets.

I received a tape of a message by one of these prophet-pastors, James Ryle, pastor of the Boulder Valley Vineyard in central Colorado. Ryle described in detail some dreams of his, which he took to be prophetic revelation from God. According to Ryle's dreams, God is getting ready to anoint Christian musicians with the same anointing that was given to the Beatles. He quotes a word from the Lord: "I called those four lads from Liverpool to myself. There was a call from God on their life; they were gifted by my hand; and it was I who anointed them, for I had a purpose, and the purpose was to usher in the charismatic renewal with musical revival around the world."

What happened? According to Ryle, God told him, "The four lads from Liverpool went AWOL and did not serve in my army. They served their own purposes and gave the gift to the other side." Ryle says God told him that in 1970 he lifted the anointing and has held it in his hand since then. But he is about to release it again in the church.[20] Ryle is young, well-educated, and articulate, and he has preached about his prophecy in numerous churches. Tapes of the messages are circulating internationally, and evidently thousands have received Ryle's prophecy as solemn truth from the Lord.

The fact remains that since the canon of Scripture was completed, *no genuine revival or orthodox movement has ever been led by people whose authority is based in any way on private revelations from God.* Many groups have claimed to receive new revelation, but all of them have been fanatical, heretical, cultic, or fraudulent. Both charismatics and non-charismatics need to consider whether there is a parallel between these groups and the modern charismatic movement.

Montanism

Montanus was a second-century heretic from Phrygia who believed he was a prophet sent by God to reform Christianity through asceticism, the practice of glossolalia, and continued prophetic revelation. He believed he was inspired by the Holy Spirit in all his teaching. Two so-called prophetesses, Priscilla and Maximilla, were instrumental in the spread of Montanism. The church father Eusebius wrote, "[Montanus] stirred up two women and filled them with the bastard spirit so that they uttered demented, absurd and irresponsible sayings."[21] Some historians have taken that to mean that those women spoke in tongues.

Hippolytus wrote of the Montanists,

> They have been deceived by two females, Priscilla and Maximilla by name, whom they hold to be prophetesses, asserting that into them the Paraclete spirit entered. . . . They magnify these females above the Apostles and every gift of Grace, so that some of them go so far as to say that in them there is something more than Christ. . . . They introduce novelties in the form of fasts and feasts, abstinences and diets of radishes, giving these females as their authority.[22]

Montanism spread rapidly throughout the early church and reached Rome in the second half of the second century. Eusebius described the birth and early growth of the movement:

> Montanus, they say, first exposed himself to the assaults of the adversary through his unbounded lust for leadership. He was one of the recent converts, and he became possessed of a spirit, and suddenly began to rave in a kind of ecstatic trance, and to babble jargon, prophesying in a manner contrary to the custom of the church which had been handed down by tradition from the earliest times.
>
> . . . Some of them that heard his bastard utterances rebuked him as one possessed of a devil . . . remembering the Lord's warning to guard vigilantly against the coming of false prophets. But others were carried away and not a little elated, thinking themselves possessed of the Holy Spirit and of the gift of prophecy.[23]

Tertullian, one of the leading church fathers, converted to Montanism in the latter years of his life, and he wrote this description of a Montanist church service:

> We have among us now a sister who has been granted gifts of revelations, which she experiences in church during the Sunday services through ecstatic vision in the Spirit. . . . And after the people have been dismissed at the end of the service it is her custom to relate to us what she has seen. . . . "Among other things," says she, "there was shown to me a soul in bodily form, and it appeared like a spirit; but it was no mere something, void of qualities, but rather a thing which could be grasped, soft and translucent and of etherial colour, in a form at all points human."[24]

Sound familiar? Tertullian sounds like he might have been describing a twentieth-century charismatic church.

Montanus and his followers claimed to receive revelation from God that supplemented the Word communicated by

Christ and the apostles. They believed the Holy Spirit spoke through the mouths of Montanus and the two prophetesses. Montanus believed he was living in the last days immediately before the return of Christ. He taught that God's kingdom would be set up in his own village of Pepuza in his lifetime, and that he would have a prominent role in it. Those and other false prophecies were among the chief reasons the rest of the church considered his movement heretical.

Montanus opposed formalism in the church and boldly intimidated Christians by claiming his followers were more spiritual than those who had only the "dead letter" of the Scriptures.

In most respects, Montanists were orthodox. But the movement was schismatic, believing only themselves to be the true church. The rest of the church branded Montanism as a serious heresy to be rejected. Augustine wrote against the movement, and the Council at Constantinople decreed that Montanism was tantamount to paganism.[25]

The contemporary charismatic movement is in many ways the spiritual heir of Montanism. In fact, it would not at all be unfair to call today's charismatic movement neo-Montanism. At least one leading charismatic writer, Larry Christenson, even claims the Montanist movement as part of the charismatic historical tradition.[26]

Roman Catholicism

The similarity between the charismatic view of revelation and the traditional teachings of the Roman Catholic Church is worth pursuing. A good place to start is with the Roman Catholic concept of tradition. Roman Catholic scholar Gabriel Moran gives these classifications:

Dogmatic tradition is the revealed truth made known by God in Scripture before the death of the last apostle. Dogmatic tradition is commonly called "primary revelation."

Disciplinary tradition includes the practices and liturgical rites of the church in apostolic or post-apostolic times that are not part of divine revelation in Scripture. Disciplinary tradition is commonly called "secondary revelation."[27]

"Tradition, then," said French Roman Catholic George Tavard, "was the overflow of the Word outside Sacred Scripture. It was neither separate from nor identical with Holy Writ. Its contents were the 'other scriptures' through which the Word made Himself known."[28]

Another Roman Catholic with a view very similar to what charismatics are saying today was Kasper Schatzgeyer (1463–1527). He taught that "An 'intimate revelation from the Holy Spirit' is an everyday possibility. Once known beyond doubt, it is as binding as the teaching that came from Christ's own mouth."[29]

All of that raises a question: "Where does the Bible end?" Because of their interpretation of the word *tradition*, Roman Catholic doctrinal teaching is open-ended. There is always the possibility of adding something that is equal in authority to the Scriptures. The Council of Trent (1545–63), which was convened to solidify Catholic opposition to the Protestant Reformation, made this summary statement regarding the equality of Scripture and tradition:

> The Holy, Oecumenical and General Synod of Trent . . . having this aim always before its eyes, that errors may be removed and the purity of the Gospel be preserved in the Church, which was before promised through the prophets in the Holy Scriptures and which our Lord Jesus Christ the Son of God first published by his own mouth and then commanded to be preached through his Apostles to every creature as a source of all saving truth and of discipline of conduct; and perceiving that this truth and this discipline are *contained in written books and in unwritten traditions,* which were received by the Apostles from the lips of Christ himself, or, by the same Apostles, at the dictation of the Holy Spirit, and were handed on and have come down to us; following the example of the orthodox Fathers, *this Synod*

receives and venerates, with equal pious affection and reverence,
all the books both of the New and the Old Testaments . . .
together with the said Traditions . . . as having been given
either from the lips of Christ or by the dictation of the Holy
Spirit and preserved in unbroken succession in the Catholic
Church.[30]

According to that, God has supposedly been giving
revelation through the Roman Catholic Church since the
New Testament era. From the "unwritten traditions, which
. . . were handed on and have come down to us," it was a
short step to the concept of the infallibility of the pope, who,
according to Roman Catholic dogma, is successor to the
apostle Peter. Roman Catholic theology teaches that when
the pope speaks *ex cathedra* (as pastor and teacher of all
Christians), he does so with supreme apostolic authority and
is infallible. Two examples of "infallible" additions to
Scripture and tradition in recent times are these:

In a papal bull of December 8, 1854, entitled *Ineffabilis Deus*
('Ineffable God'), Pius IX solemnly decreed that "the most
Blessed Virgin Mary was, from the first moment of her
conception, by the singular grace and privilege of almighty
God and in view of the merits of Christ Jesus the Savior of
the human race, preserved immune from all stain of original
sin, [that this] is revealed by God and, therefore, firmly and
constantly to be believed by the faithful."[31]

The latest addition to the long list of Roman Catholic
beliefs . . . came on November 1, 1950, with an *ex cathedra*
pronouncement by pope Pius XII from St. Peter's chair that
Mary's body was raised from the grave shortly after she died,
that her body and soul were reunited, and that she was
taken up and enthroned as Queen of Heaven. And to this
pronouncement was added the usual warning that "anyone
who may henceforth doubt or deny this doctrine is utterly
fallen away from the divine and Catholic faith."[32]

Those decrees have two important things in common. First, they are revealed outside Scripture as part of "tradition"—extrabiblical revelation. And second, Roman Catholic believers are admonished to believe them without question on threat of excommunication.

Since Roman Catholic doctrine allows for additional revelations equal to Scripture in authority, the church can spawn error after error as it conceives teachings not found in the Word of God. Once a group goes beyond Scripture and allows for any other authoritative source of truth, the gates are wide open, and anything can pour through.

Roman Catholicism has added to Scripture such traditions as penance, purgatory, papal infallibility, prayers for the dead, and an entire sacramental system. None of those things has biblical support, but they are all affirmed by the Roman Catholic faithful as truth revealed from God through the Church.

Could it be that charismatics are already building similar traditions of their own? For example, in many charismatic circles, "slain in the spirit" is a familiar expression. Those who are "slain in the spirit" are knocked unconscious or into a trance by a touch from someone who is supposedly a transmitter of divine power. The practice has more in common with occultism than with anything biblical (see chapter 7).

I talked with one charismatic who said, "Oh, yes, it's vital to be slain in the Spirit. In fact, you should never go for more than two or three weeks without being slain in the Spirit." A former charismatic told me there are no limits to it. It often becomes a contest to see who can get "slain" the most often.

I asked a charismatic friend, "Why do you do this?" His answer was, "Because this is the way the Spirit of God's power comes upon you." "According to what Scripture?" I inquired. "Well, there isn't any Scripture," he replied.

No Scripture? Then where does the authority for such a

practice come from? Pentecostal tradition? Charismatic and Roman Catholic methodology walk hand in hand at this point.

Neoorthodoxy

Neoorthodox theology claims that Scripture is not the objective Word of God, but has the potential of speaking to people's hearts in a moment of meaning as they open themselves to it. According to neoorthodoxy, God never did really speak propositionally in the Word; rather, he speaks personally in private revelation when we encounter him.

Neoorthodoxy believes that the Bible is a good model and a dynamic witness, but not intrinsically the objective Word of God. The Word must be sought in application. In other words, the Bible is not the Word of God as it sits on the shelf; it becomes the Word of God only as it speaks to the human heart. That may sound good at first, but there is a fatal flaw. This teaching relegates God's revelation entirely to the arena of the subjective. It opens the door for each individual to define truth in his or her own way, making personal feelings the ultimate rule. In the end it is simply another attempt to seek revealed truth beyond the Bible. Like the charismatic movement, it looks to human experience to find that truth.

In their excellent text *A General Introduction to the Bible*, Norman Geisler and William Nix clearly define the neoorthodox view:

> The neoorthodox view is that the Bible is a fallible human book. Nevertheless, it is the instrument of God's revelation to us, for it is a record of God's personal revelation in Christ. Revelation, however, is personal; the Bible is not a verbally inspired revelation from God. It is merely an errant human means through which one can encounter the personal revelation who is Christ. In itself it is not the Word of God; at best, the Bible only becomes the Word of God to the individual when he encounters Christ through it.[33]

The idea behind neoorthodoxy is that the Bible is inspired when it creates an experience for you. J. K. S. Reid asserts that "God marches up and down through the Bible magisterially, making His Word come to life at any point throughout its length and breadth. So too it is rightly said that the Bible *becomes* the Word of God. . . . The Bible becomes the Word of God by stated and steady appointment."[34] Emil Brunner says the Spirit of God is "imprisoned within the covers of the written word."[35] He is released in human experience.

The Bible, says neoorthodoxy, is not all there is. God is still giving revelation, still inspiring others in the same way he inspired the biblical writers. "If the Bible is indeed the 'Word of God,' it is so not as the last word," says C. H. Dodd, another prominent theologian who reflects the neoorthodox position.[36]

What happens when the inspiration of Scripture depends on subjective experience, and when the Bible itself is not the final word? There is no biblical authority! Everything else being written and said today has just as much potential as Scripture to "inspire" people. Thus virtually anything becomes a source of potential "revelation."

Are charismatics saying something similar to neoorthodoxy? I believe many of them are. An article written several years ago for *Christian Life* magazine by Charles Farah is a good example. Farah wrote, "As Christians move more and more into the New Testament world, they will rely less and less on reason and experience as ultimate ways of knowing, and more and more on pneumatic knowing."[37] And how does Farah define "pneumatic knowing"? He says it is "a knowing that is beyond all knowing, a perceiving that is beyond all perceiving, a certainty that is beyond all certainty, an understanding that is beyond all understanding."[38]

Farah's statement sounds like pure mysticism. Is he advocating a twentieth-century version of gnosticism? Gnosticism was a second-century heresy that also spoke of "pneumatic knowing," meaning secret spiritual knowledge available only to the enlightened elite.

Martin Luther's reply to the Diet of Worms is well known:

> Here it is, plain and unvarnished. Unless I am convicted of error by the testimony of Scriptures or . . . by manifest reasoning I stand convicted by the Scriptures to which I have appealed, and my conscience is taken captive by God's Word, I cannot and will not recant anything. . . . On this I take my stand. I can do no other. God help me. Amen.[39]

Luther appealed to the Word of God and to reason. Do we really need to look beyond that in search of truth? Can we possibly experience a mystical "knowing beyond knowing"? To attempt to define truth in such a way is to place truth beyond the revealed Word of God. The Bible gives certainty. The Word of God gives understanding (Ps. 119:130). Who can go beyond that? The written Word of God is sufficient for all our spiritual needs (Ps. 19:7–14). Extrabiblical revelation *always* leads to error!

The Cults

> The *Book of Mormon* makes this claim:

> Do ye not suppose that I know of these things myself? Behold, I testify unto you that I do know that these things whereof I have spoken are true. And how do ye suppose that I know of their surety? Behold, I say unto you they are made known unto me by the Holy Spirit of God . . . and this is the spirit of revelation which is in me.[40]

The Mormons also put two other books on par with Scripture: *Doctrine and Covenants* and *The Pearl of Great Price*. From these further "revelations" pour error after error concerning God, human nature, and the person and work of Christ. The result is theological chaos.

Christian Science is another cult that bases its teaching on truth supposedly given by God in addition to Scripture. The *Christian Science Journal* stated: "Because it is not a human philosophy but a divine revelation, the divinity-based reason and logic of Christian Science necessarily separates it from all other systems."[41] It calls Mary Baker Eddy "the revelator of truth for this age."[42]

Mrs. Eddy wrote, "I should blush to write of 'Science and Health with Key to the Scriptures' as I have, were it of human origin, and were I, apart from God, its author. But, as I was only a scribe echoing the harmonies of heaven in divine metaphysics, I cannot be super-modest in my estimate of the Christian Science textbook."[43]

Although the errors of Christian Science regarding God, Christ, and the Scriptures are well documented in numerous books, Mrs. Eddy was convinced she was used by God to reveal his truth for her day.

Perhaps the most visible cultists in our nation are the Jehovah's Witnesses. Tireless in their efforts, Witnesses go from door to door spreading their doctrine of salvation by works, which negates the grace of God through Christ. They claim Jesus was a created being, not God the Son. And do the Witnesses believe they have new revelation? Indeed they do! They have plainly said so in their magazine, *Watchtower*: "The *Watchtower* is a magazine without equal on earth. . . . This is not giving any credit to the magazine publishers, but is due to the great Author of the Bible with its truths and prophecies, and who now interprets its prophecies."[44]

The Worldwide Church of God is another group that teaches salvation by works and revelation from God beyond Scripture. It was founded by Herbert W. Armstrong, who also began Ambassador College, *The Plain Truth* magazine, and the radio and television programs "The World Tomorrow." Armstrong believed the Bible was written in a code only he had been able to decipher.[45]

Sun Myung Moon, self-styled messiah from Korea, claims

he is a divine messenger from God. Moon says he has the ultimate truth—not from Scripture, not from literature, and not from any person's brain. According to Moon, if his "truth" contradicts the Bible (and it does), then the Bible is wrong.

From Sola Scriptura to "Something More"

Virtually every cult and false teaching ever spawned was begun on the premise that its leader or leaders had access to new revelation. Just about every false teacher from spiritualist Edgar Cayce to L. Ron Hubbard, founder of Scientology, has claimed revelation of some kind from God. All have abandoned the tenet of *Sola Scriptura* and embarked on a dangerous quest for something more.

The charismatics' acceptance of modern "prophecy" represents a turn down a perilous road. The marker may read "Something More," but the road of new revelation is really a path to something less. It is filled with detours, dead ends, giant chuckholes—and very little else.

Some charismatics are troubled about this problem. Stephen Strang, writing in *Charisma*, says,

> When it comes to something such as personal prophecy, we believe that extremism is more deadly than when dealing with less volatile issues. That is because there is an element of control involved when one individual is able to speak for God to a group of individuals. . . . It isn't always easy to tell when a person is really speaking for God or speaking carnally. Or maybe even speaking for the enemy.
>
> We believe there are some who purport to prophesy that actually get their unusual ability to know the future, not from the Holy Spirit, but from a spirit of divination. And there are some charismatics who are so eager to know God's will or to get a word from God or to be singled out in a service where this special gift may be manifest that they are susceptible to spirits that are not from God.[46]

Strang has identified the central problem, but he offers no solution. How *do* we know if a true prophet is speaking, or if the message comes from an evil spirit of divination—or for that matter, from someone's imagination? Is discerning truth really something as subjective as upper abdominal distress? Where do we draw the line if not at the point of Scripture?

Joseph Dillow gave this account of how a charismatic brother in Christ tried to influence him at a critical point in his life:

> When I was a new Christian I met a man I'll call Bill. Bill was given to seeing visions and regularly claimed he received direct revelation from God. He saw the Lord working in every conceivable circumstance of life. Every inner impression was examined as to the Lord's leading. One night he called me at midnight because he had a message from the Lord that he had to share with me. Bill was in his forties and lived alone about an hour's drive from my house, but he still wanted to come and deliver the message in person. I was touched by his concern but told him it would be all right with me if it waited till tomorrow. He insisted, so I invited him over. When he arrived he was visibly shaken. At the time I had just decided to go to seminary. Bill was very upset about this ("The letter kills," he said, "but the Spirit gives life"), and now he had a message from the Lord warning me not to take this step. He had been reading Isaiah and the Lord gave him a special revelation that said, "If you go to seminary, your wife will be eaten by lions and you will lose your eternal salvation!" It was rather frightening but I didn't buy it. He lived in a world of superstition which his theology of tongues had fostered. The centrality of the Word had been lost in his life. The last I heard of Bill he was in jail because the "Lord had told him" that he was to disobey constituted authority and not comply with a zoning ordinance![47]

Bill is an extreme example of a questionable approach to revelation. The Mormons, Jehovah's Witnesses, and others are also extreme examples. They represent heresies that I am in no way trying to equate with charismatic Christians who love Christ and the Scriptures. But when it comes to the vital area of revelation, the parallels between charismatic claims and the ideas of the extremists are clearly there. And that is my point: *The worst extremes usually start with slight deviations.*

The price of charismatic mysticism and subjectivism is much too high. Everyone is free to do and say and teach whatever this week's personal prophecy supposedly reveals. Scholarship and careful study are swept aside in favor of private messages from God. Kenneth Hagin, for example, has written, "Theologians as a whole are not too sure who wrote Hebrews. It sounds like Paul's writings to me, and one time when Jesus appeared to me in a vision, I asked Him, and He told me that Paul wrote it. And I believe he did!"[48] No further discussion of the issue follows. Hagin's next words are, "Paul is writing here to Hebrew Christians."[49]

Scripture, of course, does not identify the author of Hebrews. Godly men who have studied the book carefully for internal evidence of its authorship generally agree that the issue cannot be settled with any biblical proof. That does not matter to Kenneth Hagin; he has his own private revelation on the matter.

The uniqueness and central authority of the Word have thus been lost, and the charismatics have developed a mystical brand of Christianity that may eventually have little biblical content or substance.

Evangelical Christianity has exploded in recent years. But our churches are being filled with people who are looking past the Scriptures for help and growth. Go into the average Christian bookstore and you will find that the overwhelming majority of books focus on feelings and experience rather than a solid study of the Bible, doctrine, or theology. Many people do not really care what Scripture says; they are sure the Bible is too simplistic or too naïve. Besides, these people are too busy looking for that elusive "something more" that they hope will solve all their problems.

The following letter written to an acquaintance of mine from a young man in the charismatic movement illustrates this indifferent attitude toward Scripture:

> The greatest experience in love I have ever had was at the foot of the cross as the blood of Jesus Christ poured out over me. He filled me with His Spirit. He brought me across the veil into the City of Jerusalem into the Holy of Holies. There I beheld myself in Him, and He in me. I received the baptism as by fire and from this His love dwells in me. From this I have communion daily.
>
> I do not feel the need for study of the Scriptures, for I know Jesus as He has revealed Himself to me within; and as He dwells in me, there is the Word.
>
> I go to scripture, and scripture is vital and necessary—but neither central nor crucial, for I have Him—rather He has me. Scriptures are a secondary source.
>
> Through the baptism of the Holy Spirit the Word in me (the very spiritual body of Jesus Christ) is primary. I say this as a living experience out of what he has given me to say.

The Reformers fought such errors with the principle of *Sola Scriptura*. Charismatics have abandoned that crucial precept. Now the true church in the twentieth century must fight for the supremacy and sufficiency of God's Word. We dare not surrender to a theology that gives tradition or experience equal weight to Scripture. The uniqueness of God's revelation in the Bible is at stake. The Bible's own claim for itself is being challenged. It is an error to which those who love the Word of God cannot acquiesce.

There is no substitute for the Word of God. There is no "something more." Don't seek energy for the spiritual walk in the empty "prophecies" of someone's imagination. Don't look for guidance in the uncertain counsel of feelings and intuition. Don't set your course by the erroneous signpost of some self-deluded prophet's exhortation. God has given us his Word, which is "profitable for teaching, for reproof, for correction, for training in righteousness; that the man of God may be adequate, equipped for every good work" (2 Tim. 3:16). That is all the truth we need—for every spiritual need in life.

— 4 —

How Should We Interpret the Bible?

Hermeneutics is a word theologians use to speak of the science of Bible interpretation. It is a crucial building block in all theology. In fact, the major streams of theology within professing Christianity (evangelicalism, liberalism, neoorthodoxy) differ largely because of the distinctive hermeneutical methods they use to make sense of what the Bible says.

Pentecostals and charismatics tend to base much of their teaching on very poor principles of hermeneutics. Gordon D. Fee has written,

> Pentecostals, in spite of some of their excesses, are frequently praised for recapturing for the church her joyful radiance, missionary enthusiasm, and life in the Spirit. But they are at the same time noted for bad hermeneutics. . . . First, their attitude toward Scripture regularly has included a general disregard for scientific exegesis and carefully thought-out hermeneutics. In fact, hermeneutics has simply not been a Pentecostal thing. Scripture is the Word of God and is to be obeyed. In place of scientific hermeneutics there developed a kind of pragmatic hermeneutics—obey what

should be taken literally; spiritualize, allegorize, or devotionalize the rest. . . .

Secondly, it is probably fair—and important—to note that in general the Pentecostals' experience has preceded their hermeneutics. In a sense, the Pentecostal tends to exegete his experience.[1]

That is not the appraisal of someone hostile to the Pentecostal and charismatic movement. Gordon Fee is himself a Pentecostal. His assessment is exactly right; he has observed from within the movement the same problem that many of us on the outside have noted.

Watch the typical charismatic television program, and you'll quickly see evidence of what Fee is talking about. I watched in horror a couple of years ago as a guest on a charismatic television network explained the "biblical basis" of his ministry of "possibility thinking." "My ministry is based entirely on my life verse, Matthew 19:26, 'With God all things are possible.' God gave me that verse because I was born in 1926."

Obviously intrigued by that method of obtaining a "life verse," the talk show host grabbed a Bible and began thumbing through excitedly. "I was born in 1934," he said. "My life verse would be Matthew 19:34. What does it say?" Then he discovered that Matthew 19 has only thirty verses. Undeterred, he flipped to Luke 19 and read verse 34: "And they said, The Lord hath need of him" (KJV).

Thrilled, he exclaimed, "Oh, the Lord has *need* of me! The Lord has need of *me*! What a wonderful life verse! I've never had a life verse before, but now the Lord has given me one! Thank you, Jesus! Hallelujah!" The studio audience began to applaud.

At that moment, however, the talk show host's wife, who had also turned to Luke 19, said, "Wait a minute! You can't use this. This verse is talking about a *donkey*!"

That incident says much about the willy-nilly way some

charismatics approach Scripture. Looking for "a word from the Lord," some play a game of "Bible roulette," flipping at random through their Bibles, looking for something that seems applicable to whatever trial or need they are facing. When they find one, they say, "The Lord gave me a verse."

That is no way to approach Bible study. Perhaps you have heard the familiar story of the man who, seeking guidance for a major decision, decided to close his eyes, open his Bible, put his finger down, and get guidance from whatever verse his finger happened to light on. His first try brought him to Matthew 27:5: "[Judas] went and hanged himself" (KJV). Thinking that that verse was really not much help, he determined to try again. This time his finger landed on Luke 10:37 and Jesus' words there: "Go, and do thou likewise" (KJV). Not ready to give up, he tried one more time. This time his finger came to rest on Jesus' words in John 13:27: "That thou doest, do quickly" (KJV).

That story, which I am sure is apocryphal, makes an important point: looking for meaning in Scripture beyond its historical, grammatical, and logical context is unwise and even potentially dangerous. It is possible, of course, to substantiate almost any idea or teaching with Scripture—if one employs proof texts apart from their intended meaning. That is precisely how most of the cults use Scripture to buttress their false doctrines.

The task of hermeneutics is to discover the meaning of the text in its proper setting; to draw meaning from Scripture rather than reading one's presuppositions into it.

The importance of careful biblical interpretation can hardly be overstated. Misinterpreting the Bible is ultimately no better than disbelieving it. What good does it do to agree that the Bible is God's final and complete revelation and then misinterpret it? The result is still the same: one misses God's truth. Interpreting Scripture to make it say what it was never intended to say is a sure road to division, error, heresy, and apostasy.

Yet how casually contemporary evangelicalism approaches Bible interpretation! Perhaps you have been in one of those "Bible studies" where everyone goes around the room and shares an opinion about the verse in question. "Well, to me this verse means such and such." In the end what you have is usually a pooling of everyone's ignorance, along with several potential interpretations of the verse, all of which may be wrong.

The truth is, it doesn't matter what a verse means to me, to you, or to anyone else. All that matters is what the verse *means*! You see, every verse has intrinsic meaning apart from any of us. It has that true meaning whether or not any of us has ever considered it. The task of Bible study is to discern that true meaning of Scripture; to understand what God is saying in the text. Sometimes the meaning is quickly evident; other times it requires a closer look at the context. I admit I have encountered some passages I simply cannot fully understand. But the fact remains: every jot and tittle of Scripture carries only the intended meaning of the author, and the task of the interpreter is to discern what that is.

Three Errors To Avoid

Second Timothy 2:15 speaks about Bible study: "Be diligent to present yourself approved to God as a workman who does not need to be ashamed, handling accurately the word of truth." Clearly, handling Scripture involves diligence and care. It must be treated accurately. Those who fail to do that will be ashamed.

Let me suggest three errors to avoid:

Refrain from making a point at the price of proper interpretation. It is easy—and often tempting—for a pastor or teacher to sneak a foreign meaning into a text to get a desired response. A good illustration of that error is found in the Talmud (commentaries on the Jewish Scriptures). A rabbi is trying to convince people that the primary issue in life is concern for human beings. He uses the stones of the Tower of Babel in Genesis 11 to support his contention, telling us that the builders of the tower were frustrated because they put material things first and people last. As the tower grew taller, it took a hod carrier many hours to carry a load of bricks to the bricklayers working at the top. If a man fell off the tower on the way down, no one paid any attention. It was only a workman who was lost. But if he fell off on the way up, they mourned because the load of bricks was lost too. That, said the teacher, is why God confused their language—because they failed to give priority to human beings.

That cannot be found in the Bible. In fact, it skews the lesson of this chapter of Genesis. While it is true that people are more important than bricks, that's not the point of the Tower of Babel. The eleventh chapter of Genesis says nothing whatever about the importance of people over bricks. The point is that *God* is more important than *idols*, and he judges idolatry. Babel was a judgment on proud men who were defying God. It is never right to come up with a good message by ignoring the real lesson in a Scripture passage.

Avoid superficial study. Accurate Bible study is hard work. As we have seen, discerning what God is saying to us through his word cannot be done by flipping through quickly and looking for messages wherever our eyes happen to settle. Nor is understanding the Bible a matter of personal opinion ("To *me* it means . . .").

Careful and accurate handling of God's Word requires diligence. If we are diligent, we can arrive at a correct interpretation of the major truths of Scripture and the general thrust of particular passages. God has not hidden his truth from us. But neither is the meaning always instantly clear. Sometimes the real meaning of a passage is revealed in an understanding of the culture to which it was addressed. Sometimes it is made clear by a simple nuance in the original language. That is why we cannot get by with the haphazard ad-libbing and flip freewheeling that is so popular in some churches today. Some differences of interpretation may never be resolved in this life, but that does not negate our responsibility to study carefully and diligently.

First Timothy 5:17 says that "double honor" is to be given to those in the church "who labor in the word and doctrine." The reason God has given teachers to the church is that understanding his Word and correctly instructing people in the Scriptures requires people who are committed to persistent, conscientious labor in response to the divine calling.

Bernard Ramm wrote,

> It is often asserted by devout people that they can know the Bible completely without helps. They preface their interpretations with a remark like this: "Dear friends, I have read no man's book. I have consulted no man-made commentaries. I have gone right to the Bible to see what it had to say for itself." This sounds very spiritual, and usually is seconded with *amens* from the audience.
>
> But is this the pathway of wisdom? Does any man have either the right or the learning to by-pass all the godly learning of the church? We think not.
>
> First, although the claim to by-pass mere human books and go right to the Bible itself sounds devout and spiritual *it is a veiled egotism*. It is a subtle affirmation that a man can adequately know the Bible apart from the untiring, godly, consecrated scholarship of men like Calvin, Bengel, Alford, Lange, Ellicott, or Moule. . . .
>
> Secondly, such a claim is the old confusion of the inspiration of the Spirit with the illumination of the Spirit. The function of the Spirit is not to communicate *new* truth or to instruct in *matters unknown*, but to illuminate what is revealed in Scripture. Suppose we select a list of words from Isaiah and ask a man who claims he can by-pass the godly learning of Christian scholarship if he can out of his own

soul or prayer give their meaning or significance: Tyre, Zidon, Chittim, Sihor, Moab, Mahershalahashbas, Calno, Carchemish, Hamath, Aiath, Migron, Michmash, Geba, Anathoth, Laish, Nob, and Gallim. He will find the only light he can get on these words is from a commentary or a Bible dictionary.[2]

What Ramm was describing—that lack of respect for the work of gifted theologians and expositors who have spent years studying and interpreting Scripture—tends to be characteristic of charismatics. Why? Is it because charismatics place more emphasis on letting people in the congregation say whatever they think the Spirit told them about a Bible verse? There is a vast difference between whimsical interpretations and the teaching of learned men who have the skills and tools to explain what the Word of God means. Unfortunately, charismatics seem too often drawn to the former.

I heard a radio interview where a charismatic woman, a pastor, was asked how she "got her sermons up." She replied, "I don't get them up; I get them down. God delivers them to me." Her words reflect an attitude all too familiar in her movement. Many actually believe it is unspiritual to study. "After all," some say (taking a verse completely out of context), "Didn't Jesus say, 'For the Holy Spirit will teach you in that very hour what you ought to say'?" (Luke 12:12).

We should be greatly concerned about this ad-lib approach to Scripture. Too many people are standing up in pulpits with little or no preparation and telling others what God is saying. Usually, it is not what God is saying at all. Many of them invent their theology as they speak.

Don't spiritualize or allegorize unless the text itself calls for it. Some people use Scripture as a fable to teach whatever point they want to put across. Instead of seeking the meaning of the biblical material, they make it an allegory to support whatever they want to teach.

An extreme example of the perils of allegorizing was the young couple that came to one of our assistant pastors to get counseling about their marital problems. He began talking with them, and after about thirty minutes he asked them, "Why did you ever get married? You are miles apart!"

"Oh" said the husband. "It was the sermon the pastor preached in our church."

"And what was it?"

"Well, he preached on Jericho."

"Jericho! What does that have to do with marriage?"

"Well, he said that God's people claimed the city, marched around it seven times, and the walls fell down. He said if a young man believed God had given him a certain young girl, he could claim her, march around her seven times, and the walls of her heart would fall down. So that's what I did, and we got married."

"That can't be true," said our assistant pastor. "You are just kidding aren't you?"

"No, it's true," said the husband. "And there were many other couples who got married because of the same sermon!"

Some people believe their marriages were made in heaven. Here was a marriage made in an allegory—and a silly one at that! That kind of interpretation has gone on since the early days of the church, and it continues today, especially in the charismatic movement. A well-known charismatic preacher, whom I have talked with often, did a series on the book of Nehemiah. As he taught, just about everything in the book represented something else or meant something symbolic. These were among his points:

Jerusalem's walls were in ruin, and that speaks of the broken-down walls of the human personality. Nehemiah represents the Holy Spirit, who comes to rebuild the walls of human personality. When he got to the king's pool (Neh. 2:14), he said this meant the baptism of the Holy Spirit; and from there he went on to teach the importance of speaking in tongues.

The book of Nehemiah has nothing to do with the walls of human personality, the baptism of the Spirit, or speaking in tongues; but when a preacher reads that kind of application into the story, some people think it is marvelous Bible teaching. I do not agree. I think it is hucksterism. It makes the Bible say what we want in place of what God is saying to us (cf. 2 Cor. 2:17).

For the correct approach to interpreting Scripture, we have the model given by Jesus himself on the road to Emmaus just after his resurrection. As he walked along with two of his disciples, he taught them: "Beginning with Moses and with all the prophets, He explained to them the things concerning Himself in all the Scriptures" (Luke 24:27). The Greek word used here for "explained" is *hermeneuō*, from which we get our English word *hermeneutics*. When Jesus taught the Scriptures, he interpreted them properly and in order. He used *hermeneuō*—hermeneutics. Jesus is the perfect model of a teacher who uses sound interpretive methods. Doing it any other way adulterates the Word of God.

Five Principles for Sound Bible Interpretation

All those suggestions are good in a general sense, but they will not give you much help with properly interpreting specific Bible passages. That is why any well-taught class on biblical hermeneutics should include the following five principles:

The literal principle. When we speak of interpreting Scripture literally, we are not talking about a slavish, rigid literalism. Literal interpretation means we understand Scripture in its normal sense, including figures of speech like parables, hyperbole, simile, metaphor, and symbolism.

Scripture is to be read naturally. In years past theologians spoke of the *usus loquendi*, meaning that the words of Scripture are to be interpreted the same way words are

understood in ordinary daily use. God has communicated his
Word to us through human language, and there is every
reason to assume he has done it in the most obvious and
simple fashion possible. His words are to be understood just as
we would interpret the language of normal discourse. Although there is occasional figurative language and symbolism
in Scripture, those things are quite evident in the places they
are employed. The first thing the careful interpreter looks for
is the literal meaning, not some mystical, deeper, hidden,
secret, or spiritualized interpretation.

Some of the apocalyptic passages, such as those in
Zechariah, Daniel, Ezekiel, Isaiah, or Revelation, contain
obvious figures and symbols that must be studied carefully to
see the literal truth they are conveying. That kind of symbolic
language, however, is not the norm in Scripture and it is
conspicuous where employed. Sometimes the symbolism is
hard to interpret, but by studying the historical setting, one
can usually discern a clear meaning. Even the figurative
language conveys clear, literal truth. Scripture is not the kind
of puzzle some people seem to want to make it.

Parables are another form of figurative language sometimes used in Scripture. Parables are stories that illustrate a
spiritual truth but whose details may not be actually historical.
The details—people, events, times, and places—may be
hypothetical, metaphorical, or simply unidentified. But the
spiritual truths illustrated by parables are always literal and
real.

Those who have abandoned literal interpretation in favor
of mystical or allegorical interpretation discard all hope of
achieving accuracy and coherence. Instead, they have a free-
for-all, where only the imagination rules. When they deny the
literal meaning, they are not serving Scripture by trying to
understand it but make it their slave by molding it to say what
they want it to say.

Some rabbis in the inter-testamental period interpreted
Scripture by numerology. That is, they would use the

numerical equivalent of each letter in the Hebrew alphabet to glean mystical meanings out of words. Their brand of interpretation led to some bizarre explanations of certain passages. For example, in the Hebrew alphabet the numerical value of the letters in Abraham's name adds up to 318. This was supposed to mean that Abraham had 318 servants! It is easy to see that when we violate the simple purpose of language, *any* interpretation is possible.

The historical principle. As we have noted, one of the crucial steps in understanding what a text means is to have some grasp of the cultural, geographical, and political setting in which the passage was written. If one understands the historical context, the passage often will practically interpret itself.

As we come to any book of the Bible, we have to understand the history involved. If it is an epistle to one of the churches, what were some of the characteristics of the city in which those believers lived? What were the political and cultural conditions at the time? Who was ruling where? What social pressures were involved and to what degree? What were the tensions, problems, and crises of the community? What was the culture of the day really like? What were the customs of the people?

For example, it is virtually impossible for the modern reader to make sense of Peter's admonition in 1 Peter 1:13: "Gird up the loins of your mind" (KJV). But when you realize that soldiers in New Testament times wore long flowing tunics, and that they had to tie them up around their waists so that they wouldn't trip over them when they went into battle, Peter's meaning becomes immediately clear. He is saying, "Prepare your minds for battle. Trim up whatever is holding you back or slowing you down."

To answer the cultural and historical questions we can use Bible dictionaries, Bible handbooks, commentaries, history books, and books about Bible customs. They enable us to reconstruct the setting of a Bible passage, and from the historical context will usually flow the clear meaning.

The grammatical principle. Often the syntactical construction of a passage is the key to its meaning. Sometimes, for example, the meaning of a sentence can hinge on something as simple as a preposition. It obviously matters a great deal whether a passage says "because of," "through," "into," "in," "by," or "with." And in some cases the original Greek word used can be translated by two or more different English words. It is important to know whether the word appearing in your English Bible has a possible alternative translation. Also, if a sentence refers to "this" or "it," it is important to know the antecedent of the pronoun.

Grammar may not be your favorite subject—it certainly isn't mine—but we need to grasp the basics when interpreting the language of Scripture. We have to follow the sequence of the words and phrases to know precisely what the Word of God says. An accurate understanding of the passage may depend on it.

People sometimes ask me, "What is the first thing you do when you prepare a message?" I tell them that I study the biblical text in the original language—Greek or Hebrew. I note the proper order of the words and sentences. I go over the sentence structure and the grammar. I want to know exactly what is being said.

This can be done by anyone willing to invest a little time and effort. Even if one does not know Greek or Hebrew, an interlinear translation, which shows the Greek or Hebrew text with corresponding English words above the original language, can be used. At the very least, a good Bible commentary can be consulted. Take note of those writers and speakers who seem to pay attention to grammar—and watch out for those who do not. Learn to do inductive Bible study by breaking down the English verses into phrases, showing nouns, verbs, modifiers, and other parts of speech to see their meaning more clearly.[3]

The synthesis principle. The Reformers used the expression *scriptura scripturam interpretatur*, or "Scripture interprets Scripture." By this they meant that obscure passages in Scripture must be understood in light of clearer ones. If the Bible is God's Word, it must be consistent with itself. No part of the Bible can contradict any other part. One divine Author—the Holy Spirit—inspired the whole Bible, so it has one marvelous, supernatural unity. The synthesis principle puts Scripture together with Scripture to arrive at a clear, consistent meaning. If we hold to an interpretation of one passage that does not square with something in another passage, one of the passages is being interpreted incorrectly— or possibly both of them. The Holy Spirit does not disagree with himself. And the passages with obvious meanings should interpret the more arcane ones. One should never build a doctrine on a single obscure or unclear text.[4]

When I teach a passage of Scripture, I often guide the congregation to different parts of the Bible to show how the passage under study fits into the total context of Scripture. In his fine book *God Has Spoken*, J. I. Packer said:

> The Bible appears like a symphony orchestra, with the Holy Ghost as its Toscanini; each instrumentalist has been brought willingly, spontaneously, creatively, to play his notes just as the great conductor desired, though none of them could ever hear the music as a whole. . . . The point of each part only becomes fully clear when seen in relation to all the rest.[5]

Peter said much the same thing when he wrote, "As to this salvation, the prophets who prophesied of the grace that would come to you . . . made careful search and inquiry, seeking to know what person or time the Spirit of Christ within them was indicating" (1 Peter 1:10–11). Even the

Bible writers did not always know the full meaning of what they wrote. Today, because the New Testament is complete, we see how the Bible connects into one glorious comprehensible whole.

The practical principle. The final question we should always ask is, "So what? What does all this have to do with me?" Second Timothy 3:16 says, "All scripture is inspired by God and is profitable." All of it applies to our lives in one way or another. It is beneficial for "teaching, for reproof, for correction, for training in righteousness."

Teaching is the basic divine truth, the principle that any passage teaches. It encompasses the principles we live by. For example, the Bible contains certain doctrine regarding marriage and the family. We are to apply that teaching to our lives. *Reproof* is how Scripture unmasks our sin, reveals our hidden guilt, and drives the skeletons out of our closets into broad daylight. When we apply teaching, the first step often is to let Scripture reprove us. Reproof leads to *correction*, which involves turning away from the sin we were reproved for. Then comes *training in righteousness*—the laying out of the new, righteous path in response to true doctrine. That is the practical work of God's Word.

One Thing More Is Needful

As valuable as the five principles of interpretation are, they are useless without the illumination of the Holy Spirit. In 1 Corinthians 2 Paul wrote:

> Now we have received, not the spirit of the world, but the spirit who is of God; that we might know the things that are freely given to us of God. . . . But the natural man receiveth not the things of the Spirit of God: for they are foolishness unto him: neither can he know them, because they are spiritually discerned (2:12, 14 KJV).

Paul was describing the Holy Spirit's ministry of *illumination*. Only the Holy Spirit can show us spiritual truth. Anyone can hear the facts, study other people's teaching, and gain something of an intellectual understanding about the meaning of Scripture. But apart from the Holy Spirit, the Bible will utterly fail to penetrate and transform the human heart. With the Spirit of God comes illumination—true understanding of what has been written. Every believer has the Holy Spirit, the One who inspired the writers of Scripture, and without His illuminating ministry to us, the truth of Scripture could not penetrate our hearts and minds.

Often when I read a book, I come to a section that I do not understand. I have often wished I had the author right there so I could ask him what he meant. But the Christian always has the Author of the Bible available. The Holy Spirit lives within and can help us understand God's Word.

Again, however, the Holy Spirit's illuminating ministry cannot replace conscientious study. They work together. We should keep in mind that God Himself requires that we be diligent (2 Tim. 3:16). As we explore Scripture carefully and thoroughly, the Holy Spirit uses whatever tools we acquire, whatever godly wisdom we expose ourselves to, as the means to illumine our hearts. Clark Pinnock put it well when he said that appealing to Scripture apart from complete dependence on the Holy Spirit is presumption. And to expect the Holy Spirit to teach us apart from Scripture is "sub-Christian fanaticism."[6]

Every Christian should guard carefully against a misunderstanding of 1 John 2:27: "The anointing which you received from Him abides in you, and you have no need for anyone to teach you; but as His anointing teaches you about all things, and is true and is not a lie, and just as it has taught you, you abide in Him."

What is that verse saying? Is it telling us that we don't need any teachers or guides in learning God's wisdom? That would be inconsistent with Ephesians 4:11–12, which says

God gave "pastors and teachers, for the equipping of the saints for the work of service, to the building up of the body of Christ."

The Holy Spirit has given to many the gift of teaching (Rom. 12:6–7) and has called on all believers to teach one another (2 Tim. 2:2). Rather than contradicting those Spirit-given instructions, John was talking here about heretics—antichrists who lead people astray. This passage doesn't give wholesale permission to everyone to do his own thing with the Bible. Rather, it is reassuring us that we can know the difference between heresy and the truth regarding the gospel of Christ (cf. 1 John 2:22) because we possess the Spirit. This is not an absolute guarantee of correct interpretation for every verse in the Bible.

Many sincere people misuse 1 John 2:27 to justify their lack of study and learning, then go on to misinterpret Scripture as they simply open their Bibles and "let the Holy Spirit tell them what it means." That attitude has led many into error—and it is precisely that kind of error for which the charismatic movement has become a breeding ground.

Four Texts Charismatics Commonly Misinterpret

It is hard to know which came first: charismatic theology or the misinterpretations of Scripture that support it. We will look at four important examples of the charismatics' free-wheeling approach to biblical interpretation.

Matthew 12:22–31. What is the sin against the Holy Spirit? Charles and Frances Hunter, a well-known charismatic husband-and-wife ministry team, have written several books and speak constantly on behalf of the charismatic experience.

While the Hunters are not scholars or theologians, they communicate readily with the average person; and their influence is widely felt wherever they give their interpretations of Scripture. In the introduction to their book *Why*

Should "I" Speak in Tongues? the Hunters liken anyone who questions tongues or other aspects of the charismatic movement to the Pharisees who criticized Jesus and attributed his work to Satan.[7] The Hunters also imply that critics of the charismatic movement may be perilously close to committing the unpardonable sin of blasphemy against the Holy Spirit.[8] Are the Hunters correct? Does a challenge to charismatic doctrine equal blasphemy against the Holy Spirit? When someone denies that tongues are for today, or that the baptism of the Spirit is a post-salvation experience, has that person committed an unforgivable sin?

The passage the Hunters referred to is Matthew 12:22–31. A demon-possessed man, born blind and dumb, was brought to Jesus and he healed the man. Verse 24 recounts: "But when the Pharisees heard it, they said, 'This man casts out demons only by Beelzebub the ruler of the demons.'" Beelzebub, the lord of the flies, was a Philistine deity. He was believed to be the prince of evil spirits, and his name became another term for Satan; so what the Pharisees were saying was that Jesus cast out demons through the power of Satan.

According to the five principles of interpretation given earlier, the first thing to do is look at the literal meaning of the passage. The Pharisees were literally saying that Christ got his power from Satan. That is simple enough, so we can move on to the historical principle.

Jesus' public ministry had been going on for over two years. During that time He had performed numerous miracles that proved to the Pharisees and all Israel that he is God. But the Pharisees claimed that Christ did what he did through satanic power.

Using the synthesis principle, we check other parts of the Bible and find that at his baptism by John (Matt. 3), Jesus received the power of the Holy Spirit: "After being baptized, Jesus went up immediately from the water; and behold, the heavens were opened, and he saw the Spirit of God descending as a dove, and coming upon Him" (Matt. 3:16).

Jesus had performed no miracles before that time. It wasn't until his ministry began, until the Father authenticated him and the Spirit came upon him at his baptism, that he began to prove who he really was. And always Jesus attributed his power to the Spirit. As Isaiah predicted, the Spirit came upon him and he preached and did wonders (Isa. 61:1–2). Yet the Pharisees concluded exactly the opposite—that his power was satanic.

Jesus replied to their claim by saying, in essence, "If I'm casting out Satan by using Satan's power, what do you think Satan is doing to himself?" (Matt. 12:25–26). Obviously the devil would be destroying his own kingdom, which would make no sense at all. The Pharisees had such hatred for Christ that their logic was twisted. Instead of being rational, they were being ridiculous.

Now consider Matthew 12:31–32, where Jesus says,

> Therefore I say to you, any sin and blasphemy shall be forgiven men, but blasphemy against the Spirit shall not be forgiven. And whoever shall speak a word against the Son of Man, it shall be forgiven him; but whoever shall speak against the Holy Spirit, it shall not be forgiven him, either in this age, or in the age to come.

One might speak against Jesus' humanness—the way he looked, spoke, or acted—but if one claimed that his miraculous works, done by the Holy Spirit to prove Christ's deity, were actually done by Satan, that person was in a hopeless state of rejection. He or she could not be saved. That is what Jesus was saying. If those Pharisees had seen and heard all that Jesus had said and done, yet still were convinced it was satanic, they were hopeless. They had concluded the opposite of what was clearly true, and had done so with full revelation.

What does this say to us? What is the application for today? In the first place, this was a unique historical event that occurred when Christ was physically on earth. That is not presently true. So in a primary sense, there is no application now. Perhaps there will be in "the age to come" (the millennial kingdom), when Christ is again on the earth.

Is there a secondary application? Was Jesus saying that if we question tongues or other practices in the charismatic movement today, we are committing blasphemy against the Holy Spirit? Neither the context nor the historical setting support that view. Jesus said, "Any sin and blasphemy shall be forgiven men." The general teaching that can apply to all ages is that unregenerate people can be forgiven anything if they are willing to repent and come to Christ. But continual, unrepentant blasphemy against the Holy Spirit, defined as knowing the facts about Jesus and still attributing his works to Satan, cannot be forgiven.

According to John 16:7–11, the Holy Spirit points to Jesus Christ, convicting the world of sin, righteousness, and judgment. Earlier, John had written that everyone needs to be "born again" of the Spirit (3:1–8). It is the Holy Spirit who is the regenerative agent of the Trinity, and sooner or later a person must respond to the Holy Spirit in order to respond to Christ for salvation. If a person determines instead to reject and scorn the convicting work of the Holy Spirit, there is no way that person can become a Christian.

The sin against the Holy Spirit was first of all a historical event. Secondarily, it can be applied to anyone who rejects the work of the Holy Spirit in presenting Christ's divine credentials. It can never be used in reference to challenging charismatic teaching.

Hebrews 13:8. Many Charismatics use Hebrews 13:8 as a proof text for their teaching. It carries a thrilling promise known and memorized by many Christians: "Jesus Christ is the same yesterday and today, yes and forever." Charles and Frances Hunter reason that "if [Jesus] baptized with the evidence of speaking in tongues yesterday, then surely He's doing the same thing today and will continue doing it tomorrow."[9]

The Hunters are saying that what happened "yesterday," during the earthly ministry of Jesus and in the apostolic age, is happening now. Revelation is happening now; tongues go on; healings continue; miracles still occur. The charismatic interpretation of Hebrews 13:8 is practically standard in all their writings. Many Pentecostal churches have the verse printed in large letters at the front of their auditoriums.

The question is, does the Pentecostal and charismatic interpretation of Hebrews 13:8 stand up to inspection according to sound hermeneutical principles? The literal meaning of the verse is plain. Jesus Christ is unchanging— yesterday, today, and forever. If the charismatics are talking about Christ's essence, then they are correct. In terms of historical manifestation, however, they need to think through their position.

Why should "yesterday" go only as far back as the earthly ministry of Jesus? What about Old Testament times? Jesus was not here in a human body, but he was here as the Angel of the Lord (see, for example, Gen. 16:1–13; Ex. 3:2–4; Judg. 6:12, 14; 13:21–22; Zech. 1:12–13; 3:1–2). What about before Old Testament times? Jesus was the Second Person of the Trinity in heaven (see Ps. 2:7; Heb. 10:5). Jesus was not "the same" in form during all those periods. Nor were the same things happening. There is no indication of tongues during the earthly ministry of Jesus, or during Old Testament times. Obviously tongues were not part of Jesus' ministry in the "yesterday" before Acts 2.

And as far as "forever" is concerned, none of the gifts is forever. First Corinthians 13:8–10 clearly says that the gifts of prophecy, tongues, and knowledge will not endure forever. When tested by sound hermeneutical principles, the charismatic interpretation of Hebrews 13:8 does not stand up. Charismatics force into the verse a meaning that is not there in order to justify their contention that tongues, miracles, and healings are happening today just as they did in the first century.

Mark 16:17–18. Another key proof text for Pentecostals and charismatics is Mark 16:17–18: "These signs will accompany those who have believed: in My name they will cast out demons, they will speak with new tongues; they will pick up serpents, and if they drink any deadly poison, it shall not hurt them; they will lay hands on the sick, and they will recover."

In his pamphlet "Our Gospel Message," Pentecostal Oscar Vouga quoted that passage, and then wrote this: "Through faith in the name of Jesus, devils are being cast out today, and many are being delivered from the powers of darkness, into the kingdom of God. Signs are following the preaching of the Gospel where it is preached in faith, and with the anointing of the Holy Spirit and power."[10]

The obvious problem with Vouga's interpretation is that he does not deal with everything mentioned in the text. He especially is silent concerning the taking up of serpents and the drinking of poison.

In their book *Why Should "I" Speak In Tongues?*, Charles and Frances Hunter dismissed the snakes and poison issue in a lighthearted but inadequate way. They assured their readers that they were not interested in handling snakes, and that they did not believe that God intends for Christians to go around putting their hands in baskets of rattlers to see whether they will bite. They referred to Paul (Acts 28:3–5), who picked up a serpent by accident. Paul did not boast of his ability to handle snakes safely, said the Hunters; he simply threw the snake into the fire and praised God for protecting him. What the Hunters implied was that protection from poisonous snakes only occurs when a person is bitten by accident.

The Hunters pursue the same "accident" concept in regard to drinking poison. People should not drink poison just to prove they are immune, but they believe that God has a protective covering ready for Christians if they need it. They write: "Do you notice the Bible says 'IF' we (accidentally) drink anything poisonous, it won't hurt us! Hallelujah! Best insurance policy we know of!"[11]

The trouble with the Hunters' interpretation is that there is no mention of "accidentally" in Mark 16:17–18. The other signs given in the passage have nothing to do with accidents. Perhaps the Hunters felt the idea of getting bitten by a snake or drinking poison accidentally would help make it clearer— and avoid steering their readers into some of the cultlike charismatic fringe groups that actually practice snake-handling to test their spirituality.

But to insert the word "accidentally" into this verse does not work either, even if one could do so. When I was young, I drank some poison and I had to have my stomach pumped. Christian people have died after accidentally drinking poison. Genuine believers have also died after accidentally being given the wrong medication (which is the same thing as being poisoned). And Christians sometimes die after being bitten by snakes. In fact, even people in the snake-handling charismatic groups sometimes die from snakebites. We read newspaper reports of such incidents at least once or twice a year.[12]

No, the Hunters' injection of the word "accidentally" in Mark 16:17–18 does not hold up. Perhaps they realize this, because they go on to talk about the biggest "snake" of all— Satan. They assure their readers that the baptism of the Holy Spirit will give them the power to handle Satan.[13] By resorting to that interpretation of the biblical text, the Hunters have used allegory to equate Satan with the serpents in this passage. That is the same kind of interpretation theological liberals use to strip Bible passages of their literal, miraculous meaning. I am certain the Hunters did not mean to do that!

One key reason the allegorical approach will not work here is that it cannot be applied consistently throughout the passage. Mark 16:17–18 tells us that believers in Christ will be able to do five things: cast out demons, speak with new tongues, handle serpents, drink deadly poison without harm, and heal the sick. If the serpents represent Satan, what do the other four represent? Can we explain them allegorically also? In what way? As we saw earlier, allegorizing is one of the easiest ways to fall into error when interpreting Scripture.

What then can we say with certainty about Mark 16:17–18? First of all, we note that there is quite a bit of debate about whether verses 9–20 are even part of the original text of Mark's gospel.[14] But let us assume that the verses are a legitimate reflection of the original, inspired manuscripts. Applying the historical principle of interpretation, the first question we must ask is, "Have all Christians of all ages, right up to the present, been able to perform the five signs?" Obviously a lot of believers—charismatic and non-charismatic—are sick. A lot of them are dying of cancer, kidney failure, heart disease, and other illnesses. A lot of Christians have died from snakebites and poisoning.

A common charismatic protest at this point is that the Christian is supposed to commit himself to the lordship of Christ and ask—even beg—for these wonderful gifts. Using the grammatical principle, we must ask, "Where does it say that in the text?" The only condition the text mentions is "believe." It does not say, "Believe extra hard." It does not say, "Submit, search, ask, or beg." Moreover, the context shows that "those who have believed" (16:17) is an expression referring to all Christians, not just those on some higher spiritual plane. The preceding verse says, "He who has believed and has been baptized shall be saved." There is no reason from the context to conclude that "those who have believed" in verse 17 means anything other than all Christians.

It quickly becomes apparent that these promises have not been fulfilled in the life of every Christian for all time. What, then, do they mean? Applying the historical and synthetic principles, we see that these signs were true of one certain group—the apostolic community. And indeed, the apostles *did* do these things, as the Book of Acts clearly reports in many places. All these wondrous signs (except the drinking of poison) can be scripturally verified as having happened during the apostolic era—but not thereafter. It is incorrect to assert that these signs should be the norm for all believers today (2 Cor. 12:12; Heb. 2:2–4).

Furthermore, it is cruel to make Christians believe that those who cannot get well do not have enough faith or are not spiritual enough to claim the signs listed in Mark chapter 16. The whole thing adds up to a tremendous guilt syndrome, and it is all based on a misinterpretation of Scripture. Either all five signs are valid for everyone today or none is valid. They were given as a unit to the apostles to confirm the gospel message and its earliest messengers.

First Peter 2:24. Charismatics often use 1 Peter 2:24 to support their strong emphasis on the gift of healing: "He Himself bore our sins in His body on the cross, that we might die to sin and live to righteousness; for by His wounds you were healed."

The grammatical principle of interpretation applies directly in regard to this verse. What is the meaning of "healed" in the context of 1 Peter 2:24? There is no mention of physical healing in this verse—or in the immediately surrounding verses. The verse says that when Christ died on the cross, he bore our sins in his own body, not our *sickness*. First Peter 2:24 says we are to live unto righteousness—not unto health—and that is an important distinction.

One other grammatical test is that the verse says, "By His wounds you *were healed*" (emphasis added). The past tense points right back to the cross, where humanity's sin-sick soul was healed. The verse does not say, "By His wounds you will be continually healed of your physical ailments."

The synthetic principle also is useful to show why the charismatic interpretation of 1 Peter 2:24 is wrong. As we check other parts of Scripture, we learn that our souls have been redeemed but our bodies have not yet fully reached a state of glory. Romans 8:23 says, "We ourselves, having the first fruits of the Spirit, even we ourselves groan within ourselves, waiting eagerly for our adoption as sons, the redemption of our body." That verse tells us we still live in a body affected by the Fall. We are still subject to sickness and other infirmities. The Spirit helps us overcome our infirmities; for example, he prays for us when we do not know how to pray as we ought (Rom. 8:26). But there is no guarantee of deliverance from disease in this life.

It is also important to note that "by whose stripes ye were healed" comes from Isaiah 53:5. Was Isaiah talking about physical healing? A study of the book of Isaiah shows that the prophet was talking about the *spiritual* healing that Israel needed so desperately. Isaiah 1:4–6 says in effect to Israel: "You are diseased with sin, there is rottenness, there is no soundness in your bones; you are polluted with sin." When Isaiah 53 talks about the suffering servant by whose stripes Israel will be healed, it is talking about spiritual healing, not physical. And when Scripture says, "He bore our sickness," it is no violation of the literal principle to recognize that it refers to the sickness of our souls.

Matthew 8:17 alludes to the fact that in a sense Christ carried our sickness by the sympathy of his heart, while Hebrews 4:15 reveals that Christ can truly sympathize with us because of his own subjection to temptation. He does not get our diseases, but he sympathizes with the pain that we have in them.[15] Ultimately, the atonement will cure all our diseases when it has wrought its final work of glorifying our bodies. Thus there *is* healing in the atonement, but only in its ultimate aspect of eternal glory in heaven (cf. Rev. 21:4).

Cutting It Straight

In 2 Timothy 2:15 Paul commanded Timothy to divide the word of truth rightly. The Greek text literally means,

"Cut it straight." Because Paul was a tentmaker, he may have been using an expression that tied in with his trade. When a tentmaker worked, he used certain patterns. In those days tents were made from the skins of animals in a patchwork design. Every piece would have to be cut and fit together properly.

Paul was simply saying, "If you don't cut the pieces right, the whole thing won't fit together properly." It's the same with Scripture. Unless one interprets correctly all the different parts, the whole message will not come through correctly. In Bible study and interpretation the Christian should cut it straight—be precise, straightforward, and accurate.

Those four frequently abused passages are not isolated examples; such misinterpretations are quite common in charismatic preaching and teaching. Too many charismatics are willing to interpret Scripture in whatever way best suits their purposes.

Where that is tolerated, false teaching, confusion, and error are bound to flourish. We dare not handle the Word of God in a careless or slipshod manner. Too much is at stake.

—— 5 ——

Does God Do Miracles Today?

What is a miracle? Is it a miracle when we pray for God to meet a financial need and the mail carrier brings a check on precisely the day the money is needed? Is it a miracle when a parking space opens up near the mall entrance right when you need one? Is it a miracle when a mother senses something wrong in an adjoining room and investigates just in time to stop her toddler from poking a paper clip into the electrical outlet? Is it a miracle when something prompts a young woman to think of a friend she hasn't seen for a long time, and she phones to discover that she has called at just the moment her friend needed encouragement?

We often call such events miracles, but they are more properly termed *acts of providence*.[1] They reveal God's working in our daily lives and often come as answers to prayer, but they are not the kind of supernatural signs and wonders Scripture classifies as *miracles* (cf. Acts 2:22).

What Are Miracles?

A *miracle* is an extraordinary event wrought by God through human agency, an event that cannot be explained by natural forces. Miracles always are designed to authenticate the human instrument God has chosen to declare a specific revelation to those who witness the miracle. In technical terms,

> A miracle is an event in nature, so extraordinary in itself and so coinciding with the prophecy or command of a religious teacher or leader, as fully to warrant the conviction, on the part of those who witness it, that God has wrought it with the design of certifying that this teacher or leader has been commissioned by Him.[2]

Miracles in Scripture are also called "signs and wonders" (Ex. 7:3; Deut. 6:22; 34:11; Neh. 9:10; Ps. 135:9; Jer. 32:21; Dan. 6:27; John 4:48; Acts 2:43; Rom. 15:19; 2 Cor. 12:12; Heb. 2:4). They involve supernatural, superhuman forces specifically associated with God's messengers and are not merely strange happenings, coincidences, sensational events, or natural anomalies.

Miracles by this definition are a subcategory of the supernatural. Creation, the Flood, natural wonders, and cataclysms show God clearly at work supernaturally interceding in human affairs, judging rebellious people, and blessing those who are faithful. Such things are not miracles by the definition we have given.

Nor are unexplainable and mysterious phenomena true miracles. Society today is obsessed with the supernatural, to the point that people are willing to interpret almost any odd phenomenon as a supernatural wonder. More and more we hear about bizarre and unusual events that are popularly misinterpreted as miracles. In 1977, for example, newspapers all across the country recorded the account of Maria Rubio, of Lake Arthur, New Mexico, who was frying tortillas in her kitchen when she noticed that one of them seemed to have the likeness of a face etched in the burn marks. She concluded that it was Jesus and even built a crude shrine for the tortilla. Thousands of people visited the Shrine of the Jesus of the

Holy Tortilla and concluded it was indeed a modern-day miracle. "I do not know why this has happened to me," Mrs. Rubio said, "but God has come into my life through this tortilla."[3]

In 1980, in Deptford, New Jersey, Bud Ward, the town's fire department photographer, was driving with his wife when he accidentally took a wrong turn. Noticing flames in an abandoned chicken coop behind the Naples Pizzeria, he pulled into the parking lot and began taking pictures. When the slides came back from K-Mart, Ward's nine-year-old daughter noticed what seemed to be an image of Christ in one of the photographs. Word of this discovery spread, and soon people from all over New Jersey were talking about the Pizza Jesus of Deptford township. Several people knelt and prayed under the image projected from the slide, and others asked that the image be projected onto their chests. Hundreds believed it was a true miracle.[4]

Such apparitions are often heralded as miracles. In August of 1986, in Fostoria, Ohio, the image of Jesus seemed to appear each night in the shadows and rust marks on the side of a soybean-oil storage tank. Hawkers sold thousands of "I saw the vision" T-shirts and coffee mugs to those who came to see the "miracle."[5]

Nearly a year later Arlene Gardner, of Estill Springs, Tennessee, noticed that when her neighbors turned on their porch light, the image of a face appeared in the glow reflecting off her freezer. She believed it was the face of Jesus, although several observers said it looked more like Willie Nelson. Arlene and her husband were so convinced it was a true miracle that they quit their church when the pastor expressed skepticism.[6]

Evidently such skepticism is a rare commodity these days, especially in Catholic and charismatic circles. The hunger that people have for mysterious and astonishing phenomena is at a level unsurpassed in the history of the church. Eager to witness miracles, many people seem willing to believe that almost anything unusual is a genuine heavenly wonder. That poses a tremendous danger for the church, because Scripture tells us that false miracles—extremely believable ones—will be a primary tool of Satan in the end times. As Jesus said, "False Christs and false prophets will arise and will show great signs and wonders, so as to mislead, if possible, even the elect." Then he added, as if knowing that many would ignore the warning, "Behold, I have told you in advance" (Matt. 24:24–25). Surely in light of those words from our Lord, some healthy skepticism on the part of Christians is warranted.

Please understand, I am not by nature a skeptic. I am by no means one of those whom C. S. Lewis called "naturalists"—people who assume miracles cannot happen.[7] I believe in miracles. I believe that every miracle recorded in the Bible literally happened exactly as the Bible describes it. I believe, for example, that Moses and the Israelites actually walked through the parted Red Sea and did not get their feet muddy (Ex. 14:21–22, 29). I believe that Elijah really raised a widow's young son from the dead (1 Kings 17:21–23) and that the fire he called down from heaven was actual heavenly fire—a genuine miracle (2 Kings 1:10, 12). I believe with absolute conviction that Elisha made an iron axe head float in water (2 Kings 6:6).

Moreover, I believe that all the healings, miracles, signs, and wonders attributed to Jesus in the four gospels happened precisely as the evangelists describe them. And I believe the apostles literally performed all the miracles Scripture indicates.

What About Modern Miracles?

I also believe that God is always operating on a supernatural level. He intervenes supernaturally in nature and in human affairs even today. I believe God can heal people apart from natural or medical remedies. I believe *all* things are possible with God (Matt. 19:26). His power has not diminished in the least since the days of the early church. Certainly salvation is always a supernatural act of God!

I do not believe, however, that God uses men and women as human agents to work miracles in the same way he used Moses, Elijah, or Jesus. I am convinced that the miracles, signs, and wonders being claimed today in the charismatic movement have nothing in common with apostolic miracles. And I am persuaded by both Scripture and history that nothing like the New Testament gift of miracles (see chapter 9 for a discussion of the gift of miracles) is operating today. The Holy Spirit has not given any modern-day Christians miraculous gifts comparable to those he gave the apostles.

Nevertheless, charismatics are making some extraordinary claims. Some believe God is raising the dead. Oral Roberts, for example, speaking at a Charismatic Bible Ministry Conference in 1987, said, "I can't tell you about [all] the dead people I've raised. I've had to stop a sermon, go back and raise a dead person."[8] No less an authority than C. Peter Wagner, professor of church growth at Fuller Seminary School of World Mission, believes such things do happen: "I, too, now believe that dead people are literally being raised in the world today. As soon as I say that, some ask if I believe it is 'normative.' I doubt if it would be normative in any local situation, but it probably is normative in terms of the universal body of Christ. Even though it is an extremely uncommon event, I would not be surprised if it were happening several times a year."[9] John Wimber lists raising the dead as one of the basic elements of the healing ministry.[10]

Surely it is significant, then, that *not one modern occurrence of raising the dead can be verified*. What about Oral Roberts' claim? Challenged to produce names and addresses of people he had raised, Roberts balked.[11] Later, he recalled only one incident—more than twenty years before—when he had

supposedly raised a dead child in front of ten thousand
witnesses

> During a healing service, he recalled, a mother in the
> audience jumped up and shouted, "My baby's dead."
> Roberts said he prayed over the child and "it jerked, it
> jerked in my hand." . . . Roberts conceded that neither that
> child nor others he said he had brought to life had been
> pronounced clinically dead. "I understand," he hedged,
> "there's a difference in a person dying and not breathing and
> [a person] being clinically dead."[12]

What are we to make of that? It is a far cry from Jesus' raising
of Lazarus, who had been four days in the grave. If, as Dr.
Wagner supposes, "dead people are literally being raised . . .
several times a year," would it not be reasonable to expect
that at least one of those miracles could be verified?

The truth is, those who claim miracles today are not able
to substantiate their claims. Unlike the miracles in the New
Testament, which were usually done with crowds of unbelievers watching, modern miracles typically happen either
privately or in religious meetings. The *types* of miracles
claimed, too, are nothing like New Testament miracles. Jesus
and the apostles instantly and completely healed people born
blind, a paralytic, a man with a withered arm—all obvious,
indisputable miracles. Even Jesus' enemies did not challenge
the reality of his miracles! Moreover, New Testament
miracles were immediate, thorough, and permanent. Our
Lord and his disciples never did a miracle slowly or incom-
pletely.[13]

By contrast, most modern miracles are nearly always
partial, gradual, or temporary. The only "instant" miracles are
healings that seem to involve forms of psychosomatic diseases.
People with visible disabilities are rarely if ever helped at all
by modern faith-healers. I recently watched a televangelist
interview a man he had supposedly "healed" of lameness. The
man said he was free from his wheel chair for the first time in

several years. Now, however, he was walking with crutches and still had heavy braces on his legs! No modern miracle worker claims the kind of unequivocal success seen in the ministries of Christ and his apostles.

What Happened to the Age of Miracles?

The late David du Plessis, known by Pentecostals and charismatics as "Mr. Pentecost," believed that the age of miracles never ended. He wrote, "The first church was a creation of the Holy Spirit, and He has not changed; but in every generation He wants to repeat what He did in the first Christian Church through the first leaders and members."[14] Du Plessis was saying that the miracles and events described in the book of Acts should be normative throughout the church's history. His view reflects the thinking of most Pentecostals and charismatics.

As Frederick Dale Bruner pointed out, "The Pentecostals frequently refer to their movement as a worthy and perhaps even superior successor to the Reformation of the sixteenth century and to the English evangelical revival of the eighteenth, and nearly always as a faithful reproduction of the apostolic movement of the first century."[15]

Pentecostals and charismatics alike believe that the Holy Spirit's methodology has never changed; but they believe that the early church did change, becoming formal and ritualistic. When that happened the church forfeited the power of the Holy Spirit. That power is finally being recovered, they believe, after almost two thousand years. Du Plessis wrote,

In miracle fashion, in many countries almost simultaneously at the turn of this century, the Holy Spirit moved upon those who were praying for revival. This happened in the United States, Europe, Asia, and Africa—on every continent and in almost every country of the world. The

> Pentecostal revival became known as the Pentecostal
> Movement.[16]

Many Pentecostals and charismatics talk about the restoration
of "New Testament Holy Spirit power" through their movement. What the apostles did in the first century, they say,
Christian believers are doing today.

Is that true? If so, why do modern revelations, visions,
tongues, healings, and miracles differ so dramatically from
those performed by the apostles? And what happened to
miracles, healings, signs, and wonders in the nineteen
hundred years since the apostles passed from the scene? Was
the Holy Spirit inactive during that time? Or was His power
for all those years manifested only among fringe groups and
fanatics? Can believers today really expect to perform the
same kind of miracles, healings, and raising of the dead seen
in the early church?

In answering those questions, it is crucial to understand
when and why miracles occurred in Scripture.

When Has God Used Miracles—and Why?

Most biblical miracles happened in three relatively brief
periods of Bible history: in the days of Moses and Joshua,
during the ministries of Elijah and Elisha, and in the time of
Christ and the apostles.[17] None of those periods lasted much
more than a hundred years. Each of them saw a proliferation
of miracles unheard of in other eras. Even during those three
time periods, however, miracles were not exactly the order of
the day. The miracles that happened involved men who were
extraordinary messengers from God—Moses and Joshua,
Elijah and Elisha, Jesus and the apostles.

Aside from those three intervals, the only supernatural
events recorded in Scripture were isolated incidents. In the
days of Isaiah, for example, the Lord supernaturally defeated
Sennacherib's army (2 Kings 19:35–36), then healed Heze-

kiah and turned the sun's shadows back (20:1–11). In the days of Daniel, God preserved Shadrach, Meshach and Abednego in the furnace (Dan. 3:20–26). For the most part, however, supernatural events like those did not characterize God's dealings with his people.

It is worth noting that charismatic theologians have recently argued that the idea of three miraculous eras is utterly baseless. Jack Deere, for example, is a former professor at Dallas Theological Seminary, now on staff at John Wimber's Anaheim Vineyard (see chapter 6). Deere says he used to teach the three-era view but now believes it cannot be substantiated biblically. Deere says he changed his mind when someone challenged him on the issue and he couldn't support his view. He says he found there are miracles everywhere in Scripture. Those he cites include Creation, the Flood, Babel, the call of Abram, and several other supernatural events and divine judgments. Deere feels such events prove signs and wonders are crucial to the program of God in every age.[18]

Most of the events Deere cites, however, are supernatural acts of God apart from any human agent. None of them are the kind of miracle Deere is attempting to defend. Worldwide cataclysms, spectacles in the heavens, and apocalyptic events are not the same as apostolic miracles. Deere's argument fails to acknowledge the distinction. He wants to enlist every supernatural act of God as support for an ongoing apostolic ministry of miracles.[19]

The reality is that though there were three eras of miracles, the first two were not like the third. The age of Christ and the apostles was unique. Nothing in all redemptive history even came close to it in the massive volume of miracles that occurred. Disease was, in effect, banished from Palestine. Demons were overwhelmed daily and the dead were raised. The flurry and scope of this miracle era pushes it far beyond the first two. There was nothing like it in all the times of Old Testament prophetic preaching and writing ministry. When the New Covenant truth came and the New Testament

Scripture with it all at once in one brief half century, God unleashed authenticating signs as never before. There had never been a time like it and there is no reason to assume there will be again.

While the supernatural flows continually through the Old Testament, miracles involving human agency are extremely rare. Notably scarce are healings and demon deliverances. That is one reason Jesus' healing ministry was such a wonder among the Jews. Not even their greatest prophets displayed the kind of power he and his disciples possessed— an ability to heal anyone and everyone (Lk. 4:40; Acts 5:16).

A look at the Old Testament record reveals that aside from those we have named—Moses, Joshua, Elijah, and Elisha—the only individual who routinely performed supernatural feats was Samson. As miracle workers go, Samson was an exception in almost every category. He taught no great truth; in fact, he was neither a preacher nor a teacher. He was unfaithful and immoral. His only role seems to have been the preservation of Israel, and his power was given to him specifically for that task. No one else in recorded history displayed physical power like his.

Samson is hardly a model of the miraculous witness charismatics say they want to have. Nevertheless, it would seem far more likely that God would raise up another Samson than that he would repeat the apostolic age.

God can, of course, interject himself into the stream of history supernaturally anytime he wishes. But he chose to limit himself primarily to three periods of biblical miracles, with very rare supernatural displays in between. The rest of the time God works through providence.

At least three characteristics of the miracles in Scripture help us understand why God has worked the way he has.

Miracles introduced new eras of revelation. All three periods of miracles were times when God gave His written revelation—Scripture—in substantial quantities. Those doing the miracles were essentially the same ones heralding an era of revelation. Moses wrote the first five books of Scripture. Elijah and Elisha introduced the prophetic age. The apostles wrote nearly all of the New Testament. Even the rare supernatural wonders that happened in other eras were associated with men who were used by God to write Scripture. Hezekiah's healing involved Isaiah, and the three men in the furnace were companions of the prophet Daniel.

Moses performed many miracles in an attempt to convince Pharaoh to let the people of Israel go. Miracles seemed to accompany the Israelites on their journey out of Egypt and through the wilderness. Then when God's written Word initially came to Moses, during the giving of the commandments on Mount Sinai, Moses' encounter with God was accompanied by signs so dramatic—fire, smoke, a trumpet, a thundering voice—that even Moses himself was fearful (Heb. 12:18–21).

Thus began the first great period of revelation. Moses recorded the entire Pentateuch, and Joshua, Moses' successor, wrote the book that bears his name. Other books were added intermittently after the time of Moses and Joshua. For example, Samuel probably wrote Judges and 1 and 2 Samuel. David wrote most of the psalms, and Solomon penned most of the wisdom literature. But those books were not accompanied by the great outpouring of miracles that had distinguished the days of Moses and Joshua.

The second major cluster of miraculous events accompanied a new era of biblical revelation—the age of the Old Testament prophets. Following Solomon's reign, the nation of Israel divided into the northern kingdom (Israel) and the southern kingdom (Judah). The northern kingdom quickly deteriorated because of idolatry, hitting a low point during the reign of King Ahab. At that time God raised up Elijah and Elisha. During their lifetimes, the prophetic office was established by many dramatic miracles. Succeeding prophets wrote all the books from Isaiah to Malachi.

As we have seen, a period of nearly four hundred years of revelatory silence occurred just prior to the time of Christ. During those final days of the Old Testament era, no one prophesied and no miracles were recorded.

Then came the beginning of the New Testament era and the third period of miracles. During this time—A.D. 33 to 96—God gave the entire New Testament.

Miracles authenticated the messengers of revelation. All the miracles served an important purpose. They were not simply divine exhibitionism; they substantiated and authenticated the prophets' claim that they spoke for God. For example, Moses' miracles confirmed first to Pharaoh, and then to the Israelites, that Moses spoke for God. Miraculous evidence thus underscored the gravity of the written law. The miracles were affirmation to all that God was speaking.

Moses and Joshua, Elijah and Elisha, and Christ and the apostles all had the ability to do frequent signs and wonders. These were designed to convince people that God was with these men and that he was speaking through them.

In 1 Kings 17, Elijah had just revived a widow's dead son. He brought the boy down from the upstairs room, delivered him to his mother, and said, "See, your son is alive" (17:23). What was the widow's reply? "Now I know that you are a man of God, and that the word of the Lord in your mouth is truth" (17:24).

In John 10, Jesus was having a confrontation with the Jewish religious leaders, who challenged, "How long will you keep us in suspense? If You are the Christ, tell us plainly." Jesus replied, "I told you, and you do not believe; the works that I do in My Father's name, these bear witness of Me" (10:24–25). Clearly Jesus' miracles served a purpose: they authenticated him and his message.

In his Pentecost sermon, Peter told the crowd that Jesus

was a man attested to them by God with miracles, wonders, and signs, which God performed through him in their midst (Acts 2:22). The same kind of power belonged to the apostles. On Paul's first missionary journey, he and Barnabas ministered in Iconium, "speaking boldly with reliance upon the Lord, who was bearing witness to the word of His grace, granting that signs and wonders be done by their hands" (Acts 14:3).

Not every believer had the power to do miracles. Victor Budgen correctly observed:

> How often people speak carelessly of the church in Acts as a wonder-working church! Yet it would be more accurate to speak of a church with *wonder-working apostles*. It is the apostles who are prominent in the initial outburst of speaking in other languages. It is their spokesman who explains this to the crowd and preaches a mighty gospel sermon. At the close of the Pentecost account, we are told that "Everyone was filled with awe, and many wonders and miraculous signs were done by the apostles" (Acts 2:43).
>
> Other scriptures confirm this: "The apostles performed many miraculous signs and wonders among the people" (Acts 5:12). "The whole assembly became silent as they listened to Barnabas and Paul telling about the miraculous signs and wonders God had done among the Gentiles through them" (Acts 15:12). . . . "The things that mark an apostle—signs, wonders and miracles—were done among you with great perseverance" (2 Cor. 12:12).[20]

Through miracles God repeatedly authenticated the messengers of his new revelation—in the time of Moses and Joshua, in the time of Elijah and Elisha, and in the New Testament times of Jesus and the apostles.

Miracles called attention to new revelation. God used the miracles to get the attention of the people to whom the message was directed so that they would know for sure it was the divine Lord speaking. Then he was able to tell them what he wanted them to do. Thus miracles have an instructive purpose that goes beyond the immediate effect of the miracle itself.

For example, the miracles Moses did in Egypt were meant to enlighten two groups of people, the Israelites and the Egyptians. In Exodus 7 we read of Moses' first miracles, and it was then that the Israelites started to believe in the power of their God. Pharaoh, however, was a hard case. It wasn't until the tenth and most terrible plague of all—the death angel passing over Egypt to take the firstborn in every Egyptian household—that Pharaoh finally let the Israelites go.

The miracles of Elijah and Elisha also were effective in convincing both believers and unbelievers that what those men spoke was the Word of God. A graphic illustration of this is found in 1 Kings 18, where Elijah defeated four hundred prophets of Baal before a large crowd of Israelites. Scripture says, "When all the people saw it, they fell on their faces; and they said, 'The Lord, He is God; the Lord, He is God.' Then Elijah said to them, 'Seize the prophets of Baal; do not let one of them escape.' So they seized them; and Elijah brought them down to the brook Kishon, and slew them there" (18:39–40).

In the New Testament, miracles and signs were again used to confirm believers and convince unbelievers. That is the theme of the gospel of John, which was written so "that you may believe that Jesus is the Christ, the Son of God; and that believing you may have life in His name" (John 20:31). The miracles and signs of Jesus were recorded so that unbelieving people might believe. The same was true of apostolic miracles (cf. Acts 5:12–14).

Are Miracles Necessary Today?

When the Old and New Testaments were complete, God's revelation was finished (cf. Heb. 1:1–2). Through many signs, wonders, and miracles God authenticated his Book. Is there an ongoing need for miracles to substantiate

God's revelation? Can anyone with faith "claim" a miracle, as some teach? Does God do miracles on demand? And do the phenomena being hailed today as signs, wonders, and healings bear any resemblance to the miracles performed by Christ and the apostles?

The answer to all those questions is no. Nothing in Scripture indicates that the miracles of the apostolic age were meant to be continuous in subsequent ages. Nor does the Bible exhort believers to seek any miraculous manifestations of the Holy Spirit. In all the New Testament epistles, there are only five commands related to the believer and the Holy Spirit:

> "Walk by the Spirit" (Gal. 5:25).
> "Do not grieve the Holy Spirit of God" (Eph. 4:30).
> "Be filled with the Spirit" (Eph. 5:18).
> "Do not quench the Spirit" (1 Thess. 5:19).
> "[Pray] in the Spirit" (Jude 20).

There is no command in the New Testament to seek miracles.

Charismatics believe that the spectacular miraculous gifts were given for the edification of believers. Does God's Word support such a conclusion? No. In fact, the truth is quite the contrary. Concerning tongues, Paul wrote in 1 Corinthians 14:22, "Tongues are for a sign, not to those who believe, but to unbelievers." Tongues never were intended to edify believers, but to convince Jewish unbelievers of the truthfulness of the gospel, as happened at Pentecost in Acts chapter 2. (For a more extensive discussion of this point, see chapter 10.)

Tongues, healings, and miracles all served as signs to authenticate an era of new revelation. As the age of revelation came to a close, the signs ceased also. Theologian B. B. Warfield wrote:

> Miracles do not appear on the pages of Scripture vagrantly, here, there, and elsewhere indifferently, without assignable

reason. They belong to revelation periods, and appear only when God is speaking to His people through accredited messengers, declaring His gracious purposes. Their abundant display in the Apostolic Church is the mark of the richness of the Apostolic age in revelation; and when this revelation period closed, the period of miracle-working had passed by also, as a mere matter of course. . . . God the Holy Spirit has made it His subsequent work, not to introduce new and unneeded revelations into the world, but to diffuse this one complete revelation through the world and to bring mankind into the saving knowledge of it.

As Abraham Kuyper figuratively expresses it [*Encyclopedia of Sacred Theology*, E. T. 1898, p. 368; cf. pp. 355 ff.], it has not been God's way to communicate to each and every man a separate store of divine knowledge of his own, to meet his separate needs; but He rather has spread a common board for all, and invites all to come and partake of the richness of the great feast. He has given to the world one organically complete revelation, adapted to all, sufficient for all, provided for all, and from this one completed revelation He requires each to draw his whole spiritual sustenance. Therefore it is that the miraculous working which is but the sign of God's revealing power, cannot be expected to continue, and in point of fact does not continue, after the revelation of which it is the accompaniment has been completed.[21]

In the seventh chapter of Acts, as Stephen preached his famous sermon, he talked about Moses, who performed "wonders and signs in the land of Egypt and in the Red Sea and in the wilderness . . . [and] received living oracles to pass on to you" (7:36–38). Note that God's Word draws the parallel between Moses' signs and his "living oracles"—direct revelation from God. Whether it was Moses, Elijah and Elisha, or Christ and the apostles, God always made it clear through signs and wonders when his messengers were bearing new revelation.

Hebrews 2:3–4 confirms that validation of the prophets was the chief purpose for biblical miracles: "How shall we escape if we neglect so great a salvation? After it was at the first spoken through the Lord, it was confirmed to us by those who heard, God also bearing witness with them, both by signs and wonders and by various miracles and by gifts of the Holy Spirit according to His own will." Again we see Scripture attesting that signs, wonders, miracles, and miraculous gifts were God's confirmation of the message of Christ and his apostles ("those who heard").

The words "it was confirmed" are in the past tense, an accurate reflection of the Greek text. Here is a clear biblical word that the miracles, wonders, and sign gifts were given only to the first-generation apostles to confirm that they were messengers of new revelation.

Does God Promise Miracles for Everyone?

Many charismatic believers insist that God wants to do miracles for every believer. They often say, "God has a special miracle just for you." Are Christians supposed to seek their own private miracles? If you study the miracles done by Jesus, you will find that not one of them was done privately.

While Jesus healed people's ailments and cured their physical suffering, those were secondary benefits. His major purpose was to authenticate his messianic claims (cf. John 20:30–31). Similarly, while the apostles also healed people, their primary purpose was to authenticate new revelation— and new revelation is never a private issue.

Those who are credulous about claims of modern miracles—especially those who are the most zealous defenders of contemporary signs and wonders—often seem reluctant to deal with the possibility, or rather the likelihood, that those marvels may actually be authenticating a diabolical variety of "revelation." Victor Budgen sees this danger clearly:

The devil wants to substitute his word for that of God. Sometimes we clearly see that Satan is doing this, for it all seems so obvious. Most Christians recognize the deception. Moses David of the Children of God claimed, "I was prophesied over many times by many prophets of God, as having been filled with the Holy Ghost from my mother's womb, and many great things were foretold that I would do . . . that I would be like Moses, Jeremiah, Ezekiel, Daniel and even David." [Quoted in *Crusade* magazine, April 1973, p. 5.] Christians reject this claim, especially in light of the group's heretical teaching. A little booklet on the rise of Sun Myung Moon and the Moonies relates that "Among some Pentecostal Christians in the underground church in Pyongyang, there had recently been prophecy of a Korean messiah. So the local populace was fertile ground for this idea." [J. Isamu Yamamoto, *The Moon Doctrine*, Intervarsity (USA), 1980, p. 4.] Yet, extreme though such groups may seem, it must not be forgotten that there are those today who compare themselves with biblical prophets, who believe in new "revelations" and who are engendering a climate where all kinds of false teachings could easily be accepted. . . . A writer on this theme can always be accused of taking extreme examples, but many palpably false movements drew in genuine Christians at first. Many temporarily entangled in the Jonestown cult, with its healings, revelations and eventual mass suicide, seem to have been earnest and genuine Christians who were deluded and led astray by the evil one. Firm biblical moorings and a belief that God has furnished a final and all-sufficient Word in Scripture alone is the only real protection and safe guidance that God has provided against deception.[22]

Indeed, Christians who pursue miraculous signs are setting themselves up for satanic deception. Paul's epistles nowhere command believers to seek the Spirit's manifestation in signs and wonders. He simply said to walk in the Spirit (Gal. 5:25) or, putting it another way, "Let the word of Christ richly dwell within you" (Col. 3:16). In other words, believers are to obey the Word in the power of the Spirit.

The book of Revelation is full of visions, wonders, and signs. It would be a perfect place for the writer to urge believers to seek such miraculous manifestations, but what did he say? "Blessed is he who *reads* and those who *hear* the words of the prophecy, and *heed* the things which are written in it" (Rev. 1:3, emphasis added).

What means has God designed to strengthen our faith? "Faith comes from hearing, and hearing by the word of Christ" (Rom. 10:17). If we want hope, if we want an anchor, if we want something to carry us through life, it is not a miracle we need. We need the Scriptures. Romans 15:4 states: "Whatever was written in earlier times was written for our instruction, that through perseverance and the encouragement of the Scriptures we might have hope."

What Made the Apostles Unique?

Some charismatics actually believe that the phenomena we are seeing today prove that God is giving new revelation, authenticated by fresh miracles, through the agency of modern apostles. That whole notion ignores the biblical role and function of the apostles. They were special men for a particular role in a unique era. The apostles were the foundation for the developing church (Eph. 2:20). That foundation is now being built upon; it cannot be laid again. There can be no modern-day apostles.

Furthermore, as we have seen, miracles were unique to the apostles and those who worked most closely with them. The average Christian had no ability to perform signs and wonders. Paul said as much in his second epistle to the Corinthians:

I have become foolish; you yourselves compelled me. Actually I should have been commended by you, for in no

respect was I inferior to the most eminent apostles, even
though I am a nobody. The signs of a true apostle were
performed among you with all perseverance, by signs and
wonders and miracles (12:11–12).

Paul was defending his apostleship to the Corinthians, some
of whom evidently doubted his apostolic authority. If doing
miracles had been the common experience of ordinary
Christians, it would be foolish for Paul to try to prove his
apostleship by citing the miracles he had done. It is obvious,
though, that even during the apostolic age Christians couldn't
do signs, wonders, and mighty deeds. Precisely because those
things were unique to the apostles, Paul could use his
experience with signs and wonders as proof of his authority.

The apostles had miraculous power as messengers of
God's Word, and that same power was sometimes given to
those who were commissioned by them, such as Stephen and
Philip (see Acts 6). But the power never went any further. In
fact, from the day the church was born at Pentecost, no
miracle ever occurred in the entire New Testament record
except in the presence of an apostle or one directly commissioned by an apostle.

One never reads in the New Testament about miracles
occurring at random among the Christian believers. Even the
miraculous granting of the Holy Spirit to the Samaritans
(Acts 8), to the Gentiles (Acts 10), and to the followers of
John the Baptist at Ephesus (Acts 19) did not occur until the
apostles were there (see Acts 8, 10, 19).

Scripture repeatedly makes it clear that the apostles were
unique. Yet charismatics are determined to resurrect the
apostolic gifts and signs. Some even believe that certain men
can legitimately lay claim to the apostolic office today. Earl
Paulk, for example, teaches that certain "anointed" individuals have been called to be apostles.[23] Jack Deere is not
certain the apostolic ministry is functioning today, but he told
a workshop in Sydney he is convinced that apostolic power is

coming, and that the new apostolic age will be greater than the first.[24]

The notion that the apostolic office might be functional today is certainly consistent with rudimentary charismatic teaching. Thus Budgen properly writes, "Anyone genuinely committed to the belief that all gifts are available today must, if they are consistent, believe that God bestows apostles on the church today."[25]

But the issue of apostolic authority has caused some struggles within the charismatic movement—and understandably so. When people claiming apostolic authority utter erroneous prophecies, when they speak "words of knowledge" that turn out to be false, and when they promise healings that never materialize, such claims of apostolic authority must be suspect.

Nevertheless, some charismatic leaders insist they are heirs to apostolic authority, and they are eager to put their authority into practice. That desire often leads to appalling abuses. Perhaps the most notorious episode developed in the 1970s, coming out of a Fort Lauderdale-based group of charismatic leaders. Known as the "Shepherding" or "Discipleship" movement, this group—influenced by the teaching of Ern Baxter, Don Basham, Bob Mumford, Derek Prince, and Charles Simpson—concluded that Scripture demands absolute submission to one's spiritual leaders. Predictably, many leaders used that teaching to maintain a cruel and tyrannical influence over their people. They insisted that their people surrender every decision to them—even questions about marriage, personal finance, and one's career. Unscrupulous men posing as spiritual leaders took advantage of their people's gullibility. Many gained a cultlike dominance over their people's lives. By now most charismatic leaders have attempted to distance themselves from the terminology and practices of the worst extremists. The cardinal teachings of the movement still live, however, disguised with names such as "church life" and "covenant life."[26]

Contrast that kind of authoritarian leadership with the style of the apostles:

> The authority was used in a gracious way. The apostles did not throw their weight around, bark out stentorian commands or draw attention to themselves. Paul seemed almost reluctant or embarrassed to exercise his powers. In his second letter to the Corinthians this emerges in his final chapter as he says, "This is why I write these things when I am absent, that when I come I may not have to be harsh in my use of authority—the authority the Lord gave me for building you up, not for tearing you down" (2 Cor. 13:10).[27]

Six biblical reasons may be given as to why the apostolic office is not for today:

The church was founded upon the apostles. As we noted briefly above, the apostolic office was foundational. Writing to the Ephesian believers, Paul said the church was "built upon the foundation of the apostles and prophets, Christ Jesus Himself being the corner stone" (Eph. 2:20). Although the point may be argued, some Greek scholars believe the best rendering of the text would be "apostles/prophets." Both words talk about the same people; "apostle" refers to their office and "prophet" to their function.[28]

Whether that view is right or not, the verse clearly teaches that the apostles were appointed to be the foundation of the church. That is, their role was to give grounding, support, direction—to provide the underpinning for a fledgling church. They were the church's founders. That role was fulfilled by them and by definition can never be repeated.

Apostles were eyewitnesses to the resurrection. When Paul was documenting his apostleship to the Corinthian church, he wrote, "Am I not an apostle? Have I not seen Jesus our Lord?" (1 Cor. 9:1). In 1 Corinthians 15:7–8 Paul records that the resurrected Christ was seen by James, then by all the apostles, and finally by Paul himself.

Some charismatics today claim to have seen the resurrected Lord (see chapter 1). Such claims can never be verified. But in the case of the biblical appearances of our risen Lord, it is clear that he appeared only a few times, usually to groups of people, such as the disciples in the upper room. Those appearances ceased with his ascension. The *only* exception (cf. 1 Cor. 15:8) was his appearance to Paul, who saw Christ on the road to Damascus (Acts 9:1–9). Even then, Paul was accompanied by others who saw the bright light and were aware that he had been struck blind in an undeniably supernatural experience. That was a unique post-ascension appearance of Christ. He later appeared to Paul on two other occasions (Acts 18:9; 23:11). There is no trustworthy evidence that he has appeared to anyone since the close of the apostolic era.

Apostles were chosen personally by Jesus Christ. Matthew 10:1–4 clearly describes the naming of the twelve apostles. Luke 6:12–16 describes the same event. Judas later betrayed the Lord and took his own life. He was replaced by Matthias in a special drawing of lots conducted by the apostles themselves. They believed Christ would providentially control the lots and thus the choice (cf. Prov. 16:33). Paul had his own unique experience with the Lord on the road to Damascus.

Jesus may have spoken Hebrew or Aramaic when he chose his apostles (scholars disagree on that point). But if he spoke in Hebrew, he would have used the word *šalîah* for "apostle." In Hebrew a *šalîah* is the proxy of the man he represents—a surrogate, a representative who stands with full authority to act on behalf of his master. The apostles were appointed by Jesus to represent him in that way.

It is true that elsewhere in the New Testament, others are called "apostles," as in 2 Corinthians 8:23 (KJV), but they are called "apostles of the church," a nontechnical term with a general meaning. It is one thing to be an apostle of the Lord, personally sent by him; it is quite another to be an apostle of the church, sent by the body of believers.[29] Also, no miracles are recorded in Scripture as having been done by any apostles of the church.

Paul made it clear to the Galatians what kind of apostle *he* was: "Not sent from men, nor through the agency of man, but through Jesus Christ, and God the Father, who raised Him from the dead" (Gal. 1:1).

The original twelve (with Matthias later replacing Judas) plus Paul had a nontransferable commission to reveal doctrine and found the church. When the pastoral epistles set forth principles for lasting church leadership, they speak of elders and deacons. They never mention apostles.

Apostles were authenticated by miraculous signs. Peter healed the crippled man at the gate to the Temple (Acts 3:3–11). He also healed many more (5:15–16), and raised Dorcas from the dead (9:36–42). Paul brought Eutychus back to life after he had fallen to his death (Acts 20:6–12). Paul was also bitten by a poisonous snake without suffering harm (28:1–6). As noted before, no such miracles were ever performed—even in the apostolic era—by anyone other than the apostles and those commissioned by them.

Apostles had absolute authority. The apostles had much more authority than other prophets, whose utterances had to be judged as to their accuracy and authenticity (see, for example, 1 Cor. 14:29–33). When the apostles spoke, there was no discussion. They were already recognized as the revelatory agents of God. In his brief letter of warning to the church, Jude said, "But you, beloved, ought to remember the words that were spoken beforehand by the apostles of our Lord Jesus Christ" (Jude 17).

Apostles have an eternal and unique place of honor. Revelation 21 describes the New Jerusalem. Part of that description reads: "The wall of the city had twelve foundation stones, and on them were the twelve names of the twelve apostles of the Lamb" (v. 14). The names of the twelve apostles are sealed forever into the wall of the New Jerusalem in heaven. (Theologians can argue whether the twelfth spot should go to Paul or Matthias or possibly to both.) Their names are unique; their office is unique; their ministry is unique; the miracles they did are unique. The apostles were unquestionably a special breed; they had no successors. The age of the apostles and what they did is forever in the past.

By the second century the apostles were gone and things had changed. Alva McClain wrote, "When the church appears in the second century, the situation as regards the miraculous is so changed that we seem to be in another world."[30]

In his *Handbook of Church History*, Samuel Green wrote:

> When we emerge in the second century, we are, to a great extent, in a changed world. Apostolic authority lives no longer in the Christian community; apostolic miracles have passed. . . . We cannot doubt that there was a Divine purpose in thus marking off the age of inspiration and of miracles, by so broad and definite a boundary, from succeeding times.[31]

The apostolic age was unique and it ended. History says it, Jesus says it, theology says it, and the New Testament itself repeatedly attests to it.

Has God's Power Diminished?

In Acts 5:16, early in the apostolic age when the church was just getting started, we read that multitudes were being healed by the apostles. Twenty-five years later Paul, the greatest of all the apostles, could not be delivered from his own troublesome thorn (see 2 Cor. 12:7–10). Though he at one time seems to have had the ability to heal others at will (Acts 28:8), as Paul neared the end of his life he showed no evidence of such a gift. He advised Timothy to take a little wine for his stomach's sake, a common way of treating illness in that day (1 Tim. 5:23). Later on, at the very end of his career, Paul left a beloved brother sick at Miletus (2 Tim. 4:20). He surely would have healed him if he could.

In the early pages of Acts, Jerusalem was filled with miracles. After the martyrdom of Stephen, however, no more miracles were recorded in that city. Something was changing.

The miracles of the apostolic age were not to be the pattern for succeeding generations of Christians. We have no mandate to seek or perform miracles. We *do* have a mandate, however, to study and obey God's Word, which is able to make us wise and mature. And we *do* have a mandate to live by faith, not by sight (2 Cor. 5:7).

John 14:12 records this promise from our Lord: "Truly, truly, I say to you, he who believes in Me, the works that I do shall he do also; and greater works than these shall he do; because I go to the Father." To listen to some contemporary advocates of signs-and-wonders ministry you would think this promise bypassed the apostolic age and is being fulfilled in their meetings.

"Greater works" does not mean more spectacular miracles; nothing in the context of John 14 speaks of supernatural signs and wonders. What is a greater work than raising the dead? John 5:20–21 indicates it is the giving of spiritual life to sinners. Of course, the apostles' works were greater in scope, not in quality, than those of Jesus. They took the Gospel to the ends of the known world in their day. But much of that was accomplished after miracles had begun to pass from the scene.

Some charismatics allege that if we concede that the age of miracles is past, we espouse a deficient concept of God. Jerry Horner, associate professor of biblical literature at Oral

Roberts University, said, "Who in the world would want a God who has lost all of His zip? Could God do one thing in one century but not in another century? . . . Has God lost all of His power?"[32]

Charismatic Russell Bixler concludes that anyone denying the normality of apostolic-style miracles today has a "faith which gives no room to a Jesus Christ who is the same yesterday and today and for ever. They are quite comfortable with a distant God who hasn't done anything significant in 2,000 years."[33]

Has God lost his zip? Has he done nothing significant in two thousand years? That's hardly the case. All around us we see evidence of God's marvelous work: in the transforming new birth in the lives of millions around the world who trust Christ; in daily answers to prayer; in the providential matching of people and resources to bring glory to himself; in the resilience of his church, which has survived ruthless persecution and various internal assaults through the centuries and continues to do so today.

But God has not placed spokesmen with miracle-working power in the church today. You can be sure that if he did, they wouldn't resemble charismatic miracle workers such as those we see on television or on the tent-meeting circuit. Why would God authenticate bad theology? Why would he give miracle power to people who teach heresy? Yet every movement today that highlights miracles as a central theme is tainted with shoddy theology, confused and inconsistent doctrine, outright heresy, or a combination of these. In the following chapter we will examine in detail the largest and most influential of the movements espousing signs-and-wonders theology.

Ephesians 3:20 gives a promise for our age: Our Lord "is able to do exceeding abundantly beyond all that we ask or think, according to the power that works within us." What God does in and through us today is not what he did in the apostolic age. He had a special purpose for the apostles and their miracles, and that purpose was served. He also has a special purpose for us, and it will be marvelous, because he is God and what he does is always marvelous.

— 6 —

What Is Behind the "Third Wave" and Where Is It Going?

Asked by one of his disciples how he prepares himself to pray for miraculous healings, John Wimber replied, "I drink a diet Coke."[1] According to the disciple, that was no flippant answer—just a normal response from someone who lives in the realm of the miraculous.[2]

Wimber is the leader and father figure for the newest major offshoot of the charismatic movement, known as "The Third Wave of the Holy Spirit," also called the Signs and Wonders movement. This latest charismatic tide seems to have swept the globe in the past decade. Is it the real thing, or just a synthetic substitute, as devoid of actual substance as a sugar-free soft drink?

The term *Third Wave* was coined by C. Peter Wagner, professor of church growth at Fuller Theological Seminary School of World Mission, author of several books on church growth—and leading proponent of Third Wave methodology.[3] According to Wagner, "The first wave was the Pentecostal movement, the second the charismatic movement, and now the third wave is joining them."[4]

While acknowledging the Third Wave's spiritual ancestry, Wagner nonetheless rejects the labels *charismatic* and *Pentecostal.*

> The Third Wave is a new moving of the Holy Spirit among evangelicals who, for one reason or another, have chosen not to identify with either the Pentecostals or the charismatics. Its roots go back a little further, but I see it as mainly a movement beginning in the 1980s and gathering momentum through the closing years of the twentieth century. . . . I see the Third Wave as distinct from, but at the same time very similar to the first and second waves. They have to be similar because it is the same Spirit of God who is doing the work. . . . The major variation comes in the understanding of the meaning of baptism in the Holy Spirit and the role of tongues in authenticating this. I myself, for example, would rather not have people call me a charismatic. I do not consider myself a charismatic. I am simply an evangelical Congregationalist who is open to the Holy Spirit working through me and my church in any way he chooses.[5]

Wagner later acknowledges that he refuses the label *charismatic* not really because of any doctrinal distinction but primarily because of the stigma attached to the name:

> We do not allow the 120 Fellowship [Wagner's Sunday school class] to be called "charismatic," nor do I accept the label personally. I have nothing but admiration and praise for the charismatic movement and for charismatics. I just prefer not to be one. . . . At this point the reason for our semantic preference is largely social. Like it or not, many mainline evangelicals have developed strongly negative attitudes toward the charismatic movement over the past twenty years. Much of this has been caused by excesses with which most charismatics would not want to identify. But the attitude unfortunately has spread to cover the entire movement. Many of these evangelicals, however, are not negative toward the movement of the Holy Spirit. This is one reason I believe he is now coming on a Third Wave,

different from the two earlier waves of Pentecostals and charismatics which continue strongly.[6]

Is it not entirely accurate, then, to view the Third Wave as part of the larger charismatic movement? While it is true that many who identify with the Third Wave avoid the usual charismatic jargon when writing or speaking about Spirit baptism, few if any Third Wave teachers treat this as anything more than a difference in terminology.[7] Wagner's differentiation between the charismatic movement and the Third Wave therefore seems little more than a semantic diversion.[8]

Indeed, most Third Wave teaching and preaching echoes standard charismatic doctrine.[9] At its core is an obsession with sensational experiences and a preoccupation with the apostolic charismata: tongues, healings, prophetic revelation, words of knowledge, and visions. Like Pentecostals and charismatics, Third Wave adherents aggressively pursue ecstatic experiences, mystical phenomena, miraculous powers, and supernatural wonders—while tending to underemphasize the traditional means of spiritual growth: prayer, Bible study, the teaching of the Word, persevering in obedience, and the fellowship of other believers.

Moreover, the Third Wave has not, as Wagner implies, managed to avoid the "excesses" of the Pentecostal and charismatic movements. On the contrary, Third Wave groups have opened their arms to some of the worst errors and most troublesome extremists from those earlier movements. The Kansas City Prophets are a case in point (see chapter 3). Wimber's books are filled with similar examples from third-world countries.[10] Chuck Smith, pastor of Calvary Chapel, Costa Mesa (with whom Wimber was once associated), told one researcher he believes "John Wimber has absorbed every aberrant teaching developed by the Pentecostals into his teaching."[11] Surely that assessment is not far from the truth.

Some men from our church staff recently visited Wimber's Vineyard in Anaheim. The evening they were there, they witnessed virtual pandemonium. Wimber tried to get everyone speaking in tongues at once. Women were convulsing on the floor; one man lay on his back in a catatonic state; and all around, hundreds of people were dancing, running, shouting, and standing on chairs.

Despite all the clear evidence to the contrary, Third Wave apologists have had astonishing success in selling their movement as a non-charismatic phenomenon. Unsuspecting churches and denominations have opened their doors—and their pulpits—to Third Wave teachers, many of whom sport very impressive academic credentials. The Third Wave is now rolling like a destructive tsunami, leaving chaos and confusion in its wake.

The effort to market the Third Wave as non-charismatic fits a pattern of shrewd promotion and semantic smoke screens that permeates Third Wave teaching. In fact, practically every Third Wave distinctive turns out on inspection to be a false promise. We will look at four of them:

Signs and Wonders?

Third Wave devotees believe that fantastic signs and wonders demonstrate the genuineness of their movement. Miraculous phenomena are the very heart of the Third Wave credo. Third Wavers are persuaded that miracles, visions, tongues, prophecies, and healings are *essential* supplements to the gospel. They view Christianity without those things as impotent, adulterated by the Western, materialistic mindset.[12]

Signs and wonders are the key to Third Wave evangelism. Some Third Wavers even say that unbelievers *must* experience the miraculous to be brought to full faith. Merely preaching the gospel message, they believe, will never reach the world for Christ. Most people will not believe without seeing miracles, they say, and those who do will be inadequately converted and therefore stunted in their spiritual growth.[13]

Wimber cites Elijah's confrontation with the prophets of Baal on Mount Carmel as a classic example of a "power encounter," where the power of God vanquishes the power of evil.[14] Similar signs and wonders, say Third Wave advocates, are the chief means we should be using to spread the gospel.

Modern miracle workers have yet to call down fire from heaven, but Third Wave aficionados tell of some fantastic signs and wonders that are happening within the movement. Wimber, for example, reported an incident where a woman's toe, which had been cut off, supposedly grew back.[15] He described another woman in Australia whose cleft palate closed up miraculously three days after God gave him a "word of knowledge" that she would be healed.[16] Wagner recounted a report from Argentine faith healer Carlos Annacondia, who told Wagner that

> Two particular manifestations of the Holy Spirit seem to impress unbelievers more than anything else in his crusades: falling in the power of the Spirit and filling teeth. On a fairly regular basis, decayed teeth are filled and new teeth grow where there were none before. Interestingly, according to Annacondia, mostly unbelievers' teeth are filled; very few believers.[17]

As we have seen, both Wagner and Wimber are convinced that many dead people are being raised (see chapter 5).

Frankly, I find all those accounts preposterous. It is difficult to resist the conclusion that they are either utter fabrications or yarns that have grown with the telling. In each case, the people to whom the miracles supposedly occurred remain anonymous. In the two cases reported by Wimber, he maintains that medical doctors witnessed the events. Yet he offers no documentation.

If Third Wave miracle workers sincerely believe their mighty works are supposed to be signs for unbelievers, why not publish proof that these events really took place? Phenomena such as digit and limb replacement, the healing of birth defects, supernatural dentistry, and raising the dead should be easy to document, especially if physicians are present. Independent validation of such wonders would make international headlines. That would certainly help bring about the kind of worldwide response Third Wavers say they are hoping to see someday.[18]

But a pattern begins to emerge from Third Wave literature: the truly spectacular miracles always seem to involve nameless people. Real people's miracles tend to be mundane and hard-to-prove—cures involving back pain, "inner healings," migraine relief, emotional deliverance, ringing in the ears, and so on. The only detailed anecdotes involving known people actually describe occasions when the healing *doesn't* come.

A prime example is Wagner's account of his friend Tom Brewster, a paraplegic who believed in healing. Brewster was so hopeful that God would heal him, he even distributed a "Declaration of Expectation" to his friends—an expression of his faith that he would one day walk. That faith never wavered, Wagner says, though it had been almost thirty years since a diving accident left him confined to a wheelchair. But the miracle never came. Brewster died after unsuccessful bladder surgery.[19]

It is difficult to read that account without noting how markedly it contrasts with the many supposed miracles Wagner, Wimber, and other Third Wave authors recount. The most dramatic miracles come with sketchy details and are nearly always anonymous. Rarely do they even involve people who are known personally to those who report the miracles. Corroborating eyewitness accounts are sometimes cited but never documented. Most UFO sightings come with more convincing evidence.

A group of five Christian medical doctors attended a recent conference led by John Wimber in Sydney, Australia.

These men were hoping to establish the truth of Wimber's claims that miraculous healings were taking place in his meetings. One of them, Dr. Philip Selden, reported,

> The fact that John Wimber knew we were present and observing may have served to "tone down" the claims which we understand were made at previous conferences. . . . Mr. Wimber himself referred to bad backs and indicated that people could expect pain relief, but no change which could be documented by a doctor. He admitted that he had never seen a degenerated vertebra restored to normal shape. . . .
> As I suspected, most of the conditions which were prayed over were in the psychosomatic, trivial, or medically difficult-to-document categories:
>   problem with left great toe
>   nervous disorders
>   breathing problems
>   barrenness
>   unequal leg lengths (my favourite—I can't measure legs accurately)
>   bad backs and neck, etc.[20]

The doctor concluded, "At this stage, we are unaware of any organic healings which could be proven."[21]

What explanation is given for people who are not healed? Wimber at first seems unequivocal on this point:

> There are many reasons that people are not healed when prayed for. Most of the reasons involve some form of sin and unbelief:
>   • Some people do not have faith in God for healing (James 5:15).
>   • Personal, unconfessed sin creates a barrier to God's grace (James 5:16).
>   • Persistent and widespread disunity, sin, and unbelief in bodies of believers and families inhibit healing in individual members of the body (1 Cor. 11:30).

• Because of incomplete or incorrect diagnoses of what is causing their problems, people do not know how to pray correctly.

• Some people assume that God always heals instantly, and when he does not heal immediately they stop praying.[22]

Oddly, however, Wimber later states, "I never blame the sick person for lack of faith if healing does not come."[23]

Perhaps Wimber has not yet thought through his own theology of healing. Evidently he rejects the biblical principle that physical ailments may be part of God's sovereign plan for believers (see chapter 9). But he struggles to explain why so many are *not* healed. "I have a continually expanding group of disgruntled people who have come for healing and don't get it," Wimber has admitted.[24]

The reality is that the Third Wave, with all its emphasis on signs and wonders, has produced nothing verifiable that qualifies in the New Testament sense as an authentic sign or wonder.

Jesus' miracles must, after all, be the standard by which we make such an evaluation. No one before or since has performed as many signs and wonders as he did during his earthly ministry (John 20:30; 21:25). His miracles were strikingly different from those produced by the modern Signs and Wonders movement. None involved psychosomatic infirmities; all were visible and verifiable. They were, in short, true signs and true wonders.

What else do we learn about miracles from our Lord's ministry? Chiefly that miracles do *not* produce real faith in an unbelieving heart. "Faith comes from *hearing*, and hearing by the *word* of Christ" (Rom. 10:17, emphasis added).

In spite of all Jesus' miracles—raising the dead, healing the sick, giving sight to the blind, and his authority over demons—Israel rejected him and crucified him. And at the time of his death, it appears he had only about 120 dedicated followers (Acts 1:15).

The gospels contain numerous examples of people who witnessed Jesus' signs and wonders, yet remained in unbelief. He rebuked the cities where he performed most of his miracles, Chorazin, Bethsaida, and Capernaum, because they did not repent (Matt. 11:20–24). John 2:23 tells us that "many believed in His name, beholding His signs which He was doing," yet Jesus did not consider them true believers (2:24). John 6:2 records that a great multitude was following him "because they were seeing the signs which He was performing on those who were sick." John 6:66 tells us that many of this same crowd "withdrew, and were not walking with Him anymore" after hearing teaching from him they could not accept. In John 11, Jesus raised Lazarus from the dead, a tremendous miracle even his enemies could not deny (11:47). But far from believing in Jesus, they began to plot His death (11:53). John 12:37 sums it all up: "Though He had performed so many signs before them, yet they were not believing in Him."

Nor were things any different in the early church. In the third chapter of Acts Peter and John healed a man who had been lame from birth. Again, the Jewish religious leaders did not deny that a miracle had occurred (Acts 4:16). But their response was far from saving faith: they ordered the apostles to stop speaking in the name of Jesus (4:18).

Examine the record of Old Testament signs and wonders. They did not produce saving faith, either. Pharaoh's heart was hardened despite the powerful signs and wonders God did through Moses. And the entire generation of Israelites, who also witnessed those miracles and many others, died in the wilderness because of their unbelief.

Despite all the miracles performed by the prophets, both Israel and Judah failed to repent and were ultimately carried away into captivity. The very account Wimber cites as biblical justification for "power encounters," Elijah's confrontation with the prophets of Baal, is an example. The revival it produced was short-lived. Within days Elijah was hiding in fear of his life (2 Kings 19:4–8), and Baal worship continued until God finally judged Israel.

The underlying assumption that drives the whole Third Wave movement is wrong. Miracles, signs, and wonders are impotent to produce either faith or genuine revival. Furthermore, power-encounter ministry misses the whole point of our witness. We are not commissioned to confront satanic power with miracle power. We are commissioned to confront satanic lies with divine truth.

That is not to say signs and wonders were unimportant. As we have seen, they had a distinctive purpose: they demonstrated that those who performed them were truly God's messengers (Heb. 2:4). And they often attracted people's attention so the gospel message could be proclaimed (cf. Acts 8:6; 14:8–18). They did not, however, generate saving faith.

Power Evangelism?

That leads to a second false promise made by the Third Wave: the "Power Evangelism" they tout is hardly evangelism at all. Third Wave methodology seriously blunts the force of the gospel. Many Third Wavers are even guilty of omitting or badly corrupting the saving message.

I realize that is a serious charge, but it is one that is borne out by abundant evidence. Third Wave books and testimonies are filled with anecdotes about people who supposedly became Christians on the basis of some miracle they witnessed—with no mention of the gospel having been proclaimed to them.[25] Perhaps the gospel *was* proclaimed—but Third Wave testimonies rarely say so. Recurring accounts like that blur the importance of the gospel message, and even make it seem superfluous. The entire movement is beset with this tendency.

Wimber's *Power Evangelism*, the movement's main textbook on evangelism, omits any reference to the cross of Christ or the doctrine of atonement. Under fire for that deficiency,

Wimber has published a new book that devotes thirteen (out of more than two hundred) pages to the cross, Christ's death, justification, regeneration, and related issues.[26] Still, soteriology (the doctrine of salvation) and an accurate gospel message can hardly be considered major thrusts of the movement, despite all its heavy emphasis on how to evangelize properly. In all the fuss about signs and wonders, the *content* of the gospel message has scarcely been a Third Wave concern.

Mark Thompson recorded his impressions of the evangelistic meeting at the Sydney conference:

> The team affirmed their concern for evangelism. John Wimber was especially at pains to deny he wanted to distract people from this task. And after all, hadn't they planned a "Healing and Evangelistic Rally" at Sydney Showground for the Thursday night?
>
> Yet two things undercut their stated concern. Firstly, the cross of Jesus got only one brief mention in all the General Meetings and workshops I attended during the conference. . . .
>
> Secondly, and even more seriously, there was no gospel in the so-called evangelistic meeting. The cross of Jesus was not central; the atonement not explained; and mankind's need and the provision of redemption not even cursorily treated. Believing himself to be following the example of Jesus and the apostles, John Wimber called out for those who needed to be healed—bad backs got a mention, short legs, neck pain and a whole host of diseases. People were asked to stand and team members dispatched to pray for them while on the stage John Wimber demanded that the Spirit come. After a few minutes of silence several screams were heard and people sobbing. A little later, Mr. Wimber declared that people had been healed and that God had given it as a token, a sign to those who did not believe. In short, they were asked to base their decision on what they had seen, or rather on Mr. Wimber's interpretation of what

they had seen. *The sacrifice of Christ for the sin of the world didn't get a guernsey.*

I was left wondering what faith people would have been converted to that night. It did not resemble New Testament Christianity except in name.[27]

Third Wave evangelistic strategy itself undermines the gospel message. The emphasis is on signs and wonders, not on preaching the Word of God. That is why Wagner can marvel at Argentine evangelist Omar Cabrera's incredible results, "People often will be saved and healed in Cabrera's meetings before he starts preaching."[28] How can anyone be saved before hearing the gospel? Wagner makes no attempt to explain what he is talking about.

Some Third Wavers give the impression that miracles are more effective than the gospel message in provoking a response of faith within the human heart. Wagner, for example, has written,

> Christianity . . . began with 120 in the upper room around 33 A.D. Within three centuries it had become the predominant religion of the Roman Empire.
>
> What brought this about?
>
> . . . The answer is deceptively simple. While Christianity was being presented to unbelievers in both word and deed, it was the deed that far exceeded the word in evangelistic effectiveness.[29]

Wagner later quotes Anglican Michael Harper, *"Miracles help people believe."*[30]

Here, then, is the key idea of "power evangelism": miracles prompt saving faith. Not only that, miracles are *more* effective than preaching in that regard. Wimber believes that those who simply preach the gospel message fall short of true evangelism. He dubs their approach "programmatic evangelism."[31] What is needed instead, he says, is "power evangelism":

By power evangelism I mean a presentation of the gospel that is rational but that also transcends the rational. The explanation of the gospel comes with a demonstration of God's power through signs and wonders. Power evangelism is a spontaneous, Spirit-inspired, empowered presentation of the gospel. Power evangelism is evangelism that is preceded and undergirded by supernatural demonstrations of God's presence.

Through these supernatural encounters people experience the presence and power of God. Usually this takes the form of words of knowledge . . . healing, prophecy, and deliverance from evil spirits. In power evangelism, resistance to the gospel is overcome by the demonstration of God's power in supernatural events, and receptivity to Christ's claims is usually very high.[32]

Two fallacies lurk in that philosophy. Both render it utterly ineffective in winning people to genuine faith in Christ. First, when modern miracles become the basis for an evangelistic invitation, the real message of the gospel—Christ's atonement for our sins and his consequent right to demand lordship over our lives (Rom. 14:9)—becomes an incidental issue. The historic and biblical Jesus is pushed aside in favor of a mystical, ethereal Jesus. The focus of faith becomes signs and wonders, not the Savior himself.

Those who put their trust in modern miracles are not saved by that faith, no matter how earnestly they invoke the name of Christ. The object of genuine saving faith is the Lord Jesus Christ, not anyone's miracles. Galatians 2:16 confirms this: "A man is not justified by the works of the Law but through *faith in Christ Jesus*, even we have *believed in Christ Jesus*, that we may be justified by *faith in Christ*, and not by the works of the Law; since by the works of the Law shall no flesh be justified" (emphasis added). No evangelist can legitimately call someone to faith in Christ until he has made clear the basic biblical and historic issues of the gospel, those which Paul said were "of first importance": "that Christ died for our sins according to the Scriptures, and that He was buried, and that He was raised on the third day according to the Scriptures" (1 Cor. 15:3-4). Paul made it his goal to "preach Christ crucified" (1 Cor. 1:23). That must be the central focus of any proclamation of the gospel. A message that excludes it cannot pretend to be evangelistic.

Second, "power evangelism" is patently unbiblical. As noted, "Faith comes from hearing, and hearing by the word of Christ" (Rom. 10:17). The gospel, not signs and wonders, is the "power of God for salvation" (Rom. 1:16). Jesus said that those who reject Scripture will not believe, even if they witness a resurrection: "If they do not listen to Moses and the Prophets, neither will they be persuaded if someone rises from the dead" (Luke 16:31).

Despite the many signs and wonders he performed, Jesus did not practice "power evangelism." He repeatedly rebuked those who demanded signs (Matt. 12:38-39; 16:1-4; Mark 8:11-12; Luke 11:16, 29; 23:8-9; John 4:48). The emphasis of Jesus' ministry was not miracles but preaching. He often preached without doing signs and wonders (cf. Matt. 13:1-52; 18:1-35; John 7:14-44).

Mark 1:29-34 records that Jesus did many miraculous healings in Galilee. Verse 37 tells us that Peter and the others found him the next morning and said excitedly, "Everyone is looking for you." They wanted Jesus to perform more signs and wonders. Jesus, however, responded: "Let us go somewhere else to the towns nearby, in order that I may preach there also; *for that is what I came out for*" (v. 38, emphasis added). For Jesus, preaching the Word was more important than performing signs and wonders. The Third Wave is advocating a different approach, erecting a facade of supernatural experience without the foundation of an appeal for repentance. It is not biblical evangelism.

phy that actions are right because they are useful. One author describes Peter Wagner's utilitarian perspective:

> Wagner makes negative assessments about nobody. He has made a career out of finding what is good in growing churches, and affirming it—without asking many critical questions. This enables him to hold up as models of church life not only Wimber's Vineyard, but Schuller's Crystal Cathedral, the entire Southern Baptist denomination, and just about any other church that is growing.[37]

Wagner is candid about his pragmatic outlook:

> I am proud to be among those who are advocating power evangelism as an important tool for fulfilling the great commission in our day. One of the reasons I am so enthusiastic is that it is working. Across the board, the most effective evangelism in today's world is accompanied by manifestations of supernatural power.[38]

Walter Chantry notes, "It appears that too much attention to church-growth statistics has led power evangelists away from the very theology the multitudes need."[39]

On the one hand Third Wavers claim they are biblical, yet on the other they admit they are pragmatic. Can both things be true? Surely not. The pragmatist is concerned primarily with *what appears to work*. The biblical thinker is concerned only with *what the Bible says*. Those approaches are usually in fundamental conflict. And in the Third Wave, when what is working conflicts with the biblical pattern, the nod nearly always goes to the pragmatic argument. Thus experience determines both the practical and the theological agendas of the movement.

Wimber says, "I have talked with many evangelical theologians who have undergone significant changes in their theology because of an experience. We are always being influenced by our experiences and need the humility to admit it. . . . Some truths in Scripture cannot be understood until we have had certain experiences."[40] But true biblicists do not alter their theology unless confronted with a more precise understanding of Scripture.

Wimber tries to synthesize that truth into his system: "God uses our experiences to show us more fully what he teaches in Scripture, many times toppling or altering elements of *our* theology and worldview."[41] The problem Wimber fails to acknowledge is that experience can be false, while God's Word cannot. The goal of a biblical perspective is to subject our experiences to the light of Scripture so that God's Word shapes our understanding. If we test Scripture by experience, we will certainly fall into error.

Despite their expressed desire to be biblical, Third Wavers have allowed their experience-centered hermeneutic—combined with a utilitarian devotion to whatever seems to work—to move them far away from biblical theology. For example, John Wimber embraces the Roman Catholic teaching on the efficacy of relics. In a healing seminar sponsored by The Vineyard in 1981, Wimber said, "It's been a rather common occurrence in the Catholic church over about a twelve-hundred-year period for people to be healed as a result of touching the relics of the saints. Now, we Protestants have difficulty with that, but we healers shouldn't, because there's nothing theologically out of line with it. Because all we're doing is giving them a point of contact for their faith."[42] Wimber also has invented some curious notions about demonology:

> There are many demons that don't have a body. Having a body [for a demon] is like having a car. They want to have a car so they can get around. If they don't have a body, they're a second-class demon. They're not first class. I'm not kidding you. That's the way it works. And so [to them] having a body is a big deal. That's why they don't want to give it up.[43]

That is fanciful, not biblical. But it works in the Third Wave because to be called *biblical*, a teaching does not need to be drawn from Scripture. It simply must avoid obvious conflict with familiar Scripture passages.

Sometimes even that guideline is not observed. Wimber's teaching regarding the person of Jesus Christ is careless at best, blasphemous at worst, but in any case clearly contradictory to Scripture. In his taped healing seminar, Wimber says, "Haven't you been taught that Jesus knows all things? There are many times in the Gospels when Jesus doesn't know, and he has to ask questions."[44] That statement denies the omniscience of Christ. Equally appalling is this: "Jesus often ministered on the faith of others. Jesus often rode the crest of the faith of others. I believe there were times when Jesus had little or no faith for the healing of the individual. I believe that there were times when he had more faith flowing than at other times."[45]

That picture of Jesus struggling with a lack of faith is totally contrary to the way the gospels portray our Lord. Out of his own imagination and experience, Wimber has spun a notion of a Jesus who has more in common with John Wimber than with the Jesus of the New Testament.

Wimber claims that various physical phenomena take place when the Holy Spirit's power comes on a person. They include shaking and trembling, falling down (being "slain in the Spirit"), a euphoric state resembling drunkenness, jumping up and down, contraction of the hands making them clawlike, facial contortions, stiffening of the body, trembling, fluttering of the eyelids, heavy breathing, sensations of heat, perspiring, and a feeling of weight on the chest.[46] Of course, the Bible nowhere associates those sensations with the working of the Spirit in a person's life. They sound more like occult phenomena or self-induced experience than the fruit of the Spirit (cf. Gal. 5:22–23).

Although Third Wave leaders want to convince Christians outside their movement that they are deeply committed to Scripture as the ultimate standard of faith and practice, they commonly build their teachings on experiences, and worry later about finding biblical support to back things up. Ken Sarles, associate professor of theology at The Master's Seminary, accurately notes, "Wimber's two major books, *Power Evangelism*, and *Power Healing*, are filled with stories, anecdotes, and illustrations. At times the stories themselves become the basis of what is taught. There are numerous Scripture references, but invariably they are explained through an illustration."[47] Undeniably, most Third Wave literature suffers from this tendency. Books touting the movement lean heavily on first-person narrative. Sometimes biblical references are woven in, but they are seldom if ever the cornerstone of any Third Wave teaching. Passages of Scripture are rarely dealt with in their proper contexts. Instead, isolated Bible stories and verses are brought in where possible as proof texts and for illustrative purposes.

Power Encounters, edited by Kevin Springer, shows this tendency throughout. It is a collection of testimonies by people who were propelled into the movement by dramatic, mystical experiences. Not one of the people featured in the book came into the Third Wave because studying Scripture convinced him or her that the movement was a work of God; all of them were swept in by an experience, or by a series of experiences.

Mike Flynn, for example, an Episcopalian rector, describes his experience during a chapel service while in seminary:

> I had decided to quit. I'm not sure exactly what or how much I quit—surely seminary, perhaps my marriage, probably religion—because I never had a chance to find out, for when I went up to the altar rail for Communion, something unbidden, unexpected, and alarming happened when the priest put the bread in my hand. Suddenly something like electricity began happening in me.

I didn't have much time to ponder that, for, as the other priest bearing the cup came closer, the sensation increased dramatically. When he was giving the cup to the person next to me, it was nearly unbearable and extremely alarming. The only reason I didn't bolt and run was shyness. As he touched the cup to my lips, the whole business climaxed: I felt as though a Vesuvius of sorts was spewing straight out of the top of my head; I was certain that I was emitting a brilliant white light and that everybody was gawking at me; and my insides were riot with that electric sensation.[48]

Flynn says he didn't understand the experience and though he sought it repeatedly after that, he finally gave up, "parked the experience in a corner," and became cynical, anti-establishment, and morally decadent.[49]

Frustrated, Flynn sought renewal. "I remember saying something like, 'All right, if it takes being an emotional idiot to get that relationship with God, then so be it.'" Suddenly he remembered his altar-rail experience: "And as I recalled that experience, the whole thing happened over again! I knew, and I knew that I knew, that my life had changed. It was August 22, 1972."[50]

But that experience wore off, too, after about six months. Finally, Flynn went to see a woman who prayed for him.

Standing behind the chair in which I was seated, she forewarned me that she shook when she prayed and that I wasn't to bother about it. So she placed her hands on my head and kept silent a while. Then she prayed that God would give me her anointing for healing of memories (inner healing, as it is called today). I was quite sure that I didn't want an anointing for *that* but was too courteous to tell her that. I drove home thinking the session had been a dead loss.

But a couple weeks later, a woman came into my office, sat down, and explained her serious marriage problems, stemming from spouse abuse. She was in need of the healing of damaged emotions. After a brief argument in my mind with God, I agreed to pray for her. But I realized with a shock that I hadn't the slightest concept of *how* to do it. I had been practicing Christ's presence visually, seeing Jesus on a throne wherever I went. So I looked at Jesus. He got off his throne, knelt down beside the woman, put his arm around her shoulders, and with his left hand reached right into her heart and pulled out what looked like black jello. This he put into his own heart where it shrank until it evaporated. Then he reached into his own heart again and took out a glob of white jello, which he carefully inserted into the woman's heart where the darkness had been. Finally he turned to me and said, "Do that." I felt rather foolish, but I described out loud in prayer what I had seen Jesus do, and the woman was rather gloriously and immediately healed.[51]

Inner healing, visualization, feelings of warmth and electricity—those things are the vocabulary of New Age and occult practices and as such have nothing to do with biblical Christianity. In fact, throughout his entire testimony, Flynn makes only one reference to Scripture; several times he cites John 15:5: "Apart from Me you can do nothing."

Near the end of his testimony, Flynn makes a telling admission: "I don't know how the word of knowledge works in you, but in me it is almost always the merest flick across my inner eye. I like to say that the Spirit speaks in a 'whis,' which is half a whisper. On an emotional level it *feels* like I'm lying when I utter a word of knowledge."[52] Obviously Flynn himself is not fully convinced these are messages from God. My judgment would be that if he *feels* like he is lying, he probably is. His attitude, however, seems frighteningly brazen. He recounts a class on signs and wonders he once taught at Fuller Seminary: "At the end of the teaching, I called the Spirit down. As my sidekick Lloyd Harris and I got in the car after the event, I joked, 'Well, I think I must have lied about twenty-five times tonight.' Lloyd laughed, knowing what I meant, for I had uttered words of knowledge about twenty-five times."[53]

Can anyone seriously argue that such an irreverent outlook aligns in any way with biblical truth?

Wimber's chronicle of his own spiritual pilgrimage shows a clear pattern of leaning heavily on experience at the expense of Scripture. Each crisis in his life, each major shift in his thinking, was prompted not by the Word of God, but by a mystical experience. His openness to charismatic gifts occurred after his wife had "a personality meltdown." He writes, "One night, through a dream, she was filled with the Holy Spirit. . . . She woke up speaking in tongues!"[54] A series of similar experiences—including healings, visions, dreams, messages from God, and miraculous events—has formed the basis for all that John Wimber teaches today.

Wagner came to his views in a similar fashion. He writes, "What brought about the change? How did I turn 180 degrees? The process took about fifteen years. First, in the later sixties, *I had an unforgettable experience*."[55] As Wagner gives his overview of those decisive fifteen years, every turning point he names is related to a person or experience that influenced him. Not one of the reasons he gives for his "worldview shift" grew out of his personal study of Scripture.

Wagner describes his friend Edward Murphy, vice president of Overseas Crusades, who once believed "that the moment the Holy Spirit entered a new Christian's life, the evil spirits, if there were any there, were automatically expelled."[56] Murphy no longer holds that view, Wagner reports. "His missionary experience . . . forced him to change his mind."[57]

Forming one's theology like that is exceedingly dangerous. The final authority in spiritual matters becomes one's subjective experience, not God's objective Word. The Bible is toppled from its proper place as the sole guide for faith and practice in the Christian life, and is relegated to the secondary role of confirming one's experience. And when an experience cannot be found in Scripture, or when it contradicts some biblical truth, the Bible is simply ignored or reinterpreted. To elevate experience above Scripture is to cast oneself adrift on a sea of mystical subjectivity.

A report on Wimber's Vineyard movement from the Christian Research Institute correctly concluded, "While there is much teaching in The Vineyard on certain practical matters . . . there appears to be little emphasis on teaching the Bible per se."[58] The report continued,

> While Bible teaching is not emphasized enough, the role of experience in the Christian life appears to be somewhat over-emphasized. People in The Vineyard frequently seem to be willing to allow their spiritual experiences to be self-authenticating. They seem too willing to assume that whatever transpires in their midst is from God. That is not to say that the leaders do not attempt to show that their experiences are scriptural, but that experience far too often is their starting point.[59]

Clearly, the Third Wave is the offspring of a fierce pragmatism married to an insatiable thirst for dramatic and spectacular experiences. Despite all the claims to the contrary, its fundamental orientation is not biblical.

An Evangelical Heritage?

Listening to the claims of Third Wave leaders, one might conclude that their movement is essentially composed of conservative evangelicals who remain strongly committed to traditional biblical theology. The facts simply do not bear this out.

Much of the Third Wave is difficult to classify doctrinally. Statements of faith and creeds simply are not an earmark of the Third Wave. Wimber's Vineyard is typical:

> Another disturbing aspect of The Vineyard's ministry is their lack of any written statement of faith. Because Vineyard members come from a variety of denominational backgrounds, the leadership has avoided setting strong doctrinal standards. This de-emphasis of doctrine is also consistent with the leadership of John Wimber and Bob Fulton (pastor of The Vineyard in Yorba Linda, California), whose backgrounds theologically include association with the Quakers, who typically stress the inner experience of God and minimize the need for doctrinal expressions of one's understanding of God.[60]

Nevertheless, Third Wavers want to position their movement in the mainstream of historic evangelicalism. Typical testimonies from Third Wavers emphasize conservative, even fundamentalist, roots. Wagner, for example, says, "My background is that of a Scofield Bible dispensational evangelical."[61] He is convinced the Third Wave is "a new moving of the Holy Spirit among *evangelicals.*"[62]

Again, the facts call such judgments into question. The Third Wave movement is broadly ecumenical, even syncretic. The truth is, the evangelical veneer of the Third Wave is a carefully crafted image, another crucial element of the skillful marketing campaign that is attempting to sell the movement to non-charismatic evangelicals. In *Power Points*, Wimber acknowledges the extreme caution that was exercised to keep the book's doctrinal content within the parameters of historic evangelicalism: "This project took a year longer than we anticipated. In part this was because of our concern to root our comments about spiritual growth in historical, orthodox theology."[63]

But is "historical, orthodox theology" really at the heart of Third Wave teaching? No.

Wimber is as comfortable with Roman Catholic dogma

as he is with evangelicalism. As we have noted, Wimber defends the Catholic claims of healing through relics. He advocates the reunification of Protestants and Catholics. A former associate says, "During a Vineyard pastors' conference, [he] went so far as to 'apologize' to the Catholic church on behalf of *all* Protestants."[64] In his seminar on church planting, Wimber stated, "The pope . . . by the way is very responsive to the charismatic movement, and is himself a born-again evangelical. If you've read any of his texts concerning salvation, you'd know he is preaching the gospel as clear as anybody is preaching it in the world today."[65]

An appendix in Wimber's *Power Evangelism* seeks to establish that signs and wonders have appeared throughout church history. Wimber cites an eclectic catalog of individuals and movements—both orthodox and heretical—as evidence. Included in these are Hilarion (a fourth-century hermit), Augustine, Pope Gregory I (The Great), Francis of Assisi (founder of the Franciscan order), the Waldenses (who opposed the Pope and were persecuted by the Dominicans), Vincent Ferrer (who was himself a Dominican), Martin Luther, Ignatius of Loyola, John Wesley, and the Jansenists (a Catholic sect).[66] In a booklet published by The Vineyard, Wimber adds the Shakers (a cult that demanded celibacy), Edward Irving (discredited leader of the Irvingite sect in nineteenth-century England), and the supposed miracles and healings worked by an apparition of the Virgin Mary at Lourdes, France![67]

Wagner credits Robert Schuller's concept of "possibility thinking" with introducing him to a whole new dimension of Christian experience. "Schuller has helped many people begin to believe God for great things," he writes.[68] He is equally comfortable endorsing Korean pastor Dr. Paul Yonggi Cho's "fourth-dimension" ideas, which are rooted in Buddhist and occult teachings.[69]

Wagner's desire to embrace and synthesize conflicting views is revealed in his own words:

> I recently took part in a symposium where six different Christian leaders addressed the meaning of spirituality. I was surprised to find how divergent their opinions were, although that divergence should have been somewhat predictable since the leaders came from different denominational backgrounds. Afterward, I found myself feeling that probably none of them was "wrong," but that each, in his or her way, was right.[70]

That epitomizes the Third Wave approach to truth: everyone is right—Catholicism is right, high-church Anglicanism is right, low-church Anglicanism is right, the Shakers are right, the Quakers are right, and evangelicalism is right, too.[71]

Third Wave teaching, however, rather quickly abandons conservative evangelicalism because Third Wavers have concluded that the power of God is missing from evangelical theology. In his foreword to Don Williams's *Signs, Wonders, and the Kingdom of God*, John White sums up the typical Third Wave perspective:

> Fundamentalist theology of the twentieth century, initially a valuable reaffirmation of the faith in the face of liberal theology, gradually took on the coloring not only of reaction against liberals but against the Pentecostal movement. In so doing it not only became more reactionary, but it threw out the baby of God's power, all the while denying that it was doing so. And the reaction at that point was less a reflection of biblical truth than of unconscious fears blinding us to some things Scripture was saying.[72]

What can free someone from these blinding, unconscious fears? Not truth but experience: "This is what has happened to Don Williams. In presenting his book, he describes the experiences which tore him out of the straightjacket of reactionary theology, a theology that had bound and emasculated him, setting him free by sovereign power."[73]

One wonders, however, whether Williams was ever committed to "fundamentalist theology" at all. Evidently his "reactionary theology" did not even include assurance that the supernatural is real. Williams describes his thinking before he joined the Third Wave: "Was it possible that the devil was a real enemy after all? Could there be a power from God to deliver and transform life at its core?"[74]

Those are not the musings of someone committed to "fundamentalist theology." Evidently Williams's theology did not allow him to be sure that conversion to Christ transforms life at its core. Perhaps his problem was not rigid, reactionary theology after all, but lip service to a creed he did not fully believe.

That, precisely, is the common denominator in virtually every published Third Wave testimony. Nearly all Third Wavers speak of theology as inherently divorced from experience, academic, straight-jacket teaching, empty creedalism, dead orthodoxy. Wimber himself notes the similar backgrounds of those featured in Springer's book, *Power Encounters*: "Almost all of them would identify themselves as evangelicals . . . [but] they recognized a large gap between what they had been taught about God and their experience. . . . [Then] they all had an encounter with God, dramatic in most instances, that caught them by surprise."[75]

The testimonies in the book tell stories of men and women whose theology *was* empty, confining, reactionary, and in some cases a total sham. These people adhered intellectually to truth that did not work its way out in their experience. Now they are looking for experiences and wanting to build a new system of truth on them.

Worse, having failed to find reality in truth they embraced only with their minds, they refuse now to believe that *anyone* can have genuine life-changing experiences in response to the same truths they found "empty" and "confining." They believe those who insist on sound doctrine are merely denouncing the possibility of *any* legitimate experience or encounter with God. Having failed to come to grips with God's power in response to objective biblical truth, they have concluded that the *real* power of God is manifested elsewhere—through miraculous, sensational, and mystical experiences. And so while claiming a commitment to evangelical theology, they scorn it as impotent and inherently flawed.

Even conversion apart from the miraculous is lame, they say. People who respond to the gospel without seeing signs and wonders "do not encounter God's power; thus frequently they do not move on to a mature faith. Because there is something inadequate about their conversion experience, later growth for many is retarded."[76]

Aside from the sheer arrogance of that perspective, the danger it poses is great. Virtually everything the New Testament says about signs and wonders in the last days is a warning against false teachers who will use miracles to deceive. Jesus said, "False Christs and false prophets will arise and will show great signs and wonders, so as to mislead, if possible, even the elect. Behold, I have told you in advance" (Matt. 24:24–25; cf. 7:22–23; 2 Thess. 2:3, 8–9).

Do not be swept away by the Third Wave. Remember, the only true test of whether a person or movement is from God is not signs and wonders, but teaching that conforms to God's Word. And the highest expression of God's power in the world today is not some spectacular and unusual sign or wonder, but the tranquil godliness of a Spirit-controlled life.

How Do
Spiritual Gifts Operate?

Benny Hinn slays people in the Spirit. When Benny feels "the anointing" come upon his hand, he touches his followers on the forehead or simply waves an arm at them and they fall down in a faint. Hinn, pastor of Orlando Christian Center, has a nationally-aired television broadcast on which people are slain in the Spirit nearly every week. Hinn occasionally "releases the anointing" on an entire auditorium, causing most of the crowd to fall backward.

Is Benny Hinn's ability a unique spiritual gift, or is he simply using the techniques of mesmerism and the power of suggestion? Surely in light of biblical warnings like Matthew 7:21–23; 24:24, Mark 13:22, and 2 Thessalonians 2:7–9, we must not automatically assume that everyone who displays signs and wonders has power from God to do so. Satanic imitations and deceptions are a very real threat to the church. One thing is certain—what Benny Hinn does is nothing like any of the spiritual gifts Scripture describes.

The charismatic practice of slaying people in the Spirit has become so commonplace that many charismatics may be surprised to learn that Scripture is utterly silent about such a gift. There is no record that any apostle or leader in the early church had the ability to knock people into a Spirit-filled catalepsy. Yet the practice typifies the charismatic movement's obsession with paranormal gifts that are displayed in public and with great commotion.

Spiritual Gifts and the Human Mind

From the earliest days of Pentecostalism, the quest for ever more unusual and spectacular manifestations of spiritual gifts has sabotaged rationality in the movement. As noted throughout this book, reports of inexplicable—even implausible—mystical phenomena are rife in the charismatic and Pentecostal tradition. No tale, it seems, is too fantastic to gain an eager following.[1] Many appear to believe that God's power can be displayed *only* in ways that are unearthly, eerie, or preposterous. As a result, some charismatics disdain logic, reason, and common sense in their eagerness to embrace such reports.

Worse, the entire movement has absorbed the erroneous notion that whatever is truly spiritual must transcend or bypass people's rational senses. Spiritual gifts supposedly operate by suspending the faculties of human reason. One might think that the strongest evidence of the Holy Spirit's power is when someone lapses into a stupor. And so the lore of the charismatic movement is filled with outrageous accounts of behavior that resembles trances, seizures, subliminal messaging, hypnosis, suspended animation, frenzy, hysteria, even dementia. These are often cited as proof that God is at work in the movement.

Kenneth Hagin, for example, claims that one night while he was preaching, a cloud of glory enveloped him and he lost track of where he was and what he was saying. "I didn't know one word I had said for 15 minutes. I had been in the glory cloud. When I found myself walking around the altar, I got so embarrassed my face got red, and I ran back on the platform, got behind the pulpit, said, 'Amen. Let's pray,' and gave the invitation."[2]

"Sometimes when I'm preaching," Hagin writes, "the Spirit of God comes on me, arrests my attention, and I can't say a word in English."[3] He goes on to tell of an incident when he was ministering with Fred Price, and he was struck with what he believes was an "anointing" during the church service. Hagin says he was unable to communicate in English for hours.[4]

In a similar vein Hagin relates this story:

> Sister Maria Woodworth-Etter was an evangelist during the early days of the Pentecostal movement in this country. I read the newspaper account concerning what happened in St. Louis, sometime before 1920. She was in her 70's, preaching in a tent which was full, when right in the middle of her sermon, with her hand uplifted to illustrate a point and her mouth open, the power of God came upon her.
>
> She froze in that position and stood like a statue for three days and three nights. Think about that: All her body had to be under the control of the Spirit of God. She had no bodily functions the three days and nights she stood there.
>
> According to the newspaper account, it was estimated that more than 150,000 people came by to see her in that three-day period. The third night, the Spirit of God released her. She thought it was the same night, and the same sermon, and she went right on preaching at the same place in her sermon.[5]

Why anyone would assume that such behavior manifests God's power is hard to comprehend. Nothing remotely like it can be found in Scripture—unless you count Lot's wife. And not to be outdone, Hagin tries to eclipse that tale with some similar anecdotes from his own experience:

> One night a 16-year-old girl was filled with the Spirit, spoke with other tongues, went into a spirit of intercession, and then with her hands raised, stood in one spot eight hours

and 40 minutes. She never batted an eye and never shifted her weight from foot to foot.

It was January, and she was standing away from the stove. Her mother, concerned about her getting cold, asked if it would be all right to move her nearer to the stove, which was in the center of the room.

"I don't know," I said. I had never seen anything like it.

The pastor, who weighed 250 pounds, said, "Brother Hagin, you get under one of her elbows, and I'll get under the other, and we'll scoot her closer to the heat."

But she could not be moved. It was as if she were nailed to the floor.[6]

Hagin continues:

On another night when we gave the altar call, I sensed the power of God was upon one of the women. She began exhorting people to be saved. I said, "Sister, go ahead and obey God."

With her eyes closed, she stepped upon the wide altar, and began walking from one end to the other, exhorting sinners to be saved. She would walk right up to the end of the altar, and you would think she was going to step off, but each time she would turn. Folks started coming to the altar. Her eyes were shut, but every time one would come, her spirit would know it, and she'd dance a little jig for joy. Then she would go right back to exhorting. When the 20th person had come—every single sinner was saved that night—God is my witness, my wife is my witness, and each person in that building is my witness, she began to dance right off the end of the altar. She stood in mid-air dancing! Her feet were not touching the floor. Everyone saw it. I could have reached out and touched her. Then she turned and danced back onto the altar, down the altar to the other end, stopped, opened her eyes, and stepped off.[7]

Frankly that sounds more like a scene from a bad horror movie than a true miracle. Levitation, altered states, feet nailed to the floor—those are the apparatus of the occult, not genuine spiritual gifts.[8]

I have not chosen isolated or atypical examples. And it is not just provincial or old-fashioned evangelists who report such spectacles. Virtually every major segment of the charismatic movement features stories like those. Even the Third Wave movement, despite strong ties to the academic community, exhibits a definite bias toward signs and wonders in which human intellect is disengaged. Carol Wimber describes the "watershed experience" that launched her husband's church into power evangelism. It was Sunday evening, Mothers' Day, 1981, and a young man whom John Wimber had invited to preach gave his testimony. At the end of his message the guest speaker invited all those under the age of twenty-five to come forward:

> None of us had a clue as to what was going to happen next. When they got to the front the speaker said, "For years now the Holy Spirit has been grieved by the church, but he's getting over it. Come Holy Spirit."
>
> And he came.
>
> Most of these young people had grown up around our home and we knew them well—we had four children between the ages of eighteen and twenty-four. One fellow, Tim, started bouncing. His arms flung out and he fell over, but one of his hands accidentally hit a mike stand and he took it down with him. He was tangled up in the cord with the mike next to his mouth. Then he began speaking in tongues, so the sound went throughout the gymnasium (by now we were meeting in a high school). We had never considered ourselves charismatics and certainly had never placed any emphasis on the gift of tongues. We had seen a few people tremble and fall over before and we had seen many healings, but this was different. The majority of the young people were shaking and falling over. At one point it looked like a battlefield scene—bodies everywhere, people weeping, wailing, and speaking in tongues, much shouting

and loud behavior. And there was Tim in the middle of it all, babbling into the microphone.[9]

Can that kind of chaos really be accepted as proof that God is working? Even John Wimber at first seemed uncertain. "He spent that night reading Scripture and historical accounts of revival," Mrs. Wimber reports. "He was afraid of doing anything that wasn't explicitly outlined in the Bible."[10] A healthy fear, but Carol Wimber says her husband's all-night study "did not yield conclusive answers."

> By 5 A.M. John was desperate. He cried out to God, "Lord, if this is you, please tell me." A moment later the phone rang and a pastor friend of ours from Denver, Colorado, was on the line. "John," he said, "I'm sorry I'm calling so early, but I have something really strange to tell you. I don't know what it means, but God wants me to say, 'It's me, John.'"
>
> That was all John needed. He didn't have to understand the trembling or why everything happened as it did; all he needed to know was Holy Spirit [sic] did it.[11]

Too bad. If John Wimber had continued reading Scripture, he might have seen that the apostle Paul reproved the Corinthians for allowing a scene not unlike the commotion that took place in Wimber's church: "If therefore the whole church should assemble together and all speak in tongues, and ungifted men or unbelievers enter, will they not say that you are mad? . . . But let all things be done properly and in an orderly manner" (1 Cor. 14:23, 40). Of course God's Word is the only reliable test of such things, and it seems clear that an honest reading of Scripture would have given Wimber the plain answer he said he was seeking. Yet Wimber took counsel instead from an unexpected telephone call. That call, of course, may have been a satanic diversion. But John Wimber decided he did not need to make sense of what was happening in his church; he did not need to reconcile it with Scripture; he did not need to understand it. He had a mystical sign, and that was enough for him. He put aside his fears about extrabiblical phenomena, deciding after one night's study that Scripture had no definitive answers for him—opting instead to accept a mystical sign as conclusive.

Spiritual Gifts or Spiritual Casualties?

This charismatic tendency to suspend the intellect and let mysticism run amok is the essence of what Paul wrote against in 1 Corinthians 14. There, condemning the Corinthians' misuse of the gift of tongues, the apostle argued that all ministry of spiritual gifts in the church should be aimed at people's *minds*: "In the church I desire to speak five words with my mind, that I may instruct others also, rather than ten thousand words in a tongue" (14:19). The principle applies to all spiritual gifts: "Since you are zealous of spiritual gifts, seek to abound for the edification of the church" (14:12).[12] "God is not a God of confusion" (14:33).

Yet confusion and chaos dominate typical contemporary charismatic meetings. Norvel Hayes describes an incident when he supposedly healed a man of deafness:

> The man fell straight forward, face down on the floor. You would have thought all his teeth would have been knocked out, but they weren't.
>
> Then he bounced and fell back down again. That impact could have broken his nose, but it didn't.
>
> Again, he bounced up off the floor and fell back. This time he laid there real quiet for about sixty seconds. Then his mouth opened and a little squeaky sound like a mouse began to come out. It got louder, sounding like a big rat, and finally sounded like a screaming hyena.
>
> In a little while the man shook his head and pushed himself up off the floor. He acted as if he had been hit in the head with a stick, but both ears had popped open and the knot in his stomach was gone!

. . . [People] jumped out of their seats and started running toward me, saying, "Pray for me!"

As I reached out and began to pray, it was as though the wind of God had come into my hands! People were lying all around on the floor, including denominational pastors. God baptized them in the Holy Ghost; and the moment they hit the floor, they started to speak in tongues.[13]

Hagin tells a series of incredible tales about unusual healings he has done when "peculiar anointings" have been manifest in his ministry:

Several times the anointing has come on me to do unusual things while praying for the sick. Sometimes I go along five or six years between times.

The first time it happened to me was in 1950. I was preaching in Oklahoma. A woman came forward for prayer. She said she was 72, but she looked like she was about to give birth to a baby. Of course, she had a tumor.

. . . .

I started to lay hands on her to pray when the Word of the Lord came to me, saying, "Hit her in the stomach with your fist."

On the inside of me, I said, "Lord, You're going to get me in trouble, going around hitting women in the stomach with my fist! I don't believe I much want to do that!"

Well, if you get to arguing about it, the anointing will leave you—it will lift from you just like a bird flying away after sitting on your shoulder. It left me.

When it left me I thought, *Well, I'll go ahead and minister with laying on of hands.* I laid hands on her again and the anointing came again and the Word of the Lord came again: "Hit her in the stomach with your fist."

I decided I had better stop and explain that to the crowd before I started doing it. So I told them what the Lord said, and I punched her in the stomach with my fist. And God and hundreds of people are my witnesses that that stomach went down like you'd stuck a pin in a balloon.[14]

Hagin tells of another man he was told to hit in the head and a young female college student he hit in the kidney.[15] Such tactics are surely dangerous, especially with elderly and infirm people, yet many other charismatics who hear Hagin's tales undoubtedly try to copy his methods.

One eighty-five-year-old woman who had come forward for a healing touch from Benny Hinn died after someone slain in the Spirit fell on her, fracturing her hip. The woman's family filed a five-million-dollar lawsuit against Hinn in the incident.[16]

Charismatic chaos is usually not physically fatal,[17] but the movement is littered with *spiritual* casualties. I received a letter from a Christian man whose wife became entangled with a fanatic charismatic assembly. He wrote me for counsel, brokenhearted. "She got involved with a group of charismatic women and they convinced her I was not saved since I didn't speak in tongues etc. as they taught her to do. . . . Finally, she left and filed for divorce two months ago. It will soon be final."

Some concerned parents wrote our church for counsel. Their daughter had become involved with a spiritual-gifts workshop in a large, well-known Third Wave church. Her mother wrote:

In December 1989, [she] began speaking in tongues. Shortly thereafter she began to see angels. An angel in armor always stands outside the front door of her home and another stands inside her living room. He has large wings. She said she asked God to send her angels for protection while her husband was on business trips.

A few months later she began to see demons also. A monkeylike demon sat on her husband's head one night and hissed at her. She sees others riding on top of cars or standing on rooftops and some in battle with the angels. She

> sometimes sees darkness around people. She believes seeing this is a God-given gift. . . .
>
> When I told her to test the spirits she got angry. . . . She said the Lord said, "Yes, it is I, the Lord." I believe they are *all* demons! I told her to read the Bible, and she said she only reads the Scripture numbers the Holy Spirit puts in her mind.
>
> We visited her . . . and attended one of her [group] meetings. A prophet . . . from Kansas City came. He said something about the past, present, or future of nearly everyone in the room—some things were incredibly true and other things have not happened yet. [Our daughter] now wants to develop this gift in herself and can now sometimes see a person's sin written on their forehead. She will then expel a demon.
>
> Since I told her to test the spirits as the Bible tells us . . . she will not tell me what she is seeing anymore. I feel that there is a wall between us.

Like so many charismatics, that young woman has come to believe that her experiences obviate Bible study and spiritual discernment. She resents and rebuffs her mother's biblical counsel (cf. 1 John 4:1: "Beloved, do not believe every spirit, but test the spirits to see whether they are from God; because many false prophets have gone out into the world"). Why should she heed her mother's entreaty when the mother cannot even *see* beings from the spirit world? Why, indeed, should she receive instruction from *anyone* whose only source of revealed truth is Scripture? This young woman believes she has a superior relationship with the Holy Spirit, and the only Scripture she needs is the occasional isolated verse that he supposedly brings to mind. Meanwhile, she is communicating with and seeing all kinds of spirits. She *knows* some of them are demonic, and she sees no need to test the others. She is trying to develop extrasensory powers. If there ever was a recipe for spiritual disaster, that young woman has found it.

The charismatic movement breeds spiritual catastrophe precisely because it discourages people from discerning truth by using Scripture and sound reason. Instead, truth is appraised subjectively, usually through signs, wonders, or other mystical means. Kenneth Hagin explains his criteria for judging between true and false spiritual gifts:

> When God moves, everybody will be blessed.
>
> If something is of the *flesh*, everybody will have a sick feeling.
>
> And if something is of the *devil*, it seems like the hair will stand up on your neck.
>
> That's a simple way everyone can judge, whether they've got any spiritual discernment or not.[18]

Whether they've got any spiritual discernment or not? There, as explicitly as it can be expressed, is a statement from a leading charismatic teacher that defines exactly what is wrong with charismatic mysticism. Spiritual discernment is deemed unnecessary. According to Kenneth Hagin, you can judge between what is true, fleshly, or demonic by a process that is really just a simplified system of biofeedback.

Again and again, charismatics hear the same message: Put your mind on hold; ignore reason; listen to your *feelings*.[19] That kind of extreme mysticism, as we have seen, contradicts everything Scripture teaches about true spiritual discernment.

Spiritual gifts are not supposed to produce mindless chaos and pandemonium in the churches. Nor are they merely for show. They are given to edify the body, not the gifted individual (1 Cor. 14:4–5, 17, 26). When you see someone using his gift selfishly or as a performance, lapsing into a spiritual daze, or putting other people into a state of unconsciousness, you can be sure that whatever he is doing, he is not using a legitimate spiritual gift.

Make no mistake, a lot of counterfeit gifts are passing for the real thing today, and the result has not been the building up of the church but the tearing apart of the body.

Gifts in the Corinthian Church

Let us take a closer look at what the apostle Paul had to say in 1 Corinthians about misuse of spiritual gifts. Abuse of the charismata was nearly as big a problem in Corinth as it is in the modern charismatic movement. Paul, who had founded the church at Corinth during his second missionary journey (Acts 18), was particularly interested in the spiritual health and life of the Corinthians. He had spent eighteen months in Corinth building up the church and protecting it from enemies without and within.

When Paul left, other pastors came to minister to the church at Corinth. Some of them gained distinction and some, notoriety. Sadly, within a few years after Paul's departure, severe moral and spiritual problems developed in the Corinthian church. The situation was so serious that Paul's first letter to the Corinthians dealt exclusively with the problems. Divisions, personality cults, cliquishness, moral compromise, and other desperate ills were afflicting the church. Carnality outweighed spirituality. Sexual perversion, fornication, incest, and adultery were being tolerated, and worldliness and materialism had set in. Church members were suing one another in secular courts. One faction was even promoting rebellion against apostolic authority. The church had utterly failed to discipline a member who had fallen into gross sin. Marital conflicts festered, and the role of single people was misunderstood. Liberty was being abused, idolatry was being practiced, selfishness ran rampant, pride was widespread, and even demon worship had crept in. People were abusing God's intended roles for men and women, cheapening the Lord's Supper, and violating the love feast. Through it all—as one might expect in such an environment—spiritual gifts were being perverted, misused, and prostituted.

This was one corrupt church. The Corinthians had managed to drag into their church life a number of vices and fallacies from their former pagan existence. Their problem was not that they *lacked* spiritual gifts. In 1 Corinthians 1:7 Paul told them, "You are not lacking in any gift." The Corinthian problem was *how* the gifts should function and how to discern true gifts from artificial or even demonic ones. This was especially true regarding the gift of tongues.

Therefore a major segment of 1 Corinthians 12–14 discusses the issue of spiritual gifts. The Corinthians held many misconceptions about the Holy Spirit. Like charismatics today, they tended to equate his work with ecstatic, involuntary, frenetic, or mysterious activity. Someone would stand up in the Corinthian assembly to give an utterance in another language, or perhaps a prophecy or interpretation. The wilder and more agitated the person was, the more godly and spiritual he was supposed to be.

Paganism at Corinth

The desire to be seen and revered by others as "spiritual" was why the gift of languages was exploited and perverted to such a great degree. Certain believers used ecstatic speech as if it were the true gift of languages. What they were doing couldn't be identified with any normal human faculty, so it was interpreted as coming from God.

It's not hard to see how that could happen. From the very start, when Paul had first preached the gospel among the Corinthians, the Holy Spirit had been doing amazing things in their midst. The Corinthians knew that the Holy Spirit was at work. But trouble started when the Corinthians started to confuse the work of the Holy Spirit with the mystical practices that they had known in their pagan religions. Aside from a core of Jews in Corinth who were part of the founding church, most of the Corinthians had been saved out of paganism.

In Corinth paganism was spelled with a capital P. The city was part of a Greek culture that was enamored with philosophy. The Corinthians loved to argue over different philosophers and even worshiped them. That is where the divisions and cliques came from that Paul speaks of in 1 Corinthians 1:11–12.

But perhaps Corinth was best known for its sexual immorality. The name of the city became a verb. To "corinthianize" meant to go to bed with a prostitute. Corinth was known throughout the world for its sexual perversions and extremes. According to Bible commentator William Barclay,

> Above the isthmus towered the hill of the Acropolis, and on it there stood the great temple of Aphrodite, the goddess of love. To that temple there were attached one thousand priestesses who were sacred prostitutes, and in the evenings they descended from the Acropolis and plied their trade upon the streets of Corinth, until it became a Greek proverb, "It is not every man who can afford a journey to Corinth."[20]

Unfortunately, the same low morality was dragged into the Corinthian church. In 1 Corinthians 5 Paul had to rebuke the church because one of their members was living sinfully with his father's wife. Marriages were in desperate trouble, and that is why Paul spent so much time discussing marriage in chapter 7.

The Influence of the Mystery Religions

At every turn, the background of the Corinthian believers worked against them. One of the greatest threats of all was the continuing influence from pagan mystery religions that they had formerly practiced. For over a thousand years these religions had dominated that part of the world.

The mystery religions have taken many forms, going back thousands of years. Many of the teachings and superstitions they espouse are common to every variety. Clearly all of them are linked together by common teachings. Much evidence indicates that they all are traceable back to a single origin—Babylon.[21] Every false system of worship has roots in the mystery religions of Babylon because all false religion started at the Tower of Babel. Babel represented the first sophisticated, organized counterfeit religion (cf. Gen. 11:1–9). Nimrod, grandson of Ham and great grandson of Noah, was the patriarchal apostate who organized and directed the building of the tower (10:9–10). Part of the whole scheme was the establishing of a false system of religion, a counterfeit to the true worship of God. Every false system of religion since that time has philosophical and doctrinal ties to that original apostasy at the Tower of Babel. Why? Because when God judged the people who built the tower, he scattered them throughout the world. They took with them the seeds of false religion that had begun at Babel. Wherever they settled, they practiced some form of Babel's false religion. They adapted it, altered it, and added to it, but every subsequent false religion is the offspring of Babel. The Babylonian heresy is alive even today, and according to Revelation 17:5, it will dominate the tribulation period in the end times. There the apostle John describes a blasphemous woman clothed in purple and scarlet as Babylon, the mother of harlots, the one with whom kings of the earth had committed fornication, the one who was full of the names of blasphemy.

Obviously in a sophisticated trade center like Corinth, they knew about and practiced every variety of mystery religion. Like false religions even today, these sects had sophisticated rites and rituals that included baptismal regeneration, sacrifices for sin, feasting, and fasts. Believers in mystery religions also practiced self-mutilation and flagellations. They believed in pilgrimages, public confession, offerings, religious ablutions, and the doing of penance to pay for sins.

But perhaps nothing was more characteristic of the mystery religions than what they called ecstasy. Believers in the mystery religions sought to cultivate a magical, sensuous communion with the divine. They would do almost anything to get themselves into a semiconscious, hallucinatory, hypnotic, or orgiastic spell in which they believed they were sensually in contact with deity. Some used wine to assist in the euphoric experience, as Paul implied in Ephesians 5:18. Whether from literal intoxication or emotional exhilaration, when worshipers fell into a state of euphoria, it was as if they had been drugged. They assumed they were in union with God.

According to S. Angus, once professor of New Testament and historical theology at St. Andrews College, Sydney, the ecstasy experienced by the mystery religion worshiper brought him into "a mystic ineffable condition in which the normal functions of personality were in abeyance and the moral strivings which form character virtually ceased or were relaxed, while the emotional and the intuitive were accentuated."[22] In other words, the worshiper would get into a state where his mind would go into neutral and his emotions would take over. The intellect and conscience would give way to passion, sentiment, and emotion. This was ecstacy, an intoxicating condition of euphoria. Angus further reported:

[Ecstasy] might be induced by vigil and fasting, tense religious expectancy, whirling dances, physical stimuli, the contemplation of the sacred objects, the effect of stirring music, inhalation of fumes, revivalistic contagion (such as happened in the Church at Corinth), hallucination, suggestion, and all the other means belonging to the apparatus of the Mysteries. . . . [One ancient writer] speaks of men "going out of themselves to be wholly established in the Divine and to be enraptured."[23]

As the mystery worshiper experienced such ecstasy, he was lifted above the level of his ordinary experience into an abnormal sense of consciousness. He experienced an exhilarating condition in which he believed his body ceased being a hindrance to his soul.

According to Angus, ecstasy could "range anywhere from nonmoral delirium to that consciousness of oneness with the Invisible and the dissolution of painful individuality which marks the mystics of all ages."[24] In other words, ecstasy could emancipate the soul from the confinement of the body and enable a person to commune with the spirit world. It created an extraordinarily buoyant sensation. In that state a person supposedly had capacity to see and understand things that only the eyes of the spirit can behold.[25]

Testimonies by Pentecostal-charismatic believers describe exactly the same kinds of experiences. Charismatics who experience various states of euphoria attribute their experiences to certain gifts of the Holy Spirit, particularly tongues. The common testimony is, "It feels so good. I never felt this way before! It *must* be of God." But does a good feeling mean their experience is from God? Not necessarily, as we are about to see from the Corinthian experience.

Visiting the First Church of Corinth

There is little doubt that various practices, rituals, attitudes, and other hangovers from the mystery religions had infiltrated the church at Corinth. Just what would it have been like to go to church there?

Imagine visiting that city in the first century and you and your family want to attend the First Church of Corinth. You arrive on time and go in to find that all the wealthy people have already been there for an hour and are just finishing the love feast (cf. 1 Cor. 11:17–22). There is nothing left for you, and you notice that a lot of the poor people, who are just arriving, will have nothing to eat, either.

Not only do you note that the wealthy people are gluttonous as they gobble the last morsels of food, but some of them are also stone drunk. And so there are two groups: the poor people who sit on one side of the room totally sober with their stomachs gnawing, and the wealthier people on the other side, stuffed with food and intoxicated with too much wine. Because of the division, there is arguing and bad feelings.

Someone announces it is time for the Lord's Supper, but this also turns into a mockery. Those who have had nothing to eat or drink become the gluttons. Next they go into their worship service, and this finds many people standing up, shouting, and talking at the same time. Some are speaking in ecstatic utterances while others are trying to give prophecies and interpret what is being said.

That is close to what it was like on a typical Sunday in the First Church of Corinth. Now you understand why Paul said in 1 Corinthians 11:17, "You come together not for the better but for the worse." Their entire worship service was a frenzied, incoherent, chaotic mess. Paul wrote in strong terms to try to straighten it all out, and he spent a great deal of time on the proper use of the gift of tongues.

The problem Paul dealt with in Corinth is the same problem that still troubles the charismatic movement today: How can you tell counterfeit gifts from genuine ones? Most charismatics will admit that when someone stands up and gives a divine utterance, they know one of two things: it is either of God or it is not.[26] How do you tell the difference? For one thing, the true gift of tongues was the ability to speak in a known foreign language (see chapter 10). Nothing in the New Testament suggests that the gift of languages was ecstatic speech. And God would not give a gift that is the same as the one used by Satan to hold people in the grip of false religions.

Corinth was filled with pagan priests and priestesses, soothsayers, and sorcerers. People in various states of ecstasy claimed divine power and divine inspiration. And because the Corinthian church had become carnal, a lot of pagan activity kept creeping in. One reason it could get in so easily was that the Corinthian believers were expecting the Holy Spirit to work only in visible, audible, and tangible ways. They believed that the outpouring of the Spirit promised in Joel

2:28 was beginning to be fulfilled, and they were looking for supernatural phenomena.

The Corinthian believers knew that Jesus had told the disciples the Spirit would come and marvelous things would follow. Undoubtedly, Paul had already told them about the amazing events at Pentecost, the early days of the church, his own conversion experience on the road to Damascus, and the wondrous signs on his first and second missionary journeys.

Satan took advantage of their enthusiasm about the miraculous working of the Holy Spirit. First Corinthians is one of the earliest letters in the New Testament. Already there were distressing problems. It did not take long for Satan to muddy the waters as well-meaning Christians fell into carnality, error, and counterfeit practices. And much of it was done under the assumption that everything mystical that was happening had to be of the Spirit.

Carried Away with False Gifts

Charismatic and Pentecostal churches today are struggling with many of the same afflictions as the church at Corinth. Ours is a pagan society whose influence on the church is strong. Carnal excesses and moral compromise have crept into the church—and some of the most disgraceful examples of immorality and corruption have surfaced at the highest levels of charismatic leadership. There are uncanny parallels in the attitudes of modern charismatics and the thinking that must have gone on in the church of Corinth.

I talked with a man who is a leader in the modern Pentecostal movement, and he said to me, "You cannot deny my experience."

I responded by saying, "Well, let me ask you this. When an experience occurs, do you always, without question, know that it is of God? Be honest."

He answered, "No."

"Could it be of Satan?" I asked.

He reluctantly replied, "Yes."

"Then how do you tell the difference?"

My charismatic friend had no answer.

That is exactly where the Corinthians were. They did not know what was of God and what was not. The work of the Spirit was confused with pagan ecstasies. They needed help.

Paul responded by saying, "Now concerning spiritual gifts, brethren, I do not want you to be unaware" (1 Cor. 12:1). Why did Paul want to be sure the Corinthians were not ignorant about spiritual gifts? Because without the proper use of their gifts, the church could not be holy and mature.

Since the church cannot function well without spiritual gifts, Satan tries to counterfeit them whenever possible. He also does everything he can to cause misunderstandings and misconceptions about spiritual gifts in order to cause confusion and chaos. It happened in Corinth, and it is happening today.

People are getting carried away in a manner similar to what Paul described in 1 Corinthians 12:2: "You know that when you were pagans, you were led astray to the dumb idols, however you were led." Paul was referring to the paganism from which the Corinthian Christians had been converted. They were "led astray"; that is, victimized by a false system. The Greek verb is *apagō*, used in the Scriptures to describe leading a person away, like a prisoner (cf. Matt. 26:57; John 19:16).

To paraphrase 1 Corinthians 12:2, Paul was telling the Corinthians that when they worshiped as pagans, they were carried away by demons in the ecstasies of their mystery religions. Now they were bringing those same old patterns into the church and letting demons invade their worship of Christ. They were unable to distinguish between what was bona fide and what was bogus, between what was divine and what was demonic. They were so eager to embrace the supernatural that they had failed to distinguish between what was of God and what was of Satan, and the result was unholy chaos. In many cases they were literally mistaking the acts of Satan for the work of the Holy Spirit.

As pagans, they used to get carried away in mindless, ecstatic, orgiastic kinds of activities, but that was not supposed to be true now. The truly spiritual person is not someone who is swept away into trances, ecstasies, and emotional frenzies. When a person is out of control, it is never because of the Spirit. Those who claim to have been slain in the Spirit may indeed have been "slain," but it is not by the Holy Spirit.

Nowhere in Scripture do we see real gifts of the Spirit operating when someone is out of control or under some sort of supernatural seizure. Nowhere does the New Testament teach that the Spirit of God causes Christians to fall into a trance, faint, or lapse into frenzied behavior. On the contrary, "The fruit of the Spirit is . . . self-control" (Gal. 5:22–23). "Therefore, gird your minds for action, keep sober in spirit, fix your hope completely on the grace to be brought to you at the revelation of Jesus Christ" (1 Peter 1:13).

We get a hint of how bizarre things had become in the Corinthian assembly in 1 Corinthians 12:3: "Therefore I make known to you, that no one speaking by the Spirit of God says, 'Jesus is accursed,' and no one can say, 'Jesus is Lord,' except by the Holy Spirit." That is an amazing statement. Apparently, some professing believers were standing up in the Corinthian assembly, supposedly manifesting the gifts of the Spirit, and *cursing Jesus!*

Now obviously, if someone says "Jesus is accursed," it is not of God. Incredibly, the Corinthians were not sure of that. Why? Could it be that they were judging the genuineness of spiritual gifts on the basis of phenomena rather than *content?* Could it be that the more ecstatic and euphoric the worship gathering was, the more it appeared to be of the Holy Spirit in their eyes? Whatever the case, the Corinthians had evidently reached a low point where they were unable to distinguish between what was of the Spirit and what was of Satan.

There are many explanations for how such a thing could have happened. Perhaps the most likely one has to do with the creeping heresy that was already at work throughout the New Testament church (see 1 John 2:22; 4:2–3). It was a heresy that denied the deity of Jesus and his sufficiency to save. In the second century, it came into full bloom as gnosticism.[27] Note that the text says, "*Jesus* [not Christ] is accursed." It is possible that in the Corinthian assembly certain people were already accepting the heresy that separated the Spirit of Christ from the human Jesus. That later became a principal teaching of the gnostics. They believed that when Jesus was baptized, the Christ Spirit descended upon him. Just prior to his death, however, the Christ Spirit supposedly left Jesus, and he died as a cursed criminal.[28]

That is the kind of error that might also have caused the Corinthians' confusion over the resurrection. Evidently some of the Corinthians were even uncertain about whether Jesus had risen bodily from the dead. To attack that poisonous confusion, Paul wrote, "If Christ has not been raised, then our preaching is vain, your faith also is vain" (1 Cor. 15:14).

Whatever specific doctrinal issues were at stake, the depth of spiritual confusion in Corinth certainly revealed that many of the ecstatic and miraculous phenomena in their midst were not true spiritual gifts.

Only What Is Valuable Is Counterfeited

In fact, it seems obvious that if people in the Corinthian assembly were calling Jesus accursed, the gifts they claimed to have received from the Holy Spirit were counterfeit. My father had a saying, "No one counterfeits what isn't valuable." One never hears about counterfeit brown paper. People do not counterfeit trash. But they do counterfeit money, diamonds, and jewelry. Counterfeiters copy what is valuable because that is the only point in counterfeiting. Satan was busy in the Corinthian church imitating spiritual gifts, and he is busy doing the same thing today.

Who can deny that the charismatic movement as a whole is suffering from exactly the same spiritual problems that Paul found in the Corinthian church? Many charismatics sincerely love the Lord and the Scriptures, but they are part of a system that has at its core the seeds of the same errors that were ruining the Corinthian church.

Non-charismatics who understand these issues cannot acquiesce quietly for the sake of external accord. The apostle Paul was bold in rebuking the Corinthians for abusing their spiritual gifts. He knew the body of Christ would suffer as long as the Holy Spirit's gifts were being counterfeited and corrupted. Satan was confusing people about spiritual gifts in Paul's time, and he is still doing it today. The tragedy in accepting the counterfeit is that we forfeit the genuine. We must see the difference. The church can be built up only when spiritual gifts are used properly, when Scripture is understood and taught accurately, and when believers are walking in the Spirit with self-control, committed to obeying the Word of God.

─── 8 ───

What Was Happening in the Early Church?

Experience, as we have noted repeatedly, is the foundation upon which much of the charismatic belief system is built. Experience is also the authority charismatics most frequently cite to validate their teachings. Their experience-centered approach to truth even influences the way charismatics handle Scripture. The book of Acts—a journal of the apostles' experiences—is where charismatics usually turn in search of biblical support for what they believe.

Acts is historical narrative, in contrast to the epistles, which are didactic. Acts is a chronicle of the infant church's experiences; the epistles contain instructions for believers throughout the church age. Historically, Christians committed to a biblical perspective have recognized the difference. That is, evangelical theologians have drawn the heart of their doctrine from Bible passages penned expressly to teach the church. They have understood Acts as an inspired historical record of the apostolic period, not necessarily viewing every event or phenomenon recorded there as normative for the entire church age.

Charismatics, however, craving the *experiences* described

in Acts, have assembled a doctrinal system that views the extraordinary events of the early apostolic age as necessary hallmarks of the Holy Spirit's working—tokens of spiritual power that are to be routinely expected by all Christians for all time.

That rather serious interpretive error undermines charismatics' comprehension of Scripture and muddies several key biblical issues crucial to a right understanding of the charismatic controversy. Gordon Fee, himself a charismatic, commented on the hermeneutical difficulties posed by the way charismatics typically render the book of Acts:

> If the primitive church is normative, *which* expression of it is normative? Jerusalem? Antioch? Philippi? Corinth? That is, why do not all the churches sell their possessions and have all things in common? Or further, is it at all legitimate to take [any] descriptive statements as normative? If so, how does one distinguish those which are from those which are not? For example, must we follow the pattern of Acts 1:26 and select leaders by lot? Just exactly what role does historical precedent play in Christian doctrine or in the understanding of Christian experience?[1]

But the book of Acts was never intended to be a primary basis for church doctrine. It records only the earliest days of the church age and shows the church in transition from the Old Covenant to the New. The apostolic healings, miracles, signs, and wonders evident in Acts were not common, even in those days. They were exceptional events, each with a specific purpose, always associated with the ministry of the apostles, and their frequency can be seen decreasing dramatically from the beginning of Acts to the end.

Written by Luke the physician, Acts covers a crucial period that started with the beginning of the church at Pentecost and ended some thirty years later with Paul in prison, following his third missionary journey. Transitions are seen from beginning to end in the book of Acts. Changes happen in almost every chapter. The Old Covenant fades away and the New Covenant comes in all its fullness. Even Paul was caught in the changes. Although he was an apostle of the new era, he still had ties to the old, as indicated by his taking Jewish vows (see Acts 18:18 and 21:26).

In Acts we move from the synagogue to the church and from law to grace. The church is transformed from a group of Jewish believers to a body made up of Jews and Gentiles united in Christ. Believers at the beginning of Acts were related to God under the Old Covenant; by the end, all believers were in Christ, living under the New Covenant, indwelt by the Holy Spirit in a new and unique relationship.

Acts, therefore, covers an extraordinary time in history. The transitions it records are never to be repeated. And so the only teachings in the book of Acts that can be called normative for the church are those that are explicitly confirmed elsewhere in Scripture.

The Charismatic Doctrine of Subsequence

Acts 2:4 is the charismatic touchstone, containing what many Pentecostals and charismatics view as the core truth of the New Testament: "They were all filled with the Holy Spirit and began to speak with other tongues, as the Spirit was giving them utterance."

Most charismatics believe this verse teaches that at conversion Christians receive the Holy Spirit only in a limited sense. Therefore, they believe, Christians need to seek Spirit baptism in order to move to a higher level of spiritual life, being supernaturally immersed in the power of God's Spirit. The experience is usually—many say *always*—accompanied by speaking in tongues and results in new spiritual motivation and power.

The notion that one gets salvation at one point and the baptism of the Spirit later is often referred to as *the doctrine of subsequence*. Gordon Fee lists two Pentecostal distinctives:

"(1) the doctrine of subsequence, i.e., that there is for Christians a baptism in the Spirit distinct from and subsequent to the experience of salvation . . . , and (2) the doctrine of tongues as the initial physical evidence of baptism in the Spirit."[2]

In his thorough investigation of Pentecostal theology, Frederick Dale Bruner wrote, "Pentecostals believe that the Spirit has baptized every believer into Christ (conversion), but that Christ has not baptized every believer into the Spirit (Pentecost)."[3] Not only do most charismatics believe that the baptism of the Spirit happens at some point after salvation, but most also believe that Spirit baptism is something Christians must seek. Bruner goes on to say,

> The most important characteristics of the Pentecostal understanding of the baptism in the Holy Spirit . . . are: (1) that the event is usually "distinct from and subsequent to" the new birth; (2) that it is evidenced initially by the sign of speaking in other tongues; (3) that it must be "earnestly" sought.[4]

Those three elements—baptism of the Spirit subsequent to conversion, the earnest seeking of those who are baptized, and the evidence of speaking in tongues—are characteristic of nearly all charismatic doctrine. In most other areas of theology, charismatics are vague, but here they usually speak a clear word regarding what they believe.

Charismatics attempt to support their doctrine of subsequence from the book of Acts. First Corinthians 12:13 ("For by one Spirit we were all baptized into one body, whether Jews or Greeks, whether slaves or free, and we were all made to drink of one Spirit") cannot be used to prove subsequence because the verse simply says that *all* believers have been baptized by one Spirit into the body of Christ. Indeed, it would seem clear that the baptism described in 1 Corinthians 12:13 *cannot* take place at a point in time after salvation. Otherwise, what Paul says could not be true of *all* Christians.

No evidence such as tongues is mentioned, and no requirement of seeking the baptism is alluded to.

Charismatics are also unable to use 1 Corinthians 14 to prove the tenets of subsequence, evidence, or seeking, because the chapter has nothing to say about any of those elements. In fact, the only passages charismatics can use to support their doctrine of subsequence are found in Acts. The epistles say nothing that can be construed to support the idea.

The truth is, even the book of Acts fails to support the charismatic view. Only four passages mention tongues or receiving the Holy Spirit: chapters 2, 8, 10, and 19. Only in Acts 2 and 8 do believers receive the Spirit *after* salvation. In Acts 10 and 19, believers were baptized in the Spirit at the moment of belief. So the doctrine of subsequence cannot be convincingly defended even from the book of Acts.

What about tongues? Believers spoke in tongues in Acts 2, 10, and 19, but there is no record of tongues in chapter 8.

What about the requirement of earnestly seeking the baptism? The believers in Acts 2 simply waited prayerfully for the fulfillment of the Lord's promise (cf. 1:4, 14). In chapters 8, 10, or 19, no seeking is mentioned.

The point is clear. To say that the book of Acts presents the normal pattern for receiving the Holy Spirit presents a problem: no consistent pattern is evident in Acts!

It is true that Christians at Pentecost (Acts 2), Gentiles in Cornelius's household (chap. 10), and the Jews at Ephesus who had only the baptism of John (chap. 19) received the Holy Spirit and tongues followed. But because those three events occurred does not mean they are to be the standard for every other Christian. In fact, none of the passages we are discussing (Acts 2, 8, 10, or 19) imply that similar experiences are to be had by anyone else.

If tongues were to be the normal experience, why were tongues not mentioned in Acts 8 when the Samaritans received the Holy Spirit? Why does the text in Acts 2 through 4 not say that everyone who believed following Peter's sermons (over five thousand people according to Acts 4:4) and received the Holy Spirit (Acts 2:38) also spoke in tongues? In order for something to be normative, it has to be common to everyone.

John Stott reasoned that

> The 3,000 do not seem to have experienced the same miraculous phenomena (the rushing mighty wind, the tongues of flame, or the speech in foreign languages). At least nothing is said about these things. Yet because of God's assurance through Peter they must have inherited the same promise and received the same gift (verses 33, 39). Nevertheless, there was this difference between them: the 120 were regenerate already, and received the baptism of the Spirit only after waiting upon God for ten days. The 3,000 on the other hand were unbelievers, and received the forgiveness of their sins and the gift of the Spirit simultaneously—and it happened immediately they repented and believed, without any need to wait.
>
> This distinction between the two companies, the 120 and the 3,000, is of great importance, because the *norm* for today must surely be the second group, the 3,000, and not (as is often supposed) the first. The fact that the experience of the 120 was in two distinct stages was due simply to historical circumstances. They could not have received the Pentecostal gift before Pentecost. But those historical circumstances have long since ceased to exist. We live after the event of Pentecost, like the 3,000. With us, therefore, as with them, the forgiveness of sins and the "gift" or "baptism" of the Spirit are received together.[5]

A Closer Look at Acts 2

Without question, the second chapter of Acts is the key passage of Scripture from which Pentecostals and charismatics develop their theology of the baptism of the Holy Spirit. As Luke recorded the birthday of the church, he reported:

> When the day of Pentecost had come, they were all together in one place. And suddenly there came from heaven a noise like a violent, rushing wind, and it filled the whole house where they were sitting. And there appeared to them tongues as of fire distributing themselves, and they rested on each one of them. And they were all filled with the Holy Spirit and began to speak with other tongues, as the Spirit was giving them utterance (2:1-4).

As noted, the Pentecostal and charismatic doctrine of subsequence is drawn primarily from that passage. Charismatics point out that the apostles and other disciples who experienced the baptism and tongues in Acts 2:1-4 had already been saved. Here at Pentecost they were receiving the power of the Holy Spirit, which they would use to change the world.

On those points the charismatic view cannot be faulted. We can be certain that the disciples mentioned in Acts 2—at least some of them—*had* experienced salvation. They probably were the same one hundred and twenty disciples, including the eleven apostles, who were gathered in the upper room in the first chapter of Acts. How do we know that some of them were already saved? Jesus had told His apostles, "Rejoice that your names are recorded in heaven" (Luke 10:20) and "You are already clean because of the word which I have spoken to you" (John 15:3). There is no doubt that he was affirming their salvation.

Most charismatics suggest that the disciples had also received the Holy Spirit before Pentecost in the upper room following the resurrection. John 20:21-22 says, "Jesus . . . breathed on them, and said to them, 'Receive the Holy Spirit.'" According to the standard charismatic interpretation of that text, since Jesus had already given the disciples the Holy Spirit, the Pentecost experience must represent something more. It was a higher-level baptism of the Spirit that gave them their real power.[6]

Is that the correct interpretation of John 20:21–22? Here the charismatic view does not hold up under scrutiny. First of all, the passage does not say that the disciples actually received the Holy Spirit. No passage says that until Pentecost. It simply says that Jesus said to them, "Receive the Holy Spirit." What did Jesus mean? The statement was a pledge or promise that would be fulfilled on the day of Pentecost. Chrysostom (A.D. 345–407) and many others have held this view. Ensuing statements in John 20 seem to confirm that the disciples did not receive the Spirit there in the upper room. Eight days later, Jesus came to them where they were hiding—full of fear—in a locked room (20:26). More than a week after Jesus breathed on them and promised the Spirit, the disciples had not gone anywhere or done anything that would manifest the Spirit's power and presence.

The strongest arguments, however, appear in the early verses of Acts 1. Just before his ascension, Jesus gathered the disciples together and told them not to leave Jerusalem but to wait for the promise of the Father (Acts 1:4). Jesus went on to say in the next verse, "John baptized with water, but you shall be baptized with the Holy Spirit not many days from now." The "promise of the Father" seems to refer back to John 14:16: "I will ask the Father, and He will give you another Helper, that He may be with you forever." It was a promise that the Holy Spirit would come. The promise was reiterated by Jesus in John 20:26 but not yet fulfilled. At this point the disciples were *still waiting* for the Holy Spirit.

Again in Acts 1:8 Jesus said, "You shall receive power when the Holy Spirit has come upon you; and you shall be My witnesses both in Jerusalem, and in all Judea and Samaria, and even to the remotest part of the earth." Clearly, the receiving of power was parallel to the receiving of the Holy Spirit. The disciples were still waiting. The promise was yet unfulfilled. If the Spirit had come upon them in John 20, the power would be there already and *there would be nothing to wait for.*

Two other passages demonstrate that the disciples did

not receive the Holy Spirit until the day of Pentecost. John 7 records Jesus stood up at the Feast of Tabernacles and offering water to anyone who wanted to come and drink. The apostle explains in verse 39 that Jesus was speaking of the Holy Spirit: "But this He spoke of the Spirit, whom those who believed in Him were to receive, for the Spirit was not yet given, because Jesus was not yet glorified." That passage explicitly states that the Spirit would not come until Jesus had been glorified, and He could not be glorified until He had ascended.[7]

Also, in John 16:7 Jesus told the disciples, "I tell you the truth, it is to your advantage that I go away; for if I do not go away, the Helper shall not come to you; but if I go, I will send Him to you." Jesus, of course, did not "go away" until he ascended, as recorded in the early verses of Acts.

And so a thorough study of Scripture points convincingly to the conclusion that what Jesus said in John 20:22 was simply a promise of the Holy Spirit; the disciples did not receive the Holy Spirit at that moment.

Remember, too, that all these events occurred in a *period of transition*. There was obviously some overlap between the Old and New Covenants. Although the disciples knew and trusted Christ, they were still Old Testament believers. They could not have understood or experienced the Spirit's permanent indwelling until the arrival of the Spirit at Pentecost.

What of the charismatic notion that Spirit baptism is something to be eagerly sought? Although the one hundred and twenty in the upper room may have been praying in a mood of anticipation and excitement (Acts 1:4), there is no evidence of their asking for or seeking the Holy Spirit. There was absolutely nothing the disciples could have done to cause this great event to occur. They were simply awaiting the sovereign fulfillment of a divine promise.

Nor is there any hint of *anyone's* seeking or asking for the Holy Spirit or tongues anywhere in the book of Acts. No one sought the Spirit in chapter 8; no one sought the Spirit in chapter 10; and no one sought the Spirit in chapter 19. Nothing in Scripture indicates that anyone in the churches at Antioch, Galatia, Philippi, Colossae, Rome, Thessalonica, or Corinth ever asked for the Holy Spirit or tongues. Study the passages in Acts where people were filled with the Spirit and spoke in tongues. *There is not once instance—even where these phenomena occurred—that indicates anyone in the early church was ever seeking such an experience.* Frederick Dale Bruner was right to ask: "Must this not affect the Pentecostal doctrine of a specifically sought baptism in the Holy Spirit with the evidence of tongues?"[8]

When the Holy Spirit came at Pentecost a new order was established. From then on the Holy Spirit came to every believer at the moment of faith and indwelt the believer in a permanent, abiding relationship. That is why Romans 8:9 says, "You are not in the flesh but in the Spirit, if indeed the Spirit of God dwells in you. But if anyone does not have the Spirit of Christ, he does not belong to Him." That is also why Paul asserts that all Christians have been baptized by the Spirit into the body of Christ and that we have all been made to drink of that one Spirit (1 Cor. 12:13).

Acts 2:3–4 records the actual reception of the Spirit. The disciples were baptized with the Spirit (verses 2–3), accompanied by a sound from heaven like a mighty rushing wind and cloven tongues as of fire, which rested upon each of them. At that point all were filled with the Spirit and began to speak in other languages. The miraculous languages, speaking the wonderful works of God to all the foreigners gathered at Jerusalem, had a definite purpose: to be a sign of judgment on unbelieving Israel, to show the inclusion of other groups in the one church, and to confirm the apostles' spiritual authority. (See chapter 10 for a thorough discussion of the purposes of tongues.)

Acts 2:5–12 reports that the Jews who were present— "devout men from every nation under heaven"—were

is that they were living in a period of transition between the covenants.

The hatred between Jews and Samaritans was well known. If these Samaritans had received the Holy Spirit at the moment of salvation without any supernatural sign or fanfare, the terrible rift between the Jews and Samaritans might have continued in the Christian church. Pentecost had been a Jewish event, and the church born at Pentecost was made up exclusively of Jewish believers in Christ. If the Samaritans had started their own Christian group, the age-old rivalries and hatreds could have been perpetuated, with a Jewish church competing against Samaritan and Gentile assemblies. Instead, God withheld the giving of the Spirit to the Samaritans until the Jewish apostles could be with them. Everyone needed to see—in a way that could not be disputed—that God's purpose under the New Covenant transcended the nation of Israel and included even Samaritans in one church.

It was also important that the Samaritans understand the power and authority of the apostles. It was important for the Jews to know the Samaritans were part of the body of Christ, and it was important for the Samaritans to know that the Jewish apostles were the channels of divine truth.

A point of grammar in Acts 8:16 makes the meaning clear: "He had not yet fallen upon any of them; they had simply been baptized in the name of the Lord Jesus." The Greek word for "not yet" is *oudepō*. The term does not simply signify something that *has not* happened, but something that *should have happened* but has not yet. In other words, the verse is saying that the Samaritans were saved, but for some peculiar reason what *should* have happened—the Holy Spirit's coming—had not yet occurred.

And so although there was an interval between the Samaritans' receiving Christ and their receiving the Holy Spirit—subsequence, in a sense—it was due to the crucial transition that was going on in the early church. The gap allowed everyone to see clearly that God was doing a new thing in the church. It proved to the apostles and all the other Jewish believers who were witnesses, that the Samaritans were accepted by God into the church the same as Jewish believers. They had the same Christ, the same salvation, the same acceptance by God, and the same Holy Spirit; and they were under the same apostolic authority.

Frederick Dale Bruner underscored the significance of the inclusion of the Samaritans in the church when he wrote:

> This was no casual event. Only the accession of the Gentiles (ch. 10) can be compared with it. Samaria was both a bridge to be crossed and a base to be occupied. A bridge to be crossed because Samaria represented the deepest of clefts: the racial-religious. A base to be occupied because the church no longer resides in Jerusalem or among Jews alone, but becomes a mission.
>
> We know from other accounts in the New Testament of the feeling of the Jew for the Samaritan, and we know from the important records in Acts 10–11 and 15 of the painful and critical decision which the reception of the Gentiles posed for the Jewish church. The reason behind the absolutely unique division of what everywhere else since Pentecost is one—Christian baptism and the gift of the Spirit—may most satisfactorily be found in the divine will to establish unequivocally for the apostles, for the despised Samaritans, and for the whole church present and future that for God no barriers existed for his *gift* of the Spirit; that wherever faith in the gospel occurred, there was the *work* of God's Spirit and there accordingly God purposed to give the *gift* of His Spirit; that baptism in the name of Christ as everywhere else now even in Samaria must include the gift of the Spirit; in a word, that the gift of God's Holy Spirit was free and for all. To teach this basic and important fact—it was the fact of the gospel—God withheld His gift until the apostles should see with their own eyes and—let it not be overlooked—be instrumental with their own hands

in the impartation of the gift of God (v. 20), merited by nothing, least of all by race or prior religion. [10]

The amazing revival in Samaria was followed by the gift of the Holy Spirit to these outcast people—and in just the same way as it had initially happened with Jewish believers. This was not a "Samaritan Pentecost" but a crucial step of growth for the church. There was only one Pentecost, and this added nothing to that. But it served as an audio-visual lesson to the whole church that the middle wall of partition had indeed been broken down (cf. Eph. 2:14–15). Merrill Unger commented on this by saying,

> The events in Samaria cannot be called a "Samaritan Pentecost" for the following reasons: (a) Pentecost is unrepeatable, since it represents the advent and taking up of permanent abode of the Spirit in the church. The Spirit could not again arrive and take up residence. This was once-for-all for the new age. (b) Neither could the Spirit be given, received, and deposited again as was the gift initially so given, received, and deposited once-for-all for the age at Pentecost. (c) Pentecost, therefore, was the beginning of a new age. By contrast the Samaritan Revival was the entrance into the spiritual blessings of that age, not the inaugurating of that age.
>
> The Samaritan event represented growth, not birth. It was the extension of gospel privilege to another people (the Samaritans), not—as at Pentecost—the introduction of gospel privilege to Jews alone. [11]

It is interesting that in Acts 8 there is no mention of tongues or fire or the sound of wind, although some supernatural sign must have occurred, as indicated by Simon's reaction (8:18–19). What was really crucial was that everyone present knew there were not two churches. There was only one, with the same Holy Spirit under the same apostolic authority.

A Closer Look at Acts 10

A third passage often cited as support for the Pentecostal and charismatic doctrine of subsequence is Acts 10, which records the salvation and receiving of the Holy Spirit by Cornelius and other Gentiles at Caesarea Philippi. The gospel was truly now reaching "even to the remotest parts of the earth" (Acts 1:8).

If there was a rift between the Samaritans and Jews, a practically unbridgeable chasm had developed between Gentiles and Jews. When a Jew came back from traveling in a Gentile country, he would shake the dust off his feet and his clothes because he did not want to drag Gentile dirt into Judea. A Jew would not enter the house of a Gentile, and would not eat a meal cooked by Gentile hands. Some Jews would not even buy meat cut by a Gentile butcher.

Nevertheless, the Lord gave Peter a vision that taught him God was no respecter of persons. Right after Peter had the vision, three men came to the house where he was staying and explained that they had been sent by Cornelius, who wanted to see Peter and learn more about God.

Remembering the vision he had just experienced, Peter swallowed his Jewish prejudice and agreed to accompany the Gentiles back to Caesarea, where Cornelius lived. Once there, Peter presented the gospel. Cornelius and the rest of the people present believed. Peter and the other Jews who had accompanied him to Cornelius's home were astonished "because the gift of the Holy Spirit had been poured out upon the Gentiles also" and they heard "them speaking with tongues and exalting God" (Acts 10:45–46). Peter concluded, "Surely no one can refuse the water for these to be baptized who have received the Holy Spirit just as we did" (10:47).

Two things are noteworthy here in regard to charismatic doctrine. One is that no interval passed between Cornelius's trusting Christ and his receiving of the Holy Spirit. Second,

Peter and the Jews who were with him were all astonished. Why? Because they heard the Gentiles speak with tongues and magnify God. Although tongues were primarily a sign of judgment to unbelieving Israel (1 Cor. 14:21–22), God here repeated the phenomenon as a way to demonstrate to believing Jews that the Holy Spirit had come to the Gentiles just as he had to them.

The same thing was happening here that happened in Samaria. This was the time of transition. Had there been no visible evidence of the Holy Spirit, Peter and the others would not have been as quickly convinced that Gentiles were now a part of the body of Christ. As it was, the Jewish believers saw an irrefutable demonstration that these Gentiles were in Christ. Peter immediately concluded that they should be baptized (10:47). Obviously Peter was equating receiving the Holy Spirit with salvation. The Gentiles had received the same Holy Spirit who had come to the Jews. Peter knew beyond doubt that they were saved and should be baptized.

This all came out beautifully in the next chapter of Acts, where Peter reported his experience to the church council at Jerusalem. As he explained to his Jewish brethren what had happened, he said,

> As I began to speak, the Holy Spirit fell upon them, just as He did upon us at the beginning. And I remembered the word of the Lord, how He used to say, "John baptized with water, but you shall be baptized with the Holy Spirit." If God therefore gave to them the same gift as He gave to us also after believing in the Lord Jesus Christ, who was I that I could stand in God's way? (Acts 11:15–17).

This scene is almost comical. It is as if Peter were saying, "I'm sorry, guys, I couldn't help it. God was doing it and I couldn't stop it!"

Shocked as they were, the council members could not deny what had happened. They held their peace, glorified God, and acknowledged that God had graciously granted to the Gentiles also the repentance that leads to life (Acts 11:18). The church was one—Jew and Gentile (cf. Gal. 3:28; Eph. 2:14–18).

These events were happening for specific reasons in this period of historical transition. The Gentiles received the Holy Spirit at the time of conversion. They spoke with tongues, as proof to everyone that they were now part of the church, but there is no subsequence here! Unger said, "As Pentecost was introductory in the sense of inaugurating a new age, so Acts 10 is terminal in the sense of marking the consummation of the introductory period and the establishment of the normal course of the new age."[12]

The norm is salvation and reception of the Spirit *at the same time*. The apostle Peter was present, and therefore he could report to the church council (made up of Jews) that the Gentiles were true believers. At the same time, the Gentiles would recognize apostolic authority because Peter had been with them and had led them to Christ. Most important, both groups knew that they had the same Holy Spirit and were part of the same body.

A Closer Look at Acts 19

Acts 19 continues to show the church in transition. Here again is another basic charismatic proof text that shows people being baptized by the Spirit and speaking in tongues. Again there is no subsequence, no interval between salvation and Spirit baptism. Some charismatics and Pentecostals would like to claim that these people had been believers in Christ prior to the encounter recorded here, but a study of the text shows clearly that they were not.

Acts 19 records Paul's arrival at Ephesus on one of his missionary journeys and that there he found "some disciples" (19:1). "Did you receive the Holy Spirit when you believed?" Paul wanted to know (v. 2).

The reply by the disciples from Ephesus is peculiar: "No, we have not even heard whether there is a Holy Spirit."

"Into what then were you baptized?" was Paul's next question (v. 3).

They replied, "Into John's baptism."

Then Paul understood their problem. And so he said, "John baptized with the baptism of repentance, telling the people to believe in Him who was coming after him, that is, in Jesus" (v. 4).

The disciples at Ephesus were not Christians. They were believers in the Old Testament sense. The sum of their spiritual knowledge stopped with John the Baptist, and somehow they were not familiar with the ministry of Christ. Once they heard about Jesus, they believed and were baptized in his name. When Paul laid hands on them, the Holy Spirit came upon them, and they began speaking in tongues and prophesying (vv. 5–6).

Obviously, these disciples were not seeking the Holy Spirit or tongues. Paul initiated the conversation about the Holy Spirit. They had not heard about any of the phenomena associated with the coming of the Spirit. Most translations of Acts 19:2 do not fully capture the implications of the Ephesian believers' reply to Paul's question. In essence they said, "We did not so much as hear whether the Holy Spirit was given." It is likely that they knew of the Holy Spirit. If they were followers of John's baptism, they had heard him talk about the Spirit (for example, see Luke 3:16). But they had not heard whether or not the Holy Spirit had ever been given. Why? Because they had not yet heard anything about Jesus Christ.

As soon as Paul heard their response, he began to probe. He soon realized they were disciples, not of Jesus Christ, but of John the Baptist. They were people in transition, remnants of the Old Testament saints, still hanging on, still looking for their Messiah twenty years after John the Baptist had died.

Paul's next move was quite predictable. He said, in

effect, "You people are to be commended. You repented as John taught, but now you've got to take the next step: believe in the One who came after John—Jesus Christ."

Note that after Paul realized who these disciples were, he spoke about Jesus Christ, not the Holy Spirit. Paul knew that all they had was the baptism of John. If they had confessed faith in Christ and been baptized, they would have had the Holy Spirit. Paul implied that when he asked, "Well, if you haven't received the Spirit, what kind of baptism have you had?" Paul knew that receiving the Spirit at the moment of belief in Christ was the normal pattern for the church after Pentecost.

Paul was not trying to teach the Ephesian disciples how to press on to a second level or get something more than salvation through Christ. He realized that what was missing for the people at Ephesus was not information about the baptism of the Holy Spirit, but information about Jesus Christ.

So Paul presented Christ to the Ephesian disciples, they believed, and they were baptized in the name of the Lord Jesus. And when Paul laid hands on them, they spoke in tongues and prophesied.

Why did Paul lay hands on them? It seems he did it to demonstrate that they were no longer to follow John the Baptist's teaching, but that of the apostles. And why were the Ephesian believers given tongues? The tongues demonstrated that although they had first come into their relationship with God under the Old Covenant, they were now part of the church with everyone else. Like those who had experienced Pentecost, they were now living under the New Covenant.

Actually the whole theme of the book of Acts is to show how Jesus' prayer in John 17:21 was being answered. There Jesus prayed "that they may all be one; even as Thou, Father, art in Me, and I in Thee, that they also may be in Us; that the world may believe that Thou didst send Me." As all believers were becoming one, a transition was taking place between the two covenants. Pentecost illustrated what was happening. Samaria illustrated it. The salvation of Cornelius and the other Gentiles illustrated it. And here in Acts 19 we find a unique group of followers of John at Ephesus. They all became one in the Spirit through faith in the Lord Jesus Christ, and their oneness was demonstrated graphically by the same miraculous phenomena witnessed three times before. These events were not supposed to be a pattern for the church as a whole; they did not even reflect the normal experience of Christians in the first-century church. They were exceptional, one-time signs, involving only a limited number of believers, and showing brilliantly the process that was taking place as all believers became one in Christ.

To claim that the norm is for people to believe in Christ and at a later time get the baptism of the Holy Spirit with the evidence of tongues is to force the book of Acts through a theological grid of one's own making. The events in Acts simply do not back up the Pentecostal and charismatic view.

Joseph Dillow summarized our responsibility when he said:

> We must not make the tragic mistake of teaching the experience of the apostles, but rather we must experience the teaching of the apostles. The experience of the apostles is found in the transitional book of Acts, while the teaching of the apostles is set forth clearly in the epistles, which are our guide for our Christian experience today.[13]

Acts reveals how a new epoch began—the church age, the era of the Holy Spirit. We Christians who live in that age receive the Spirit when we believe in Jesus Christ as Lord and Savior. The Spirit is a gift from God for every believer. That is taught again and again in the New Testament epistles. Yet nowhere do they substantiate the Pentecostal and charismatic doctrine of a second work of grace that is sought by the believer and evidenced by speaking in tongues.

Paul wrote about the Holy Spirit many times. He dealt at length with the subject of spiritual gifts. Strangely enough, at no time did he even hint that the normative Christian experience is to be similar to what is described in the second, eighth, tenth, and nineteenth chapters of Acts.

Paul, by the way, had his own experience, recorded for us in Acts. He met the Lord Jesus Christ on the road to Damascus and was immediately changed from a murderer of Christians to a servant of the Lord. Paul was blind for three days, after which Ananias came to him and laid hands on him that he might receive his sight and "be filled with the Holy Spirit" (Acts 9:17). Interestingly, Acts 9 does not mention that Paul spoke in tongues at that time. Yet later he told the Corinthians that he spoke in languages more than all of them (1 Cor. 14:18).

Paul was well aware of the varieties of experiences that had happened to people as recorded in Acts. He was right in the middle of them. But in none of his epistles did he ever hint that one must be saved first and then experience the baptism of the Spirit sometime down the road. The same is true in the writings of Jude, James, and Peter. No apostolic writer taught the charismatic and Pentecostal doctrine of subsequence.

Seek the Power or Release It?

Acts 8:19 records Simon's seeking to buy the power of the Holy Spirit. Peter said in reply, "May your silver perish with you, because you thought you could obtain the gift of God with money!" (Acts 8:20).

Simon wanted power, but he sought it in the wrong way. Christians today want power, too. They want to be able to live better Christian lives. They want power to witness, to make disciples, to reach the world with the gospel as they have been commissioned to do, and that is certainly not wrong.

Yet as this incident with Peter and Simon shows, some people seek spiritual power out of wrong or impure motives. Simon presumed to seek by human effort the spiritual power that God gives freely—and that revealed his sinful heart. Many charismatics appear to be seeking spiritual power for the same selfish reasons that Simon displayed—and often by similar kinds of human effort.

Michael Green, who is certainly not unfriendly to the charismatic position, commented on the Corinthian charismatics:

> The charismatics were always out for *more*, and Paul was always insisting that Christ and Christ alone was the blessing for Christians. Any doctrine that adds something to Christ, as some charismatics do in their cry, "Christ, yes, but beyond Christ you need the Spirit," stands self-condemned.
>
> The charismatics were always out for *power*; they were elated by spiritual power, and were always seeking short cuts to power. It is the same today. Paul's reply is to boast not of his power but of his weakness, through which alone the power of Christ can shine. Paul knew all about the marks of an apostle, in signs, wonders and mighty deeds (2 Corinthians 12:12) but he knew that the power of an apostle, or of any other Christian, came from the patient endurance of suffering, such as he had with his thorn in the flesh, or the patient endurance of reviling and hardship such as he was submitted to in the course of his missionary work (1 Corinthians 4). The charismatics had a theology of the resurrection and its power; they needed to learn afresh the secret of the cross and its shame . . . which yet produced the power of God (1 Corinthians 1:18).
>
> The charismatics were always out for *evidence*. That is why tongues and healings and miracles were so highly esteemed among them. But Paul knows that we walk by faith while we are in this life, not by sight. There are many

times when God calls upon us to trust Him in the dark, without any supporting evidence.[14]

Charismatics today share those same shortcomings. The thirst for something more, the quest for greater power, and the desire to see evidences are as familiar today as they were in Corinth. Yet they are more compatible with the spirit of Simon than with the Spirit of God. To deny what is clearly taught in God's Word, to question God's promise, and to seek by human effort what he has already given is wrong, no matter how euphoric an experience might be. Instead of seeking power and miraculous evidences, all Christians—charismatic and non-charismatic alike—should seek to *know* him, including the fellowship of his suffering and conformity to his death (cf. Phil. 3:10–11). That is what releases the power of his resurrection, which God has given us already (cf. Rom. 6:4–5).

Is Spirit Baptism a Fact or a Feeling?

The charismatic notion of subsequence leads to other errors. The belief that Spirit baptism is a second work of grace has become a cardinal doctrine of the charismatic movement. As we have seen, charismatic writers and teachers generally agree that "the baptism," evidenced by speaking in tongues, is a crucial next step after salvation.

Turning to the epistles yields quite a different view. For example, as 1 Corinthians 12:13 makes clear, Spirit baptism is actually an integral part of every Christian's salvation experience. Paul wrote, "By one Spirit we were *all* baptized into one body, whether Jews or Greeks, whether slaves or free, and we were all made to drink of one Spirit" (emphasis added). That passage has nothing to do with water baptism. Paul was not talking about the sacrament or ordinance of water baptism, important as that is in another context. Paul was talking about the indwelling presence of the Spirit of

God. He used the word *baptizō*, which is the same Greek term used in Romans 6:3–4 and Galatians 3:27 to refer to spiritual immersion.

Spirit baptism brings the believer into a vital union with Christ. To be baptized with the Holy Spirit means that Christ immerses us in the Spirit, thereby giving us a common life principle. This spiritual baptism is what connects us with all other believers in Christ and makes us part of Christ's own body. Baptism with the Spirit makes all believers one. It is a fact, not a feeling.

Unfortunately, the tremendous truth of that verse has been greatly misunderstood. Paul was blending two vital thoughts here. One is that the church, the body of Christ, is formed through Spirit baptism, and the other is that the life of the body is sustained as we all are made to drink of one Spirit. The twin ideas of immersion by the Spirit and drinking of the Spirit picture the all-sufficient relationship with the Spirit of God that bonds each believer to Christ and the rest of the body.

First Corinthians 12:13 opens with the phrase, "For by one Spirit." That is where much of the charismatic confusion begins. The Greek text uses the tiny preposition *en*. This term can be translated "at," "by," or "with"—and some scholars might even translate it "in." Greek prepositions are translated differently depending on the case endings of the words that follow the prepositions. An accurate translation in 1 Corinthians 12:13, and the most consistent in the context of the New Testament, would use either *by* or *with*. In other words, at conversion, we are baptized *by* or *with* the Holy Spirit.

This must not be taken to mean that the Holy Spirit is the One who *does* the baptizing. Nowhere in the Bible is the Holy Spirit spoken of as the baptizer. In Matthew 3:11, for example, John the Baptist told the Pharisees and Sadducees he could baptize them with water, but someone was coming later who would "baptize [them] with the Holy Spirit and fire. And His winnowing fork is in His hand, and He will thoroughly clear His threshing floor; and He will gather His wheat into the barn, but He will burn up the chaff with unquenchable fire" (Matt. 3:11–12).

A common charismatic interpretation of that verse takes "fire" as a reference to the cloven tongues of fire seen on the day of Pentecost. But it is obvious from verse 12 that John was referring to the fires of judgment, the unquenchable fires of hell. Obviously the cloven tongues like fire at Pentecost cannot be equated with the unquenchable fire that burns up chaff. This is clearly a fire of judgment, and its agent is not the Holy Spirit but Christ (see John 5:22). So what John was really saying here is that there are only two kinds of people in the world: those who will be baptized with the Holy Spirit, and those who will be baptized with the unquenchable fire of hell.

Mark 1:7–8 and Luke 3:16 contain similar expressions. Likewise, John 1:33 says of Christ, "This is the one who baptizes in the Holy Spirit." In all those passages, Jesus does the baptizing.

In his sermon on the day of Pentecost, Peter said of Christ, "Therefore having been exalted to the right hand of God, and having received from the Father the promise of the Holy Spirit, He has poured forth this which you both see and hear" (Acts 2:33). Again, we see Christ as the baptizer, who "pours forth" the Spirit in the miraculous events of Pentecost.

In Romans 8:9 Paul says, "If anyone does not have the Spirit of Christ, he does not belong to Him." If we take away the concept that every believer is baptized and indwelt by the Holy Spirit, we destroy the doctrine of the unity of the body. Why? Because we have some people who aren't "in." Where are they? What kind of limbo is it to be saved but not be a part of the body of Christ? Is it possible to be a Christian and not a part of Christ? No. Paul's whole point in 1 Corinthians 12:12–13 is that *all* Christians are baptized with one Spirit into one body. We are all in one body possessing one life source, indwelt by one Christ.

The charismatic view of Holy Spirit baptism actually redefines the doctrine of salvation. According to that view, salvation does not really give us everything we need for spiritual victory. We are still lacking; we need something more. Although they sometimes concede that every believer has the Holy Spirit to a limited degree, they believe the full power of the Spirit is withheld from those who have not yet experienced Spirit baptism with the evidence of tongues. That is the perspective of Larry Christenson, a noted Lutheran Charismatic.[15] Yet his point of view seems to overlook the clear meaning of 1 Corinthians 12:13. Christenson has stated:

> Beyond conversion, beyond the assurance of salvation, beyond having the Holy Spirit, there is a *baptism* with the Holy Spirit. It might not make sense to our human understanding any more than it made sense for Jesus to be baptized by John. . . . We are not called to understand it, or justify it, or explain it, but simply to enter into it in humble obedience and with expectant faith.[16]

Is Christenson embracing something that does not make sense rather than admitting the truth of 1 Corinthians 12:13, which clearly *does* make sense? Jesus' baptism by John certainly *did* make sense. In being baptized, Jesus identified himself with the repenting Israelites who were looking for their Messiah. Christenson went on to say:

> Sometimes the baptism with the Holy Spirit occurs spontaneously, sometimes through prayer and the laying on of hands. Sometimes it occurs after water baptism, sometimes before. Sometimes it occurs virtually simultaneously with conversion, sometimes after an interval of time. . . . But one thing is constant in the Scripture, and it is most important: It is never merely *assumed* that a person has been baptized with the Holy Spirit. When he has been baptized with the Holy Spirit the person *knows* it. *It is a definite experience.*[17]

In making those claims Christenson was trying to base truth on experience. As we shall see, the baptism with the Holy Spirit is a spiritual fact, not a physical experience related to some emotional feeling.

What Is the Difference Between the Baptism and the Filling?

As I continue to talk with charismatics and study their writings, it becomes more and more apparent that they are confusing Spirit baptism, which places the Christian in the body of Christ, and the fullness of the Spirit, which produces effective Christian living (see Eph. 5:18–6:11).

Charles and Frances Hunter, for example, lead seminars instructing people how to be baptized with the Holy Spirit. Charles Hunter has written:

> Picture yourself in the position of being one to whom we are ministering. Here is how we lead people into the baptism:
> "You are about to receive what the Bible calls the baptism with the Holy Spirit, or the gift of the Holy Spirit. Your spirit, the same size as your body, is about to be filled completely with God's Spirit, and just as Jesus instructed, you will speak in a spirit language as the Holy Spirit gives the utterance."[18]

In the first place, the idea that one's spirit is the same size as one's body is absurd. A spirit, being nonmaterial, has no size.[19] Second, and more significantly, Hunter speaks of the baptism with the Holy Spirit and the *fullness* of the Holy Spirit as if they were the same. They are not.

Pentecostal Evangel magazine, the denominational magazine of the Assemblies of God, has published a creed in its masthead every week for decades, saying in part, "We believe . . . the baptism in the Holy Spirit, according to Acts 2:4, is given to believers who ask for it." But Acts 2:4 simply says, "They were all filled with the Holy Spirit and began to speak with other tongues, as the Spirit was giving them utterance."

Nothing in all of Acts chapter 2 says believers asked for the Holy Spirit.

Acts 2:1–4 teaches two distinctive truths. At Pentecost, Christian believers were *baptized* with the Holy Spirit into the body. Then the Holy Spirit *filled* those believers to give a miraculous testimony—the ability to speak in other languages. Believers since that time have all been baptized with the Holy Spirit by the Lord Jesus Christ at conversion. How are we filled? When we yield to the Spirit, who is already there, we have access to the Spirit's power and fullness. Paul told the Ephesians to be kept filled with the Spirit as a constant pattern for living (5:18).

Nowhere in Scripture is the Christian taught to tarry and wait for the baptism. Nowhere in Scripture are we taught to get with a group of people who can teach us to speak in tongues. Christians are admonished to keep being filled with the Spirit, but that is not the same thing as waiting to be baptized by the Spirit. There is one simple key to knowing the fullness and power of the Holy Spirit in your life: obeying the Lord. As you walk in obedience to the Word of God, the Spirit of God fills you and energizes your life (see Gal. 5:25).

Not only have believers been placed into Someone (Christ), but they have had Someone placed into them (the Holy Spirit). As Christians we have the Holy Spirit. Our bodies are temples of the Holy Spirit (1 Cor. 6:19). God himself indwells our bodies (2 Cor. 6:16). All the resources we need are there. The promise of the Holy Spirit has already been fulfilled for us. The Bible is absolutely clear on that point. There is nothing more to wait for. The Christian life consists of yielding to the control of the Spirit who is *already* in us. We do that through obedience to the Word (Col. 3:16).

Significantly, charismatic writers are not all agreed on how believers are to receive the baptism of the Spirit. Why all the confusion and contradiction? Why is it that charismatic writers do not quote the Bible plainly and let it go at that?

The reason no charismatic writer can do that is the Bible never tells *how* to get the baptism of the Spirit; it only tells believers that they are already baptized with the Spirit.

One of the greatest realities the Christian will ever have is contained in two brief and fulfilling statements. One is by Paul, the other is by Peter:

"In Him you have been made complete" (Col. 2:10).

"His divine power has granted to us everything pertaining to life and godliness" (2 Peter 1:3).

How? Through "the knowledge of God and of Jesus our Lord" (2 Peter 1:2). There is no point in seeking what is already ours.

── 9 ──

Does God Still Heal?

Hobart Freeman believed God had healed him of polio. Nonetheless, one of Freeman's legs was so much shorter than the other that he had to wear corrective shoes—and still he walked only with great difficulty. Freeman was a pastor. He began his ministry as a Baptist and even wrote a commendable and doctrinally orthodox textbook, *An Introduction to the Old Testament Prophets*.[1] But in the mid-1960s Freeman's fascination with faith healing moved him into the charismatic movement, and then further and further toward the fringe. He started his own church in Claypool, Indiana, known as Faith Assembly, which grew to more than two thousand members. Meetings were held in a building Freeman called The Glory Barn. Church services were closed to non-members.

Freeman and the Faith Assembly congregation utterly disdained medical treatment, believing that modern medicine was an extension of ancient witchcraft and black magic. To submit to a doctor's remedies, Freeman believed, was to expose oneself to demonic influence. Expectant mothers in Freeman's congregation were told that they must give birth at home, with the help of a church-sponsored midwife, rather than go to a hospital delivery room. Obedience to that teaching cost a number of mothers and infants their lives. In fact, over the years, at least ninety church members died as a result of ailments that would have been easily treatable. No one really knows what the actual death toll would be if nationwide figures could be compiled on all who followed Freeman's teaching.

After a fifteen-year-old girl whose parents belonged to Faith Assembly died of a medically treatable malady, the parents were convicted of negligent homicide and sentenced to ten years in prison. Freeman himself was charged with aiding and inducing reckless homicide in the case. Shortly afterward, on December 8, 1984, Freeman died of pneumonia and heart failure, complicated by an ulcerated leg.[2]

Hobart Freeman's theology did not allow him to acknowledge that polio had left one of his legs disfigured and lame. "I have my healing," is all he would say when anyone pointed out the rather conspicuous inconsistency between his own physical disabilities and his teaching. Ultimately his refusal to acknowledge his obvious infirmities cost him his life. He had dutifully refused treatment for the ailments that were killing him. Medical science could easily have prolonged his life. But in the end, Freeman was the victim of his own teaching.

Freeman is not the only so-called faith healer who has succumbed to sickness without finding healing. William Branham, father of the post-World War II healing revival, a man reputed to have been instrumental in some of the most spectacular healings the movement has ever seen, died in 1965 at age 56 after suffering for six days from injuries received in an automobile accident. Though his followers were confident that God would raise him up, the resurrection never happened. A. A. Allen, famed tent evangelist and faith healer, died of sclerosis of the liver in 1970, having secretly struggled with alcoholism for many of the years he was supposedly healing others. Kathryn Kuhlman died of heart problems in 1976. She had battled heart disease for nearly twenty years.[3] Ruth Carter Stapleton, faith-healing sister of former United States President Jimmy Carter, refused medical treatment for cancer because of her belief in faith healing.[4] She died of the disease in 1983.

Even John Wimber struggles with chronic heart problems. He begins his book *Power Healing* with "A Personal Note from John Wimber," which says in part:

> In October 1985 I was in England for three weeks, teaching at conferences in London, Brighton, and Sheffield. Many people were healed. One was not—me.
>
> During the previous two years I had suffered minor chest pains every four or five months. I suspected they had something to do with my heart but did nothing about them. Nobody, not even Carol, my wife, knew about my condition. But in England I could no longer hide it from her. On several occasions when we were walking I had to stop abruptly because of the chest pains. I was very tired for most of the trip. I had what doctors later suspected were a series of coronary attacks.
>
> When we returned home . . . a series of medical tests . . . confirmed my worst fears: I had a damaged heart, possibly seriously damaged. Tests indicated that my heart was not functioning properly, a condition complicated and possibly caused by high blood pressure. These problems, combined with my being overweight and overworked, meant I could die at any time.[5]

Wimber sought God and says God told him "that in the same way that Abraham waited for his child I was to wait for my healing. In the meantime, he told me to follow my doctor's orders."[6] Since then, Wimber has seen improvements followed by setbacks, but he believes the Lord has given him reassurance that he will eventually be healed.

"I wish I could write that at this time I am completely healed, that I no longer have physical problems. But if I did, it would not be true," Wimber admits.[7]

Why is it that so many of the leading advocates of faith healing are themselves in need of healing? Annette Capps, daughter of faith healer Charles Capps and also a faith-healing minister, raised that question in her book, *Reverse the Curse in Your Body and Emotions.* She wrote,

> People have stumbled over the fact that the so-called "healing minister" later became ill or died. They say, "I don't understand this. If the power of God came into operation and all those people were healed, why did the evangelist get sick? Why did he or she die?"
>
> The reason is because healings that take place in meetings like that are a special manifestation of the Holy Spirit. This is different from using your own faith. . . .
>
> The evangelist who is being used by God in the gifts of healing is still required to use his own faith in the Word of God to receive divine health and divine healing for his own body. Why? Because the gifts of healings are not manifested for the individual who is ministering. They are for the benefit of the people.
>
> . . . .
>
> Over the years I have seen various manifestations of the gifts of healing in my own ministry, but I have always had to use my own faith in God's Word for my healing. There have been times that I have been attacked with illness in my body, but as I ministered, many were healed, even though I did not feel well. I had to receive *my* healing through faith and acting on God's Word.[8]

Thus she concludes—astonishingly—that if a faith healer gets sick it is because his or her personal faith is somehow deficient.

Perspectives on faith healing often seem as varied as the number of faith healers. Some say God wants to heal *all* sickness; others come close to conceding that God's purposes may *sometimes* be fulfilled in our infirmities. Some equate sickness with sin; others stop short of that but still find it hard to explain why spiritually strong people get sick. Some blame the devil. Some claim to have *gifts* of healing; others say they have no unusual healing ability—they simply are used of God to show people the way of faith. Some use a physical touch or anointing oil; others claim they can "speak forth" healings or simply pray for healing and get results.

At one time in his ministry, Oral Roberts declared that God had called him to build a massive hospital that would blend conventional medicine and faith healing. Later, in the face of huge financial losses, he said God was telling him to close it down. I recently visited the site. An enormous sculpture of praying hands stood in front of a monolithic but virtually empty building in the middle of a lot overgrown with weeds. It is a monument to the unfulfilled promises of faith healing.

Faith healing and the charismatic movement have grown up together. Charles Fox Parham, father of the contemporary Pentecostal movement, came to the conviction that divine healing is God's will for all true believers. He then developed an entire system of Pentecostal beliefs around that conviction. Aimee Semple McPherson, E. W. Kenyon, William Branham, Kathryn Kuhlman, Oral Roberts, Kenneth Hagin, Kenneth Copeland, Fred Price, Jerry Savelle, Charles Capps, Norvel Hayes, Robert Tilton, Benny Hinn, and Larry Lea have all headlined healing in their public meetings. Catholic charismatics, such as Father John Bertolucci and Francis MacNutt, have followed suit, seeing the charismatic healing emphasis as a natural extension of Roman Catholic tradition. Third Wave leaders, most notably John Wimber, have made healing a central element in their repertoire.

The claims and methods of faith healers range from the eccentric to the grotesque. A few years ago I received in the mail a "miracle prayer cloth" from a faith-healing charismatic leader. With it came this message:

> Take this special miracle prayer cloth and put it under your pillow and sleep on it tonight. Or you may want to place it on your body or on a loved one. Use it as a release point wherever you hurt. First thing in the morning send it back to me in the green envelope. Do not keep this prayer cloth; return it to me. I will take it, pray over it all night. Miracle power will flow like a river. God has something better for you, a special miracle to meet your needs.

Interestingly enough, the sender of the prayer cloth feels he has a biblical support for what he is doing. While Paul was in Ephesus, God performed extraordinary miracles through him "so that handkerchiefs or aprons were even carried from his body to the sick, and the diseases left them and the evil spirits went out" (Acts 19:12). As we have seen, however, Paul and the other apostles had been given unique power. Nothing in the New Testament suggests that anyone else could send out handkerchiefs to work healing miracles.

Kenneth Hagin tells of one faith healer he heard of who used a method I have never personally witnessed:

> He'd always spit on them—every single one of them. He'd spit in his hand and rub it on them. That's the way he ministered. . . . If there was something wrong with your head, he'd spit in his hand and rub it on your forehead. If you had stomach trouble he'd spit in his hand and rub it on your clothes and on your stomach. If you had something wrong with your knee, he'd spit in his hand and rub it on your knee. And all the people would get healed.[9]

Other gimmicks not quite that uncouth but every bit as outlandish parade across Christian television daily. Oral Roberts asks for "seed-faith offerings"—money donated to him that is in effect a down-payment on your own personal miracle or healing. Robert Tilton regularly devises similar ploys, pledging special healings and financial miracles to people who send him money—the larger, more sacrificial the gift, the better the miracle. Pat Robertson peers into the camera, and as if he can see into people's living rooms, describes people who are being healed that very moment. Benny Hinn recently healed fellow faith healer and talk-show host Paul Crouch live on the Trinity Broadcasting Network. After Hinn "released his anointing" on a roomful of people, Crouch stepped forward to testify that he had been miraculously cured of a persistent ringing in the ears he had been suffering from for years. The list of fantastic claims and incredible stories of healings grows at a frantic pace—but real evidence of genuine miracles is conspicuously absent.

Everywhere I go, I am asked questions about miracles and healings. Is God restoring these marvelous gifts? What about such-and-such a healing? From all sides come confusion, questions, and contradictions.

As we study the Scriptures, we find three categories of spiritual gifts. In Ephesians 4 there is the category of *gifted men*: apostles, prophets, evangelists, teaching pastors, and teachers. The men themselves are described as gifts from Christ to his church. Second, there are the *permanent edifying gifts*, including knowledge, wisdom, prophecy (authoritative preaching), teaching, exhortation, faith (or prayer), discernment, showing mercy, giving, administration, and helps (see Rom. 12:3–8; 1 Cor. 12:8–10, 28). Third, there were the *temporary sign gifts*. These were specific enablements given to certain believers for the purpose of authenticating or confirming God's Word when it was proclaimed in the early church before the Scriptures were written. The temporary sign gifts included prophecy (revelatory prophecy), miracles, healings, tongues, and interpretation of tongues. The sign gifts had a unique purpose: to give the apostles credentials, that is, to let the people know that these men all spoke the truth of God. Once the Word of God was inscripturated, the sign gifts were no longer needed and they ceased.

What Was the Biblical Gift of Miracles?

Miracles and healing were both extraordinary sign gifts given to confirm God's revelation. Miracles could include healing, and the cures wrought by people with the healing gift were all miraculous, so in a sense the two gifts overlapped.

The great miracle worker was the Lord Jesus Christ himself. Basically, Jesus did three types of miracles: healings (including raising the dead—the ultimate healing); casting out demons (which often resulted in healing); and miracles of nature (such as multiplying loaves and fishes, stilling the sea, and walking on water). The gospels are full of Jesus' miracles from each of these categories. John wrote, "There are also many other things which Jesus did, which if they were written in detail, I suppose that even the world itself would not contain the books which were written" (John 21:25). All those miracles were signs pointing to the reality of Jesus' claim to be God (see John 2:11; 5:36; 20:30–31; Acts 2:22).

Once Christ's work was finished, the apostles had the task of proclaiming and recording his message in Scripture. To authenticate their work, God gave them the ability to do miracles of healing and casting out demons. Nothing in the New Testament indicates that anyone other than Jesus did miracles of nature. The apostles never created food, stilled the sea, or walked on water by themselves. (When Peter walked on water—one time—Jesus was present and helped him. Nothing suggests he ever repeated the experience.)

As we noted in our earlier discussion of miracles (chapter 5), the power to perform miracles was given specifically and exclusively to the apostles and their closest associates. Jesus' simple promise to the twelve is recorded in Matthew 10:1: "Having summoned His twelve disciples, He gave them authority over unclean spirits, to cast them out, and to heal every kind of disease and every kind of sickness." As the Spirit was given and the church age began, the apostles continued to manifest those two supernatural gifts. In fact, the apostles were so associated with such miracles that Paul reminded the believers at Corinth that "the signs of a true apostle were performed among you with all perseverance, by signs and wonders and miracles" (2 Cor. 12:12).

Miracle powers, then, were limited in scope and restricted to apostolic ministry. They were not given to the average Christian (Mark 16:20; Heb. 2:3–4), though some who were commissioned by an apostle shared in the ministry of miraculous gifts (such as Philip; Acts 8:6–7). The astute theologian B. B. Warfield correctly observed that the miraculous gifts

> were not for the possession of the primitive Christian as such; nor for that matter of the Apostolic Church or the Apostolic age for themselves; they were distinctively the authentication of the Apostles. They were part of the credentials of the apostles as the authoritative agents of God in founding the church. Their function thus confined them to distinctively the Apostolic Church, and they necessarily passed away with it. [10]

The Greek word translated "miracles" (*dunamis*) literally means "power." It is found some 118 times in the New Testament (the verb form another 209 times). It is the word used for the gift of miracles in 1 Corinthians 12:10 in the phrase "the effecting of miracles" (literally, "the energizing of the powerful works").

Dunamis is the same word translated "power" throughout the gospels. It is really the gift of "powers," then. What does that mean?

Jesus provided the clearest pattern for understanding it. Throughout his life and ministry, Jesus encountered Satan and defeated him by his *dunamis*, his power (Luke 4:13–14, 36; 6:17–18). Constantly we find Jesus casting out demons by his "power" (see Matt. 8, 9, 12; Mark 5, 6, 7; Luke 9). In every case Jesus' gift of power was used to combat Satan's kingdom. The gift of "powers," then, is the ability to cast out

demons. That is what the apostles did (Acts 19:12) and what
Philip did (Acts 8:6–7).

So apostolic miracles were limited to healing and casting
out demons. Claims by some today to be able to do miracles of
nature beyond healing and casting out demons do not have
apostolic precedent. Further, they are out of harmony with
God's intended purpose for miracles: to confirm new scriptural
revelation.

Today we deal with evil spirits not by finding someone
with the gift of powers to cast them out, but by following the
instructions of 2 Corinthians 2:10–11; Ephesians 6:11–18;
2 Timothy 2:25–26; James 4:7; and 1 Peter 5:7–9. All those
verses teach us how we can triumph over Satan.[11]

Often the gift of miracles was closely related to healing,
since disease could be brought on by satanic or demonic
influence.

Disease—A Universal Problem

Since the Fall of man in the garden of Eden, disease has
been a terrible reality. For millennia the search for cures to
alleviate illness and suffering has consumed humankind.
Sickness and death have distressed and ultimately conquered
every person since Adam. Only Enoch and Elijah have
escaped death (Gen. 5:24; 2 Kings 2:11). Only Jesus has
conquered death and risen again in glory. Aside from them
and people still living within a normal life span, every one of
the millions of people who have ever been born has ultimately
perished, either from sickness, injury, or some kind of
infirmity. No one—not even those who claim gifts of
healing—is exempt.

May I admit something? If I could choose one spiritual
gift beyond the ones given me, I would ask for the gift of
healing. On innumerable occasions I have wished I could
heal. I have stood with weeping parents in a hospital room
watching a precious child die of leukemia. I have prayed with

a dear friend as inoperable cancer ate at his insides. I have stood by helplessly as a young person fought for life in the intensive care unit; I have seen teenagers crushed in automobile accidents; I have watched people lie comatose while machines kept their vital signs alive; I have watched a close friend weaken and die after an unsuccessful heart transplant; I have seen friends in terrible pain from surgery; I know people who are permanently disabled through sickness and injury; I see babies born with heartbreaking deformities; I have helped people learn to cope with amputations and other tragic losses. And through it all I have wished I could heal people with a word, with a touch, with a command—but I cannot.

Think of how thrilling and rewarding it would be to have the gift of healing! Think of what it would be like to go into a hospital among the sick and dying and just walk up and down the hall touching people and healing them! It would be wonderful to gather groups of people with the gift of healing and fly them into the great pockets of disease in the world. They could walk through the crowds, healing everyone of cancer, tuberculosis, AIDS, and countless other ailments.

Why is it that charismatic healers have not attempted that? Why not assemble all those who say they have gifts of healing and have them go out to minister where the worst needs are? They could start in the hospitals and sanitariums in their own area, and then move beyond to the four corners of the earth. Opportunities to heal the sick are unlimited. And if, as charismatics often claim, such miracles are signs and wonders designed to convince unbelievers, would that kind of ministry not accomplish the purpose best?[12]

But strangely, the healers rarely if ever come out of their tents, their tabernacles, or their television studios. They always seem to exercise their gift only in a controlled environment, staged their way, run according to their schedule.[13] Why do we seldom hear of the gift of healing being used in hospital hallways? Why aren't more healers using their gift on the streets in India and Bangladesh? Why aren't they in the leper colonies and AIDS hospices where masses of people are racked by disease?

It is not happening. Why? Because those who claim the gift of healing do not really have it. The gift of healing was a temporary sign gift for the authenticating of the Scriptures as the Word of God. Once that authenticity was established, the gift of healing ceased.

Scripture teaches that although God is concerned about our bodies, he is infinitely more concerned about our souls (Matt. 10:28). We must realize that even if Christians could heal everyone at will the way Jesus did, the masses still would not believe the gospel. After all Jesus' marvelous healings, what did the people do? They crucified him. The apostles fared no better. They did miracle after miracle of healing. And what happened? They were jailed, persecuted, and even killed. Salvation does not come through experiencing or seeing physical healing. Salvation comes through hearing and believing the gospel (Rom. 10:17).

The gift of healing, however, has been claimed through the centuries by Christians and pagans alike. Historically, the Roman Catholic Church has led the way in claiming the power to heal. They have boasted of healing people with the bones of John the Baptist, or Peter, fragments of the cross, or even vials of Mary's breast milk. Lourdes, a Catholic shrine in France, has supposedly been the site of countless miraculous healings. Medjugorje, in Yugoslavia, has drawn more than fifteen million people in less than a decade. They come in search of a miracle or healing from an apparition of the Virgin Mary, who supposedly appeared to six children there in 1981.

Oriental psychic healers say they can do "bloodless surgery." They wave their hands over afflicted organs and say incantations. Supposedly people are cured.

Witch doctors and shamans even claim to raise the dead. Occultists use black magic to do lying wonders in the healing arts. Mary Baker Eddy, founder of Christian Science, claimed to have healed people through telepathy. Satan has always held people in his dominion by means of counterfeit healings. Raphael Gasson, a former spiritualist medium who was converted to Christ, said, "There are many, many Spiritualists today who are endowed with this remarkable gift of power by Satan, and I myself, having been used in this way, can testify to having witnessed miraculous healings taking place at 'healing meetings' in Spiritualism."[14]

And from the ranks of Christianity, particularly the Pentecostal and charismatic movements, come continuing claims of the power to heal. Turn on your television or radio. Chances are, whatever time of day or night it is, you can hear somebody promising to heal you from a distance, even if the program is tape delayed.

I once spoke to a man who told me his wife had been marvelously healed of cancer by his pastor.

"How is your wife doing now?" I asked.

"Oh, she is dead," the man said.

"She died?" I asked. "How long after the healing?"

He replied, "One year."

Stories like that are common in the movement. Kenneth Hagin tells of a pastor who supposedly was totally healed of deafness in a large healing meeting. "But by the time the meeting was dismissed, he couldn't hear a thing." Hagin writes, "He put his hearing aid back on."[15]

Charismatic television programs exhibit a "Can you top this?" mentality toward miracles and healings. One pastor on a popular charismatic television show explained that his gift of healing worked this way: "In the morning services the Lord tells me what healings are available. The Lord will say 'I've got three cancers available; I've got one bad back; I've got two headache healings.' I announce that to the congregation and tell them that anyone who comes at night with faith can claim those that are available for that evening."

A Closer Look at Healers and Healing

Although the methods and activities of those claiming the gift of healing do not match with Scripture, it cannot be denied that things happen at their services. People fall over, "slain in the Spirit." People jump up from wheelchairs, shouting that they are healed. Is there an explanation for those things?

You might think a tremendous amount of evidence exists to buttress the claims healers make. Not so. Most of the "evidence" healers cite as their proof cannot be tested. It is conjecture or subjective opinion. One man, William Nolen, a medical doctor but not an evangelical, tested the claims of faith healers. He wrote a book called *Healing: A Doctor in Search of a Miracle*. He included a section on charismatic healers, with particular reference to Kathryn Kuhlman, whom he studied in detail. Nolen gave this account of a healing service:

> Finally it was over. There were still long lines of people waiting to get onto the stage and claim their cures, but at five o'clock, with a hymn and final blessing, the show ended. Miss Kuhlman left the stage and the audience left the auditorium.
>
> Before going back to talk to Miss Kuhlman I spent a few minutes watching the wheelchair patients leave. All the desperately ill patients who had been in wheelchairs were still in wheelchairs. In fact, the man with the kidney cancer in his spine and hip, the man whom I had helped to the auditorium and who had his borrowed wheelchair brought to the stage and shown to the audience when he had claimed a cure, was now back in the wheelchair. His "cure," even if only a hysterical one, had been extremely short-lived.
>
> As I stood in the corridor watching the hopeless cases leave, seeing the tears of the parents as they pushed their crippled children to the elevators, I wished Miss Kuhlman had been with me. She had complained a couple of times

during the service of "the responsibility, the enormous responsibility," and of how her "heart aches for those that weren't cured," but I wondered how often she had really looked at them. I wondered whether she sincerely felt that the joy of those "cured" of bursitis and arthritis compensated for the anguish of those left with their withered legs, their imbecilic children, their cancers of the liver.

I wondered if she really knew what damage she was doing. I couldn't believe that she did.

. . . .

Here are some aspects of the medical healing process about which some of us know nothing and none of us know enough. To start with the *body's ability to heal itself*: Kathryn Kuhlman often says, "I don't heal; the Holy Spirit heals through me." I suspect there are two reasons why Miss Kuhlman continually repeats this statement: first, if the patient doesn't improve, the Holy Spirit, not Kathryn Kuhlman, gets the blame; second, she hasn't the foggiest notion of what healing is all about and once she puts the responsibility on the shoulders of the Holy Spirit she can answer, if questioned about her healing powers, "I don't know. The Holy Spirit does it all."[16]

Dr. Nolen went on to explain that physicians as well as charismatic healers can often influence a patient and cure symptoms of disease by suggestion, with or without the laying on of hands. Such cures are not miraculous but result from the functioning of the patient's own autonomic nervous system.

Nolen also mentioned that all healers—faith healers and medical doctors—use the power of suggestion to some extent. Nolen admitted that when he gives a person a pill or a shot, he often makes a point of telling the patient that the medicine will make him feel better in twenty-four to forty-eight hours. He gets far better results than if he gave the patient an uncertain message. As Nolen points out, there is a lot of power in an optimistic attitude, especially where functional disorders are concerned.[17]

Dr. Nolen explains the important distinction between functional disease and organic disease: A functional disease is one in which a perfectly good organ does not function properly. An organic disease is one in which the organ is diseased, maimed, physically impaired, or even defunct. "Infections, heart attacks, gallstones, hernias, slipped discs, cancers of all kinds, broken bones, congenital deformities, [and] lacerations" are all included in the organic disease class.[18] Nolen claims faith healers cannot cure organic diseases.

In a magazine article, Nolen made the point that Miss Kuhlman did not understand "psychogenic disease"—disease related to the mind.[19] In simple terms, a functional disease might be a sore arm. An organic disease would be a withered arm or no arm at all. A psychogenic disease would be *thinking* your arm was sore. Nolen wrote,

> Search the literature, as I have, and you will find no documented cures by healers of gallstones, heart disease, cancer or any other serious organic disease. Certainly, you'll find patients temporarily relieved of their upset stomachs, their chest pains, their breathing problems; and you will find healers, and believers, who will interpret this interruption of symptoms as evidence that the disease is cured. But when you track the patient down and find out what happened later, you always find the "cure" to have been purely symptomatic and transient. The underlying disease remains.[20]

When faith healers try to treat serious organic diseases, they often are responsible for untold anguish and unhappiness. Sometimes they keep patients away from effective and possibly lifesaving help.

Several years ago, after I preached a message in which I said many of the things contained in this chapter, a young man came up to me and said, "You'll never know what that message meant in my life. I had fallen down some stairs and as a result I injured my head and had terrible headaches. Some people prayed for me and told me I was healed and my headaches went away. But since that time the headaches have come back and I have felt guilty, as if I had not accepted a healing from God. So I've been refusing to go to a doctor, but this morning you've freed me to understand that I must go to a doctor." A physician was able to find organic causes for his headaches and treat them effectively.

But What About All the Evidence?

Undoubtedly, many who have placed their faith in charismatic healers will protest that Dr. Nolen does not know what he's talking about. After all, he is not an evangelical and perhaps not prone to believe in miracles. How objective was his research? Dr. Nolen had Miss Kuhlman herself send him a list of the cancer victims she had seen "cured," and this is what the doctor discovered:

> I wrote to all the cancer victims on her list—eight in all— and the only one who offered cooperation was a man who claimed he had been cured of prostatic cancer by Miss Kuhlman. He sent me a complete report of his case. Prostatic cancer is frequently very responsive to hormone therapy; if it spreads, it is also often highly responsive to radiation therapy. This man had had extensive treatment with surgery, radiation and hormones. He had also been "treated" by Kathryn Kuhlman. He chose to attribute his cure—or remission, as the case may be—to Miss Kuhlman. But anyone who read his report, layman or doctor, would see immediately that it is impossible to tell which kind of treatment had actually done most to prolong his life. If Miss Kuhlman had to rely on his case to prove that the Holy Spirit "cured" cancer through her, she would be in very desperate straits.[21]

Dr. Nolen did further follow-up work on eighty-two cases of Kathryn Kuhlman's healings, using names she supplied. Of the eighty-two, only twenty-three responded and were interviewed. Nolen's conclusion at the end of the entire investigation was that not one of the so-called healings was legitimate.[22]

> Kathryn Kuhlman's lack of medical sophistication is a critical point. I don't believe she is a liar or a charlatan or that she is, consciously, dishonest. . . . I think she sincerely believes that the thousands of sick people who come to her services and claim cures are, through her ministrations, being cured of organic diseases. I also think—and my investigations confirm this—that she is wrong.
>
> The problem is—and I'm sorry this has to be so blunt— one of ignorance. Miss Kuhlman doesn't *know* the difference between psychogenic and organic diseases. Though she uses hypnotic techniques, she doesn't know anything about hypnotism and the power of suggestion. She doesn't *know* anything about the autonomic nervous system. Or, if she does know something about these things, she has certainly learned to hide her knowledge.
>
> There is one other possibility: It may be that Miss Kuhlman doesn't *want* to learn that her work is not as miraculous as it seems. For this reason she has trained herself to deny, emotionally and intellectually, anything that might threaten the validity of her ministry.[23]

More recently, James Randi, a professional magician known as The Amazing Randi, has written a book in which he examines the claims of faith healers.[24] Randi is the man who exposed television evangelist Peter Popoff's fakery in 1986 on "The Tonight Show." (Popoff claimed to be getting "words of knowledge" from God about people in his audience, and his details were incredibly accurate. It turned out he was merely repeating information he received from his wife via a hidden receiver in his ear. She read him the information off inquirers' cards and crib sheets assembled from informal conversations with people before the services began.)

Randi is openly antagonistic to Christianity.[25] Nevertheless, he seems to have done his investigation thoroughly and fairly. He asked scores of faith healers to supply him with "direct, examinable evidence" of true healings.[26] "I have been willing to accept just *one* case of a miracle cure so that I might say in this book that at least on one occasion a miracle occurred," he wrote.[27] But not one faith healer anywhere gave him a single case of medically confirmed healing that could not be explained as natural convalescence, psychosomatic improvement, or outright fakery. Randi's conclusion? "Reduced to its basics, faith-healing today—as it has always been—is simply 'magic.' Though the preachers vehemently deny any connection with the practice, their activities meet all the requirements for the definition. All of the elements are present, and the intent is identical."[28]

Many faith healers, of course, equivocate about the claims they make. Some even deny that they claim to be able to heal. "I don't heal," they will say. "The Holy Spirit does." But all the showmanship, bravado, and gimmickry deny that. If these people do not claim to heal, why do hopeful people flock to *their* services? And why do they continually tell fantastic stories of people who were supposedly healed in their meetings?

What of the healings we hear about? Are *any* of them genuine? Perhaps not. Where are the healings of shattered bones? When have we heard of a faith healer taking someone who had been in a car accident and straightening out a lacerated face or a shattered skull? Where are the healings of the terminally ill? Where are the restored limbs for amputees, or former quadriplegics who now function normally? Instead, what we see mostly seem to be imagined illnesses, imaginarily healed.

Not one of today's self-styled healers can produce irrefutable proof of the miracles they claim to have wrought.

Many of them are transparently fraudulent, and the healings they display are clearly suspect. Yet thousands of intelligent people continue to go to their services. Why? Because desperation often accompanies disease. Sickness drives people to do frantic and extreme things they normally would not do. People who are ordinarily clear-minded, intelligent, and balanced become irrational. Satan knows that, which is why he said, "Skin for skin! Yes; all that a man has he will give for his life" (Job 2:4).

The most desperate, heartbreaking cases involve people who are incurably, organically ill. Others are not really sick at all. They have psychosomatic disorders or minor functional diseases of some kind. Still others are so full of doubts that they have to run from meeting to meeting to have their faith reinforced by seeing what they believe to be miracles. The tragedy is that no good is done for any of these people—no one's faith is really strengthened, no one's diseases are really healed. Multitudes go away shattered, disconsolate, feeling either that they have failed God or that he has failed them.

There is much confusion, guilt, and heartache among charismatics and non-charismatics because of what they have been told about healing. The agony of disease and illness is only intensified when people feel that they are not healed because of their sin, their lack of faith, or God's indifference to them. They reason that if healing is available and they do not get it, it is either their fault or God's. Thus faith healers have left untold wreckage in their wake.

God Does Heal—His Way

Does God heal? I believe He does. I do not automatically discount all claims of supernatural healings just because some are false. But I am convinced that dramatic, miraculous, immediate intervention by God is quite rare—and never dependent on some supposedly gifted person who acts as an agent of healing. Genuine healings may come as a result of prayer and most often involve simple natural processes. Other times, God speeds up the recovery mechanisms and restores a sick person to health in a way that medicine cannot explain. Sometimes he overrules a medical prognosis and allows someone to recover from a normally debilitating disease. Healings like that come ' in response to prayer and the sovereign will of God and can happen at any time. But the gift of healing, the ability to heal others, special anointings for healing ministry, healings that can be "claimed," and other typical faith-healing techniques have no biblical sanction in the post-apostolic era.

Certainly God heals. He heals in answer to prayer and in order to reveal his glory. But there is a vast difference between the healings done in the days of Jesus and his disciples and the "healings" being offered today on television, on the radio, through direct-mail gimmicks, and from some pulpits across the land. A look at Scripture shows the distinction starkly.

How Did Jesus Heal?

To make a comparison between the gift of healing being claimed today and what the Bible teaches, we simply have to go back and look at Jesus' ministry. Our Lord set the pattern for the apostolic gifts, and he did a massive amount of healing. In Jesus' day the world was full of disease. Medical science was crude and limited. There were more incurable diseases than we have now. Plagues could wipe out entire cities.

Jesus healed disease to demonstrate his deity. How did he do it? Scripture reveals six noteworthy characteristics of Jesus' healing ministry:

First, *Jesus healed with a word or a touch.* Matthew 8 relates that as Jesus was entering Capernaum, a centurion came to Jesus and asked him to help his servant, who was lying paralyzed at his home and suffering great pain (vv. 6–7). Jesus told the centurion he would come and heal the servant, but the centurion protested, pointing out that if Jesus would just say the word, his servant could be healed (v. 8).

The Lord was amazed at the centurion's faith, particularly because he was a Roman soldier, and not of the house of Israel. Jesus said to the centurion, " 'Go your way; let it be done to you as you have believed.' And the servant was healed that very hour" (v. 13).

When Jesus fed the five thousand (John 6), he had spent most of the day healing people in the crowd who were sick. Scripture does not tell us how many were healed—it could have been thousands. But whatever the number, Jesus healed them with a word. There were no theatrics, no special environment.

Jesus also healed with a touch. For example, in Mark 5:25–34 we find the account of a woman with chronic bleeding who was healed simply by touching Jesus' robe.

Second, *Jesus healed instantly*. The centurion's servant was healed "that very hour" (Matt. 8:13). The woman with the bleeding problem was healed "immediately" (Mark 5:29). Jesus healed ten lepers instantaneously right on the road (Luke 17:14). He touched another man with leprosy and "immediately the leprosy departed from him" (Luke 5:13). The crippled man at the pool of Bethesda "immediately became well," took up his pallet, and began to walk (John 5:9). Even the man born blind, who had to go and wash his eyes, was healed instantly—though for his own purposes, Jesus accomplished that miracle in two distinct stages (John 9:1–7). The healing was no less instantaneous.

People often say, "I've been healed, and now I'm getting better." Jesus never did "progressive" healing. If Jesus had not healed instantly, there would have been no miraculous element sufficient to demonstrate his deity. His critics could easily have said the healing was just a natural process.

Third, *Jesus healed totally*. In Luke 4, Jesus left the synagogue and came to Simon Peter's home. Peter's mother-in-law was there, suffering from a high fever. Possibly she was dying. Jesus stood over her, "rebuked the fever," and immediately she was well (v. 39). In fact, she then she got up and began to wait on them. There was no recuperation period. Jesus did not advise her to sip a little honey in hot water and take it easy for a few weeks. Nor did he goad her to "claim the healing by faith" despite unrelenting symptoms. She was immediately well and knew it. Her healing was instantaneous and it was total. That was the only kind of healing Jesus ever did.

Fourth, *Jesus healed everyone.* Unlike healers today, Jesus did not leave long lines of disappointed people who had to return home in their wheelchairs. He did not have healing services or programs that ended at a certain time because of airline or television schedules. Luke 4:40 tells us, "And while the sun was setting, all who had any sick with various diseases brought them to Him; and laying His hands on *every one* of them, He was healing them" (emphasis added). Luke 9:11 records a similar example.

Fifth, *Jesus healed organic disease.* Jesus did not go up and down Palestine healing lower back pain, heart palpitations, headaches, and other invisible ailments. He healed the most obvious kinds of organic disease—crippled legs, withered hands, blind eyes, palsy—all healings that were undeniably miraculous.

Sixth, *Jesus raised the dead.* Luke 7:11–16 tells us that while Jesus was at a city called Nain, he came upon a funeral procession as a widow went out to bury her only son. Jesus stopped the procession, touched the coffin, and said, "Young man, I say to you, arise!"—and the dead man sat up and began to speak! He also raised a synagogue ruler's daughter in Mark 5:22–24, 35–43.

People who tout the gift of healing today do not spend much time in funeral parlors, funeral processions, or cemeteries. The reason is obvious.

Some charismatics, as we have already noted, claim that people today do sometimes come back from the dead. Those cases, however, are nothing like the biblical examples. It is one thing to revive someone whose vital signs stopped on a surgeon's table. It is entirely another matter to come out of the grave four days after being buried (see John 11) or to climb out of one's casket at the funeral (see Luke 7). Those are resurrections that cannot be challenged. Charismatics who make such claims today do so on hearsay and with scant evidence. They are guilty of trivializing our Lord's miraculous works. Why is it that the only miracles ever done on television are the kind that involve no visible evidence?

Note, by the way, that Jesus did virtually all his healing and raising the dead in public—often before vast crowds of people. His gift of healing was an authenticating gift. He used it to confirm his claims that he was the Son of God in a way that also displayed his divine compassion. Dispelling demons and diseases was Christ's way of proving that he was God in human flesh. John's gospel clearly demonstrates that truth. John said all the signs and miracles Jesus wrought validated his deity (John 20:30–31).

How Did the Apostles Heal?

As we have seen, Jesus set the standard for the healing gift. Someone might argue that healers today operate at a different level of power. After all, they are not God.

But how did the apostles and others use the gifts of healing that were bestowed on them by Christ? Christ gave the gift of healing to all twelve apostles (Luke 9:1–2). Later, Jesus extended the gift to seventy others whom he sent out two-by-two to preach the gospel and heal the sick (Luke 10:1–9). Did anyone else in the New Testament have the ability to heal? Yes, there were a few close companions of the apostles who also received the gift, namely Barnabas (Acts 15:12), Philip (8:7), and Stephen (6:8). But we never see the gift being used at random in the churches. It is a gift associated only with Christ, the twelve (plus Paul), the seventy, and some who were intimate co-workers with the apostles.

The third chapter of Acts clearly illustrates how the gift of healing helped the apostles proclaim their message. Peter and John were going into the temple to pray when a lame man asked them for alms. Peter replied by saying he had no money, but what he did have he would give the man. Then he said, "In the name of Jesus Christ the Nazarene—walk!" (Acts 3:6).

Immediately the man leaped to his feet and began walking and praising God. Word passed quickly, and soon a huge crowd had gathered. Everyone knew of the lame man who had been begging at the temple gate for years. Peter seized the opportunity and addressed the crowd, telling them they should not marvel at what they had seen. What had been done had not been through the power of Peter or John but through the power of Jesus Christ, the One whom the people had just crucified.

It is crucial to understand the impact of what Peter said and the effect of the healing miracle on his audience. Peter was talking to Jewish people who had been looking eagerly for their Messiah all their lives. Suppose Peter had walked in and simply told them, "Jesus Christ, the one you crucified a few months ago—he was your Messiah. Believe in Him."

We cannot begin to imagine how shocking and repulsive that message would have been to a first-century Jew. It would have been utterly unthinkable to him that his Messiah would be crucified like a common criminal. A typical Jew believed the Messiah was to come in power and glory to sweep away the bondage of the hated Romans, who held Palestine in their grip.

Had Peter not performed the miracle of healing the lame man, he would have had little or no audience. As it was, many were shaken and pierced to their hearts. According to Acts 4:4, "Many of those who had heard the message believed; and the number of the men came to be about five thousand."

At Pentecost the church was born. A new era had come, and God gave miraculous abilities to his apostles to help them proclaim their message. In fact, we can see that the same six characteristics of the miracles of healing done by Jesus Christ also characterized the apostles' healing.

The apostles healed with a word or a touch. In Acts 9:32–35 Peter healed a man named Aeneas, who had been bedridden eight years because he was paralyzed. All Peter said was, "Aeneas, Jesus Christ heals you; arise, and make your bed" and immediately Aeneas was healed (v. 34).

In Acts 28 we see Paul on the island of Malta, and he healed with a touch. Publius, one of the leading men on Malta, was hosting Paul and his companions. Publius's father was lying in bed with a bad case of fever and dysentery. Paul went in to see him, prayed, laid his hands on him, and healed him (v. 8).

The apostles healed instantly. The beggar at the temple gate came *immediately* to his feet and started leaping, walking, and praising God (Acts 3:2–8). There was no need for any therapy, no extra rehabilitation. The man was cured at once after a lifetime of lameness.

The apostles healed totally. We see this in the account of the lame man in the third chapter of Acts, and also in the healing of Aeneas in chapter 9. Acts 9:34 is most insightful when it says, "Jesus Christ maketh thee whole" (KJV). Like every healing Jesus did, every healing of the apostles was complete. There was no progression, no talk of recurring symptoms or slow improvement.

The apostles were able to heal anyone. Acts 5:12–16 reports that the apostles did many signs and wonders, and the people held them in high esteem. They carried the sick out into the streets and laid them on pallets so that when Peter came by, his shadow might fall on them. In addition, people from surrounding cities brought those who were sick to be healed and "they were all being healed" (Acts 5:16).

In Acts 28:9 we learn that after Paul healed Publius's father, "the rest of the people on the island who had diseases were coming to him and getting cured." No one was left out.

The apostles healed organic disease. They did not deal in functional, symptomatic, or psychosomatic problems. The man at the temple gate was probably in his forties, crippled from birth. Publius's father had dysentery, an infectious organic disease.

Finally, *the apostles raised the dead.* Acts 9:36–42 tells how Peter brought Dorcas (Tabitha) back to life. Note especially verse 42: "It was known throughout all Joppa; and many believed in the Lord." Again we see a miracle giving credence and impact to the gospel message. In Acts 20:9–12 a young man named Eutychus died in a fall, and Paul brought him back to life.

Despite all the claims being made today, no one is exhibiting those six traits in any healing ministry.

Let me suggest a final point: According to Scripture, those who possessed miraculous gifts could use their gifts at will. Contemporary healers do not heal at will. They cannot. They do not have the biblical gift of healing. They are forced to dodge the difficulty by saying, "It's not my doing; it's the Lord's." Thus God—or the person seeking healing—is blamed for the repeated failures.

The Gift of Healing Is Gone, but the Lord Continues to Heal

The gift of healing was one of the miraculous sign gifts given to help the apostolic community confirm the authority of the gospel message in the early years of the church. Once the Word of God was complete, the signs ceased. Miraculous signs were no longer needed. The apostles used healing only as a powerful sign to convince people of the validity of the gospel message.

In Philippians 2:25–27 Paul mentioned his good friend Epaphroditus, who had been very sick. Paul had previously displayed the gift of healing. Why did he not simply heal Epaphroditus? Perhaps the gift was no longer operational. Or perhaps Paul simply refused to pervert the gift by using it for his own ends. Either way, healing Epaphroditus was beyond the purpose of the gift of healing. The gift was not given to keep Christians healthy. It was to be a sign to unbelievers to convince them that the gospel was divine truth.

We find a similar case in 2 Timothy 4:20, where Paul mentioned that he had left Trophimus sick at Miletus. Why should Paul leave one of his good Christian friends sick? Why didn't he heal him? Because that was not the purpose of the healing gift. (See also 1 Tim. 5:23 and 2 Cor. 12:7.)

Healing was a miraculous sign gift to be used for special purposes. It was not intended as a permanent way to keep the Christian community in perfect health. Yet today most charismatics teach that God wants every Christian well. If that is true, why does God allow Christians to get sick in the first place?

In a world where believers are subject to the consequences of sin, why should we assume that suffering is excluded? If every Christian were well and healthy, if perfect health were a guaranteed benefit of the atonement, millions of people would be stampeding to get saved—but for the wrong reason. God wants people to come to him in repentance for sin, and for his glory, not because they see him as a panacea for their physical and temporal ills.

What Is the Explanation for Charismatic Healings?

Charismatics often respond to biblical and theological reasoning by appealing to experience. They plead, "But incredible things are happening; how do you explain it?" I hear the same refrain constantly from charismatic friends: "I know this lady whose son who had cancer and—" "My friend's mother was so bent over with arthritis she couldn't move and—"

In reply I say: "Since no charismatic healer can come up with genuinely verifiable cases of instant healing involving organic disease; since no charismatic healer heals everyone who comes for healing and hundreds go away from their services as sick or as crippled as when they came; since no charismatic healer raises the dead; since the Word of God needs no confirmation outside itself and is sufficient to show the way of salvation; since charismatic healings are based on a questionable theology of the atonement and salvation; since charismatic writers and teachers appear to disallow God his own purposes in allowing people to be sick; since charismatic healers seem to need their own special environment; since the evidence they bring forth to prove healings is often weak, unsupported, and over-exaggerated; since charismatics are not known for going into hospitals to heal though there are plenty of faithful people in hospitals; since most instances of healings by charismatics can be explained in ways other than God's unquestioned supernatural intervention; since charismatics get sick and die like everyone else; since so much confusion and contradiction surrounds what is happening—let me ask the return question: How do *you* explain it? It certainly is not the biblical gift of healing!"

Healings *are* occurring today. But the biblical gift of healing is not present. God heals whom he wills, when he wills, and there have been many times when my human wisdom might want to second-guess him. Like any pastor, I have seen the most tragic, unexplainable, and seemingly needless cases of suffering involving committed Christians. I have prayed earnestly with families for the recovery of loved ones only to see the answer come back no. Charismatic pastors—if they are honest—will admit they have the same experiences.

But what is the typical explanation charismatic teachers, healers, and leaders give for the multitudes who are not healed? "They didn't have enough faith." That kind of reasoning is neither kind nor accurate.

Why Do Christians Get Sick?

We should not neglect an essential question: Why do Christians get sick? There are several reasons.

Some sickness comes from God. In Exodus 4:11 God told Moses: "Who has made man's mouth? Or who makes him dumb or deaf, or seeing or blind? Is it not I, the Lord?" Stated that simply and directly, the idea sounds repulsive. Would a loving God want anyone to suffer? Why would he make a man dumb, deaf, or blind? Yet again and again in Scripture we see that there is far more to God's sovereign plan than our finite minds can comprehend. God made the disabled and infirm. Babies are born every day with defects. Many children grow up with congenital deformities. Some people have illnesses that last for years. While it is unexplainable according to our human logic, it is all God's plan and a gift of God's love.[29]

Some sickness comes from Satan. Luke 13:11–13 is the account of how Jesus healed a woman who "for eighteen years had had a sickness caused by a spirit; and she was bent double, and could not straighten up at all." When Jesus saw her he said, "Woman, you are freed from your sickness."

God may let Satan cause someone to be sick for his own reasons. The classic biblical example is Job (see Job 1).

Some sickness is chastening for sin. In the twelfth chapter of Numbers we see Miriam getting leprosy because of disobedience to the Lord. And then we see her being healed because of her repentance. In Deuteronomy 28:20–22 God warned the Israelites that he would smite them with pestilence if they sinned. In 2 Kings 5 Gehazi, the servant of Elisha, gets leprosy because of his greed.

The psalmist wrote, "Before I was afflicted I went astray, but now I keep Thy word" (Ps. 119:67).

When one is sick, every area of life should be checked for unconfessed sin. If there is unconfessed sin, there is a need to repent and experience God's forgiveness. Be careful in counseling others who are sick, however. Inquiries or accusations about sin in the life of someone else should not be made without careful, prayerful self-examination. It is far too easy to abuse this biblical principle and falsely accuse someone of sin (cf. John 9:1–3).

It may well be that in some cases a person is sick because of sin, and God is chastening him or her. But is that *always* the problem? By no means. And suggesting that someone's sickness is necessarily related to personal sin is as unfeeling and cruel as telling people they are not healed because they do not have enough faith. We need to avoid the error of Job's friends (cf. Job 42:7–8).

Has God Promised to Heal All Who Have Faith?

Charismatics who claim that God wants every believer well are clearly in error. Still, we can be equally positive that God has promised that he *does* heal. He does not promise he will *always* heal, but the Christian has a right to look to heaven for relief during any illness. There are at least three reasons for this:

God heals because of his person. In Exodus 15:26 God told the Israelites, "I, the Lord, am your healer." The words for Lord here are *Yahweh Ropeca*, which means "the Lord who heals thee." And so the Christian has a right to look to God in times of illness.

God heals because of his promise. God has promised that whatever we ask in his name and in faith will be done (Matt. 21:22; John 14:13–14; 16:24; 1 John 5:14). That means our requests must be according to his will. If we ask for healing and it is according to his will, God will heal us.

God heals because of his pattern. We see the pattern of God's mercy and grace in Jesus. So if you want to know how God feels about human suffering and disease, look at Jesus. He went everywhere healing. He could have confirmed his claim to be God in other ways, but he chose the compassionate means of alleviating pain and suffering "in order that what was spoken through Isaiah the prophet might be fulfilled, saying, 'He Himself took our infirmities, and carried away our diseases'" (Matt. 8:17). As we pointed out in our discussion of 1 Peter 2:24 (see chapter 4), that does not mean healing for every sickness in this age is guaranteed as part of the atonement. But it confirms the healing pattern in Christ's work on our behalf and assures us of ultimate, eternal deliverance from the sicknesses and infirmities of this present world. There will be no sickness or death in our eternal home.

Should Christians Go to Doctors?

While the Bible teaches that God definitely heals, Scripture also gives ample evidence that Christians should go to doctors. Isaiah chapter 38 relates the story of how King Hezekiah was deathly ill. The king wept bitterly and beseeched the Lord in prayer for healing. God granted his request, but note how the healing took place: "Now Isaiah had said, 'Let them take a cake of figs, and apply it to the boil, that he may recover'" (Isa. 38:21). Why was a poultice needed if God had granted the healing? God was laying down a principle here. When you get sick, do two things: pray for healing and go to a doctor.

Jesus confirmed that same idea in Matthew 9:12 when he

said, "It is not those who are healthy who need a physician but those who are ill." Granted, Jesus was speaking of the problem of sin, but he was using an analogy that everyone understood. Sick people need a doctor. By those words, our Lord affirmed that medical treatment is consistent with the will of God.

We observed that many came to be healed after Paul miraculously healed Publius's father in Acts 28. The Greek word used of Paul's healing of Publius's father in verse 8 is the regular term for healing, while the one used in verse 9 for everyone else's healing is a word for medical cures. We get the word *therapeutic* from it. It may well have been that Paul healed miraculously, and his companion Luke, who was a physician (Col. 4:14), healed medically. What a team they would have made!

The principle is clear: When we get sick, we should pray; we should seek help from competent doctors; and we should wholeheartedly rest in the perfect will of God. After all, adversity is for our good in time (James 1:2–4; 1 Peter 5:10) and for our glory in eternity (Rom. 8:18; 1 Peter 1:6–7). It is helpful to remember that because of the Fall, we are all ultimately going to die (except for the elect who are alive when Christ returns). Every Christian's hope should be that his death would, as Jesus told Peter, "glorify God."

In illness, as in everything else, the Christian should keep a biblical perspective and seek to glorify God. God heals in his own time, by his own means, for his own glory, and according to his own sovereign will and pleasure. Would we have it any other way?

— 10 —

Is the Gift of Tongues for Today?

Someone sent me a sample of some charismatic Sunday school literature designed to teach kindergarten children to speak in tongues. It is titled "I've Been Filled with the Holy Spirit!!!" and is an eight-page coloring book. One page has a caricature of a smiling weight-lifter with a T-shirt that says "Spirit-Man." Under him is printed 1 Corinthians 14:4: "He that speaks in an unknown tongue builds himself up."

Another page features a boy who looks like Howdy Doody with his hands lifted up. A dotted outline pictures where his lungs would be. (This evidently represents his spirit.) Inside the lung-shaped diagram is printed "BAH-LE ODOMA TA LAH-SE-TA NO-MO." A cartoon-style balloon coming from his mouth repeats the words, "BAH-LE ODOMA-TA LAH-SE-TA NO-MO." A brain-shaped cloud is drawn in his head, with a large question mark in the cloud. Also inside the cloud is printed, "MY MIND DOESN'T UNDERSTAND WHAT I'M SAYING." Under the boy 1 Corinthians 14:14 is printed: "For if I pray in an unknown tongue, my spirit prayeth, but my understanding is unfruitful."

270

That expresses the typical charismatic perspective. The gift of tongues is viewed as a wholly mystical ability that somehow operates in a person's spirit but utterly bypasses the mind. Many charismatics are even told that they must purposefully switch off their minds to enable the gift to function. Charles and Frances Hunter, for example, hold "Healing Explosion" meetings, attended by as many as fifty thousand people at a time. At those seminars the Hunters "teach" people how to receive the gift of tongues. Charles Hunter tells people,

> When you pray with your spirit, you do not think of the sounds of the language. Just trust God, but make the sounds when I tell you to.
>
> In just a moment when I tell you to, begin loving and praising God by speaking forth a lot of different syllable sounds. At first make the sounds rapidly so you won't try to think as you do in speaking your natural language. . . . Make the sounds loudly at first so you can easily hear what you are saying.[1]

Hunter does not explain what point there is in *hearing* what one is saying, since the mind is supposed to be disengaged anyway. He continually reminds his audience that they are not supposed to be thinking: "The reason some of you don't speak fluently is that you tried to think of the sounds. So when we pray this prayer and you start speaking in your heavenly language, don't try to think."[2] Later, he adds, "[You] don't even have to think in order to pray in the Spirit."[3]

Arthur L. Johnson, in his excellent exposé of mysticism, calls the charismatic movement "the zenith of mysticism"[4]—and with good reason. This desire to switch off the mind and disconnect from all that is rational was, as we noted previously (see chapter 7), one of the primary characteristics of the pagan mystery religions. Nearly all the teachings distinctive to the charismatic movement are unadulterated mysticism, and nothing illustrates that more perfectly than the way charismatics themselves depict the gift of tongues.

Charismatics typically describe tongues as an ecstatic experience without parallel that arouses the spirit in a way that must be experienced to be appreciated. One author quotes Robert V. Morris:

> For me . . . the gift of tongues turned out to be the gift of praise. As I used the unknown language which God had given me I felt rising in me the love, the awe, the adoration pure and uncontingent, that I had not been able to achieve in thought-out prayer.[5]

A newspaper article on tongues quoted the Reverend Bill L. Williams, of San Jose:

> "It involves you with someone you're deeply in love with and devoted to. . . . We don't understand the verbiage, but we know we're in communication."
>
> That awareness is "beyond emotion, beyond intellect," he said. "It transcends human understanding. It is the heart of man speaking to the heart of God. It is deep, inner heart understanding."
>
> "It comes as supernatural utterances, bringing intimacy with God."[6]

The article also quoted the Reverend Billy Martin, of Farmington, New Mexico: "It's a joyous, glorious, wonderful experience." And the Reverend Darlene Miller, of Knoxville, Tennessee: "It's like the sweetness of peaches that you can't know until you taste it yourself. There['s] nothing ever to compare with that taste."[7] Other tongues-speakers would echo sentiments similar to those.

And what could possibly be wrong with such an experience? If it makes a person *feel* good, closer to God, spiritually stronger, or even delirious with joy, can it in any way be dangerous or deceptive?

It can, and it is. The late George Gardiner, a pastor and

former tongues-speaker who left the Pentecostal movement, poignantly described the danger of surrendering one's mind and abandoning control of oneself for the sake of the euphoria of a tongues experience:

> The enemy of the soul is ever ready to take an advantage of an "out of control" situation and thousands of Christians can testify with regret to the end results.
>
> Such experiences not only give Satan an opening he is quick to exploit, they can be psychologically damaging to the individual. Charismatic writers are constantly warning tongues-speakers that they will suffer a letdown. This is ascribed to the devil and the reader is urged to get refilled as soon as possible. . . .
>
> So the seeker for experience goes back through the ritual again and again, but begins to discover something; ecstatic experience, like drug-addiction, requires larger and larger doses to satisfy. Sometimes the bizarre is introduced. I have seen people run around a room until they were exhausted, climb tent poles, laugh hysterically, go into trances for days and do other weird things as the "high" sought became more elusive. Eventually there is a crisis and a decision is made; he will sit on the back seats and be a spectator, "fake it," or go on in the hope that everything will eventually be as it was. The most tragic decision is to quit and in the quitting abandon all things spiritual as fraudulent. The spectators are frustrated, the fakers suffer guilt, the hoping are pitiable and the quitters are a tragedy. No, such movements are not harmless![8]

Many who speak in tongues will understand the tensions Gardiner has described. He is not the only tongues-speaker to turn against the practice and expose its dangers. Wayne Robinson, who served as editor-in-chief of publications in the Oral Roberts Evangelistic Association, was an enthusiastic tongues-speaker at one time. In the preface of his book *I Once Spoke in Tongues*, he wrote:

In the past few years, I have become more and more convinced that *the* test, not only of tongues but of any religious experience, cannot be limited to the logic and truthfulness supporting it. There is also the essential question, *"What does it do in one's life?"* More specifically, does it turn a person inward to self-concern and selfish interests, or does it open him up to others and to their needs?

I know people who testify that speaking in tongues has been the great liberating experience of their lives. But juxtaposed with them are a great many others for whom speaking in tongues has been an excuse to withdraw from confronting the realities of a suffering and divided world. For some, tongues has been the greatest thing ever to happen; others have seen it disrupt churches, destroy careers, and rupture personal relationships.[9]

Ben Byrd, another former charismatic, writes,

To say that speaking in tongues is a harmless practice and is all right for those who want to IS AN UNWISE position when information to the contrary is evident. . . . Speaking in tongues is addictive. The misunderstanding of the issue of tongues and the habit plus the psychic high it brings plus the stimulation of the flesh equals a practice hard to let go of. . . . [But to] equate much speaking in tongues with advanced spirituality is to reveal one's misunderstanding of Bible Truth and to reveal one's willingness to be satisfied with a deceptive and dangerous counterfeit.[10]

Others who practice tongues can turn the phenomenon on and off mechanically, without feeling anything emotional. Having learned the familiar sounds to repeat, they have honed the ability and can speak fluently and effortlessly—yet dispassionately.

The Biblical Gift of Tongues

Tongues are mentioned in three books of the Bible: Mark (16:17); Acts (2, 10, 19); and 1 Corinthians (12–14).[11] In chapter 8 of this book we looked at the Acts passages, noting that Acts is primarily historical narrative and the extraordinary, miraculous events it recounts do not represent a normative pattern for the entire church age. The disputed text of Mark 16:17 simply mentions tongues as an apostolic sign (see chapter 4). That leaves 1 Corinthians 12–14, the only passage of Scripture that talks about the role of tongues in the church. Note that Paul wrote those chapters to reprove the Corinthians for their *misuse* of the gift. Most of what he had to say *restricted* the use of tongues in the church.[12]

In 1 Corinthians 12 Paul discussed spiritual gifts in general, how they are received, and how God has ordered the gifts in the church. In the fourteenth chapter of that book he demonstrated the inferiority of tongues to prophecy. There he also gave guidelines for the proper exercise of the gifts of tongues and interpretation.[13] Right in the middle of those two chapters—in 1 Corinthians 13—Paul discussed the proper motive for using the gifts—namely, love. Usually dealt with apart from its context, 1 Corinthians 13 has been called a hymn of love. It is undeniably a supreme literary achievement, and it deals profoundly and beautifully with the subject of genuine love. But it is helpful to remember that it is first of all a crucial point in Paul's discussion of the adulteration of tongues.

In 1 Corinthians 13:1–3 Paul affirms the preeminence of love. Verse 1 plainly states that miraculous languages without love are nothing. Paul was rebuking the Corinthians for using gifts of the Spirit selfishly and without love. They were more interested in inflating their own egos or in enjoying a euphoric experience than they were in serving one another with the self-sacrificing concern that characterizes *agapē* love.

"If I speak with the tongues of men and of angels . . ." is

how Paul begins the chapter. "Tongues" is from the Greek word *glōssa*, which, like our word *tongue*, can refer either to the physical organ or to a language. Paul is clearly referring to a gift of *languages*. Note that Paul had personally spoken in tongues (1 Cor. 14:18). He was not condemning the practice itself; he was saying that if the gift of tongues is used in any other way than God intended, it is only noise—like the rhythm band in a kindergarten class.

Are Tongues a Heavenly Language?

What did Paul mean by the "tongues of . . . angels?" Many believe Paul was suggesting that the gift of tongues involves some kind of angelic or heavenly language. Indeed, most charismatics believe that the gift of tongues is a private prayer language, a heavenly language known only to God, celestial speech, or some other kind of unearthly idiom. There is no warrant in the text itself for such a view, however. Paul was making a hypothetical case,[14] just as in the subsequent verses, where he speaks about knowing all mysteries and knowledge (even Paul could not literally make that claim), giving all his possessions to the poor, and giving his body to be burned. Paul was speaking theoretically, suggesting that even if those things *were* true, without love they would be meaningless. To make his point about the necessity for love, Paul was trying to stretch his examples to the outer limits.

Besides, there is no evidence in Scripture that angels use a heavenly language. Whenever angels appear in Scripture, they communicate in normal human language (e.g., Luke 1:11–20, 26–37; 2:8–14).

Nowhere does the Bible teach that the gift of tongues is anything other than human languages. Nor is there any suggestion that the true tongues described in 1 Corinthians 12–14 were materially different from the miraculous languages described in Acts 2 at Pentecost. The Greek word in both places is *glōssa*. In Acts it is clear that the disciples were speaking in *known* languages. Unbelieving Jews who were in Jerusalem at the time "were bewildered, because they were each one hearing them speak in his own language" (2:6). Luke went on to name some fifteen different countries and areas whose languages were being spoken (vv. 8–11).

Furthermore, the Greek word *dialektos*, from which we get the English word "dialect," is also used in reference to the languages in Acts 2:6, 8. Unbelievers present at Pentecost heard God's message proclaimed in their own local dialects. Such a description could not apply to ecstatic speech.

Many charismatics point out that the King James Version of 1 Corinthians 14 repeatedly uses the expression "an unknown tongue." That, they say, describes a language that is not of this world. The word *unknown*, however, was supplied by translators and does not appear in the Greek text.[15] That is why the King James Version shows the word in italics. Therefore, 1 Corinthians 13:1 cannot be used to prove that Paul is advocating meaningless, ecstatic speech or some kind of heavenly or angelic language.

Moreover, Paul insisted that when tongues were spoken in the church, someone should interpret (14:13, 27). Such a command would not be apropos if Paul had in mind the ecstatic babbling of a "private" prayer language or spontaneous celestial sounds. The Greek word for interpretation is *hermeneuō*, which means "translation." (It is so used in John 9:7 and Heb. 7:2.) The gift of interpretation was a supernatural ability to translate a language one had never learned so that others might be edified by the message (1 Cor. 14:5). You cannot translate ecstatic speech or gibberish.

Still another indication that Paul had in mind human languages is his statement in 1 Corinthians 14:21–22 that tongues were given as a sign to unbelieving Israel: "In the Law it is written, 'By men of strange tongues and by the lips of strangers I will speak to this people, and even so they will not listen to Me,' says the Lord." Paul was referring to Isaiah 28:11–12, a prophecy telling the nation of Israel that God would speak his revelation in Gentile languages. That was a rebuke to Israel in their unbelief. In order to be a meaningful sign, these must have been Gentile foreign languages, not some kind of angelic speech.

Counterfeit Tongues

Clearly, true biblical tongues are not gibberish, but languages. What passes for tongues in the Pentecostal and charismatic movements, however, are not true languages. Modern tongues-speaking, often called *glossolalia*, is not the same thing as the biblical gift of languages. William Samarin, professor of linguistics at the University of Toronto, wrote:

> Over a period of five years I have taken part in meetings in Italy, Holland, Jamaica, Canada, and the United States. I have observed old-fashioned Pentecostals and neo-Pentecostals; I have been in small meetings at private homes as well as in mammoth public meetings; I have seen such different cultural settings as are found among the Puerto Ricans of the Bronx, the snake handlers of the Appalachians [and] Russian Molakans in Los Angeles. . . . Glossolalia is indeed like language in some ways, but this is only because the speaker (unconsciously) wants it to be like language. Yet in spite of superficial similarities, glossolalia is fundamentally *not* language.[16]

William Samarin is one of many men who have made studies of glossolalia. The studies all agree that what we are hearing today is not language; and if it is not language, then it is not the biblical gift of tongues.

As we have seen (chapter 7), the mystery religions in and around Corinth in the first century made wide use of ecstatic speech and trancelike experiences. It seems some of the Corinthians had corrupted the gift of tongues by using the ecstatic counterfeit. What they were doing was very similar to modern-day glossolalia. Paul was trying to correct them by telling them that such practices circumvented the whole point of the gift of tongues. If they used tongues that way, they would do harm and not good for the cause of Christ.

The Abuse of Tongues at Corinth

Note that in 1 Corinthians 14:2 Paul was *criticizing* the Corinthians for using their "gift of tongues" to speak to God and not to men: "One who speaks in a tongue does not speak to men, but to God; for no one understands, but in his spirit he speaks mysteries."[17] Paul's comment is not suggesting that tongues should be used as a "prayer language"; he was using irony, pointing out the futility of speaking in tongues without an interpreter, because only God would know if anything was said. Spiritual gifts were never intended to be used for God's benefit, or for the benefit of the gifted individual. Peter made that clear in 1 Peter 4:10: "As each one has received a special gift, employ it in serving one another."

Paul further added in 1 Corinthians 14:4, "One who speaks in a tongue edifies himself, but one who prophesies edifies the church." Again, Paul was not commending the use of tongues for self-edification, but condemning people who were using the gift in violation of its purpose and in disregard of the principle of love ("[Love] does not seek its own."—1 Cor. 13:5). The word "edify" in 14:4 means "to build up." It might carry either a positive or a negative connotation, depending on the context.[18] The Corinthians were using tongues to build themselves up in a selfish sense. Their motives were not wholesome but egocentric. Their passion for tongues grew out of a desire to exercise the most spectacular, showy gifts in front of other believers. Paul's point was that no one profits from such an exhibition except the person speaking in tongues—and the chief value he gets out of it is the building of his own ego. In 1 Corinthians 10:24 Paul had already made clear this principle: "Let no one seek his own good, but that of his neighbor."

Tongues posed another problem: used as they were in Corinth, they obscured rather than clarified the message they were intended to convey. In 1 Corinthians 14:16–17, Paul wrote, "If you bless in the spirit only, how will the one who fills the place of the ungifted say the 'Amen' at your giving of thanks, since he does not know what you are saying? For you are giving thanks well enough, but the other man is not edified." In other words, the tongues-speakers in Corinth were being selfish, ignoring the rest of the people in the congregation, muddying the message the gift was designed to communicate, and doing it all just to gratify their own egos, to show off, and to demonstrate their spirituality to one another.

In light of all that, we might wonder about Paul's apparent command in 1 Corinthians 12:31: "But earnestly desire the greater gifts." The way that verse is usually translated presents some serious interpretive problems. Since Paul stresses God's sovereignty in distributing the gifts, and he writes to castigate the Corinthians for favoring the showy gifts, why would he command them to seek "the greater" gifts? Wouldn't that just encourage them to continue competing for status?

But in fact the verse is not actually a command at all. The English translation is misleading as to Paul's meaning. The verb form used here can be either indicative (a statement of fact) or imperative (a command). The indicative form makes better sense. The *New International Version* offers the indicative as an alternate reading: "But you are eagerly desiring the greater gifts." Albert Barnes takes the indicative view, pointing out that many of his fellow commentators in the mid-nineteenth century (Doddridge, Locke, and Macknight) did likewise. Barnes observes that the Syriac New Testament renders the verse, "Because you are zealous of the best gifts, I will show to you a more excellent way."[19]

In other words, Paul was actually saying, "But you are jealously coveting the showy gifts." That is a rebuke, which makes better sense of Paul's next words: "I show you a still more excellent way." He is not commanding them to seek certain gifts, but condemning them for seeking the showy ones. The "more excellent way" he speaks of is the way of love he then goes on to describe in 1 Corinthians 13.

The Corinthians were selfishly seeking the most prominent, most ostentatious, most celebrated gifts. They coveted others' admiration. They craved the applause of men. They desired to be seen as "spiritual." Evidently, people had even gone to the extreme of using counterfeit tongues. The abuse of tongues in Corinth was threatening that church.

Sadly, the very same problems are threatening the church today.

Tongues Will Cease

In 1 Corinthians 13:8 Paul made an interesting, almost startling, statement: "Love never fails; but if there are gifts of prophecy, they will be done away; if there are tongues, they will cease; if there is knowledge, it will be done away." In the expression "love never fails," the Greek word translated "fails" means "to decay" or "to be abolished." Paul was not saying that love is invincible or that it cannot be rejected. He was saying that love is eternal—that it will be applicable forever and will never be passé.

Tongues, however, "will cease." The Greek verb used In 1 Corinthians 13:8 (*pauō*) means "to cease permanently." It implies that when tongues ceased, they would never start up again.[20]

Here is the problem this passage poses for the contemporary charismatic movement: if tongues were supposed to cease, has that already happened, or is it yet future? Charismatic brothers in Christ insist that none of the gifts have ceased yet, so the cessation of tongues is yet future. Most non-charismatics insist that tongues have already ceased, passing away with the apostolic age.

Who is right?

I am convinced by history, theology, and the Bible that tongues ceased in the apostolic age. And when it happened, they terminated altogether. The contemporary charismatic movement does not represent a revival of biblical tongues. It is an aberration similar to the practice of counterfeit tongues at Corinth.

What evidence is there that tongues have ceased? First, tongues was a miraculous, revelatory gift, and as we have noted repeatedly, the age of miracles and revelation ended with the apostles. The last recorded miracles in the New Testament occurred around A.D. 58, with the healings on the island of Malta (Acts 28:7–10). From A.D. 58 to 96, when John finished the book of Revelation, no miracle is recorded. Miracle gifts like tongues and healing are mentioned only in 1 Corinthians, an early epistle. Two later epistles, Ephesians and Romans, both discuss gifts of the Spirit at length—but no mention is made of the miraculous gifts. By that time miracles were already looked on as something in the past (Heb. 2:3–4). Apostolic authority and the apostolic message needed no further confirmation. Before the first century ended, all the New Testament had been written and was circulating through the churches. The revelatory gifts had ceased to serve any purpose. And when the apostolic age ended with the death of the apostle John, the signs that identified the apostles had already become moot (cf. 2 Cor. 12:12).

Second, as we noted, tongues were intended as a sign to unbelieving Israel. They signified that God had begun a new work that encompassed the Gentiles. The Lord would now speak to all nations in all languages. The barriers were down. And so the gift of languages symbolized not only the curse of God on a disobedient nation, but also the blessing of God on the whole world.

Tongues were therefore a sign of transition between the Old and New Covenants. With the establishment of the church, a new day had dawned for the people of God. God would speak in all languages. But once the period of transition was past, the sign was no longer necessary. O. Palmer Robertson aptly articulated the consequence of that:

> Tongues served well to show that Christianity, though begun in the cradle of Judaism, was not to be distinctively Jewish. . . . Now that the transition [between Old and New Covenants] has been made, the sign of transition has no abiding value in the life of the church.
>
> Today there is no need for a sign to show that God is moving from the single nation of Israel to all the nations. That movement has become an accomplished fact. As in the case of the founding office of apostle, so the particularly transitional gift of tongues has fulfilled its function as covenantal sign for the Old and New Covenant people of God. Once having fulfilled that role, it has no further function among the people of God.[21]

Moreover, the gift of tongues was inferior to other gifts. It was given primarily as a sign (1 Cor. 14:22) and cannot edify the church in a proper way. It is also easily misused to edify self (14:4). The church meets for the edification of the body, not self-gratification or personal experience-seeking. Therefore, tongues had limited usefulness in the church, and so it was never intended to be a permanent gift.

History records that tongues did cease.[22] Again, it is significant that tongues are mentioned only in the earliest books of the New Testament. Paul wrote at least twelve epistles after 1 Corinthians and never mentioned tongues again. Peter never mentioned tongues; James never mentioned tongues; John never mentioned tongues; neither did Jude. Tongues appeared only briefly in Acts and 1 Corinthians as the new message of the gospel was being spread. But once the church was established, tongues were gone. They stopped. The later books of the New Testament do not mention tongues again. Nor did anyone in the post-apostolic age. Cleon Rogers wrote, "It is significant that the gift of tongues is nowhere alluded to, hinted at or even found in the Apostolic Fathers."[23]

Chrysostom and Augustine—the greatest theologians of the eastern and western churches—considered tongues obsolete. Chrysostom stated categorically that tongues had ceased by his time. Writing in the fourth century, he described tongues as an obscure practice, admitting that he was not even certain about the characteristics of the gift. "The obscurity is produced by our ignorance of the facts referred to and by their cessation, being such as then used to occur but now no longer take place," he wrote.[24]

Augustine wrote of tongues as a sign that was adapted to the apostolic age:

> In the earliest times, "the Holy Ghost fell upon them that believed: and they spake with tongues," which they had not learned, "as the Spirit gave them utterance." *These were signs adapted to the time.* For there behooved to be that betokening of the Holy Spirit in all tongues, to shew that the Gospel of God was to run through all tongues over the whole earth. *That thing was done for a betokening, and it passed away.* In the laying on of hands now, that persons may receive the Holy Ghost, do we look that they should speak·with tongues? [To this rhetorical question Augustine obviously anticipated a negative reply.] . . . If then the witness of the presence of the Holy Ghost be not now given through these miracles, by what is it given, by what does one get to know that he has received the Holy Ghost? Let him question his own heart. If he love his brother, the Spirit of God dwelleth in him.[25]

Augustine also wrote,

> How then, brethren, because he that is baptized in Christ, and believes on Him, does not now speak in the tongues of all nations, are we not to believe that he has received the Holy Ghost? God forbid that our heart should be tempted by this faithlessness. . . . Why is it that no man speaks in the

tongues of all nations? Because the Church itself now speaks in the tongues of all nations. Before, the Church was in one nation, where it spoke in the tongues of all. By speaking then in the tongues of all, it signified what was to come to pass; that by growing among the nations, it would speak in the tongues of all.[26]

During the first five hundred years of the church, the only people who claimed to have spoken in tongues were followers of Montanus, who was branded a heretic (see chapter 3).

The next time any significant tongues-speaking movement arose within Christianity was in the late seventeenth century. A group of militant Protestants in the Cevennes region of southern France began to prophesy, experience visions, and speak in tongues. The group, sometimes called the Cevennol prophets, are remembered for their political and military activities, not their spiritual legacy. Most of their prophecies went unfulfilled. They were rabidly anti-Catholic, and advocated the use of armed force against the Catholic church. Many of them were consequently persecuted and killed by Rome.

At the other end of the spectrum, the Jansenists, a group of Roman Catholic loyalists who opposed the Reformers' teaching on justification by faith, also claimed to be able to speak in tongues in the 1700s.

Another group that practiced a form of tongues was the Shakers, an American sect with Quaker roots that flourished in the mid-1700s. Mother Ann Lee, founder of the sect, regarded herself as the female equivalent of Jesus Christ. She claimed to be able to speak in seventy-two languages. The Shakers believed sexual intercourse was sinful, even within marriage. They spoke in tongues while dancing and singing in a trancelike state.

Then in the early nineteenth century, Scottish Presbyterian pastor Edward Irving and members of his congregation practiced speaking in tongues and prophesying. Irvingite prophets often contradicted each other, their prophecies failed to come to pass, and their meetings were characterized by wild excesses. The movement was further discredited when some of their prophets admitted to falsifying prophesies and others even attributed their "giftedness" to evil spirits. This group eventually became the Catholic Apostolic Church, which taught many false doctrines, embracing several Roman Catholic doctrines and creating twelve apostolic offices.

All of those supposed manifestations of tongues were identified with groups that were heretical, fanatical, or otherwise unorthodox. The judgment of biblically orthodox believers who were their contemporaries was that all those groups were aberrations. Surely - that should also be the assessment of any Christian who is concerned with truth. Thus we conclude that from the end of the apostolic era to the beginning of the twentieth century there were no genuine occurrences of the New Testament gift of tongues. They had ceased, as the Holy Spirit said they would (1 Cor. 13:8).

New Testament scholar Thomas R. Edgar makes this observation:

> Since these gifts and signs did cease, the burden of proof is entirely on the charismatics to prove their validity. Too long Christians have assumed that the noncharismatic must produce incontestable biblical evidence that the miraculous sign gifts did cease. However, noncharismatics have no burden to prove this, since it has already been proved by history. It is an irrefutable fact admitted by many Pentecostals. Therefore the charismatics must prove biblically that the sign gifts will start up again during the Church Age and that today's phenomena are this reoccurrence. In other words they must prove that their experiences are the reoccurrence of gifts that have not occurred for almost 1,900 years.[27]

A Final Outpouring?

Has the gift of tongues resumed in the twentieth century? Pentecostals and charismatics treat that question in one of two ways. Some claim that the gift never ceased—it just declined—and therefore the groups who claimed to speak in tongues were forerunners of those contemporary Pentecostal and charismatic movements.[28] In taking that position they put themselves in a heretical tradition.

On the other hand, many charismatics concede that tongues *did* cease after the apostolic era, but they believe the contemporary manifestations of the charismata are a final outpouring of the Spirit and his gifts for the last days.

A key text for Pentecostals and charismatics who take this second view is Joel 2:28: "It will come about after this that I will pour out My Spirit on all mankind; and your sons and daughters will prophesy and your old men will dream dreams, your young men will see visions."

According to Joel 2:19–32, before the final Day of the Lord, God's Spirit will be poured out in such a way that there will be wonders in the sky, and on the earth—blood, fire, and columns of smoke: "The sun will be turned into darkness, and the moon into blood, before the great and awesome day of the Lord comes" (v. 31). That is obviously a prophecy of the coming millennial kingdom and cannot refer to anything earlier. The context of the Joel passage makes this the only plausible interpretation.

For example, Joel 2:20 refers to the defeat of "the northern army" that will attack Israel in the end-time apocalypse. Verse 27 of Joel 2 speaks of the great revival that will bring Israel back to God. That is another feature of the Great Tribulation and is not yet fulfilled. Joel 3 (vv. 2, 12, 14) describes the judgment of the nations, an event that comes after Armageddon and in connection with the establishment of the earthly, millennial kingdom of the Lord Jesus Christ. Later in chapter 3, Joel gives a beautiful description of the millennial kingdom (v. 18). Clearly, Joel 2 is a kingdom prophecy, which was not completely fulfilled at Pentecost (Acts 2) or on any occasion since. It must refer to an era that is still future.

There is still, however, the question of what Peter meant when he quoted Joel 2:28–32 on the day of Pentecost (Acts 2:17–21). Some Bible teachers say that Peter was pointing to Pentecost as a fulfillment of Joel 2:28. But on the day of Pentecost there were no wonders in the heavens and signs in the earth; no blood and fire and vapors of smoke; the sun did not turn to darkness and the moon to blood and the great and terrible day of the Lord did not come. The prophecy was not fully realized; Pentecost was only a partial fulfillment, or better, a preview of the prophecy's ultimate culmination. The parallel to that is the Transfiguration, in which our Lord's glory was briefly revealed as it will be seen fully throughout the millennial kingdom.

Peter was simply telling those present at Pentecost that they were getting a preliminary glimpse, a projection of the kind of power that the Spirit would release in the millennial kingdom. What they were seeing in Jerusalem among a handful of people was a sign of what God's Spirit would someday do on a worldwide basis.

One of the fine Bible scholars of the nineteenth century, George N. H. Peters, wrote, "The Baptism of Pentecost is a *pledge* of fulfillment in the future, *evidencing* what the Holy Ghost will *yet perform* in the coming age."[29] The miracles that began on the day of Pentecost are light on the horizon, heralding the coming earthly kingdom of Jesus Christ.

Some charismatics spiritualize "the former rain and the latter rain" of Joel 2:23 (KJV). They argue that the former rain refers to Pentecost, when the Spirit came, and the latter rain to his outpouring in the twentieth century.

Throughout the Old Testament, "the former rain" refers to the autumn rains and "the latter rain" to the spring rains. Joel was actually saying that in the millennial kingdom both rains will come "as before"[30] (v. 23). His point was that God will make crops grow profusely in the kingdom. Joel 2:24–26 makes that abundantly clear: "And the threshing floors will be full of grain, and the vats will overflow with the new wine and oil. Then I will make up to you for the years that the swarming locust has eaten, the creeping locust, the stripping locust, and the gnawing locust, My great army which I sent among you. And you shall have plenty to eat and be satisfied, and praise the name of the Lord your God, who has dealt wondrously with you; then My people will never be put to shame."

The "former and latter rain," then, have nothing to do with Pentecost, the twentieth century, or the Holy Spirit. Pentecostals and charismatics cannot use Joel 2:28 as a basis for saying tongues have been poured out a second time. In the first place, Joel did not even mention tongues. In the second place, the outpouring of the Spirit at Pentecost was not the ultimate fulfillment of Joel's prophecy.

Thomas Edgar makes this significant observation:

> There is no biblical evidence that there will be a reoccurrence in the church of the sign gifts or that believers will work miracles near the end of the Church age. However, there is ample evidence that near the end of the age there will be false prophets who perform miracles, prophesy, and cast out demons in Jesus' name (cf. Matt. 7:22–23; 24:11, 24; 2 Thess. 2:9–12).[31]

We do well to be on guard.

What Kind of Tongues Are Being Spoken Today?

How are we to explain the charismatic experience? Countless charismatics testify that speaking in tongues has enriched their lives. For example:

> "What's the *use* of speaking in tongues?" The only way I can
> answer that is to say, "What's the use of a bluebird? What is
> the use of a sunset?" Just sheer, unmitigated uplift, just joy
> unspeakable and with it health and peace and rest and
> release from burdens and tensions.[32]

And this:

> When I started praying in tongues I felt, and people told me
> I looked, twenty years younger. . . . I am built up, am given
> joy, courage, peace, the sense of God's presence; and I
> happen to be a weak personality who needs this.[33]

Those testimonies make a powerful sales pitch for speaking in
tongues. If tongues can give health and happiness and make
you look younger, the potential market is unlimited.

On the other hand, the evidence to support such claims
is dubious. Would anyone seriously argue that today's tongues-
speakers live holier, more consistent lives for Christ than
believers who do not speak in tongues? What about all the
charismatic leaders in recent years whose lives have proved to
be morally and spiritually bankrupt? And does the evidence
show that charismatic churches are, on the whole, spiritually
stronger and more solid than Bible-believing churches that do
not advocate the gifts? The truth is, one must look long and
diligently to find a charismatic fellowship where spiritual
growth and biblical understanding are genuinely the focus. If
the movement does not produce more spiritual Christians or
believers who are better informed theologically, what fruit is it
producing after all? And what of the many former tongues-
speakers who testify that they did *not* experience genuine
peace, satisfaction, power, and joy until they came out of the
tongues movement? Why does the charismatic experience so
often culminate in disillusionment as the emotional high from
initiatory ecstatic experiences becomes harder and harder to
duplicate?

Without question, many people who speak in tongues say

they find the practice beneficial to one degree or another. But normally—as in the testimonies cited above—they are speaking of how it makes them *feel* or *look*, not how it helps them be better Christians. Yet improved looks and feelings were never results of the New Testament gift.

It is significant to note that Pentecostals and charismatics cannot substantiate their claim that what they are doing is the biblical gift of tongues. We know of no authentic, proven cases where any Pentecostal or charismatic has actually spoken in an identifiable, translatable language.[34] The linguist William Samarin wrote, "It is extremely doubtful that the alleged cases of xenoglossia [real languages] among charismatics are real. Any time one attempts to verify them he finds that the stories have been greatly distorted or that the 'witnesses' turn out to be incompetent or unreliable from a linguistic point of view."[35] "Charismatic proponents have given no evidence, other than their assumption, that these are the same phenomena" as the New Testament gift.[36]

So how can the phenomenon be explained?

A number of possibilities arise. First, *tongues may be satanic or demonic.* Some critics of the movement want to write off all supposed tongues as the work of the devil. While I am not ready to do that, I am convinced that Satan is often the force behind phenomena that pass as gifts of the Spirit. After all, he is behind every false religion (1 Cor. 10:20), and he specializes in counterfeiting truth (2 Cor. 11:13–15). Many in the church these days are susceptible to his lies: "The Spirit explicitly says that in later times some will fall away from the faith, paying attention to deceitful spirits and doctrines of demons" (1 Tim. 4:1).

Former tongues-speaker Ben Byrd believes some of his extraordinary abilities were "psychic and possibly satanic powers":

Many, many times I have walked down ministry lines praying for people with my eyes closed while I prayed with tongues. I was able to function as if my eyes were open. I was aware of everything happening around me, BUT MY EYES WERE CLOSED. I felt as though I were in a strange, but very vivid dream state . . . almost asleep in my body, but very aware and alert in my mind. Functioning through another realm IS POSSIBLE. But PLEASE REMEMBER THAT ALL GIFTS ARE NOT FROM GOD.[37]

Ecstatic speech is common in false religions. Current editions of the *Encyclopedia Britannica* contain helpful articles on glossolalia among pagans in their worship rites. Reports have come from East Africa telling of persons possessed by demons who speak fluently in Swahili or English, although under normal circumstances they would not understand either language. Among the Thonga people of Africa, when a demon is exorcised, a song is usually sung in Zulu even though the Thonga people do not know Zulu. The one doing the exorcising is supposedly able to speak Zulu by a "miracle of tongues."

Today, ecstatic speech is found among Muslims, Eskimos, and Tibetan monks. A parapsychological laboratory at the University of Virginia Medical School reports incidents of tongues-speaking among those practicing the occult.[38]

Those are only a few examples of the centuries-old tradition of glossolalia that continues today among pagans, heretics, and worshipers of the occult. The possibility of satanic influence is a serious issue, and one which charismatics ought not brush aside without somber reflection.

Another possibility is that *tongues is a learned behavior.* Most contemporary glossolalia, I am convinced, falls into this category. As we have seen, charismatic leaders like Charles and Frances Hunter hold seminars to *instruct* people about how to receive the gift of tongues. How can that be viewed as anything other than learned behavior? The Hunters jump-start people emotionally by getting them to shout prayers and praise; they suggest sample syllables to prime the pump; and they encourage people to repeat "funny little sounds."[39] That's clearly *not* how a spontaneous gift operates. Nor is that kind of tongues-speaking by any stretch of the term a "supernatural" experience. It is not a miracle. It is something almost anyone can learn to do. It is striking that many of the different tongues-speakers use the same terms and sounds. They all speak essentially the same way. Anyone who hears it enough can do it.

In his book *The Psychology of Speaking in Tongues*, John Kildahl concluded after much study of the evidence that glossolalia is a learned skill.[40] Kildahl, a clinical psychologist, and his partner Paul Qualben, a psychiatrist, were commissioned by the American Lutheran Church and the National Institute of Mental Health to do a long-range study on tongues. After all their work, they came to the firm conviction that it was nothing more than a "learned phenomenon."[41]

A more recent study conducted at Carleton University, Ottawa, demonstrated that virtually anyone can learn to speak in tongues with minimum instruction and modeling. Sixty subjects who had never spoken in tongues or heard anyone else do it were used in an experiment. After two brief training sessions including audio- and videotaped samples of tongues speaking, all the subjects were asked to attempt to speak glossolalia for thirty seconds. Every subject in the test was able to speak passable glossolalia throughout the thirty-second test, and seventy percent were able to speak fluently.[42]

A man in our church who used to speak in tongues admitted to me, "I learned to do it. I'll show you." Then he started speaking in tongues. The sounds I heard coming from him were exactly like other tongues I had heard from others. Yet the claim is constantly made that each charismatic is supposed to receive his own "private" prayer language.

I overheard a zealous charismatic trying to teach a new believer to speak in tongues. It struck me as odd that this man felt he needed to labor so industriously to help this baby

Christian receive the gift of tongues. Why a person would have to *learn* how to receive a gift from the Holy Spirit is baffling. Nonetheless the charismatic movement is full of people who will gladly "teach" you how to speak in tongues.

While researching for this book, I was watching a charismatic talk show on television. One person confessed to having spiritual problems. Another charismatic said to him, "Have you used your tongue every day? Have you spoken in your language every day?"

"Well, no, I haven't," the person admitted.

To which the other one replied, "Well, that's your problem. You have to get into it every day, and it doesn't matter how it starts. Just get it started and once you get it started, the Holy Spirit will keep it going."

That conversation is revealing on several counts. For one, if the Holy Spirit has given someone the gift of tongues, why does that person have to make an effort to get it started?

Within the charismatic movement, there is great peer pressure to belong, to perform, to have the same gifts and power that everyone else has. The "answer" to spiritual problems is tongues. It is easy to see why tongues has become the great common denominator, the universal test of spirituality, orthodoxy, and maturity for charismatics. But it is a faulty test.

Kildahl and Qualben wrote,

> Our study produced conclusive evidence that the benefits reported by tongue-speakers which are subjectively real and continuous are dependent upon acceptance by the leader and other members of the group rather than upon the actual experience of saying the sounds. Whenever a tongue-speaker broke off the relationship with the leader of the group, or felt rejected by the group, the experience of glossolalia was no longer so subjectively meaningful.[43]

They also reported a widespread disillusionment among the subjects of their study. People who spoke in tongues realized instinctively that what they were doing was learned behavior. There was nothing supernatural about it. Soon they found themselves facing the same problems and hangups they had always had. According to Kildahl and Qualben, the more sincere a person was when starting to speak in tongues, the more disillusioned he could be when he stopped.

One more possibility has been suggested: *tongues can be psychologically induced.* Some of the strangest cases of tongues have been explained as psychological aberrations. The tongues-speaker goes into motor automatism, which is clinically described as radical inward detachment from one's conscious surroundings. Motor automatism results in disassociation of nearly all voluntary muscles from conscious control.

Have you ever watched a newscast that showed young teenage girls at a rock concert? In the excitement and the emotion, the fervor and the noise, they literally give up voluntary control of their vocal chords and their muscles. They fall to the floor in a paroxysm.

Most people, at one time or another, experience moments when they feel a little detached, a little woozy, and a little faint. Given the right set of conditions, particularly where there is a great deal of emotional fervor involved, a person can easily slip into a state where he or she is no longer consciously in control. In such a state, glossolalia can be the result.

The condition in which most people sense the euphoria of the tongues experience seems to be closely related to the hypnotic state. Kildahl and Qualben stated from their studies that "hypnotizability constitutes the *sine qua non* of the glossolalia experience. If one can be hypnotized, then one is able under proper conditions to speak in tongues."[44]

After extensive study of tongues-speakers, Kildahl and Qualben concluded that people who were submissive, suggestible, and dependent on a leader were those most likely to speak in tongues.[45] William Samarin agreed that "people of a certain type are *attracted* to the kind of religion that used tongues."[46] Obviously, not every tongues-speaker would fit into this category, but many if not most of them do. Watch almost any charismatic program on television. The people in the audiences nod and *amèn* everything that is said from the platform, even novel and bizarre teachings. They submit easily to the power of suggestion and do whatever is being suggested. When emotions get high and the pressure mounts, anything might happen.

There is no way to analyze each speaker in tongues and come up with a clear reason for his behavior. But as we saw, there are many possible explanations for the glossolalia among modern charismatics. Dr. E. Mansell Pattison, a member of the Christian Association for Psychological Studies, said:

> The product of our analysis is the demonstration of the very natural mechanisms which produce glossolalia. As a psychological phenomenon, glossolalia is easy to produce and readily understandable.
>
> . . . .
>
> I can add my own observations from clinical experiences with neurological and psychiatric patients. In certain types of brain disorders resulting from strokes, brain tumors, etc. the patient is left with disruptions in his automatic, physical speech circuit patterns. If we study these "aphasic" patients we can observe the same decomposition of speech that occurs in glossolalia. Similar decomposition of speech occurs in schizophrenic thought and speech patterns, which is structurally the same as glossolalia.
>
> This data can be understood to demonstrate that the same stereotypes of speech will result whenever conscious, willful control of speech is interfered with, whether by injury to the brain, by psychosis, or by passive renunciation of willful control.[47]

As we have seen, would-be tongues-speakers are often explicitly instructed to enter into "passive renunciation of willful control." They are told to release themselves, give up control of their voice. They are coached to say a few syllables, just to let them flow. They are not to think about what they are saying.

Charles Smith, the late dean of The Master's Seminary, offered an entire chapter of possible explanations for the modern tongues phenomenon. He suggested that tongues can be produced by "motor automatism," "ecstasy," "hypnosis," "psychic catharsis," "collective psyche," or "memory excitation."[48] The point is that tongues can have many explanations. One cannot escape the conclusion that tongues exist today in many counterfeit forms, apart from the Holy Spirit, just as they did in first-century Corinth.

But Why Are Tongues So Popular?

Christians from every denomination continue to speak in tongues and new people seek the experience every day. Charismatic teachers and writers claim this is the work of the Holy Spirit, that it is a sweeping new burst of power that has come upon the church in the last days.

How can that be? The tongues being spoken today are not biblical. Those who speak in tongues are not practicing the gift described in Scripture. Then why do so many pursue this practice with such fervor? Why do they seek to convince and intimidate others to start doing the same thing? A basic reason is spiritual hunger. People hear that tongues is a way to have a wonderful spiritual experience. They fear that if they have not spoken in tongues, they may be missing something. They want "something more."

Also, many people are hungry to express themselves spiritually. They have been coming to church for years, but they really have not been involved. They have not been recognized as particularly spiritual or holy; and because they hear that tongues-speakers are thought to be holy and spiritual, they try it.

Another basic reason for the growth of tongues is the

need for acceptance and security. People need to be in the "in group." They want to be among the ones who "have it," and they cringe at the thought of being among the have-nots who are on the outside looking in. It is very satisfying for some to be in the charismatic movement. It is a form of self-actualization to be able to say, "I am a charismatic." It makes many people feel like they are somebody, like they belong to something, like they have something others do not have.

Another explanation is that the charismatic movement is a reaction to the secularized, mechanized, academic, cold, indifferent society in which we live. The tongues-speaker feels like he or she is directly in touch with the supernatural. Here is something tangible that they can experience. This is not dry and academic. It feels real!

Probably the key reason tongues have exploded on the scene with such force is the need for an alternative to the cold, lifeless Christianity that permeates so many churches. People who join the charismatic movement often are those who are looking for action, excitement, warmth, and love. They want to believe that God is really at work in their lives—right here and now. Dead orthodoxy can never satisfy, and that is why many people look for satisfaction in the charismatic movement.

We can thank God for charismatic and Pentecostal people who believe in the Word of God. We can be grateful that they believe the Bible and hold it up as authoritative, though we are concerned about their view of revelation. We can also praise God that they believe in the deity of Jesus Christ, his sacrificial death, his physical resurrection, salvation by faith not works, and the need to live in obedience to Christ, fervently love their fellow man, and proclaim the faith with zeal.

Some might say, "Why criticize them?" We do so because it is scriptural to be concerned about whether our brothers and sisters are walking in the truth. Although it may not seem very loving to some, the Bible is clear that we are to "speak the truth in love" (Eph. 4:15). True love must act on the truth.

—— 11 ——

What Is True Spirituality?

"Be transformed by the renewing of your mind," Paul wrote in Romans 12:2. Many charismatics believe you can renew your mind and achieve holiness without any conscious effort. Sanctification, they believe, can come to you all at once through an experience, or effortlessly through subliminal conditioning.

My first exposure to the notion of subliminal spirituality came a few years ago when I received a flyer advertising "subliminal neckties." They were handsome paisley ties, quite normal-looking at a casual glance. "But," the ad copy informed prospective buyers, "hidden in the fabric—almost totally undetectable to the human eye, are the words—'JESUS SAVES JESUS SAVES.'" The ties, "made from anointed cloth" and offered by a charismatic enterprise, could be "yours for a tax-deductible love gift of $30.00." You could also buy seven "for a tax-deductible gift of $200 to help us feed the hungry."

"For years Russian and communist scientists have experimented with subliminal advertising—designed to influence unsuspecting consumers to their ideology and propaganda," the flyer said. "Now. . . the Lord has revealed to His people HOW to use it For His Glory!!!" A magnified picture of one of the ties revealed that, indeed, the words "JESUS SAVES JESUS SAVES JESUS SAVES JESUS SAVES JESUS SAVES" were woven throughout the fabric. "When worn," the leaflet promised, "the words 'JESUS SAVES' are actually being planted in the subconscious minds of everyone who sees it." In other words, you could do your witnessing without ever having to say a word to anyone!

At the time, that struck me as a bizarre, atypical oddity. In retrospect, I see that it was a harbinger of one of the latest fads in the charismatic movement. Subliminal messaging, despite its New Age and occult overtones, is quickly becoming a popular means of addressing spiritual, emotional, and health problems among charismatics. At the outset of this book, I mentioned the subliminal "Word Therapy" tapes offered by Rapha Ranch as a means of healing cancer patients. Rapha offers single cassette tapes for $14.95. Although that seems high, thousands of people desperately seeking cures for cancer have evidently been willing to pay the price. Linda Fehl explains how the tapes were born:

> In 1983 God healed me of breast cancer and called me to "Raise up a place where cancer victims can come and be healed." In obedience to that call our family of four moved to 70 acres of land in a small rural community in northwest Florida. There we began construction on the 5,000 square foot Rapha Ranch Lodge.
>
> After almost two years we received our first cancer patients and quickly realized our commission would not be an easy one. Over the next two years we learned much but continued to see the great majority of our guests die with cancer.
>
> . . . .
>
> We continuously cried out to God to show us how to get the Word in His precious people in their crisis situation.

Then one day we stumbled onto a television program describing how the subliminal process was helping masses of people using positive affirmations.

The idea came! Could the pure Word of God be used in a similar fashion? After two months of some research and much prayer we knew we had not only a creative idea but a mandate from God to produce a tool that would help heal the sick.

The Lord said that I was to be the voice since He could trust my Spirit and to use Christian musicians, engineers and studio to create this marvelous new tape.

In June 1988 the Word Therapy Healing tape was released and healing reports were immediate. Within two weeks a woman was healed of cancer.[1]

To those who might have fears that subliminal therapy is of the devil, Mrs. Fehl writes,

Your cautions are justified as you approach subliminal tapes, but be assured of this: There is no need to fear our tapes. They are holy and have the blessing of the Lord upon them.

We use no hypnosis, no relaxation techniques, no New Age or deceptive practices. Simply a modern technological method of multi-track duplication of the pure Word of God. Your first tape will convince you as the anointing will destroy the yoke. . . . If the Apostles were alive today, they would consider Word Therapy *a scroll of the 90's.*[2]

Several charismatic ministries offer subliminal tapes. One group, Renew Ministries, offers continuous-play tapes ($19.95 apiece, but you do not have to rewind) promising "freedom from: Doubt, Fear, Failure, Fear of Death, Guilt, Grief, Depression, Temper, Pride, Lust, Temptation, Pornography, Procrastination, Unforgiveness, Rejection, Drugs, Alcohol, Smoking, Anger, Rebellion, Anxiety and Panic, Judging, Homosexuality, Scars of Child Abuse & Molestation."[3] Other Renew tapes promise to "speak into being: Prosperity, Weight Loss, Peace, Healing, Self Esteem, Salvation, Marital Harmony, Surrender to God, Acceptance of God's Love, A Closer Walk With God!"⁴ According to Renew, "Bible-based subliminal messages hit controlling spirits where they live and command them to leave in Jesus' name. Then the void is filled with the *Word of God!*"⁵

What are the mechanics of such tapes? Renew puts multiple voices on different tracks simultaneously chanting a message aimed at indwelling demons. For example, one tape designed for people struggling with homosexuality includes this message: "I speak to you, spirits of homosexuality . . . I curse you and cast you down in the name of Jesus." That message is followed by Scripture verses relating to moral purity.⁶ Other companies use variations of that approach. Lifesource, an El Paso-based ministry, uses an audible track of ocean waves. Inaudible subliminal background tracks carry Scripture verses.⁷ Healing evangelist Vicki Jamison-Peterson, of Tulsa, Oklahoma, plays a reading of the entire King James Version New Testament at a rapid speed on a sixty-minute cassette. Her brochures promise that "positive suggestions (thoughts) are being stored in your belief system at the rate of 100,000 suggestions per hour."⁸

It is all so easy, so effortless. Supposedly you can absorb Scripture without even paying attention to it. Fervent prayer, diligent holiness, earnest devotion, careful study, and conscientious meditation are all rendered unnecessary by this approach. It used to be that losing weight required self-control and discipline. Now, we are told, a continuous-play tape can exorcise demons of fat and gluttony for you, and there is nothing to it. More important, it used to be that faith, spiritual understanding, and righteousness were pursued through disciplined lives of devotion and study. Now, proponents of subliminal therapy promise, holiness can happen to you while you sleep!

Subliminal sanctification and the charismatic movement fit each other perfectly. From the beginning, the charismatic movement has flourished primarily because it promises a shortcut to spiritual maturity. One of the greatest attractions of that movement has always been that it offers believers power, understanding, and spirituality immediately through an experience—without the time, pains, and struggles that are a natural part of any growth process.

But is there *really* a shortcut to sanctification? Can a believer receive subliminal messages, a divine jolt, or some other kind of quick power boost, and be instantly brought out of infancy and into maturity? Not according to Scripture.

The Zapped and the Unzapped

For the typical charismatic, the gateway to spirituality is through an experience, usually speaking in tongues. The term actually used by some charismatics is "zapped." It accurately describes the way most charismatics view sanctification. People in my congregation tell me that they have talked with charismatics about spirituality; and when they admitted they had never had an ecstatic experience, the charismatic person would say, "Well, may Jesus zap you."

Charismatic evangelist Norvel Hayes explained what happened when he got his zap: "God came on me so strong and started blessing me so much, I just fell on my knees and started crying and weeping and getting blessed. I found out God loves me and He was petting me because I obeyed the Holy Spirit."[9]

Unfortunately, the charismatic movement has divided Christianity into two levels of believers—the zapped and the unzapped. The zapped believe they are at least a bit more spiritual than the unzapped; and like it or not, the effect has been schismatic. Some of the unzapped wonder why they do not have the kind of experiences charismatics describe. Charismatics argue that unless you have had the baptism of the Spirit with tongues, you cannot function the way God really wants you to. You are missing something. You are an eight-cylinder engine firing on four, or possibly six at the most. You are just not quite there.

A good example of this viewpoint is in Melvin Hodges' book *Spiritual Gifts*:

> While the full manifestation of a person's gift and ministry must await the fullness of the Spirit, there may be a partial measure of spiritual ministry and incomplete manifestation of spiritual gifts or endowments before the culmination of the Pentecostal gift is experienced. . . . We must not lose sight of the fact that in the New Testament, the baptism in the Holy Spirit [by this, Hodges means a charismatic experience] is considered an essential and a primary requisite for a fully developed spiritual life and ministry.[10]

Are the charismatics correct? Is there a gap between Christians? Are there two levels—the zapped and the unzapped? Are non-charismatic Christians mired in a second-class Christianity? The unzapped will be glad to hear that the Scriptures allot them no such fate.

The Natural Man Versus the Spiritual Man

A foundational teaching on Christian spirituality is in 1 Corinthians 2:14–15: "A natural man does not accept the things of the Spirit of God; for they are foolishness to him, and he cannot understand them, because they are spiritually appraised. But he who is spiritual appraises all things, yet he himself is appraised by no man." Paul spent most of 1 Corinthians 2 discussing the difference between the natural (unregenerate) person and the spiritual (saved) person. The natural person does not know God; he is unsaved, isolated in his humanness. He cannot understand the things of the Spirit. In contrast, the spiritual person knows God and understands spiritual things.

According to 1 Corinthians 2, all Christians are spiritual—at least that is our position in Christ. All Christians are spiritual because they possess the Holy Spirit. To be "spiritual" simply means to possess the Holy Spirit, as Romans 8:6–9 clearly indicates.[11]

But while all Christians are spiritual *positionally*, they are not always spiritual *practically*. That is, we do not always *act* spiritual. That is why Paul wrote about spiritual babies in 1 Corinthians 3:1–3. Paul said that he should have been able to talk to the Corinthians as spiritual men, but they were not acting like spiritual men. They were not receiving the Word, and there was unholiness in their lives. They were behaving carnally, requiring him to deal with them as babes in Christ.

The Corinthians were not unique. All Christians face the same problem. All Christians are "spiritual" because they know Christ as Savior and have the Holy Spirit dwelling within, but all Christians do not always act spiritual. Sometimes we act in very carnal and natural ways.

A good illustration of that is the apostle Peter. In Matthew 16 Peter recognized Christ as the Son of the living God. Jesus immediately responded, "Blessed are you, Simon, and now I am going to change your name to Peter [the word meant "rock"]. You are going to be a new person, solid as a rock" (see 16:17–18). But in the twenty-first chapter of John, Jesus met Peter on the shore of the Sea of Galilee, following Peter's failure on the night before the crucifixion. There Jesus called him Simon, because Peter had been acting like his old self—like the man he was before he believed in Christ.

What Peter had done—and what all of us do from time to time—was temporarily cease following closely after Christ. Even after Pentecost, Peter continued to struggle occasionally with fleshly behavior. At one time even Paul had to rebuke him face to face (see Gal. 2:11–21).

Paul himself understood firsthand the Christian's unrelenting struggle with the flesh, and wrote movingly of it in Romans 6–7. The point is, spirituality is not a permanent state you enter into the moment you get "zapped" with some kind of spiritual experience. Spirituality is simply receiving the living Word daily from God, letting it dwell in you richly, and then living in obedience to it through a moment-by-moment walk in the Spirit. Paul said as much in Galatians 5:16: "Walk by the Spirit, and you will not carry out the desire of the flesh."

The word "walk" is a very important word in the New Testament. To walk speaks of moment-by-moment conduct. Paul taught the church to walk in accord with the Holy Spirit: "If we live by the Spirit, let us also walk by the Spirit" (Gal. 5:25). Walking speaks of a measured pace, taking one step at a time. That is, after all, how true spirituality functions: one step, one moment at a time.

Marks of True Spirituality

A basic mark of true spirituality is a deep awareness of sin. In Scripture those who most despised their sinfulness were often those who were the most spiritual. Paul said he was the chief of sinners (1 Tim. 1:15). Peter said, "Depart from me, for I am a sinful man, O Lord!" (Luke 5:8). Isaiah said, "Woe is me . . . because I am a man of unclean lips" (Isa. 6:5). Spiritual people realize they are in a death struggle with sin. Paul said that he died to himself daily (1 Cor. 15:31).

The ultimate objective of spirituality is to be like Christ. Paul emphasized that truth repeatedly (1 Cor. 11:1; Gal. 2:20; Eph. 4:13; Phil. 1:21). For Paul, ultimate spirituality was to be like Jesus; and that is not something you could attain by any one-time experience or through some subliminal technique. It is a constant, unremitting pursuit:

> Not that I have already obtained it, or have already become perfect, but I press on in order that I may lay hold of that for which also I was laid hold of by Christ Jesus. Brethren, I do not regard myself as having laid hold of it yet; but one thing I do: forgetting what lies behind and reaching forward to

what lies ahead, I press on toward the goal for the prize of the upward call of God in Christ Jesus (Phil. 3:12–14).

Many charismatics, however, insist that once you get the baptism of the Spirit, spirituality is yours. Unfortunately, it does not work that way. When the glow of one experience fades, they are forced to find another, and then another. They find that a second work of grace is not enough; they need a third, a fourth, a fifth, and so on. In their effort to seek something more, charismatics often unwittingly abandon the Bible and the true path of spirituality to run errantly down the road of experience to its inevitable dead end.

Gifts Do Not Guarantee Spirituality

Charismatic books, pamphlets, and articles are filled with testimonies of how a certain special experience brought a new degree of spirituality. The testimonies usually follow the same general pattern: "When I was baptized by the Spirit, when I spoke in tongues—then I began to live a more holy life. I had more power and freedom and joy than ever before. I had more love, more fulfillment as a Christian."

Although charismatics are not consistent on the point, most strongly emphasize the gift of tongues as a means of obtaining spirituality. Scripture, however, does not support that idea. For example in 1 Corinthians 1:7 Paul commended the church at Corinth by saying, "You are not lacking in any gift." The Corinthians had all the spiritual gifts: prophecy, knowledge, miracles, healing, tongues, interpretation of tongues, and more. They also had just about every spiritual problem possible. They were spiritual in a positional sense, but their actions had thrown the church into carnal chaos.

The Corinthian believers of the first century were not unique. Christians today face similar problems. We are saved and have the Holy Spirit. We have certain spiritual gifts, but we also still struggle with the flesh (see Rom. 7). No spiritual gift can guarantee that we will win the struggle once and for all in this life. The only way we can win is by consistently walking in the Spirit and not fulfilling the lusts of the flesh (Gal. 5:16).

Any discerning charismatic will admit that he or she has just as much trouble with the appetites of the flesh as the rest of us. Enthusiasm, euphoria, fervor, excitement, and emotion—all the things charismatics tend to equate with spiritual intensity—have no power to restrain lust, pride, selfishness, or greed. Charismatics whose only strength is drawn from the high of their latest experience are in fact more likely to be spiritually weak and immature. The history of the movement proves this is so.[12] The trap too many fall into is believing that their charismatic experience solves the struggle with the flesh. It does not. To compound the difficulty, when they stumble, charismatics are unlikely to take the responsibility for the failure. They will blame demonic power rather than reexamine their theology of sanctification.

With all their claims of new power and a new level of spirituality, the charismatics have absolutely no guarantee that any of their ecstatic experiences will put them in a new and lasting spiritual state. No matter what kind of experience they think they have had, no matter how often they speak in tongues or get slain in the Spirit, they still face the same challenge given to every Christian: the need to walk by the Spirit in obedience to the Word and die to self and sin daily.

Charismatic testimonies and teaching rarely are honest on that point. And because of that, charismatics often foster a strong escapist mentality. How many people join the movement because they have been promised an easy answer to problems or a quick and easy path to godliness?

Sanctification or Superficiality?

Yet much of what goes on in the charismatic movement is more giddy than godly. The Christian television station in my area features a live talk and variety program every night of the week. The program is broadcast nationwide and features some of the biggest names in the charismatic movement. Turn it on almost any night of the week and you will see the same thing. The emphasis is almost totally on amusement and frivolity. There is a lot of laughing and breathless gushing. The time is normally filled with entertainment, buffoonery, silliness, and shallow talk. The expensive, lavish clothing, thick makeup, behavior, and talk of most of the women who appear clearly violate every possible interpretation of 1 Peter 3:3–6 and 1 Timothy 2:9–10. Frankly, I am embarrassed to know that many unbelievers get their idea of Christianity from people like that. And I am not talking about unknowns or fringe charismatics; these are people at the forefront of the movement's visible leadership.

There is nothing wrong with being happy; there is nothing wrong with praising God and feeling fulfilled. Unfortunately, however, many in the charismatic movement seem so determined to pursue the emotional high, the quick thrill, the exciting event, the electrifying moment, the exhilarating conference—that they have given up the rich rewards of a consistent walk with God in favor of the superficial gaiety of a public spectacle.

But gaiety is no substitute for godliness. And real godliness does not always carry with it an emotional high. According to Scripture, the Spirit-filled person pursues righteousness with a burning sense of conviction and with a deep awareness of his or her own sin. Where the Spirit is at work, there is deep joy; but there is also profound sorrow. As Walter Chantry has aptly written,

> When the Holy Spirit comes to sinful men, he initially brings sorrow. But in [charismatic] circles . . . there is only the boast of rapid transport to joy and peace. Any religious experiences which bring immediate rejoicing and uninterrupted cheerfulness are not to be trusted. There is much

more to spirituality than a lifting of the spirits, an entering into the exuberant life, and an extending one's succession of thrilling experiences. Yet in many of the popular neo-pentecostal societies you will look in vain for anything else.

. . . .

No one who has God's Spirit can walk through our world without deep groanings of sorrow and distress. When the stench of immorality fills his nostrils, the Spirit-filled man cannot be happy, happy, happy, all the day. . . . If the Spirit were to come powerfully [today] it would not be to make men clap their hands for joy but to make them smite their breasts in sorrow.[13]

Chantry adds, "He is not the 'Jolly Spirit' but the Holy Spirit."[14]

Charismatics usually give the impression that the Spirit is more jolly than holy. If anyone protests all the hoopla, the shouting, the giddiness, the silliness, the flippancy, and the false promises—he is looked upon askance. Meanwhile the self-indulgence and immoderation gets louder, gaudier, flashier, and more eccentric. That trend is not the fruit of genuine godliness.

Paul Versus the Superapostles

One of the most unfortunate characteristics of the charismatic movement is a continual emphasis on the astonishing, dramatic, sensational events that are supposed to be part of the charismatic's everyday experience. The effect is to intimidate anyone who is not getting these same kinds of results—the tongues, the prophecies, the spiritual pyrotechnics, the miraculously filled fuel tanks, the audible instructions from God, and so on. Those who are getting less spectacular results (or who perhaps are in a dry spell where no results seem to come) feel relegated to second-class status.

The apostle Paul knew what it was like to be scorned and

intimidated by people who felt they had attained a higher level than he. In the last four chapters of 2 Corinthians, Paul discussed the new superapostles in Corinth who had come to town and taken over while he was gone. The new teachers loved to extol themselves. They claimed that their powers, experiences, and ecstasies had swept the Corinthian believers off their feet. It got back to Paul that his spirituality was now in question. He simply did not measure up to the new superstars who had taken his place.

How did Paul answer that? Read 2 Corinthians 11–12. Paul didn't rattle off a list of healings or other miracles he had performed. Instead, he presented what might be called his spiritual "rap sheet." Five times he had received thirty-nine lashes; three times he had been beaten with rods; once he had been stoned and left for dead; three times he had been shipwrecked; he had spent a night and a day in the open sea.

Paul had been through it all. He had gone hungry and sleepless and had been in danger from robbers, Gentiles, and even his own countrymen. He had been run out of town more times than he could remember. His thorn in the flesh (which God would not take away although Paul had asked him to on three different occasions) was a severe torture for him to endure. And what did Paul have to say about all that?

> Therefore I am well content with weaknesses, with insults, with distresses, with persecutions, with difficulties, for Christ's sake; for when I am weak, then I am strong. I have become foolish; you yourselves compelled me. Actually I should have been commended by you, for in no respect was I inferior to the most eminent apostles, even though I am a nobody (2 Cor. 12:10–11).

It seems doubtful that Paul would have made a good impression on many charismatic television shows. Instead of being slain in the Spirit, he was almost slain in the body time and time again. Paul could not even remember his visions very well. In 2 Corinthians 12:1–4 he mentioned being caught up to the third heaven some fourteen years before. But he could not seem to remember the fine details. Instead of emphasizing his miraculous trip to the third heaven and back, Paul preferred to talk about his weaknesses and how they gave glory to God.

The kind of true spirituality Paul talked about would not do much on current Christian bestseller charts. According to Paul, his life was weak and wretched and desperate and humble. He was in a constant state of trouble, perplexity, persecution, and even imprisonment from the time he came to Christ until he was beheaded by a Roman executioner (2 Cor. 4:8–11). The same is true of the other apostles, who also knew something about suffering and true spirituality— notably Peter, James, and John.

Nowhere in Scripture can you find even a hint that there is an escape from the realities and struggles and difficulties of the Christian life. Speaking in tongues will not result in true spirituality; it may, however, lead you down the wrong road from where true spirituality lies. The right road to true spirituality is the one marked "Walk by the Spirit."

What Does It Mean To Be Filled with the Holy Spirit?

As we have seen, the Bible gives no command to experience a "baptism of the Spirit." The Christian is baptized with the Holy Spirit into the body of Christ at the moment of belief (1 Cor. 12:13; Rom. 8:9). There are seven references in the New Testament to the baptism with the Spirit. It is significant that those references are all in the indicative mood. Not one of them is a command.

But Scripture is full of commands about how to live the Christian life. The Christian's marching orders are found primarily in the epistles, particularly those written by Paul. In Ephesians 4:1 the apostle entreated us "to walk in a manner worthy of the calling with which you have been called." In

Ephesians 5:18 he told us how to achieve that worthy walk: by being filled with the Spirit.

Paul began with an exhortation: "Do not get drunk with wine, for that is dissipation." We're to avoid anything that leads to excess, degeneration, wastefulness, or a lack of self-control.

After Paul gave his contrasting command, "Be filled with the Spirit," he spent the next several paragraphs of his letter explaining what being filled is all about. There is no mention of getting high with wild, ecstatic religious experiences. Instead, being filled involves submitting to one another, loving one another, obeying one another, seeking the best for one another.

When Paul said, "Be filled with the Spirit," he used terms that speak of being continuously filled. Paul was not giving an option or suggestion. His choice of words was framed as a command. We are to be continuously filled with the Spirit. What did Paul mean? Was he demanding that we achieve some kind of superspiritual state from which we never stray? Was he suggesting that we be perfect?

Paul never said, "Be baptized in the Spirit." He was not championing a second work of grace. What Paul was talking about is a continual, daily filling. You can be filled today, but tomorrow is another story. That is why the whole concept of a "second blessing" is inadequate. When the "second blessing" wears off, the charismatic believer is left wrestling with the same basic problems faced by all Christians. Although he is saved, he still exists in a human body that has a strong propensity towards sin. As the Israelites gathered manna daily, the Christian must be kept filled by the Spirit daily.

You Are Not Filled Up, but Through

It is important to get the precise meaning of the word "filled" as Paul used it. When we think of filling, we usually picture a container into which something is poured or shoveled until it is full. That is not what Paul had in mind here. Paul was not speaking of being filled *up*; he had in mind the idea of being filled *through*, or permeated by the Holy Spirit's influence.

We often speak of people being "filled" with anger or "filled" with joy. We mean they are totally under the control of those things. That is what Paul had in mind; we are to be utterly controlled by the Holy Spirit.

Scripture often uses the word "filled" in that sense. For example, when Jesus told his disciples he was going to have to leave them, they were "filled" with sorrow (John 16:6). Sorrow dominated and consumed them at that moment. In Luke 5, Jesus healed a man with the palsy and all the people were amazed. They were "filled with fear" (v. 26). Most of us have been filled with fear. Fear is an emotion you do not share with other feelings. When you're afraid, there is only fear, period! In Luke's sixth chapter, Jesus argued with the Pharisees about their legalism and then healed a man with a withered hand on the Sabbath. The result was that the Pharisees were "filled with madness," and they started planning what they could do to Jesus to destroy him (6:11). In other words, the Pharisees were furious! When you are full of madness, or fury, or rage, those things can consume you. That is why anger can be so dangerous. It is possible for one's sense of reason to be utterly blinded by such passions.

The word *filled*, then, is used in Scripture of those who are totally controlled by an emotion or influence. Scripture means exactly the same thing when it talks about being filled with the Holy Spirit. We see that in Acts 4:31: "When they had prayed the place where they had gathered together was shaken, and they were all filled with the Holy Spirit, and began to speak the word of God with boldness."

Obviously, a lot of believers are *not* filled with the Spirit. Moreover, a lot of charismatics who claim to have had the experience show no evidence of being filled, or controlled, by the Spirit. They choose not to let the Holy Spirit permeate their lives. They get preoccupied with themselves, with others, or with things. They succumb to pride, self-centeredness, anger, depression, and many other things that bring spiritual emptiness.

How To Be Filled with the Spirit

The first step in being filled with the Spirit is to yield to the Spirit in our daily walk. According to Ephesians 4:30 a Christian can "grieve" the Spirit of God. First Thessalonians 5:19 says likewise that we can "quench" the Spirit. If it is possible to grieve and quench the Spirit, it is equally possible to treat the Spirit with respect—to yield and allow him to work in our lives. We do that by surrendering our wills, our minds, our bodies, our time, our talents, our treasures—every single area—to the control of the Holy Spirit.

This is a purposeful act; a commitment to yield to the Spirit in every area of life. As temptations come, we refuse to yield. Every time sin beckons, we turn away. Every time something comes to distract us from the Spirit of God's influence, we put it aside. We do not seek amusements or diversions or friends that distract us from the things of God. And when we fail, we confess and forsake our sin. Then as the Spirit of God stays in control, we experience his filling, his joy, and his power. That is the abundant life (John 10:10).

If you live that kind of life, it will show, because Spirit-filled persons bear the fruit of righteousness in their lives.

What Happens When You Are Filled?

Nothing in Scripture teaches that the filling of the Spirit is accompanied by ecstatic experiences or external signs. To be sure, being filled with the Spirit does bring the believer tremendous exhilaration and joy, but the New Testament epistles reveal that being filled with the Spirit brings forth the fruit of the Spirit, not the gifts of the Spirit.

Ephesians 5:19–6:9 gives a list of specifics: A Spirit-filled person sings psalms, hymns, and spiritual songs, making melody in his or her heart to the Lord. A Spirit-filled person always gives thanks for all things in the name of Christ. Spirit-filled Christians are subject to one another, they listen to one another, and bow to one another's authority. Spirit-filled wives submit to their husbands, and Spirit-filled husbands love their wives as Christ loves the church. Spirit-filled children honor and obey their parents, and Spirit-filled parents bring up their children in the discipline and instruction of the Lord without exasperating them in the process. A Spirit-filled employee obeys his or her employer and does good work. And the Spirit-filled employer is fair and understanding with employees. Those are all manifestations of the Spirit-filled life.

A parallel passage, Colossians 3:16–22, ascribes the blessed manifestations of being filled with the Spirit to letting "the Word of Christ richly dwell within you" (3:16). Since being filled with the Spirit and letting the Word of Christ dwell within both produce the same results, a Spirit-filled Christian is one in whom the Word of Christ dwells. A Spirit-filled Christian is a Christ-conscious Christian. A Spirit-filled Christian is consumed with learning everything he or she can about Jesus and obeying everything that Jesus said. That is what it means to "let the word of Christ richly dwell within you." To be filled with the Spirit is to be totally and richly involved in all there is to know about Jesus Christ.

Peter—A Pattern for Being Filled

A perfect example of how this works is the apostle Peter. Peter loved to be near Jesus. He didn't want to be away from his Lord for a moment. And when Peter was near Jesus, he said and did amazing things. In Matthew 16 Jesus asked his disciples who he was, and Peter answered, "You are the Christ, the Son of the living God" (v. 16). Jesus told Peter he did not think of that by himself; the Father in heaven told him that (v. 17).

In Matthew 14 we find the disciples in their boat in rough seas. They saw Jesus walking on the water toward them. Peter wanted to be sure it was Jesus so he said, "Lord, if it is really You, command me to come to You on the water" (v. 28). Jesus said, "Come," and Peter stepped right out on the water. Once outside the boat, Peter had second thoughts and started to sink; but Jesus held him up. Whenever Jesus was near, Peter could do amazing things.

Another example is the account of the arrest of Jesus in the Garden of Gethsemane. A band of armed men came to arrest Jesus, but Peter showed no fear. In fact, he rashly whipped out his sword and slashed off the ear of Malchus, the high priest's servant. Jesus reproved Peter for being violent and healed Malchus's ear on the spot. While what Peter did was wrong, it does show that when he was with Jesus, he felt invincible.

But what happened just a few hours later? Jesus was on trial, and Peter was no longer in his presence. Three times he was asked whether he knew Jesus. Three times he denied his Lord completely. The crucifixion hours must have been particularly hard for Peter as he watched his beloved Master going through the agonies of the cross.

But Jesus rose from the dead, and a few weeks later he ascended into heaven. Now what would Peter do? The Lord was not just a few feet or miles away; he was completely gone into heaven. In the second chapter of Acts we get our answer. Peter stood before a hostile crowd in downtown Jerusalem and preached a mighty sermon that convinced many to turn to Jesus Christ. Soon he would be used to heal a lame man and speak with great boldness before the angry Sanhedrin. What was the difference? Peter had received the Holy Spirit and had been filled by him. When Peter was filled with the Spirit of God, he had the same abilities, the same boldness and power that he had when he was in Jesus' bodily presence.

To be filled with the Spirit means to live every moment as if we were standing in the presence of Jesus Christ. It means practicing Christ-consciousness. How do we do that? Well, for one thing, when we are conscious of someone, we communicate. The same is true if we practice Christ-consciousness. We should start our day by saying, "Good morning, Lord, this is your day and I just want you to keep reminding me all day that you are right beside me."

When we are tempted, we should talk to the Lord. When we have decisions to make, we should ask the Lord to show us the way. Our minds and hearts cannot be filled with an awareness of Jesus and sinful thoughts at the same time. Jesus and sin do not occupy the same place at the same time. One or the other will be squeezed out. When we fail to remember Christ's presence, our sinful flesh has the upper hand. As we remember his presence and are conscious that he is with us, we are filled with his Spirit.

How Can You Know You Are Filled?

How can you really know you are filled with the Spirit? Here are some questions to ask yourself:

Do I sing? According to Scripture, you will share psalms, hymns, and spiritual songs as you let the Word of Christ dwell in you richly (Col. 3:16). That suggests that daily Bible reading and communion with the Lord are not fads or legalistic regimens but natural aspects to being Spirit-filled.

Am I thankful? Scripture teaches us to give thanks always (Eph. 5:20; 1 Thess. 5:18). What characterizes your life: complaints or thanksgiving? It is true that there is much to complain about in this fallen world. We all have problems, irritations, frustrations, and crises. But we have so much to be thankful for! Are you thankful for God's presence? For salvation in Christ? For victory over death? For victory in daily living? For health? Family? Friends? The list is practically endless. Never forget to count your blessings.

Am I getting along with my spouse, children, friends, co-workers, and neighbors? Go down the line on what Paul taught in Ephesians 5:21–6:9. Can you submit to others? Can you follow as well as lead? If you are a wife, are you submitting to your husband's leadership? If you are a husband, are you loving your wife sacrificially, emulating Christ's love for his church?

Am I being a trustworthy and obedient employee? Can you be counted on to do a day's work for a day's pay? If you are an employer, are you being fair and just? Are you seeking the good of your employees rather than simply trying to come out ahead on the bottom line of the profit sheet?

Is there unconfessed sin in my life? One sure sign of being filled with the Spirit is a sense of sinfulness. Peter told Jesus, "Depart from me; for I am a sinful man, O Lord" (Luke 5:8). The closer you are to the Lord, the more you will be aware of your sin and your need of him. Whenever you become aware of sin in your life, immediately confess it and turn from it. Is there anything you are harboring or grasping? Is there any material thing that you want more than you want the filling of the Spirit?

Am I living some kind of lie? Am I self-centered? Am I failing to pray, read the Bible, or share the gospel of Christ? Whatever is wanting in your life, you can turn it over to Christ and let the Holy Spirit take control right now. Simply tell the Lord you want to be totally under his influence. Then discipline yourself to be obedient to his Word.

Yielding to the Spirit and being filled by him brings different reactions in different people. Some find it exhilarating, joyous, as if a load has been lifted. Others may find that nothing spectacular seems to happen emotionally, but they feel a peace and a satisfaction that can come no other way. Whatever your reaction might be, the Scriptures make it plain that a "divine zap" is not the long-range answer.

Being truly spiritual is simply being true to Christ and yielding to him day by day and moment by moment, consistently, steadily, over time. It doesn't all come at once; rather it comes in painfully small amounts, a bit at a time. But no matter how it comes, there are no shortcuts to spirituality. There is no easy way, no single spiritual "zap" that does the job.

It is a process of renewing the mind (Rom. 12:2), and there is no subliminal tape or effortless method that can accomplish that for you. You must study to show yourself approved (2 Tim. 2:15). You must be diligent and steadfast, and "bear fruit with perseverance" (Luke 8:15). Peter outlined the constant and demanding process of spiritual growth:

> Applying all diligence, in your faith supply moral excellence, and in your moral excellence, knowledge; and in your knowledge, self-control, and in your self-control, perseverance, and in your perseverance, godliness; and in your godliness, brotherly kindness, and in your brotherly kindness, love. For if these qualities are yours and are increasing, they render you neither useless nor unfruitful in the true knowledge of our Lord Jesus Christ (2 Peter 1:5–8).

Never try to trade that for a quick fix.

Aesop told of a dog who was crossing a bridge with a bone in his mouth. He looked over the edge and saw his reflection in the clear stream. The bone in the water looked better than the one in his mouth; so he gave up the reality for the reflection. My great fear is that there are many Christians who, with great zeal but lacking knowledge, are doing the very same thing.

Does God Promise
Health and Wealth?

One of the most unusual legacies of World War II has been the cargo cults of the South Pacific. Many aboriginal island peoples ranging from north Australia to Indonesia were first exposed to modern civilization through the Allied armed forces during the war. The American military in particular often used the remote islands that dot that part of the globe as sites for temporary landing strips and supply depots.

White men came bearing cargo; then they left as quickly as they had come. The tribal peoples had no time to learn the ways of civilization. But for a brief time they saw high technology up close. Cargo planes would swoop from the sky, land, leave their payload, then take off. Island natives saw cigarette lighters produce fire instantly and believed it to be miraculous. They saw large machinery push aside whole forests to build airstrips. They saw for the first time jeeps, modern weaponry, refrigerators, radios, power tools, and many varieties of food. They were fascinated by all of that and many concluded that the white men must be gods. When the war was over and the armies were gone, tribesmen built shrines to the cargo gods. Their tabernacles were perfect replicas of cargo planes, control towers, and airplane hangars—all made of bamboo and woven material. These structures all looked exactly like the real thing, but they were nonfunctional except for their use as temples to the cargo gods.

On some of the more remote islands, the cargo cults still thrive today. Some have personified all Americans in one deity they call Tom Navy. They pray for holy cargo from every airplane that flies over. They venerate religious relics—such as Zippo lighters, cameras, eyeglasses, ballpoint pens, nuts and bolts, and so on. As civilization has begun to penetrate some of these cultures, their fascination for cargo has not diminished. Missionaries who have been sent to areas where cargo cults have flourished receive a warm reception at first; the cargo cultists view their arrival as a sort of second coming. But the cultists are looking for cargo, not the gospel, and missionaries have found it very difficult to penetrate the materialism that is the very essence of the islanders' religion.

In recent years the charismatic movement has spawned its own variety of cargo cult. The Word Faith movement, known otherwise as the Faith movement—or Word, Faith-Formula, Word of Faith, Hyper-Faith, Positive Confession, Name It and Claim It, or Health, Wealth, and Prosperity teaching—is a subdivision of the charismatic movement that is every bit as superstitious and materialistic as the cargo cults in the South Pacific. The leaders of the Word Faith movement, including Kenneth Hagin, Kenneth and Gloria Copeland, Robert Tilton, Fred Price, and Charles Capps, promise each believer financial prosperity and perfect health. Anything less, they argue, is not God's will.

False and True Religion

Virtually every false religion ever spawned by man worships a god whose function is to deliver some sort of cargo. That is, human religions invent gods for utilitarian reasons;

the deities exist to serve men, rather than the other way around. Word Faith theology has turned Christianity into a system no different from the lowest human religions—a form of voodoo where God can be coerced, cajoled, manipulated, controlled, and exploited for the Christian's own ends.

I received a mailing sent out by one rather extreme Word Faith teacher named David Epley. A brochure was included with "a bar of prayer-blessed soap." "We are going to WASH away all BAD LUCK, SICKNESS, MISFORTUNES and EVIL! Yes, even that evil person you want out of your life! Jesus helped a man wash blindness from his eyes. I want to help you concerning Hexs [sic], Vexs [sic], Home Problems, Love, Happiness and Joy!" the brochure said. Inside were testimonies from people who had been blessed by that ministry: "Door opens to NEW JOB!"; "An $80,000 dollar dream comes true!"; "Couldn't use my hand for 12 years!" Also inside was a "personal" letter from Epley, closing with a full page of instructions on how to use the soap for healing or a "money miracle": "Now, after you wash the poverty from your hands . . . take out the largest bill or check you have . . . that $100, $50, or $20 bill. . . . Hold it in your clean hands and say, 'In Jesus' Name I dedicate this gift to God's work . . . and expect a miracle return of money.'" Of course, your "largest bill or check" must be sent to Epley's organization.

The last paragraph in the letter said,

> Through this Gift of Discernment I see someone sending a $25.00 offering and God is showing me a large check coming to them in the next short while. I *mean* LARGE . . . it looks like over a $1000 dollars. I know this sounds strange but you know me well enough to know I have to obey God when He speaks.
>
> I'll be here waiting for your answer.

That sounds more like black magic than faith. It is certainly a more outrageous example than most. Still, it reflects a *style* that is typical of nearly all Word Faith ministries. If it were merely hucksterism, that would be bad enough. But Word Faith teachers have corrupted the heart of New Testament Christianity, moving the believer's focus off sound doctrine, worship, service, sacrifice, and ministry; shifting it instead to promised physical, financial, and material "blessings." Those blessings are the cargo that God is expected to deliver to those who know and follow the Word Faith formulas.

Word Faith writings carry titles like "How to Write Your Own Ticket with God,"[1] "Godliness Is Profitable,"[2] "The Laws of Prosperity,"[3] "God's Creative Power Will Work for You,"[4] "Releasing the Ability of God Through Prayer,"[5] "God's Formula for Success and Prosperity,"[6] "God's Master Key to Prosperity,"[7] and "Living in Divine Prosperity."[8]

In Word Faith religion, the believer uses God, whereas the truth of biblical Christianity is just the opposite: God uses the believer. Word Faith theology sees the Holy Spirit as a power to be put to use for whatever the believer wills. The Bible teaches, however, that the Holy Spirit is a *Person* who enables the believer to do *God's* will.[9] Many Word Faith teachers claim that Jesus was born again so that we might become little gods. Scripture, however, teaches that Jesus is God, and it is *we* who must be born again.

I have little tolerance for the deceptions, corruptions of Scripture, and false claims of the Word Faith movement. The movement closely resembles some of the destructive greed sects that ravaged the early church. Paul and the other apostles were not accommodating to or conciliatory with the false teachers who propagated such ideas. Rather, they identified them as dangerous false teachers and urged Christians to avoid them. Paul warned Timothy, for example, about

> men of depraved mind and deprived of the truth, *who suppose that godliness is a means of gain.* . . . But those who want to get rich fall into temptation and a snare and many foolish and harmful desires which plunge men into ruin and

destruction. For the love of money is a root of all sorts of evil, and some by longing for it have wandered away from the faith, and pierced themselves with many a pang. But flee from these things, you man of God; and pursue righteousness, godliness, faith, love, perseverance and gentleness (1 Tim. 6:5, 9–11, emphasis added).

Jude wrote of the greed-mongers,

Woe to them! For they have gone the way of Cain, and *for pay* they have rushed headlong into the error of Balaam, and perished in the rebellion of Korah. These men are those who are hidden reefs in your love feasts when they feast with you without fear, caring for themselves; clouds without water, carried along by winds; autumn trees without fruit, doubly dead, uprooted; wild waves of the sea, casting up their own shame like foam; wandering stars, for whom the black darkness has been reserved forever. These are grumblers, finding fault, following after their own lusts; they speak arrogantly, flattering people for the sake of gaining an advantage (Jude 11–16, emphasis added).

Peter wrote,

But false prophets also arose among the people, just as there will also be false teachers among you, who will secretly introduce destructive heresies, even denying the Master who bought them, bringing swift destruction upon themselves. And many will follow their sensuality, and because of them the way of the truth will be maligned; and *in their greed they will exploit you with false words*; their judgment from long ago is not idle, and their destruction is not asleep. For speaking out arrogant words of vanity *they entice by fleshly desires, by sensuality*, those who barely escape from the ones who live in error, promising them freedom while they themselves are slaves of corruption; for by what a man is overcome, by this he is enslaved (2 Peter 2:1–19, emphasis added).

Paul said covetousness is idolatry (Eph. 5:5) and forbade the Ephesians to be partakers with anyone who brought a message of immorality or covetousness (vv. 6–7).

How closely do modern Word Faith teachers resemble the greedy false teachers the apostles decried? Is it fair to write the movement off as sub-Christian or heretical?

I hesitate to label the Word Faith movement a cult only because its boundaries are as yet somewhat hazy. Many sincere believers hover around the periphery of Word Faith teaching, and some in the movement who adhere to the core of Word Faith teaching reject some of the most extreme teachings of the group. Nevertheless, all the elements that are common to the cults exist within the movement: a distorted Christology, an exalted view of man, a theology based on human works, a belief that new revelation from within the group is unlocking "secrets" that have been hidden from the church for years, extrabiblical human writings that are deemed inspired and authoritative,[10] the use and abuse of evangelical terminology, and an exclusivity that compels adherents to shun any criticism of the movement or teaching that is contrary to the system. Without some exacting corrections in the movement's doctrinal foundations, the movement is well on its way to being established as a false cult in every sense of the term. It is, I am convinced, the closest thing on earth to the greed cults of the New Testament era, which the apostles bluntly labeled heresy.

I realize that is a grave verdict, but abundant evidence bears it out. At almost every crucial point, the Word Faith movement has tainted, twisted, garbled, misunderstood, corrupted, or obliterated the crucial doctrines of our faith.

As I noted in this book's introduction, I will quote frequently from Word Faith teachers' tapes and television broadcasts as well as from the published literature of the movement. Because their own words are so incriminating, I expect that some of these men will want to distance themselves from what they have said. Most of them desperately need support from mainstream evangelicals to keep their programs on the air. Consequently, some will do whatever damage control is necessary to sidestep critical or biblical analysis of their doctrine. Even though most of these men have assured people that their teachings are infallible truth revealed to them personally by God, and even though they have been teaching these things consistently and clearly for many years, don't be surprised if some of them respond now by claiming they have been misunderstood, or that they have modified their views since making the statements I quote in this chapter.

But don't be misled by shallow disclaimers or shrewd maneuvering. The only trustworthy evidence that these preachers have really embraced historic biblical Christianity will be when they publicly renounce the heresies they have been teaching for so long and actually begin preaching sound biblical doctrine.

The Wrong God

The god of the Word Faith movement is not the God of the Bible. Word Faith teaching, in effect, sets the individual believer above God and relegates God to the role of a genie, or Santa Claus, or a valet who is at the Christian's beck and call. Word Faith believers are their own supreme authority. As we will note, disciples in this movement are explicitly taught and encouraged to act like little gods.

Word Faith teaching has no concept of God's sovereignty. Scripture says, "The Lord has established His throne in the heavens; and His sovereignty rules over all" (Ps. 103:19). God is "the blessed and *only* Sovereign, the King of kings and Lord of lords" (1 Tim. 6:15). Yet in the volumes of Word Faith material I have read, I have not found one reference to the sovereignty of God. The reason is clear: Word Faith teachers do not believe God is sovereign. Jesus, according to Word

Faith theology, has no authority on earth, having delegated it all to the church.[11]

Furthermore, Word Faith theology teaches that God is bound by spiritual laws that govern health and prosperity. If we say the right words, or believe without wavering, God is forced to respond in whatever way we determine. Robert Tilton claims that God is already committed to his part of a covenant relationship with us. We can make whatever commitment or promise to him we want, "then we can tell God on the authority of his word what we would like him to do. That's right! You can actually tell God what you would like his part in the covenant to be!"[12]

In the Word Faith system God is not Lord of all; he is not able to work until we release him to do so. He is dependent on human instruments, human faith, and above all human words to get his work done. "It is in your power to release the ability of God," Charles Capps has written.[13] On the other hand, according to Capps, "Fear activates the devil."[14] If you succumb to fear—even doubting a little—

> You've moved God out of it. . . . *You have stopped God's ability immediately.* Maybe it was just about to come into manifestation, but now you have established satan's word in the earth—that it's not getting any better, it's getting worse. *YOU have established his word.*[15]

According to Capps, God has turned over his sovereignty— including his creative authority—to people. Capps has written:

> In August of 1973, the Word of the Lord came unto me saying, "If men would believe me, long prayers are not necessary. Just speaking the Word will bring you what you desire. My creative power is given to man in Word form. I have ceased for a time from my work and have given man the book of MY CREATIVE POWER. That power is STILL IN MY WORD.

"For it to be effective, man must speak it in faith. Jesus spoke it when He was on earth and as it worked then so it shall work now. *But it must be spoken by the body.* Man must rise up and have dominion over the power of evil by my Words. It is my greatest desire that my people create a better life by the spoken Word. For my Word has not lost its power just because it has been spoken once. It is still equally as powerful today as when I said, 'Let there be light.'

"But for my Word to be effective, *men must speak it,* and that creative power will come forth performing that which is spoken in faith."[16]

Why pray at all if our words have so much creative force? Indeed, some Word Faith teachers come dangerously close to explicitly denying the need to seek any help from God through prayer. Norvel Hayes says it is better to talk to your checkbook, your disease, or whatever predicament you are in than to turn to God in prayer:

You aren't supposed to talk to Jesus about it. You're supposed to talk directly to the mountain in Jesus' name— whatever the mountain is in your life.

. . . Stop talking to Jesus about it. Stop talking to anybody else about it. Speak to the mountain itself in Jesus' name!

Don't say, "Oh, God, help me. Remove this sickness from me." Say, "Flu, I am not going to let you come into my body. Go from me in the name of Jesus! Nose, I tell you to stop running. Cough, I tell you to leave in Jesus' name." Say, "Cancer, you can't kill me. I will never die of cancer in Jesus' name."

Do you have a financial mountain in your life? Start talking to your money. Tell your checkbook to line up with God's Word. Talk to your business. Command customers to come into your business and spend their money there. Talk to the mountain![17]

Hayes also teaches that believers can exercise dominion over their guardian angels. "Since Angels are ministering spirits sent to minister to and for us Christians," he reasons, we can learn "how to put them into action on our behalf."[18] "We believers ought to be keeping those angelic creatures busy!" Hayes writes. "We ought to have them working for us all the time."[19]

And so Word Faith theology denies God's sovereignty, removes the need to pray to God for any relief from burdens or needs, and gives the Christian himself both dominion and creative power.

Indeed, by far the most controversial teaching of the Word Faith movement is their notion that God created mankind to be a race of "little gods." Kenneth Copeland has explicitly stated what many Word Faith teachers more subtly imply:

> He imparted in you when you were born again—Peter said it just as plain, he said, "We are partakers of the divine nature." That nature is life eternal in absolute perfection. And that was imparted, injected into your spirit man, and you have that imparted into you by God just the same as you imparted into your child the nature of humanity. That child wasn't born a whale! [It was] born a human. Isn't that true?
>
> Well, now, you don't *have* a human, do you? You *are* one. You don't *have* a god in you. You *are* one.[20]

Copeland teaches that Adam was "created in the god class," that is, he was a reproduction of God. "He was not *subordinate* to God, even. . . . [Adam] was walking as a god. . . . What he said, went. What he did, counted. [And when he] bowed his knee to Satan and put Satan up above him, then there wasn't anything God could do about it, because a *god* had placed [Satan] there."[21] Adam, remember, was "created in the god class, but when he committed high treason, he fell below the god class."[22]

On the cross, according to Copeland, Jesus won the right

for believers to be born again back into the "god class." Jesus' deity, according to Copeland, encompasses "healing . . . deliverance . . . financial prosperity, mental prosperity, physical prosperity, [and] family prosperity."[23] Because believers are in the "god class," they are guaranteed those blessings here and now:

> He said He'd meet my needs according to His riches in glory by Christ Jesus, and I'm walking around and saying, "Yes! My needs are met according to His riches in glory by Christ Jesus! Glory to God! . . . I'm covenanting to the need meeter. I'm covenanting to the I AM!" Hallelujah.
>
> And I say this with all respect, so that it don't upset you too bad. But I say it anyway: When I read in the Bible where He says, "I Am," I just smile and say, "Yes, I Am, too."[24]

That is so blasphemous it ought to make every true child of God cringe. Yet it is typical of Word Faith teaching. In the face of criticism for some of his statements about the deity of the believer, Copeland appeared with Paul and Jan Crouch on the Trinity Broadcasting Network's nationwide program "Praise the Lord" to defend and explain his teaching. The following conversation ensued:

> PC: [God] doesn't even draw a distinction between Himself and us.
>
> KC: Never, Never! You never can do that in a covenant relationship.
>
> PC: Do you know what else that has settled, then, tonight? This hue and cry and controversy that has been spawned by the devil to try and bring dissension within the body of Christ that we are gods. I *am* a little god!
>
> KC: Yes! Yes!
>
> JC: Absolutely! (giggling) He gave us His name.
>
> KC: The *reason* we are—
>
> PC: I have His name. I'm one with Him. I'm in covenant relations—I *am* a little god! Critics, be gone!

> KC: You are anything that He is.
>
> PC: Yes.[25]

Paul Crouch, head and on-air host of Trinity Broadcasting Network and therefore one of the most powerful and influential people in religious broadcasting today, has reaffirmed repeatedly his commitment to the "little gods" doctrine of the Word Faith:

> That new creation that comes into new birth is created in His image. . . . It is joined, then, with Jesus Christ. Is that correct? And so in that sense—I saw this many years ago—whatever that union is that unites Father, Son, and Holy Spirit, He says, "Father, I want them to be one with Me even as You and I are one in Us." So apparently, what He does, He opens up that union of the very godhead, and brings us into it![26]

Other Word Faith teachers have reiterated the heresy. Charles Capps writes, "I have heard people say, 'Those who confess God's Word and say the promises of God over and over are just trying to act like God!' Yes! That's exactly what we're trying to do: *Act as God would in a similar situation*. . . . What did He do? *He spoke the thing desired*."[27] Earl Paulk wrote, "Until we comprehend that we are little gods and we begin to act like little gods, we cannot manifest the kingdom of God."[28] Robert Tilton also calls the believer "a God kind of creature . . . designed to be as a god in this world . . . designed or created by God to be the god of this world."[29] And Morris Cerullo had this televised conversation with Dwight Thompson:

> MC: See, when God created us in His image, He didn't put any strings on us, did He? He didn't make us puppets.
>
> DT: No, not at all.
>
> MC: He didn't say—He didn't say, Morris, raise your hand. Raise your—You know, and then here we are, we have no absolute—no control over us, so—
>
> DT: No. No. No.

MC: He made Dwight Thompson, He made Morris Cerullo a *small, miniature god.* Of course! The Bible says we are created in the image of God. His likeness. Where is that godlikeness? He gave us power . . . He gave us authority, He gave us dominion. He didn't tell us to act like a man! He told us to act like a *god!*[30]

Benny Hinn adds, "The new creation is created after God in righteousness and true holiness. The new man is after God, like God, godlike, complete in Christ Jesus. The new creation is just like God. May I say it like this: 'You are a little god on earth running around'?"[31] Hinn responded to criticism of such teaching this way:

> Now are you ready for some *real* revelation knowledge? OK. Now watch this: He laid aside His divine form . . . so one day I would be clothed on earth with the divine form.
>
> Kenneth Hagin has a teaching. A lot of people have problems with it. Yet it is absolute truth. Kenneth Copeland has a teaching. Many Christians have put holes in it, but it's divine truth. Hagin and Copeland say: You are god. Ye are gods.
>
> "Oh! I can't be god." Hold it. Let's bring balance to this teaching. The balance is being taught by Hagin. It's those that repeat him that mess it up. The balance is being taught by Copeland, who is my dear friend, but it's those that repeat what he says that are messing it up.
>
> You see there brother? When Jesus was on earth, the Bible says that first He disrobed Himself of the divine form. He, the limitless God, became a man, that we men, may become as He is.[32]

Hagin, whom most major Word Faith teachers acknowledge as a major influence in shaping their theology, has said, "If we ever wake up and realize who we are, we'll start doing the work that we're supposed to do. Because the church hasn't realized yet that they are Christ. That's who they are. They are Christ."[33]

Thus have the Word Faith teachers deposed God and put the believer in his place. From that basic error nearly all their other fallacies flow. Why do they teach that health and prosperity are every Christian's divine right? Because in their system, Christians are gods, deserving of those things. Why do they teach that a believer's words have creative and determinative force? Because in their system, the believer is sovereign, not God.

They have bought Satan's original lie: "The serpent said to the woman, 'You surely shall not die! For God knows that in the day you eat from it your eyes will be opened, and you *will be like God*, knowing good and evil'" (Gen. 3:4–5, emphasis added). The idea that any created being can be like God is and always has been a satanic lie. In fact, it was the very lie that brought the devil himself down (cf. Isa. 14:14).

Two proof texts are often used by the Word Faith teachers as support for their teaching. In Psalm 82:6, God says to the rulers of earth, "You are gods, and all of you are sons of the Most High." A simple reading of the psalm, however, reveals that those words were spoken to unrighteous rulers on the verge of their judgment. God was deriding them for their haughtiness. It was *they* who thought they were gods. Read verses 6 and 7 together: "You are gods . . . nevertheless you will die like men." There was a clear note of irony in God's condemnation of them. Far from affirming their godhood, he was condemning them for thinking too highly of themselves!

Word Faith teachers will immediately turn to their other favorite proof text, where Jesus himself quoted Psalm 82 in defense of his deity: "The Jews answered Him, 'For a good work we do not stone You, but for blasphemy; and because You, being a man, make Yourself out to be God.' Jesus answered them, 'Has it not been written in your Law, "I said, you are gods"?'" (John 10:33–34). But do not fail to notice Jesus' purpose for choosing that verse. It would have been a familiar one to the scribes and Pharisees, who understood its meaning as a condemnation of evil rulers. Jesus was echoing the irony of the original psalm. Walter Martin wrote,

> Jesus mocks the people as if to say, "You all think you're gods yourselves. What's one more god among you?" Irony is used to provoke us, not to inform us. It is not a basis for building a theology.
>
> It is also pertinent to an understanding of John 10 that we remember that Satan is called "the ruler of this world" by no less an authority than the Lord Jesus Christ (John 14:30, NASB). And Paul reinforces this by calling him "the god of this age" (2 Corinthians 4:4). We can make a "god" out of anything—money, power, status, position, sex, patriotism, family, or, as in Lucifer's case, an angel. We can be our own "god." But to *call* something deity or to worship it or treat it as divine is quite another thing than its being by nature and in essence deity.[34]

God said to the rebellious Israelites, "You turn things around! Shall the potter be considered as equal with the clay?" (Isa. 29:16). According to the Word Faith movement, the answer is yes. But according to Scripture, there is only one God, and beside him there is no other (Deut. 5:35, 39; 32:39; 2 Sam. 7:22; Isa. 43:10; 44:6; 45:5–6, 21–22; 1 Cor. 8:4).

The Wrong Jesus

It should come as no surprise that the Jesus of the Word Faith movement is not the Jesus of the New Testament. Word Faith teachers say Jesus gave up his deity and even took on Satan's nature in order to die for our sins. Kenneth Copeland, defending his infamous "prophecy" that seemed to call doubt on the deity of Christ (see chapter 2), wrote, "Why didn't Jesus openly proclaim Himself as God during His 33 years on earth? For one single reason. He hadn't come to earth as God, He'd come as man."[35]

The Word Faith Jesus often sounds like nothing more than a divinely empowered man:

> [Most Christians] mistakenly believe that Jesus was able to work wonders, to perform miracles, and to live above sin because He had divine power that we don't have. Thus, they've never really aspired to live like He lived.
>
> They don't realize that when Jesus came to earth, He voluntarily gave up that advantage, living His life here not as God, but as a man. He had no innate supernatural powers. He had no ability to perform miracles until after He was anointed by the Holy Spirit as recorded in Luke 3:22. He ministered as a man anointed by the Holy Spirit.[36]

Evidently it matters little to Copeland's system whether Jesus was God or man:

> The Spirit of God spoke to me, and He said, "Son, realize this."
>
> (Now follow me in this. Don't let your tradition trip you up.)
>
> He said, "Think this way: A twice-born man whipped Satan in his own domain."
>
> And I threw my Bible and I sat up like that. I said, "What?"
>
> He said, "A born-again man defeated Satan. The first-born of many brethren defeated him." He said, "You are the very image and the very copy of that one."
>
> I said, "Good-ness gracious sakes alive!" I began to see what had gone on in there. And I said, "Well, now You don't mean—You couldn't *dare* mean that I could've done the same thing."
>
> He said, "Oh yeah! If you'd known that—had the knowledge of the Word of God that he did, you could've done the same thing. Because you're a reborn man, too." He said, "The same power that I used to raise him from the dead, I used to raise you from your death in trespasses and sins." He said, "I had to have that copy and that pattern to

establish judgment on Satan so that I could recreate a child
and a family and a whole new race of mankind." And he
said, "You are in his likeness."[37]

That utterance is glaringly blasphemous.[38] It is astonishing to
me that anyone with the barest knowledge of biblical truth
could accept it as true revelation. But judging from the
response to Copeland's ministry, hundreds of thousands do.

The atonement of Christ—his sacrificial death on the
cross—was the primary work our Lord came to earth to
accomplish. The atonement is a major emphasis of the New
Testament and is central to all that we believe and teach as
Christians. Yet the Word Faith movement's teachings about
the work of Christ are aberrant to the point of blasphemy.
Copeland says,

> Jesus was the first man to ever be borned [sic] from sin to
> righteousness. He was the pattern of a new race of men to
> come. Glory to God! And you know what he did? The very
> first thing that this reborn man did—See, you have to
> realize that he died. You have to realize that he went into
> the pit of hell as a mortal man made sin. But he didn't stay
> there, thank God. He was reborn in the pit of hell.
>
> . . . .
>
> The righteousness of God was made to be sin. He
> accepted the sin nature of Satan in his own spirit, and at the
> moment that he did so, he cried, "My God! My God! Why
> hast Thou forsaken me?"
>
> You don't know what happened at the cross. Why do you
> think Moses, upon the instruction of God, raised a serpent
> up on that pole instead of a lamb? That used to *bug* me. I
> said, "Why in the world have you got to put that snake up
> there—the sign of Satan. Why didn't you put a lamb on
> that pole?"
>
> The Lord said, "Because it *was* the sign of Satan that was
> hanging on the cross." He said, "I accepted in my own spirit
> spiritual death, and the light was turned off."[39]

Later in that same message Copeland adds:

> The spirit of Jesus accepting that sin, and making it to be
> sin, he separated from his God, and in that moment, he's a
> mortal man. Capable of failure. Capable of death. Not only
> that, he's fixing to be ushered into the Jaws of hell. And if
> Satan is capable of overpowering him there, he'll win the
> universe, and mankind is doomed. Don't get the idea that
> Jesus was incapable of failure, because if he had been, it
> would have been illegal.[40]

Illegal? Copeland has embraced a heresy known as the
Ransom theory of the atonement. It is the view that Christ's
death was a ransom paid to Satan to settle the legal claim the
devil had on the human race because of Adam's sin. That
view contradicts the clear biblical teaching that Christ's death
was a sacrifice offered to God, not to Satan (Eph. 5:2).

Moreover, Copeland and the Word Faith teachers move
outside of orthodoxy with their teaching that Christ actually
died spiritually. We sometimes refer to Christ's separation
from the Father on the cross (cf. Matt. 27:46) as spiritual
death. It is error to teach, however, that Christ's spirit ceased
to exist ("the light was turned off"), or that the Trinity was
somehow broken up ("he separated from his God, and in that
moment, he's a mortal man"). Nor was Jesus dragged into hell
by Satan and tormented for three days and three nights, as
Fred Price wrote in a newsletter:

> Do you think that the punishment for our sin was to die on a
> cross? If that were the case, the two thieves could have paid
> your price. No, the punishment was to go into hell itself and
> to serve time in hell separated from God. . . . Satan and all
> the demons of hell thought that they had him bound, and
> they threw a net over Jesus, and they dragged Him down to
> the very pit of hell itself to serve our sentence.[41]

Could a *zillion* thieves on the cross have paid the price of our
sin? Of course not. Jesus' deity and his sinlessness qualified

him alone to be our Great High Priest (Heb. 4:14–15) and perfect sacrifice ("You were not redeemed with perishable things like silver or gold from your futile way of life inherited from your forefathers, but with precious blood, as of a lamb unblemished and spotless, the blood of Christ. For He was foreknown before the foundation of the world, but has appeared in these last times for the sake of you" [1 Peter 1:18–20]). Depreciating the death of Christ is serious error indeed.

Nevertheless, Copeland boldly preaches an aberrant view similar to Price's:

> Jesus had to go through that same spiritual death in order to pay the price—Now it wasn't the physical death on the cross that paid the price for sins, because if it had've been, any prophet of God that had died for the last couple of thousand years before that could've paid that price. It wasn't the physical death. Anybody could do that.[42]

Worse, Copeland teaches that Jesus made himself "obedient to Satan . . . [and took] on his nature."[43] Copeland continues, "He allowed the devil to drag Him into the depths of hell as if He were the most wicked sinner who ever lived. He submitted Himself to death. He allowed Himself to come under Satan's control. . . . For three days in the belly of the earth, He suffered as if He'd sinned every sin that exists."[44]

Once again, Kenneth Hagin's influence is behind all these teachings. Hagin says,

> Jesus tasted death—*spiritual* death—for every man. See, sin is more than a physical act, it's a spiritual act. And so, He became what we were, that we might become what He is. Praise God. And so therefore, His spirit was separated from God.
>
> . . . .
>
> Why did He need to be begotten, or born? Because He became like we were: separated from God. Because He tasted spiritual death for every man. And His spirit and

inner man went to hell. In my place. Can't you see that?
Physical death wouldn't remove your sins. "He's tasted
death for every man"—He's talking about tasting spiritual
death.

Jesus is the first person that was ever born again. Why did
His spirit need to be born again? Because it was estranged
from God.[45]

And so the Word Faith movement has concocted a theology
that makes sinners gods and requires the sinless Son of God to
be born again. Moreover, it sees Satan as the righteous judge
who exacts payment for sin from Christ. Such teaching is
convoluted and totally unbiblical. It demeans our Lord and
his work. Jesus does not merely *have* eternal life, nor did He
buy it for us by paying off the devil. He *is* eternal life. As He
said in John 14:6, "I am the way, and the truth, and the life"
(cf. John 1:4; 5:26; 11:25). Although Jesus took upon himself
human nature in the Incarnation, and although he bore our
sins on the cross, he never ceased to be God.

Furthermore, the atonement did not take place in hell. It
was completed on the cross when Jesus cried, "It is finished"
(John 19:30). First Peter 2:24 says that Christ "bore our sins
in His body *on the cross*," not in hell. Colossians 2:13–14 says
he canceled the debt of our sin "and He has taken it out of the
way, having nailed it to the cross." Ephesians 1:7 says "We
have redemption through His blood ['blood' here refers to his
physical death—the actual shedding of his blood on the
cross], the forgiveness of our trespasses" (cf. Matt. 26:28; Acts
20:28; Rom. 3:25; 5:9; Eph. 2:13; Col. 1:20; Heb. 9:22;
13:12; 1 Peter 1:19; 1 John 1:7; Rev. 1:5; 5:9). Jesus
promised the repentant thief on the cross, "Today you shall be
with Me in Paradise" (Luke 23:43). Clearly, he was not
preparing to serve a sentence in hell. Instead, he served *notice*
to hell that the powers of evil were defeated (cf. 1 Peter
3:19). The Bible knows nothing of the kind of atonement that
the Word Faith movement describes. That is because the Jesus

of the Bible is not the Jesus Word Faith teachers are talking about.

The Wrong Faith

Word Faith teaching sees faith as an immutable, impersonal "law" that, like gravity or the laws of thermodynamics, rules the universe: a principle that works regardless of who is exercising it—or for what. Pat Robertson, asked if the laws of the kingdom work, even for non-Christians, wrote, "Yes. These are not just Christian and Jewish principles, any more than the law of gravity is Christian and Jewish. . . . The laws of God work for anybody who will follow them. The principles of the Kingdom apply to all of creation."[46] Applied to the "law" of faith, that reasoning means all who claim a blessing without doubting, can have whatever they claim—whether they are Christians or not.

Faith, according to Word Faith doctrine, is not submissive trust in God; faith is a formula by which to manipulate the spiritual laws Word Faith teachers believe govern the universe. "Words governed by spiritual law become spiritual forces working for you. Idle words work against you. The spirit world is controlled by the word of God. The natural world is to be controlled by man speaking God's words."[47]

As the name "Word Faith" implies, this movement teaches that faith is a matter of what we *say* more than whom we trust or what truths we embrace and affirm in our hearts. A favorite term in the Word Faith movement is "positive confession." It refers to the Word Faith teaching that words have creative power. What you *say*, Word Faith teachers claim, determines everything that happens to you. Your "confessions," that is, the things you say—especially the favors you demand of God—must all be stated positively and without wavering. Then God is required to answer.

Kenneth Hagin writes, "You can have what you say. *You can write your own ticket with God.* And the first step in writing your own ticket with God is: *Say it.*"⁴⁸ He adds later, "If you talk about your trials, your difficulties, your lack of faith, your lack of money—your faith will shrivel and dry up. But, bless God, if you talk about the Word of God, your lovely Heavenly Father and what He can do—your faith will grow by leaps and bounds."⁴⁹

Those ideas have bred festering superstition within the movement. Word Faith disciples believe, in effect, that all their words are magical incantations, determining their fate. Charles Capps warns against the dangers of speaking a negative confession, albeit unintentionally:

> We have programmed our vocabulary with the devil's language. We have brought sickness and disease into our vocabulary, and even death. The main word so many people use to express themselves is death—the word, *"death."*
>
> *"I'm just dying to do that."* They will say, *"I'm going to die if I don't. That just tickled me to death."*
>
> Now that, my friend, is *perverse speech.* That is contrary to God's Word. *Death is of the devil.* . . . We need not *buddy-up* with death. All men are going to die soon enough, so don't start *buddying up* with it now.⁵⁰

That is superstition, not biblical faith.

Positive confession would seem to rule out confession of sin. Indeed, Word Faith books on prayer and spiritual growth are utterly lacking in any teaching on confessing one's sin. They have undermined the crucial teaching of 1 John 1:9, which indicates believers should be constantly confessing their sin.

In fact, positive-confession teaching actually *encourages* believers to ignore and deny the reality of their sins and limitations. It has produced multitudes who perpetually wear emotionless smiles out of fear that a negative confession will bring them bad fortune.⁵¹ Hagin admits he feels that way himself:

I wouldn't tell anybody if I had a doubt-thought, or a fear-thought. I wouldn't accept it. I wouldn't tell somebody if the thought came to me—and you know the devil can put all kinds of thoughts in your mind.

We are a product of WORDS. Did you ever stop to think that the Bible teaches that there is health and healing in your tongue? Did you notice that he said here, [Prov. 12:18] *"the tongue of the wise is health"*?

I never talk sickness. I don't believe in sickness. I talk health. . . . I believe in healing. I believe in health. I never talk sickness. I never talk disease. I talk healing.

I never talk failure. I don't believe in failure. I believe in success. I never talk defeat. I don't believe in defeat. I believe in winning, hallelujah to Jesus![52]

That perspective is rife with obvious problems. Bruce Barron tells of one Word Faith church where

the pastor rose sheepishly to instruct his congregation on a ticklish concern. Some of the church members, he had heard, were spreading contagious diseases among the church's little ones by bringing their sick babies to the nursery. Against the nursery volunteers' protests, these parents were positively confessing that their children were well. Since the parents had claimed their healing, there was nothing to worry about. They may have been dismissing those persistent whines and coughs as lying symptoms, but those lying symptoms proved to be contagious, and only an announcement from the pulpit could succeed in putting an end to the problem.[53]

In addition, the Word Faith denial of diseases and problems as "lying symptoms" robs believers of an opportunity to minister with compassion and understanding to suffering people. How can you help someone whose symptoms you believe are lies of Satan—or worse, the result of sinful unbelief in the sick person's life? Consequently, many Word Faith devotees tend to be unfeeling, even to the point of being coarse and abrasive toward people they assume do not have enough faith to claim a healing.

Barron tells of a pastor and his wife, unable to bear children, who "were told by a member of their church that they needed to 'confess' a pregnancy and display their faith by purchasing a baby stroller and walking down the street with it!"[54] A few years ago I received a heart-rending letter from a dear woman who, deceived by "positive confession" theology, believed God wanted her to write everyone she knew with a baby announcement for the child she was hoping to conceive. Tragically, that poor woman was physically incapable of bearing children. Months later she had to write to everyone again to explain that the expected "faith baby" had not arrived. She was quick to add that she was still claiming a pregnancy by faith, however. She was obviously fearful that someone might take her second letter as a "negative confession."

Hagin seems callous even about the death of his own sister from lingering cancer:

> My sister got down to 79 pounds. The Lord kept telling me that she was going to die. I kept asking the Lord why I couldn't change the outcome. He told me she had had five years in which she could have studied the Word and built up her faith (she was saved), but she hadn't done it. He told me she was going to die, and she did. This is a sad example, but it's so true.[55]

Word Faith theology makes the healer a hero when miraculous cures are claimed, but always blames the seeker for a lack of faith when a healing does not happen. Hagin describes an incident when he was attempting to heal an arthritic woman. Her disease had crippled her so badly that she was unable to walk. Hagin became frustrated at her unwillingness to let go of her wheel chair.

I pointed my finger at her and said, "Sister, you don't have an ounce of faith, do you?" (She was saved and baptized with the Holy Spirit, but I meant she didn't have faith for her healing.)

Without thinking, she blurted out, "No, Brother Hagin, I don't! I don't believe I'll ever be healed. I'll go to my grave from this chair." She said it, and she did it.

We weren't to blame.[56]

Remember, positive confession teaches people that their words are determinative. God is no longer the object of faith; Word Faith devotees learn to put their faith in their own words—or as Hagin bluntly puts it, "faith in [their] own faith."[57] Try to follow his logic as he attempts to substantiate that concept:

Did you ever stop to think about having faith in your own faith? Evidently God had faith in His faith, because He spoke the words of faith and they came to pass. Evidently Jesus had faith in His faith, because He spoke to the fig tree, and what He said came to pass.

In other words, *having faith in your words is having faith in your faith.*

That's what you've got to learn to do to get things from God: *Have faith in your faith.*

It would help you to get faith down in your spirit to say out loud, "Faith in my faith." Keep saying it until it registers on your heart. I know it sounds strange when you first say it; your mind almost rebels against it. But we are not talking about your head; we're talking about faith in your heart. As Jesus said, ". . . *and shall not doubt in his heart.* . . ."[58]

Notice that once again Hagin manages to depreciate the Father and Son (Does God have faith? Can we accurately speak of the *faith* of an omniscient, sovereign God?) and deify himself as a worthy object of trust. Moreover, he turns faith into a magical formula and our words into some kind of abracadabra by which one may "get things from God."[59]

There is no biblical basis for any of those ideas. The only appropriate objects for our faith are God and his infallible Word, certainly not our own words.

Nevertheless, Word Faith believers view their positive confessions as an incantation by which they can conjure up *anything* they desire. "Believe it in your heart; say it with your mouth. That is the principle of faith. *You can have what you say*," Kenneth Hagin claims.[60] Quoting John 14:14 ("If you ask Me anything in My name, I will do it"), ignoring the plain implications of the phrase "in My name," they take that verse to be an unqualified promise they can use in extorting from God whatever kind of cargo they fancy.

Such teachings have led many Word Faith proponents into the grossest kind of materialism. John Avanzini, one of the lesser-known Word Faith teachers, spent an evening on Trinity Broadcasting Network arguing that Jesus was actually quite wealthy during his earthly ministry.[61] He pointed to Judas's role as treasurer and said, "You've got to handle lots of money to need a treasurer."[62] More recently, as a guest on Kenneth Copeland's broadcast, Avanzini said he believes Scripture teaches that Jesus had a big house and wore designer clothes.[63] All of that is touted as justification for the Word Faith teachers' own lavish lifestyles and materialistic philosophies.

Robert Tilton goes a step further: "Being poor is a sin, when God promises prosperity."[64] "My God's rich! And He's trying to show you how to draw out of your heavenly account that Jesus bought and paid for and purchased for you at Calvary."[65] Tilton says, "New house? New car? That's chicken feed. That's nothing compared to what God wants to do for you."[66]

How is this cargo to be obtained? Tilton suggests that his followers make a "vow of faith" in the form of a gift to his ministry:

I like a thousand-dollar vow, because I like—don't like—
half-hearted people, lukewarm, just, "Well, I'll do a
little. . . ." I like a thousand-dollar vow of faith. . . . I'm
not talking to you that's got it. You that's got it don't pay a
bit of attention to me. I'm talking to you that don't have it,
and I'm showing you how you can get it! Yes, the Lord's
work gets a portion of it. But you get the biggest portion.
You get the biggest blessing. I'm trying to talk you out of
that dump you're in! I'm trying to talk you into a decent
car! . . . I'm trying to help you! Quit cursing me! Quit
cursing me! God, what will pull this blessing from you? I am
a blessing. I have been blessed supernaturally by God. I
bring a blessing to you this day, and I know it, and my
responsibility is to take it to you.[67]

Tilton encourages his listeners to pray the prayer of faith;
"not one of those, 'Lord, if it be Thy will—' I *know* what the
will of God is when it concerns healing, and prosperity, and
divine direction. . . . I don't have to pray a prayer of doubt
and unbelief."[68] In other words, Robert Tilton wants you to
make a thousand-dollar vow of faith to his ministry, especially
if you *can't* afford to give away that much money. He doesn't
want you to pray for God's will on the matter. After all, you
can demand what you want and God must give it to you. Set
your vow at a thousand, and demand that God provide the
money. That's deceitful, blasphemous folly, but literally
millions are sucked into such traps.

Richard Roberts, echoing his father's "seed-faith" concept, urged viewers to "sow a seed on your MasterCard, your
Visa or your American Express, and then when you do, expect
God to open the windows of heaven and pour you out a
blessing."[69] Oral Roberts once mailed out plastic bags full of
"holy water" from the River of Life Fountain at Oral Roberts
University. To demonstrate how to use the stuff, he poured a
bag of it over his own wallet on his television program.[70]

If it is that simple to get the cargo, why do so many Word

Faith believers "claim" material blessings they never receive?[71] Fred Price explains:

> If you've got one-dollar faith and you ask for a ten-thousand-dollar item, it ain't going to work. It won't work. Jesus said, "according to your [faith]," not according to God's *will for you*, in His own good time, if it's according to His will, if He can work it into His busy schedule. He said, "According to *your* faith, be it unto you."
>
> Now, I may want a Rolls Royce, and don't have but bicycle faith. Guess what I'm going to get? A bicycle.[72]

Thus God's ability to bless us supposedly hangs on our faith.

Note that both Price and Tilton recoil from praying, "If it be Thy will." That is a common characteristic of Word Faith teachers. As we noted, they love to quote John 14:14: "If you ask Me anything in My name, I will do it." But 1 John 5:14 is noticeably missing from their database: "This is the confidence which we have before Him, that, if we ask anything *according to His will*, He hears us" (emphasis added). Hagin goes so far as to claim that no such truth is taught in the New Testament:

> Because we didn't understand what Jesus said, and because we've been religiously brainwashed instead of New Testament-taught, we watered down the promises of God and tacked on something that Jesus didn't say, and added on something else to it: "Well, He will all right if it's His will, but it might not be His will," people have said. And yet, you don't find that kind of talk in the New Testament.[73]

Hagin has also written, "It is unscriptural to pray, 'If it is the will of God.' When you put an 'if' in your prayer, you are praying in doubt."[74]

Yet 1 John 5:14 clearly includes an "if." Furthermore, Romans 8:27 tells us that even the Holy Spirit "intercedes for the saints *according to the will of God*" (emphasis added).

And what will the Word Faith movement do with James

4:13–16? Does not their most fundamental teaching utterly contradict this passage?

> Come now, you who say, "Today or tomorrow, we shall go to such and such a city, and spend a year there and engage in business and make a profit." Yet you do not know what your life will be like tomorrow. You are just a vapor that appears for a little while and then vanishes away. Instead, you ought to say, "If the Lord wills, we shall live and also do this or that." But as it is, you boast in your arrogance; all such boasting is evil.

What of the Word Faith movement's emphasis on material wealth and prosperity? Is that what real faith is all about? Hardly.

Far from stressing the importance of wealth, the Bible warns against pursuing it. Believers—especially leaders in the church (1 Tim. 3:3)—are to be free from the love of money (Heb. 13:5). Love of money leads to all kinds of evil (1 Tim. 6:10). Jesus warned, "Beware, and be on your guard against every form of greed; for not even when one has an abundance does his life consist of his possessions" (Luke 12:15). In sharp contrast to the Word Faith gospel's emphasis on gaining money and possessions in this life, Jesus said, "Do not lay up for yourselves treasures upon earth, where moth and rust destroy, and where thieves break in and steal" (Matt. 6:19). The irreconcilable contradiction between the Word Faith gospel and the gospel of our Lord Jesus Christ is best summed up in the words of Jesus in Matthew 6:24: "You cannot serve God and mammon [riches]."

Christian Sense or Christian Science?

The concept that the universe (including God)[75] is governed by impersonal spiritual laws is not biblical. It is a denial of God's sovereignty and providence. It is nothing less than deism. Furthermore, the notion that we can use words mystically to control reality is far removed from the biblical pattern of faith, especially as revealed in Hebrews 11.[76] Both ideas have more in common with the cult of Christian Science than with biblical truth.

Most Word Faith teachers vehemently deny that their teachings have anything to do with Christian Science or the other metaphysical cults. Charles Capps has written,

> You see, sometimes when I start teaching on this folks will say it sounds like *Christian Science.* One lady punched her husband in a service in Texas and said, (My wife overheard them.) *"That sounds like Christian Science."*
>
> It's not *Christian Science.* I like what Brother Kenneth Hagin says, *"IT'S CHRISTIAN SENSE"*![77]

Later he adds, "No, it's not Christian Science. I don't deny the existence of disease. I deny the right of that disease to exist in this body, because I'm the Body of Christ."[78]

Still, the distinction is a fine one. It is a simple matter of fact that many of the doctrines central to Word Faith teaching are similar to those of Christian Science. There is a reason for that. A direct line of relationship ties the modern Word Faith movement to the metaphysical cults that flourished earlier in this century, including Christian Science.

That connection has been carefully and conclusively documented in an excellent critique of the Word Faith movement, *A Different Gospel* by D. R. McConnell.[79] McConnell chronicles the development of the Word Faith movement, showing that nearly every major figure in the movement was mentored by Kenneth Hagin or one of his close disciples. Every doctrinal distinctive of the movement is traceable to Hagin.

Moreover, McConnell demonstrates convincingly that Word Faith teachings are not original with Hagin; Hagin gleaned them from the writings of a faith evangelist named E. W. Kenyon.[80] Hagin borrowed not only the *ideas* from Kenyon; McConnell includes several pages of column-by-column text that proves beyond question that Hagin has repeatedly plagiarized long sections of his writings *word-for-word* from Kenyon's material.[81]

Why is that significant? Because McConnell also reveals that Kenyon's roots were in the metaphysical cults. He was a faith-healer not in the Pentecostal tradition, but in the tradition of Mary Baker Eddy and Christian Science. He attended a college that specialized in training lecturers for the metaphysical science cults. And he imported and adapted into his system most of the essential ideas these cults propagated.[82] Hagin absorbed them from there.[83]

In short, McConnell's book is a devastating exposé of the Word Faith movement. It demonstrates irrefutably that Word Faith teachers owe their ancestry to groups like Christian Science, Swedenborgianism, Theosophy, Science of Mind, and New Thought—not to classical Pentecostalism. It reveals that at their very core, Word Faith teachings are corrupt. Their undeniable derivation is cultish, not Christian.

The sad truth is that the gospel proclaimed by the Word Faith movement is not the gospel of the New Testament. Word Faith doctrine is a mongrel system, a blend of mysticism, dualism, and neo-gnosticism that borrows generously from the teachings of the metaphysical cults. Its perverse teachings are causing untold harm to the church in general and charismatics in particular. Word Faith is, in the words of the apostle Peter a "destructive heresy" (2 Peter 2:1). No wonder it is as riddled with greed and materialism—and as spiritually bankrupt—as the crudest cargo cult.

The Word Faith movement may be the most dangerous false system that has grown out of the charismatic movement so far. Because so many charismatics are unsure of the finality of Scripture, and because they feel they cannot discount tales of people who claim to have had visitations from Christ, they are particularly susceptible to the movement's lies—and often at a loss to answer them.

Despite what Word Faith teachers say, however, our God

is not merely a source of cargo. We are his servants, not he ours. He has called us to lives of loving service and worship, not godlike supremacy. He blesses us, but not always materially. In no way can we "write our own ticket" and expect him to follow our script—nor should any real believer ever desire such a scenario. The life of the Christian is a life spent in pursuit of God's will—not a strategy to get him to go along with ours. No one who rejects that fundamental truth can genuinely live unto God's glory. And no one who has known the emancipation from sin and selfishness wrought by God's grace should ever be willing to exchange that freedom for the cheapened cargo of the Word Faith doctrines.

Epilogue:
How Should We Respond
to the Charismatic Movement?

As I said at the outset of this book, I know many charismatics who are committed, consistent, honorable believers devoted to the Word of God. Numerous charismatic churches and individual charismatic believers reject many of the errors I have highlighted in this book. By no means am I attempting to color all charismatics the same. Obviously there are many extremes within the movement and many hues of charismatic doctrine, ranging from evangelical orthodoxy to rank heresy.

Confronting Error

I am grateful for those charismatics who have the courage to confront error in their movement and call all charismatics to a biblical perspective—and I fervently wish more charismatics would join their ranks. Certainly there are some important and very effective voices within the charismatic movement who have shown more willingness than most noncharismatics to confront the heresies bred by the charismatic movement. The most thorough critiques of the Word Faith movement, for example, have come from a handful of charismatic authors.[1] Chuck Smith, charismatic pastor of Calvary Chapel in Costa Mesa, California, has written a very straightforward critique of charismatic extremism.[2] John

Goodwin, pastor of Calvary Chapel, San Jose, has written a brief but excellent critique of the Third Wave movement.[3]

I thank God for those men and their courage. I am convinced, nevertheless, that the seeds of the errors they wish to fight are inherent in the very doctrines that distinguish the charismatic position: the idea that God is still revealing truth beyond Scripture; the teaching that Spirit baptism is subsequent to and separate from salvation, thus creating two classes of believers; and the mysticism that is innate in charismatic teaching, which encourages people to denigrate reason, elevate feeling, and open their minds and spirits to powers they cannot understand. As long as those ideas lie at the core of charismatic belief, error and extremism will continue to overgrow the movement.

This book is an appeal to my charismatic friends to reexamine what they believe. It is also an appeal to non-charismatics who imagine that the differences between charismatic and non-charismatic doctrine are inconsequential or petty. All true believers can agree that a proper understanding of Scripture is one thing worth guarding aggressively. Like the noble-minded Bereans, let us each examine the Scriptures carefully and diligently "to see whether these things [are] so" (Acts 17:11). Ask yourself in all honesty: *Am I putting my emphasis on God's living Word in the Scriptures, or on my feelings and experiences?*

A Final Word

Many who read a book like this will be concerned about its effect on unity in the body of Christ. Please understand that I have no desire to place a gulf between charismatic and non-charismatic believers. No such rift can possibly exist between believers when they meet on the common ground of God's Word. Harmful division germinates only when someone turns away from the Word and lets error creep in to threaten the flock. My principal concern is to call the church to a firm commitment to the purity and authority of the Scriptures, and thereby *strengthen* the unity of the true church.

Perhaps the most serious damage done to the church by the charismatic movement has been precisely in this matter of unity. Who knows how many thousands of churches have split over charismatic teaching? The number would surely be staggering. Charismatic doctrine itself is schismatic, as we have seen, because it erects a fence between the common believer and those who think they have attained a higher level of spirituality. Thus the partition between charismatics and non-charismatics was actually put there by ideas intrinsic to the charismatic system.

Many charismatics, I'm sure, are keenly aware of that difficulty. But it is compounded by a second tendency, and that is the disposition of many charismatics who, in the name of unity, are willing to embrace anyone and everyone—even if it means overlooking grossly errant doctrinal perspectives—as long as the person has manifested some outward evidence of the charismata.

Because of this penchant for doctrinal ambiguity, inclusiveness, and altruism toward others of different backgrounds, the charismatic movement has unwittingly succeeded in becoming the kind of worldwide ecumenical force many liberals originally envisioned the World Council of Churches might one day become.[4] Catholics, Eastern Orthodox Christians, Protestants, and many sects are already uniting under the charismatic banner. Far from being a positive corollary to the movement's growth, this ecumenical influence may well prove to be the most potentially disastrous long-term effect of the twentieth-century charismatic phenomenon.

One writer pointed out the irony of the charismatic movement's marriage with ecumenism:

> Is it not inconsistent that a movement which claims to be in direct contact with the Holy Spirit, to have all the gifts such as prophecy, apostleship, and the word of knowledge, to

communicate directly with God by tongues-speaking and other means, can at the same time include Roman Catholics, conservative and liberal Protestants, amillennialists, premillennialists, Calvinists, Arminians, those who deny the verbal inspiration of the Bible, and those who reject Christ's vicarious atonement on the cross?

Apparently the Holy Spirit is not concerned with communicating any information to correct all these differences, many of which are crucial and some of which are incorrect. All this direct communication with the Spirit has apparently done nothing to correct even basic errors. It has not produced unity among charismatics regarding the nature and purpose of many of the gifts. This movement has solved no theological issue, produced no advance in biblical knowledge, and has not produced more spiritual Christians. Would such an effusion of the genuine Spirit of God produce so little?[5]

Gordon Clark has also written about the dangers of charismatic ecumenism. He quoted an article[6] from a charismatic magazine celebrating the inroads Pentecostalism was making into Catholicism, then said:

Several things immediately strike any reader who is not asleep. First, the tongues experience is tremendously important. If it is not true to say that nothing else matters, it nonetheless seems true to say that nothing else matters very much. Speaking in tongues is the chief mark of a dedicated Christian. The clear implication is that the worship of the virgin Mary is unobjectionable, if one speaks in tongues. There is little point in justification by faith alone, one can accept merit from the treasury of the Saints, transubstantiation can be acknowledged; if only one speaks in tongues. Still more fundamental, one can place tradition on a level with Scripture and even assert new revelations from God, if only one speaks in tongues. The Pentecostalist minister [mentioned in the article in question], note well, said, "There has been no attempt [by Protestant Charismatics] to proselyte [Roman Catholic Charismatics]." In other words, Romanism is acceptable, if only one speaks in tongues.[7]

Charismatic ecumenism is steadily eroding any claim the charismatic movement ever had to biblical orthodoxy. In Asia shocking new charismatic cults are springing up, blending Buddhism, Taoism, Confucianism, and other false teachings with the teachings of Western Charismatics.[8] The charismatic movement as a whole is entirely unequipped to defend against such influences. How can they confront errant groups—even ones that are overtly heathen? For in the charismatic movement, unity is a question of shared religious experience, not commonality of teaching. If doctrine really does not matter, why *not* embrace Buddhist charismatic groups? In effect that is precisely what is happening.

And so while charismatic doctrine tends to be divisive among groups that are orthodox, it has had the opposite effect among groups that are not. Charismatics are building bridges with groups and individuals whom Christians are commanded to shun (2 John 9–11). Sadly, many charismatics have thereby become participants in the evil deeds of those who deny the teaching of our Lord (v. 11).

I suspect charismatics—even many who acknowledge the severity of these problems—will claim that their movement's legacy has been more positive than negative. As evidence, they will point to the widespread effects of the so-called charismatic renewal, and to the movement's numerical growth worldwide. They will say that charismatic ministry is revitalizing churches and reaching the lost, even to the uttermost parts of the earth. But the ecumenical nature of much of that renewal and expansion negates the claim that it is God's work.

The sad truth is, the legacy of the charismatic movement has been mostly one of chaos and doctrinal confusion. The charismatic approach to spirituality is unsound and fraught with potential disillusionment. On both sides of the charismatic fence are Christian believers who are unsure, disappointed, defeated. Some are even desperate. The spiritual "good life" they hear about in sermons and Sunday school lessons seems to be passing them by. Where can they find the key to living out their Christian faith on a realistic, practical day-to-day basis?

The only appropriate response is and always has been a return to the Word of God. For it is there that God has revealed to us all the truth we need to serve him and live for his glory. Unfortunately, as we have seen so often, the charismatic movement tends to turn people inward, toward mysticism and subjectivity, and away from the Word of God. Don't heed that siren call.

> His divine power has granted to us everything pertaining to life and godliness, through the true knowledge of Him who called us by His own glory and excellence. For by these He has granted to us His precious and magnificent promises, in order that by them you might become partakers of the divine nature, having escaped the corruption that is in the world by lust. Now for this very reason also, applying all diligence, in your faith supply moral excellence, and in your moral excellence, knowledge; and in your knowledge, self-control, and in your self-control, perseverance, and in your perseverance, godliness; and in your godliness, brotherly kindness, and in your brotherly kindness, love. For if these qualities are yours and are increasing, they render you neither useless nor unfruitful in the true knowledge of our Lord Jesus Christ (2 Peter 1:3–8).

Notes

Introduction

1. John F. MacArthur, Jr., *The Charismatics: A Doctrinal Perspective* (Grand Rapids: Zondervan, 1978).

2. It seems ironic that critics of charismatic extremism are so frequently scolded for being unloving and divisive. Listen to these comments by charismatic Benny Hinn: "Somebody's attacking me because of something I'm teaching. Let me tell you something, brother: You watch it! . . . You know, I've looked for one verse in the Bible; I just can't seem to find it. One verse that said 'If you don't like them, kill them.' I really wish I could find it! . . . You stink, frankly—that's the way I think about it! . . . Sometimes I wish God will give me a Holy Ghost machine gun; I'll blow your head off!" ["Praise-a-thon" broadcast on the Trinity Broadcasting Network (November 8, 1990).]

Paul Crouch is scarcely more charitable. Of his critics, he said, "I think they're damned and on their way to hell and I don't think there's any redemption for them. . . . I say, To hell with you! Get out of my life! Get out of the way! . . . And I want to say to all you scribes, Pharisees, heresy hunters—all of you that are going around picking little bits of doctrinal error out of everybody's eyes. . . . Get out of God's way; quit blocking God's bridges, or God's going to shoot you if I don't. . . . Get out of my life! I don't want to even talk to you or hear you! I don't want to see your ugly face! Get out of my face in Jesus' name." ["Praise the Lord" broadcast on the Trinity Broadcasting Network (April 2, 1991).]

Hinn's and Crouch's railings were aimed at godly men and women (many of them fellow charismatics) who had raised valid *biblical* questions about some of the novel Word Faith teachings (see chapter 12) frequently aired on Crouch's television network. Crouch called his critics' analyses "doctrinal doodoo."

I am not aware of a single incident anywhere—certainly not on live international television—where *anyone* has publicly spoken disparagingly of charismatics in the kind of savage and caustic language used in those two samples. Why would anyone consider it unloving or ungracious to examine doctrine biblically, but acceptable to defend oneself with such philistine threats?

3. MacArthur, *The Charismatics*, 58.

4. Jan Crouch, "Costa Ricans Say 'Thank You for Sending Christian Television!' " "Praise the Lord" newsletter (September 1991), 4.

5. "Choose Your Weapons, Saints of God" (advertisement), *Charisma* (September 1989), 14–15.

6. "The Prophet of Prosperity," *Dallas Times Herald* (June 24, 1990), A1.

7. See pages 291–92.

8. In its context this verse forbids physical violence against kings. In no way does it condemn careful scrutiny or criticism of preachers and teachers. Such an application would violate the clear command of 1 Thessalonians 5:21: "Examine everything carefully."

9. Howard M. Ervin, *These Are Not Drunken, As Ye Suppose* (Plainfield, N.J.: Logos, 1968), 3–4.

10. J. Rodman Williams, *Renewal Theology* (Grand Rapids: Zondervan, 1990), 326 (emphasis in original).

11. Frederick Dale Bruner, *A Theology of the Holy Spirit* (Grand Rapids: Eerdmans, 1970), 33.

12. For this account see Dennis Bennett, *Nine O'Clock in the Morning* (Plainfield, N.J.: Logos International, 1970).

13. John L. Sherrill, *They Speak with Other Tongues* (Old Tappan, N.J.: Spire, 1964), 51.

14. I do not say that charismatics knowingly or willingly foster duplicity or hypocrisy. In any philosophy that tends to gauge spirituality by external standards—be it fundamentalist legalism, sanctimonious asceticism, communal pietism, religious institutionalism, hard-line pharisaism, wild-eyed mysticism, or rigid monasticism—keeping up appearances tends to take priority over openness and honesty. In the charismatic movement,

sensational spiritual experiences are more highly valued than quiet devotion. Is it any wonder if some people are tempted to exaggerate or pretend?

1. Is Experience a Valid Test of Truth?

1. Gordon L. Anderson, "Pentecostals Believe in More Than Tongues," in Harold B. Smith, ed., *Pentecostals from the Inside Out* (Wheaton, Ill.: Victor, 1990), 55.

2. Kenneth Copeland, *Laws of Prosperity* (Fort Worth: Kenneth Copeland Publications, 1974), 65.

3. Mary Stewart Relfe, "Interview with Dr. Percy Collett," *Relfe's Review* (Report #55, August 1984), 3.

4. Ibid., 1–8.

5. Ibid., 5.

6. Ibid.

7. Ibid., 5–6.

8. Ibid., 7.

9. Ibid.

10. Ibid.

11. Some charismatic leaders acknowledge this problem. Kenneth Hagin, an advocate of the charismatic Word Faith message (see chapter 12), wrote, "A minister who at one time was very sound said, 'I don't need that book any more. I am beyond that.' Then he threw the Bible on the floor. 'I have the Holy Ghost. I am a prophet. God sends my instructions direct' " *The Gift of Prophecy* (Tulsa: Kenneth Hagin Ministries, 1969), 24.

12. Roberts Liardon, "I Saw Heaven," (Tulsa: Harrison House, 1983), 6, 19 (emphasis in original).

13. Ibid., 16–20. About this last item, Liardon writes, "I thought, *My land, overdoses will kill people.* But then I thought, *Well, the Holy Ghost won't kill you. He'll just translate you!*" He adds, "When Jesus saw me look at that bottle, He laughed. And when He laughs, it's the most hilarious thing you'll ever see and hear. He leans back and roars with laughter. You'd think He was going to collapse from laughing, He gets into it so much! That's one reason He's so strong: He laughs so hard. You see, the joy of the Lord is His strength!" (Ibid., 20.)

14. Ibid., 16–17.

15. Ibid., 22.

16. Ibid., 26.

17. Not to be outdone, Aline Baxley, "an ex-alcoholic and drug addict," says she has been to hell, and "God brought her back to tell her story." She advertises a free tract that tells her story. ["I Walked in Hell and There Is Life After Death" (advertisement), *Charisma* (November 1990), 145.]

Aline Baxley's testimony may be the vanguard of a new charismatic fad. Recently I watched a broadcast of The 700 Club featuring a woman who claimed to have experienced hell in a near-death experience during surgery. The following week, a charismatic friend sent me a book that purports to be divinely inspired, detailing yet another woman's visions and out-of-body experiences in hell. [Mary Kathryn Baxter, *A Divine Revelation of Hell* (Washington: National Church of God, n.d.).]

18. See John 5:28–29 and 1 Thessalonians 4:16–17.

19. For a helpful discussion on the relationship between Roman Catholic theology and Charismatic thinking, see Gordon H. Clark, *I Corinthians: A Contemporary Commentary* (Philadelphia: Presbyterian and Reformed, 1975), 223–227.

20. Vinson Synan, "The Touch Felt Around the World" *Charisma* (January 1991), 80.

21. Ibid., 81–82.

22. Ibid., 82.

23. Ibid.

24. Ibid., 83.

25. Ibid.

26. Ibid.

27. Ibid. Regarding the application to missions, Synan adds, "The major significance of this event to Parham lay in his belief that tongues were 'xenoglossolalia,' or known languages, which the Lord would give to prospective missionaries for use in evangelizing foreign lands. This was further confirmed in his mind when linguists, foreigners and government interpreters visited the school and claimed that at least 20 languages and dialects were perfectly spoken and understood." [Ibid.]

As far as I know, however, none of that has ever been independently confirmed. If true, it is difficult to explain the school's failure later in the year. It would seem that Bethel should have become one of the greatest missionary training schools in church history. But I know of not one missionary—from Bethel or any other charismatic organization—who has used tongues in the way Parham envisioned.

28. Dennis Bennett, *Nine O'Clock in the Morning* (Plainfield, N.J.: Logos, 1970).

29. Frederick Dale Bruner, *A Theology of the Holy Spirit* (Grand Rapids: Eerdmans, 1970), 21 (emphasis in original).

30. Henry Frost, *Miraculous Healing* (New York: Revell, 1939), 109–110.

31. Charles Farah, "Toward a Theology of Healing," *Christian Life* 38 (September 1976), 78.

32. John R. W. Stott, *Your Mind Matters* (Downers Grove, Ill.: InterVarsity, 1972), 7.

33. Ibid., 10.

34. James Orr, *The Christian View of God and the World* (New York: Scribner's, n.d.), 21.

35. For an evaluation of existentialism see C. Stephen Evans, *Existentialism* (Grand Rapids: Zondervan, 1984).

36. Clark H. Pinnock, *Set Forth Your Case* (Chicago: Moody, 1967), 69–70. Pinnock himself evidently no longer holds this view. He has certainly denied its implications by abandoning his commitment to absolute biblical inerrancy and by endorsing the charismatic movement because of his own experience. [Clark H. Pinnock, "A Revolutionary Promise," *Christianity Today* (August 8, 1986), p. 19.]

37. For an evaluation of humanism see Norman L. Geisler, *Is Man the Measure?* (Grand Rapids: Baker, 1983).

38. For a discussion of the absolute nature of truth see William Barrett, *Irrational Man* (Garden City, N.Y.: Doubleday, 1962), and Francis A. Schaeffer, *How Should We Then Live?* (Old Tappan, N.J.: Revell, 1976).

39. S. Angus, *The Mystery-Religions and Christianity* (New York: Dover, 1975), 66–67.

40. Eugene H. Peterson, "Baalism and Yahwism Updated," *Theology for Today* (July 1972), 139–141.

41. Pinnock, *Case*, 73.

42. Harold Lindsell, *The Battle for the Bible* (Grand Rapids: Zondervan, 1976).

43. Robert K. Johnson, "Of Tidy Doctrine and Truncated Experience," *Christianity Today* (February 18, 1977), 11.

44. Larry Christenson, *Speaking in Tongues* (Minneapolis: Dimension Books, 1968), 40.

45. Michael Harper, *A New Way of Living* (Plainfield, N.J.: Logos, 1973), 12.

46. J. Rodman Williams, *The Era of the Spirit* (Plainfield, N.J.: Logos, 1971), 55.

47. Ibid.

2. Does God Still Give Revelation?

1. "Oral Roberts: Victory Out of Defeat," *Charisma* (December 1989), 88.

2. "The Tapes That Are Healing the Nations" (advertisement), *Charisma* (October 1988), 69.

3. Occasionally, one of the "inspired" books finds a publisher. David Wilkerson, *The Vision* (Old Tappan, N.J.: Spire, 1974) is one such example. The book was subtitled "A Thrilling Prophecy of the Coming of Armageddon." "Deep in my heart I am convinced that this vision is from God, that it is true, and that it will come to pass," Wilkerson wrote [12]. It did not. Wilkerson predicted, "Nature will release its fury with increasing intensity over the next decade. There will be short periods of relief, but almost every day mankind will witness the wrath of nature somewhere in the world" [36]. Wilkerson predicted a cataclysmic earthquake that would start a panic somewhere in the United States—"the biggest, most disastrous in its history" [32]. He foresaw many catastrophes, including worldwide financial calamity. Perhaps most ironic of all, Wilkerson predicted a decline of the "positive thinking" doctrines [25].

I recently received another supposedly inspired book by mail. An endorsement on the book's back cover, written by Dr. T. L. Lowery, senior pastor of the National Church of God in Washington, D. C., says, "Unlike other books, I believe that the Holy Spirit has brought this writing into being for time and eternity. The experiences and the message are of utmost importance to the body of Christ. I believe that God's anointing will rest upon this book and minister to every person who reads these contents." Clearly, Pastor Lowery believes the book is on par with Scripture. But I thumbed through the 171-page book and found it to be filled with speculation, bizarre fantasy, and much teaching that is inconsistent with Scripture. [Mary Kathryn Baxter, *A Divine Revelation of Hell* (Washington: National Church of God, n.d.).]

4. "Pentecostals Set Priorities," *Charisma* (January 1991), 44.

5. "The Strongman of Greed," *Charisma* (March 1991), 40 (italics in original).

6. Kenneth E. Hagin, "The Glory of God" (Tulsa: Faith Library, 1987), 14–15 (emphasis added).

7. Ibid., 15–16.

8. Ibid., 16.

9. J. Rodman Williams, *The Era of the Spirit* (Plainfield, N.J.: Logos, 1971), 16.

10. Edward N. Gross, *Miracles, Demons, & Spiritual Warfare* (Grand Rapids: Baker, 1990), 150–52.

11. Thomas A. Thomas, *The Doctrine of the Word of God* (Philadelphia: Presbyterian and Reformed, 1972), 8–9.

12. Dewey Beegle, *The Inspiration of Scripture* (Philadelphia: Westminster, 1963), 140 (emphasis in original).

13. Ibid., 141.

14. Dewey Beegle, *Scripture, Tradition, and Infallibility* (Grand Rapids: Eerdmans, 1973), 308.

15. Ibid.

16. Ibid., 309.

17. A recent *Charisma* article recommended this: "To meditate on our personal prophecies, we should record them if at all possible. If someone approaches us saying he or she has a word from God, we should ask the person to wait a moment until we can get an audio recorder, or else ask the person to write it down. If the word comes from someone on the platform during a meeting that is not being recorded, we must try to write down as much as possible, getting at least the main points." [Bill Hamon, "How to Receive a Personal Prophecy," *Charisma* (April 1991), 66.]

18. Williams, *Era*, 16 (emphasis added).

19. Ibid (emphasis in original).

20. Ibid., 27–28.

21. Ibid., 29.

22. J. Rodman Williams, "Opinion," *Logos Journal* (May–June, 1977), 35.

23. Kenneth Copeland, "Take Time to Pray," *Voice of Victory* (February 1987), 9.

24. Ibid.

25. Larry Lea, "Are You a Mousekateer?" [sic], *Charisma* (August 1988), 9.

26. Melvin L. Hodges, *Spiritual Gifts* (Springfield, Mo.: Gospel Publishing House, 1964), 19–20.

27. "Bernard Jordan Presents the Monthly School of the Prophet" (advertisement), *Charisma* (December 1990), 31.

28. "Do Only Prophets Hear God's Voice? No!" (advertisement), *Charisma* (December 1990), 112.

29. René Pache, *The Inspiration and Authority of Scripture* (Chicago: Moody, 1969), 319.

30. Henry Alford, *Alford's Greek Testament*, vol. IV (Grand Rapids: Baker, 1980), 530.

31. George L. Lawlor, *Translation and Exposition of the Epistle of Jude* (Philadelphia: Presbyterian and Reformed, 1972), 45.

32. For a helpful discussion of the Apocrypha, see Norman L. Geisler and William E. Nix, *A General Introduction to the Bible* (Chicago: Moody, 1986), chaps. 15, 17.

33. For a more detailed treatment of the canon, see Geisler and Nix; and F. F. Bruce, *The Canon of Scripture* (Downers Grove, Ill.: InterVarsity, 1988).

34. It is not accurate to use Agabus to support theories of continuing revelation. Agabus's only recorded prophecies were given while the canon was still open.

3. Prophets, Fanatics, or Heretics?

1. David Pytches, *Some Said It Thundered* (Nashville: Oliver Nelson, 1991).

2. Ibid., 109.

3. Bob Jones, "The Shepherd's Rod" cassette tape (Kansas City, Mo.: Kansas City Fellowship, October 1989).

4. Ibid.

5. Ibid. Bickle no longer defends Jones so staunchly as he once did. In November 1991, John Wimber distributed a letter to

Vineyard churches and constituents notifying them that Jones
was undergoing a process of "restoration" after having confessed
to sexual misconduct and abuses of his prophetic gifting.

6. Wimber offered to take the Kansas City Prophets into the
Vineyard in order to correct their excesses, disciple them, and
hold them accountable. But almost immediately he began using
them to teach.

7. John White, Foreword to David Pytches, *Some Said It
Thundered*, ix-x.

8. Ibid., xix.

9. Ibid., xi–xii.

10. Ibid., xiii (emphasis in original).

11. Ibid., xvi (emphasis in original). White seeks support
for his statement in a dubious interpretation of 1 Kings 13:7–32.
The passage is sometimes thought to relate the account of a true
prophet who prophesied falsely. But note that the false prophet in
that narrative is never identified as a "man of God," while the
honest (but disobedient) prophet in that passage is. Second Kings
23:17 identifies the false prophet as "the prophet who came from
Samaria." He may well have been an unbelieving seer whose
powers were demonic—hence his superstitious request (1 Ki.
13:31). Note also that he was not immediately punished for his
lying, even though the "man of God" he duped died for his
disobedience.

There are several examples in Scripture where unrighteous
men sometimes prophesied accurately. But there is no clear
example in Scripture of a true, righteous prophet of God who
ever uttered false prophecy while purporting to be speaking for
God.

12. Some imagine that the distinction between Old Testament and New Testament prophecy negates the principle of
Deuteronomy 3:1–5; 18:20–22. They claim that prophets in the
church age are not to be judged according to the truthfulness of
their prophecies, for New Testament prophecy is different in
character from Old Testament prophecy. Wayne Grudem [*The
Gift of Prophecy in the New Testament and Today* (Wheaton:
Crossway, 1988)], for example, argues for two levels of New
Testament prophecy. One is apostolic prophecy, which is
infallible and on a par with both Old Testament prophecy and

the inerrant written Word of God. The other is the gift of prophecy, which is meant to edify, encourage, and comfort. I would agree. But unlike Grudem I do not believe this second level of prophecy is revelatory.

Grudem believes prophets today speak messages revealed to them supernaturally from God. Yet he believes these messages may not always be one hundred percent accurate. Unfortunately, Grudem never answers the obvious dilemma his position raises: How can *any* message revealed by God contain error? False prophecy by definition cannot be from God.

For a fine discussion of whether inspired prophecy in the New Testament was always infallible, see appendix 3, "Is the New Testament Gift of Prophecy Fallible?" in Norman Geisler, *Signs and Wonders* (Wheaton, Ill.: Tyndale, 1988), 157–162.

13. Bill Hamon, "How to Receive a Personal Prophecy," *Charisma* (April 1991), 63.

14. Ibid., 65.

15. Ibid. (emphasis in original).

16. Hamon's view puts God at the mercy of happenstance. It characterizes him as capricious—adapting his Word to events beyond his control—as if he were unable to know or control the future. This view is obviously the product of a theology that rejects the biblical teaching about God's sovereignty.

17. Ibid., 66 (italics in original). See also endnote 17, page 366.

18. Ibid.

19. Ibid., 68.

20. James Ryle, "Sons of Thunder," (Longmont, Colo.: Boulder Valley Vineyard), preached 1 July 1990.

21. Cited in Henry Bettenson, ed., *Documents of the Christian Church* (London: Oxford, 1963), 77.

22. Ibid.

23. Ibid.

24. Ibid., 78.

25. Earle E. Cairns, *Christianity Through the Centuries* (Grand Rapids: Zondervan, 1954), 110–11.

26. Larry Christenson, "Pentecostalism's Forgotten Forerunner," in Vinson Synan, ed. *Aspects of Pentecostal–Charismatic Origins* (Plainfield, N.J.: Logos, 1975), 32–34.

27. Gabriel Moran, *Scripture and Tradition* (New York: Herder and Herder, 1963), 20.

28. George Tavard, *Holy Writ or Holy Church* (New York: Harper, 1959), 8.

29. Ibid., 164.

30. Bettenson, ed., *Documents*, 261 (emphasis added).

31. Richard P. McBrien, *Catholicism* (Oak Grove, Minn.: Winston, 1981), 880.

32. Loraine Boettner, *Roman Catholicism* (Philadelphia: Presbyterian & Reformed, 1962), 162.

33. Norman L. Geisler and William E. Nix, *A General Introduction to the Bible* (Chicago: Moody, 1986), 175.

34. J. K. S. Reid, *The Inspiration of Scripture* (London: Methuen, 1957), 278–79 (emphasis in original).

35. Cited in R. A. Finlayson, "Contemporary Ideas of Revelation," in Carl F. H. Henry, ed. *Revelation and the Bible* (Grand Rapids: Baker, 1974), 225.

36. C. H. Dodd, "The Bible as 'the Word of God,'" in Millard J. Erickson, ed. *The Living God: Readings in Christian Theology* (Grand Rapids: Baker, 1973), 273.

37. Charles Farah, "Toward a Theology of Healing," *Christian Life* 38 (September 1976), 81.

38. Ibid.

39. Bettenson, ed., *Documents*, 201.

40. *Book of Mormon*, Alma 5:45–46. Cf. the Mormons' seventh article of faith: "We believe in the gift of tongues, prophecy, revelation, visions, healing, interpretation of tongues, etc." James E. Talmage, *The Articles of Faith* (Salt Lake City: The Church of Jesus Christ of Latter-Day Saints, 1972), 2.

41. *The Christian Science Journal* (July 1975), 362.

42. Ibid., 361.

43. Mary Baker Eddy, *The First Church of Christ, Scientist, and Miscellany* (Boston: First Church of Christ, Scientist, 1941), 115.

44. *Watchtower* (April 15, 1943), 127.

45. Herbert W. Armstrong, *Mystery of the Ages* (New York: Dodd, Mead, 1985), xiii.

46. Stephen Strang, "A Caution on Personal Prophecy," *Charisma* (September 1989), 9.

47. Joseph Dillow, *Speaking in Tongues* (Grand Rapids: Zondervan, 1975), 190.

48. Kenneth E. Hagin, "The Gifts and Calling of God" (Tulsa: Faith Library, 1986), 12.

49. Ibid., 13.

4. How Should We Interpret the Bible?

1. Gordon D. Fee, "Hermeneutics and Historical Precedent—a Major Problem in Pentecostal Hermeneutics," in Russell P. Spittler, ed., *Perspectives on the New Pentecostalism* (Grand Rapids: Baker, 1976), 119–122.

2. Bernard Ramm, *Protestant Biblical Interpretation* (Grand Rapids: Baker, 1970), 17–18 (emphasis in original).

3. An excellent handbook on inductive Bible Study is Richard Mayhue, *How To Interpret the Bible for Yourself* (Chicago: Moody, 1986). See also Irving L. Jensen, *Independent Bible Study* (Chicago: Moody, 1963).

4. Some of the cults have done this with 1 Corinthians 15:29, which speaks of baptism for the dead. Admittedly this is a difficult verse to understand, and there are at least thirty possible interpretations offered to explain what it is saying. The verse should not be used as a launching point for a new doctrine. Rather, we should understand it in light of Scriptures that are clear.

5. J. I. Packer, *God Has Spoken* (London: Hodder and Stoughton, 1965), 74.

6. Clark H. Pinnock, *Biblical Revelation* (Chicago: Moody, 1971), 216.

7. Charles and Frances Hunter, *Why Should "I" Speak in Tongues?* (Houston: Hunter Ministries, 1976).

8. Ibid., 7–8.

9. Ibid., 13.

10. Oscar Vouga, "Our Gospel Message" (Hazelwood, Mo.: Pentecostal Publishing House, n.d.), 20.

11. Hunter and Hunter, *Why Should "I"?*, 9–10.

12. See endnote 17, p. 381.

13. Hunter and Hunter, *Why Should "I"?*, 10.

14. For a helpful discussion of this issue, see William Hendriksen, *The Gospel of Mark* (Grand Rapids: Baker, 1979), 682–687.

15. This use in no way contradicts the primary interpretation of Matthew 8:17, as aptly indicated by William Hendriksen:

The question might be asked, however, "In what sense is it true that Jesus took the infirmities and diseases upon himself, and thus off the shoulders of those whom he befriended?" Certainly not in the sense that when, for example, he healed a sick person he himself became afflicted with that very sickness. The true answer can be reached only by examining what Scripture itself says about this. Two things stand out: (a) He did so by means of his deep *sympathy* or *compassion*, thus entering fully and personally into the sorrows of those whom he came to rescue. Again and again this fact is mentioned. Jesus healed because he pitied. See the following passages: Matt. 9:36; 14:14; 20:34; Mark 1:41; 5:19; cf. 6:34; Luke 7:13. This note of compassion enters even into his parables (Matt. 18:27; Luke 10:33; 15:20–24, 31, 32). At least just as important is (b) He did it by means of his *vicarious suffering for sin*, which—and this, too, he felt very deeply—was the root of every ill, and dishonored his Father. Thus whenever he saw sickness or distress he experienced Calvary, *his own* Calvary, his own bitter, vicarious suffering throughout his life on earth but especially on the cross. That is why it was *not easy* for him to heal (Mark 2:9; Matthew 9:5). That also accounts for the fact that at the tomb of Lazarus he was deeply moved and agitated in the spirit.

It was in this twofold sense that the Lord took our infirmities upon himself and carried our diseases. Our physical afflictions must never be separated from that without which they never would have occurred, namely our sins. Note how very closely the Isa. 53:4, 5 context connects these two; for verse 4—"Surely, our diseases he has borne. . . ."—is immediately followed by: "He was wounded for our transgressions; he was bruised for our iniquities." [William Hendriksen, *The Gospel of Matthew* (Grand Rapids: Baker, 1973), 400–401.]

5. Does God Do Miracles Today?

1. Providence is God's supernatural, sovereign control over all natural events so that his plan and purposes are achieved.

2. Augustus H. Strong, *Systematic Theology* (Philadelphia: Judson, 1907), 118.

3. Bob Greene, "Jesus on a Tortilla: Making of Miracle?" *Chicago Tribune* (July 11, 1978), B1

4. Joe Diemer, "Jesus' Image Seen in Fire," *The Gloucester County Times* (December 23, 1980), A1.

5. Gregory Jaynes, "In Ohio: A Vision West of Town," *Time* (September 29, 1986), 8–14.

6. "Maybe It's Not the Freezer of Turin, but Arlene Gardner Says She Sees Jesus on Her G.E." *People* (June 29, 1987), 80.

7. C. S. Lewis, *Miracles* (New York: Macmillan, 1960), 5.

8. Kenneth L. Woodward with Frank Gibney, Jr., "Saving Souls—Or a Ministry?" *Newsweek* (July 13, 1987), 52.

9. C. Peter Wagner, *The Third Wave of the Holy Spirit* (Ann Arbor: Vine, 1988), 112.

10. John Wimber, *Power Healing* (San Francisco: Harper & Row, 1987), 38, 62.

11. Norman Geisler, *Signs and Wonders* (Wheaton, Ill.: Tyndale, 1988), 119.

12. Woodward and Gibney, "Saving Souls," 52.

13. For a thorough discussion of this issue, including a look at all the biblical passages that are commonly used to refute this claim, see appendix 2, "Are Miracles Always Successful, Immediate, and Permanent?" in Geisler, 149–155.

14. David du Plessis, *The Spirit Bade Me Go* (Oakland: du Plessis, n.d.), 64.

15. Frederick Dale Bruner, *A Theology of the Holy Spirit* (Grand Rapids: Eerdmans, 1970), 27.

16. du Plessis, *Spirit*, 64.

17. A fourth period of miracles yet to come is described in the book of Revelation.

18. Jack Deere, "God's Power for Today's Church" (tape 1), (Nashville: Belmont Church, n.d.).

19. Deere is so determined to find biblical support for an ongoing ministry of signs and wonders that he misreads Jeremiah 32:20: "[God] has set signs and wonders in the land of Egypt and

even to this day both in Israel and among mankind; and Thou hast made a name for Thyself, as at this day." Deere believes Jeremiah was saying signs and wonders continued in Egypt and Israel after the Exodus and that Jeremiah was acknowledging their existence even in his day. What Jeremiah actually wrote, of course, was that God had made a name for himself through the signs and wonders he performed in Egypt, and that his name was known "even to this day" both in Israel and among the Gentiles. Anyone familiar with Old Testament history knows that the miracles of the Exodus were unique, and the Israelites always recalled them as evidence of their God's greatness.

20. Victor Budgen, *The Charismatics and the Word of God* (Durham, England: Evangelical Press, 1989), 99 (italics in original).

21. B. B. Warfield, *Counterfeit Miracles* (Carlisle, Pa.: Banner of Truth, 1918), 25–27.

22. Budgen, *The Charismatics*, 243–213.,

23. Robert M. Bowman, Jr., Craig S. Hawkins, and Dan Schlesinger, "The Gospel According to Paulk" Part 2, *Christian Research Journal* (Summer 1988), 16.

24. Graham Banister, "Spiritual Warfare: The Signs & Wonders Gospel," *The Briefing* (April 24, 1990), 15.

25. Budgen, *The Charismatics*, 91.

26. Robert M. Bowman, Jr., Craig S. Hawkins, and Dan Schlesinger, "The Gospel According to Paulk" Part 1, *Christian Research Journal* (Winter/Spring 1988), 13.

27. Budgen, *The Charismatics*, 94.

28. See, for example, Charles R. Smith, *Tongues in Biblical Perspective* (Winona Lake, Ind.: BMH, 1972), 60.

29. For a defense of the view that the apostles of Christ were limited to the twelve (and Paul), see J. Norval Geldenhuys, *Supreme Authority* (Grand Rapids: Eerdmans, 1953).

30. Alva McClain, *The Greatness of the Kingdom* (Grand Rapids: Zondervan, 1959), 409.

31. Samuel Green, *A Handbook of Church History* (London: Religious Tract Society, 1913), 22.

32. Cited in Charles and Frances Hunter, *Why Should "I" Speak in Tongues?* (Houston: Hunter Ministries, 1976), 74–75.

33. Russell Bixler, *It Can Happen to Anybody* (Monroeville, Pa.: Whitaker, 1970), 59.

6. *What Is Behind the "Third Wave" and Where Is It Going?*

1. Don Williams, *Signs, Wonders, and the Kingdom of God* (Ann Arbor: Vine, 1989), 19.

2. Ibid.

3. Wagner writes, "The label 'Third Wave' surfaced while I was being interviewed on this subject by *Pastoral Renewal* magazine. So far as I can tell, it has no relationship to the title of Alvin Toffler's best-selling book, *The Third Wave*. It is simply a term which I found convenient at the moment, and which others now have picked up, to describe this new activity of the Holy Spirit." [C. Peter Wagner, *The Third Wave of the Holy Spirit* (Ann Arbor: Vine, 1988), 15.]

4. Ibid., 13.

5. Ibid., 18–19.

6. Ibid., 54.

7. See, for example, John Wimber, *Power Evangelism* (San Francisco: Harper & Row, 1986), 136–51.

8. Even Wimber seems to agree: "I believe Dr. Wagner's 'third wave' is not so much another wave as the next stage of development in the charismatic renewal. Perhaps both Pentecostal and charismatic movements are part of one great movement of the Holy Spirit in this century. In this perspective the similarities between the movements outweigh their differences." [Ibid., 122.]

9. It is difficult to characterize Third Wave doctrine in a way that is fair to all who identify with the movement. I do not mean to imply in this chapter that everyone in the Third Wave is guilty of all the errors I have highlighted. One Third Wave distinctive is the downplaying of doctrinal differences (see endnote 71, pages 378–79). Consequently, dissenting views within the movement often go unexpressed. Peter Wagner, for example, has assured me privately that he does not necessarily share some of the views propounded by other Third Wave leaders.

10. *Power Evangelism*'s Appendix B, "Signs and Wonders in the Twentieth Century" [Ibid., 175–185], furnishes ample evidence of this.

11. Cited by Robert Dean, "Don't Be Caught in the Undertow of the Third Wave," *Biblical Perspectives* (May–June 1990), 1.

12. Wimber, *Power Evangelism*, 39–41.

13. Ibid., 46.

14. Ibid., 17.

15. Cited in Wagner, *The Third Wave*, 35.

16. CT Institute symposium, "The Holy Spirit: God at Work," *Christianity Today* (supplement March 19, 1990), 29–30.

17. Wagner, *The Third Wave*, 96. Why decaying teeth are filled instead of being restored to health is a question Wagner does not address.

18. Andrew Shead, "Spiritual Warfare: The Critical Moment," *The Briefing* (April 24, 1990), 7, summarizes what Wimber told the Sydney Spiritual Warfare Conference: "We are at a crisis point in history. In the next decade, the world will turn to Jesus as never before in any era. Neutrality toward the gospel will be a thing of the past. How will this happen? Through a revitalized church which by its unity, faith and godliness will recover the lost apostolic powers and with them will cure AIDS, emancipate the underprivileged, and impress the gospel upon hundreds of millions of people."

19. Wagner, *The Third Wave*, 123–25. Cf. also Wimber's account of his late friend David Watson in John Wimber, *Power Healing* (San Francisco: Harper & Row, 1987), 147–49. Wimber dedicated *Power Healing* to Watson.

20. Philip Selden, "Spiritual Warfare: Medical Reflections," *The Briefing* (April 24, 1990), 19.

21. Ibid., 20.

22. Wimber, *Power Healing*, 152.

23. Ibid., 174.

24. CT Institute symposium, 33.

25. See, for example, Wimber, *Power Evangelism*, 18–19. See also Wimber's incredible "evangelistic" encounter with a man and his wife on an airplane (ibid., 32–34). Wimber says he saw the word *adultery* written across the man's forehead so he boldly confronted him about that sin. Supposedly the man repented and even led his wife to Christ, though Wimber does not say he ever shared the gospel with the couple.

26. John Wimber, *Power Points* (San Francisco: Harper, 1991), 103–16.

27. Mark Thompson, "Spiritual Warfare: What Happens When I Contradict Myself," *The Briefing* (April 24, 1990), 12 (emphasis added).

28. Wagner, *The Third Wave*, 99.

29. Ibid., 79.

30. Ibid., 92 (italics in original).

31. Wimber, *Power Evangelism*, 45.

32. Ibid., 35.

33. Wimber, *Power Points*, 31–51.

34. Cited in Thompson, "Spiritual Warfare," 11. Deere has elsewhere repeated the charge that those who reject "fresh revelation from heaven" are satanically deceived (Jack Deere, "God's Power for Today's Church" [tape 1], Nashville: Belmont Church, n.d.).

35. For a more complete treatment of the sufficiency of Scripture, see John F. MacArthur, Jr., *Our Sufficiency in Christ* (Dallas: Word, 1991).

36. John Wimber, "Zip to 3,000 in 5 Years," *Christian Life* (October 1982), 20.

37. Tim Stafford, "Testing the Wine from John Wimber's Vineyard," *Christianity Today* (August 8, 1986), 18.

38. Wagner, *The Third Wave*, 87.

39. Walter Chantry, "Powerfully Misleading," *Eternity* (July–August 1987), 29.

40. Wimber, *Power Evangelism*, 88.

41. Ibid, 89 (emphasis in original).

42. John Wimber, "Healing Seminar" (3 tapes) 1981 edition (unpublished), tape 1.

43. Ibid., tape 2.

44. Ibid., 24.

45. Ibid.

46. Wimber, *Power Healing*, 215–23.

47. Ken L. Sarles, "An Appraisal of the Signs and Wonders Movement," *Bibliotheca Sacra* (January–March 1988), 70 (footnote 52).

48. Mike Flynn, "Come, Holy Spirit," Kevin Springer, ed., *Power Encounters* (San Francisco: Harper & Row, 1988), 139–40.

49. Ibid., 140.

50. Ibid., 141.

51. Ibid., 142–43.

52. Ibid., 147–48 (italics in original).

53. Ibid., 147.

54. Wimber, *Power Healing*, 31.

55. Wagner, *The Third Wave*, 22 (emphasis added).

56. Ibid., 73.

57. Ibid.

58. Elliot Miller and Robert M. Bowman, Jr., "The Vineyard," CRI paper (February 1985), 1.

59. Ibid., 2.

60. Ibid. More than six years after the CRI paper made that observation, The Vineyard still has no statement of faith.

61. Cited in Wimber, *Power Evangelism*, 39.

62. Wagner, *The Third Wave*, 18 (emphasis added).

63. Wimber, *Power Points*, xiii.

64. John Goodwin, "Testing the Fruit of the Vineyard," *Media Spotlight Special Report: Latter-Day Prophets* (Redmond, Wash.: Media Spotlight, 1990), 24. Goodwin was a Vineyard pastor for eight years and traveled extensively with John Wimber.

65. John Wimber, "Church Planting Seminar" (5 tapes) 1981 edition (unpublished), tape 2.

66. Wimber, *Power Evangelism*, 157–74.

67. John Wimber, *A Brief Sketch of Signs and Wonders Through the Church Age* (Placentia, Calif.: The Vineyard, 1984), 41–46.

68. Wagner, *The Third Wave*, 38.

69. Ibid., 40. The occult roots of Cho's methodology are documented in "Occult Healing Builds the World's Largest Church," and "East Wind Blows West," *Sword and Trowel* (November 7, 1987), 13–20.

70. Wagner, *The Third Wave*, 127.

71. Wagner, in fact, says one of five identifying factors of the Third Wave is "avoidance of divisiveness at almost any cost."

[C. Peter Wagner, "Third Wave," *Dictionary of Pentecostal and Charismatic Movements* (Grand Rapids: Zondervan, 1988), 844.]

72. John White, foreword in Williams, *Signs, Wonders*, viii.

73. Ibid., ix.

74. Ibid., 10.

75. John Wimber, foreword in Springer, ed., *Power Encounters*, xxxii.

76. Wimber, *Power Evangelism*, 46.

7. How Do Spiritual Gifts Operate?

1. "There is no doubt that charismatic teaching results in a considerable lowering of the credulity threshold of all its adherents. . . . The practice of tongues, the relegation of the understanding to a minor place, the diet of miracles, and the extreme subjectivity of charismatic thinking all combine to produce this effect quickly and inevitably. Once people have been mentally conditioned by a charismatic environment, they are able to take seriously such amazing ideas as Oral Roberts' claim to have seen a vision of Jesus, 900 feet tall. Charismatic practices loosen up the mind in such an unhealthy way that people will believe almost anything." [Peter Masters and John C. Whitcomb, *The Charismatic Phenomenon* (London: The Wakeman Trust, 1988), 67.]

2. Kenneth E. Hagin, *Understanding the Anointing* (Tulsa: Faith Library, 1983), 48.

3. Ibid., 82.

4. Ibid., 82–83.

5. Kenneth E. Hagin, "Why Do People Fall Under the Power?" (Tulsa: Faith Library, 1983), 4–5. Though Hagin refers to newspaper reports that corroborate this story, he does not substantiate his claims with specific citations. I found no reference to this incident in Wayne E. Warner, "Woodworth-Etter, Maria Beulah," Stanley M. Burgess and Gary B. McGee, *Dictionary of Pentecostal and Charismatic Movements* (Grand Rapids: Zondervan, 1988), 900–901. Warner does, however, record that Mrs. Woodworth-Etter "often went into trances . . . during a service, standing like a statue for an hour or more with her hands raised while the service continued. . . . She was dubbed the 'trance evangelist.' Later she was called the 'priestess

of divine healing' and the 'voodoo priestess.' A frequent charge
was that she hypnotized the people. Two doctors in St. Louis
tried to have her committed as insane during a service she
conducted there in 1890." [Ibid., 901.] Hagin's report has all the
earmarks of a legend that has been embellished with the passing
of time.

6. Hagin, "Why Do People Fall?," 9–10.

7. Ibid., 10–11.

8. As Masters and Whitcomb have written, "If Christians
believe the unsubstantiated claims of present-day charismatic
leaders they will believe anything! If they believe the ludicrous
and extravagant yarns of extrovert, spiritually-deluded showmen,
how will they stand against the lying wonders to be unleashed by
the devil during the final apostasy?" [Masters and Whitcomb, *The
Charismatic Phenomenon*, 68.]

9. Carol Wimber, "A Hunger for God," Kevin Springer,
ed., *Power Encounters* (San Francisco: Harper & Row, 1988), 12.

10. Ibid., 13.

11. Ibid.

12. "Whenever the word translated *edify* (meaning—to
build up) is used in the Greek New Testament it is used in a
context which has to do with learning some tangible truth,
dispelling all mystery, superstition or confusion. Edification may
be accomplished by words of instruction, encouragement or
testimony, or even by the power of example, but in every case a
definite and describable lesson is received by those who benefit,
so that their understanding is built up. Beyond all controversy it
means—to build up the understanding. (See Romans 14:19;
15:2; 1 Corinthians 8:1; 10:23; 14:3 and 12; 2 Corinthians 10:8;
12:19; 13:10; Ephesians 4:12–16; 1 Thessalonians 5:11; 1 Timothy 1:4–5)." [Masters and Whitcomb, *The Charismatic Phenomenon*, 50–51.]

13. Norvel Hayes, "What To Do for Healing" (Tulsa:
Harrison, 1981), 13–14.

14. Hagin, *Understanding the Anointing*, 114–115.

15. Ibid., 116–117.

16. "Elderly Woman 'Killed' by a Person 'Slain in the Spirit'
Falling on Her," *National & International Religion Report* (September 21, 1987), 4.

17. Fatality rates in snake-handling churches, however, can be quite high. Snake-handlers are charismatics who interpret to a literal extreme the words of Mark 16:17–18 (see chapter 4). Charles Prince of Canton, North Carolina, was a snake-handling preacher who defied state authorities and held public services where deadly snakes were handled and poison was imbibed. Prince died in August of 1985 after a rattlesnake bit him and he drank strychnine in a church service in Greenville, Tennessee. Nearly every year, the news media carry reports of snake-handling worshipers who die from poison or snakebites. It is a high price to pay for misunderstanding Scripture.

18. Kenneth E. Hagin, "Learning to Flow with the Spirit of God" (Tulsa: Faith Library, 1986), 23.

19. Kenneth Copeland has written, "Believers are not supposed to be led by logic. We are not even to be led by good sense. . . . The ministry of Jesus was never governed by logic or reason." [Kenneth Copeland, "The Force of Faith" (Ft. Worth: Kenneth Copeland Ministries, n. d.), 10.]

20. William Barclay, *The Letters to the Corinthians* (Philadelphia: Westminster, 1975), 3.

21. See, for example, Alexander Hislop, *The Two Babylons* (Neptune, N.J.: Loizeaux, 1959 reprint).

22. S. Angus, *The Mystery-Religions and Christianity* (New York: Dover, 1975), 100–101.

23. Ibid., 101.

24. Ibid.

25. For further information on tongues speaking and ecstasies in the pagan world, see the Encyclopedia Britannica articles "Mystery Religions," "Mysteries," "Religions of Primitive People," and "Gift of Tongues." See also A. R. Hay, "Counterfeit Speaking in Tongues" in *What is Wrong in the Church?* Vol. 2 (Audubon, N.J.: New Testament Missionary Union, n.d.), 15–53.

26. Cf. Melvin L. Hodges, *Spiritual Gifts* (Springfield, Mo.: Gospel Publishing House, 1964), chap. 4.

27. Gnosticism denied the reality of the Lord Jesus Christ as presented in Scripture. For an excellent discussion of gnosticism, see A. F. Walls, "Gnosticism," in Merrill C. Tenney, ed. *The*

Zondervan Pictorial Encyclopedia of the Bible, Vol. 2 (Grand Rapids: Zondervan, 1975), 736ff.

28. Some of these same elements of the gnostic heresy are echoed in certain contemporary charismatic false teachings. (See chapter 12).

8. What Was Happening in the Early Church?

1. Gordon D. Fee, "Hermeneutics and Historical Precedent—a Major Problem in Pentecostal Hermeneutics," in Russell P. Spittler, ed., *Perspectives on the New Pentecostalism* (Grand Rapids: Baker, 1976), 123.

2. Ibid., 120.

3. Frederick Dale Bruner, *A Theology of the Holy Spirit* (Grand Rapids: Eerdmans, 1970), 60.

4. Ibid., 61.

5. John R. W. Stott, *Baptism and Fulness* (Downers Grove, Ill.: InterVarsity, 1976), 28–29.

6. For a presentation of this view, see Howard M. Ervin, *These Are Not Drunken, As Ye Suppose* (Plainfield, N.J.: Logos, 1968), 31–32.

7. The ascension was on Jesus' mind when he prayed in John 17 asking the Father to give him back the glory he had with the Father before the world began (verses 1–5). According to John 7:39, then, the Spirit would not come until after Jesus had ascended to receive that glory.

8. Bruner, *A Theology*, 165.

9. Merrill F. Unger, *New Testament Teaching on Tongues* (Grand Rapids: Kregel, 1971), 17–18.

10. Bruner, *A Theology*, 175–76 (emphasis in original).

11. Unger, *New Testament Teaching*, 36–37.

12. Ibid., 54–55. Unger went on to say: "To reason that Cornelius and his household were 'saved' (despite Acts 11:14) before Peter came to open the gift of the Spirit and common New Testament salvation to them and that therefore what happened to him and his household was a second experience after salvation which is normative for believers today is a serious mistake. It not only violates the time-setting of the event and distorts its meaning in general, but it misinterprets the significance of the manifestation of tongues in connection with it in particular. To

treat Cornelius and his household as 'saved' before Peter came to bring them New Testament salvation (Acts 11:14) is to fail to see what New Testament salvation is or to differentiate it from Old Testament salvation." [Ibid., 55.]

13. Joseph Dillow, *Speaking in Tongues* (Grand Rapids: Zondervan, 1975), 66.

14. Michael Green, *I Believe in the Holy Spirit* (Grand Rapids: Eerdmans, 1975), 208–209.

15. cf. Larry Christenson, *Speaking in Tongues* (Minneapolis: Dimension, 1968), 37.

16. Ibid.

17. Ibid., 38.

18. Charles Hunter, "Receiving the Baptism with the Holy Spirit," *Charisma* (July 1989), 54.

19. Why does Hunter believe he knows this detail about people's spirits? He writes, "I saw my spirit out of my body in 1968 and it was identical to my body; even my face was the same, except that I could see through my spirit like a thin fog or cloud." [Ibid.] Hunter makes the typical charismatic error of drawing doctrine from his experience.

9. *Does God Still Heal?*

1. Hobart Freeman, *An Introduction to the Old Testament Prophets* (Chicago: Moody, 1969).

2. Cf. Chris Lutes, "Leader's Death Gives Rise to Speculation About the Future of His Faith-healing Sect," *Christianity Today* (January 18, 1985), 48.

3. Jamie Buckingham, *Daughter of Destiny* (Plainfield, N.J.: Logos, 1976), 282 ff.

4. Frances Bixler, "Ruth Carter Stapleton," Stanley M. Burgess and Gary B. McGee, *Dictionary of Pentecostal and Charismatic Movements* (Grand Rapids: Zondervan, 1988), 810.

5. John Wimber, *Power Healing* (San Francisco: Harper & Row, 1987), xv.

6. Ibid., xvii.

7. Ibid., xviii.

8. Annette Capps, *Reverse the Curse in Your Body and Emotions* (Broken Arrow, Okla.: Annette Capps Ministries, 1987), 91–92.

9. Kenneth E. Hagin, *Understanding the Anointing* (Tulsa: Faith Library, 1983), 114.

10. B. B. Warfield, *Counterfeit Miracles* (Carlisle, Pa.: Banner of Truth, 1918), 6.

11. For a more thorough discussion of spiritual warfare, see John MacArthur, *Our Sufficiency in Christ* (Dallas: Word, 1991), 211–237.

12. Interestingly, that is precisely the kind of ministry Third Wave prophet Paul Cain has "prophetically" foreseen: "Cain describes his vision of an army of children that will parade down the streets, healing whole hospital wards. He foresees news broadcasts where the anchors report no bad news because everyone is in sports arenas hearing the gospel. Over a billion will be saved. The dead will be raised; limbs will be restored; those with handicaps will jump from their wheelchairs and crutches will be cast aside; and those in the stadiums will go for days without food or water and never notice." [Michael G. Maudlin, "Seers in the Heartland," *Christianity Today* (January 14, 1991), 21.]

13. Although Jamie Buckingham is sympathetic to Kathryn Kuhlman, he recounts an incident in her biography, which reveals, among other things, the degree of control she insisted on having over her meetings:

> A former supper club singer, who had been saved and healed in Miss Kuhlman's ministry, was on stage. As the service was ending she moved to one of the stage mikes so it would pick up her voice and began singing "Alleluia." Kathryn was displeased. To put a stop to it she reached over and touched the woman, praying for her. She went down under the power. Then Kathryn turned, gripped my arm, and pushed me toward the microphone. If there was to be any song leading, she wanted it to come from someone who was familiar, not a stranger.
>
> The people were singing, but listlessly, Kathryn was moving back and forth across the stage, saying all her favorite phrases. They seemed empty. The singer had climbed to her feet and Kathryn touched her again. Nothing happened this time. In a desperate move I heard her say, "The Spirit is all over you, Jamie." She swept toward me, putting her hands on my jaw as I sang. There had been times in the past when,

if she even got close to me, I would go down "under the power." But that day it was just Kathryn—with her hands on my jaw. I loved her too much to disappoint her. With a sigh of resignation, I fell backwards into the arms of the man behind me. As the man helped me to my feet Kathryn moved in again, "I give you glory. I give you praise." But this time I simply could not. I just stepped back when she touched me. She whirled and moved to the other side of the platform. Moments later she disappeared through the stage door. [Buckingham, *Daughter of Destiny*, 280–81.]

14. Raphael Gasson, *The Challenging Counterfeit* (Plainfield, N.J.: Logos, 1966), 109.

15. Kenneth Hagin, "How to Keep Your Healing," (Tulsa: Rhema, 1989), 20–21. Hagin explains why he believes the healing did not take: "*If you don't have enough faith in you to hold on to what you have, the devil is going to steal it away from you.*" [Ibid, emphasis in original.]

16. William Nolen, *Healing: A Doctor in Search of a Miracle* (New York: Random House, 1974), 60, 239.

17. Ibid., 256–57.

18. Ibid., 259.

19. William Nolen, "In Search of a Miracle," *McCall's* (September, 1974), 107.

20. Nolen, *Healing*, 259–260.

21. Nolen, "Search," 107.

22. Ibid., 106.

23. Ibid., 107.

24. James Randi, *The Faith Healers* (Buffalo: Prometheus, 1987).

25. Remember, however, that even Jesus' most vehement critics could not dispute or deny the miracles he had done.

26. Randi, *The Faith Healers*, 287.

27. Ibid., 25.

28. Ibid., 35.

29. For a touching insight into why illness and suffering happen, see Margaret Clarkson, *Grace Grows Best in Winter* (Grand Rapids: Zondervan, 1972).

10. Is the Gift of Tongues for Today?

1. Charles Hunter, "Receiving the Baptism with the Holy Spirit," *Charisma* (July 1989), 54.

2. Ibid.

3. Ibid.

4. Arthur L. Johnson, *Faith Misguided: Exposing the Dangers of Mysticism* (Chicago: Moody, 1988), 113.

5. John L. Sherrill, *They Speak with Other Tongues* (Old Tappan, N.J.: Spire, 1964), 83.

6. "Speaking in Tongues—Believers Relish the Experience," *Los Angeles Times* (September 19, 1987), B2.

7. Ibid.

8. George E. Gardiner, *The Corinthian Catastrophe* (Grand Rapids: Kregel, 1974), 55.

9. Wayne Robinson, *I Once Spoke in Tongues* (Atlanta: Forum House, 1973), 9–10.

10. Ben Byrd, *The Truth About Speaking in Tongues*, (Columbus, Ga.: Brentwood, 1988), 49 (emphasis in original).

11. Some charismatics point to Romans 8:26–27 as another New Testament reference to tongues: "We do not know how to pray as we should, but the Spirit Himself intercedes for us with groanings too deep for words; and He who searches the hearts knows what the mind of the Spirit is, because He intercedes for the saints according to the will of God."

Regarding that passage Kenneth Hagin has written: "P. C. Nelson, a scholar of the Greek, said that the Greek literally reads here, 'The Holy Ghost maketh intercession for us in groanings that cannot be uttered in articulate speech.' Articulate speech means our regular kind of speech. He went on to point out how the Greek stresses that this not only includes groanings escaping our lips in prayer, but also praying in other tongues." [Kenneth E. Hagin, "Why Tongues" (Tulsa: Faith Library, 1975), 19.]

That is a tortured interpretation of the passage and an unscholarly handling of the Greek text. Nothing in the Greek suggests the idea of praying in tongues; Nelson and Hagin are reading it in. Even if inarticulate speech could be read into this term, that does not correspond to the New Testament description of the gift of tongues. "Groanings," however, *is* accurate. The word is *stenazō*. A standard New Testament dictionary says, "Paul uses the term exclusively in the sense of sighing in the sense of longing for something." [Thomas McComiskey, "*Stenazō*," Colin Brown, ed. *Dictionary of New Testament Theology*, Vol. 2 (Grand Rapids: Zondervan, 1976), 425.]

12. For a detailed exposition of 1 Corinthians 12–14 see John F. MacArthur, Jr., *The MacArthur New Testament Commentary: 1 Corinthians* (Chicago: Moody, 1984).

13. Paul Van Gorder offered this list of limitations on the use of tongues in the church from 1 Corinthians 14:

● Tongues were for a sign to unbelievers (verse 22).

● Tongues were to be used for the edification of the church (verse 26).

● No more than three people in the assembly were to speak in tongues during a service, and then, each in his turn (verse 27).

● There was to be no speaking in tongues unless they should be interpreted (verse 28).

● Any confusion or disorder in the assembly was an indication of something that did not originate from God (verse 33).

● In the apostolic church, women were to keep silent and not to speak in tongues (verse 34).

● To recognize these regulations as the commandments of the Lord was imperative (verse 37).

● Though not forbidding tongues in the apostolic assembly, the predominant command was "covet to prophesy" (verse 39).

Most contemporary charismatics violate every one of the apostle's guidelines. [Paul R. Van Gorder, "Charismatic Confusion" (Grand Rapids: Radio Bible Class, 1972), 33.]

14. The Greek verbs in 1 Corinthians 13:2–3 are subjunctive. The subjunctive mood is used to indicate the imaginary or a situation contrary to fact. A standard Greek grammar explains, "While the indicative assumes reality, the subjunctive assumes unreality. It is the first step away from that which is actual in the direction of that which is only conceivable" [H. E. Dana and J. R. Mantey, *A Manual Grammar of the Greek New Testament* (Toronto: Macmillan, 1957), 170.]

15. *Glōssa* always appears in the plural form throughout Acts, indicating multiple languages. In 1 Corinthians 14, however, Paul employed both the singular and plural forms. One

possible explanation is that when he used the singular "tongue" in verses 2, 4, 13, 14, and 19, he was referring to the counterfeit pagan babbling that some of the Corinthian believers were evidently using instead of the true gift of languages. Meaningless, ecstatic speech was fundamentally all the same, so the plural form was unnecessary. When Paul was clearly referring to the authentic gift of languages, however, he used the plural "tongues." The only exception is 1 Corinthians 14:27, where Paul describes one man speaking one language, so the singular 'tongue' was necessary there, too.

The KJV supplies the word *unknown* only where the form of *glōssa* is singular. If this differentiation between the singular "tongue" and the plural "tongues" signifies the difference between a real language and mere gibberish, perhaps the King James translators were correct to supply the term after all. Thus understood, the "unknown tongue" is not a manifestation of the true spiritual gift but a pagan corruption.

16. William J. Samarin, *Tongues of Men and Angels* (New York: Macmillan, 1972), xii, 227. For an expansion of that claim, see pp. 103–28.

17. Because of the absence of any definite article in the Greek text, it is also possible to translate this verse as, "One who speaks in a tongue does not speak to men but to *a god*" —referring to a pagan deity. Either way, 1 Corinthians 14:2 is condemnation, not commendation. The context demands that.

18. In 1 Corinthians 8:10, for example, the same Greek word is used to speak of "strengthening" someone's conscience to do evil.

19. Albert Barnes, *Notes on the New Testament: 1 Corinthians* (Grand Rapids: Baker, 1975 reprint), 240. Charismatic commentator Gordon Fee acknowledges the legitimacy of the indicative view [Gordon D. Fee, *The First Epistle to the Corinthians* (Grand Rapids: Eerdmans, 1987), 624.] Fee also gives the following list of scholars who support that view: Arnold Bittling-er, *Gifts and Graces, A Commentary on 1 Corinthians 12–14* (Grand Rapids: Eerdmans, 1967), 73–75; Ralph P. Martin, *The Spirit and the Congregation: Studies in 1 Corinthians 12–15* (Grand Rapids: Eerdmans, 1984), 34–35; D.L. Baker, "The Interpreta-tion of 1 Corinthians 12–14," *Evangelical Quarterly* 46 (1974):

226–27; G. Iber, "Zum Verständnis von I Cor. 12:31," *Zeitschrift für die neutestamentliche Wissenschaft* 54 (1963): 42–52; M.A. Chevallier, *Esprit de Dieu, Paroles d'Hommes* (Neuchâtel, 1963): 158–63.

20. The passage does not say *when* tongues were to cease. Some commentators believe verse 10 sets the timing: "When the perfect comes, the partial will be done away." Many suggestions have been made as to the meaning of "the perfect." Some believe it is the complete New Testament; thus they conclude this passage is saying that tongues would cease when the canon was closed. Various others say the perfect thing is the maturing of the church, the rapture, or the second coming. But it seems that the perfect thing Paul has in mind must be the eternal state—"face to face" in verse 12 can best be explained as being with God in the new heavens and new earth. It is only in glory that we will know as we are known (v. 12).

The language of the passage puts tongues in a category apart from prophecy and knowledge. Verse 8 says prophecy and knowledge will be "done away" (Gk., *katargeō*), but tongues "will cease" (*pauō*, "stop"). *Katargeō* appears as a passive verb, meaning that the subject of the sentence receives the action: Prophecy and knowledge will be "done away" by "the perfect." *Pauō*, however, appears in the Greek middle voice, which here seems to signify a reflexive action: The gift of tongues will "stop itself." *When* is not stipulated, but they won't be around when the perfect thing arrives. History suggests that tongues ceased shortly after Paul wrote this epistle, as we shall see in the following pages.

Incidentally, knowledge and prophecy need not be understood in this context exclusively as miraculous or revelatory gifts. The non-revelatory gifts of knowledge (the ability to grasp the meaning of God's revelation) and prophecy (the ability to proclaim truth powerfully) continue today and will not pass away until the ultimate perfection of the eternal state causes them to be "done away."

21. O. Palmer Robertson, "Tongues: Sign of Covenantal Curse and Blessing," *The Westminster Theological Journal* 38 (Fall 1975–Spring 1976): 53.

22. For helpful discussions of the historical evidence for the cessation of tongues, see Robert G. Gromacki, *The Modern*

Tongues Movement (Phillipsburg, N.J.: Presbyterian and Reformed, 1967); Victor Budgen, *The Charismatics and the Word of God* (Durham: Evangelical Press, 1989); Thomas R. Edgar, *Miraculous Gifts: Are They for Today?* (Neptune, N.J.: Loizeaux Brothers, 1983).

23. Cleon L. Rogers, "The Gift of Tongues in the Post-Apostolic Church," *Bibliotheca Sacra* 122 (April–June 1965): 134.

24. Chrysostom, "Homilies in First Corinthians," Philip Schaff, ed., *The Nicene and Post-Nicene Fathers of the Christian Church*, Vol. 12 (Grand Rapids: Eerdmans, 1956), 168.

25. Augustine, "Ten Homilies on the First Epistle of John," Philip Schaff, ed., *The Nicene and Post-Nicene Fathers of the Christian Church*, Vol. 7 (Grand Rapids: Eerdmans, 1956), 497 (emphasis added).

26. Augustine, "Lectures or Tractates on the Gospel According to St. John," Ibid., 195.

27. Thomas R. Edgar, "The Cessation of the Sign Gifts," *Bibliotheca Sacra* (October–December 1988), 374.

28. John Wimber, for example, takes this position. See John Wimber, *A Brief Sketch of Signs and Wonders Through the Church Age* (Placentia, Calif.: The Vineyard, 1984), 41–46.

29. George N. H. Peters, *The Theocratic Kingdom* (Grand Rapids: Kregel, 1972), 66 (emphasis in original).

30. The literal Hebrew meaning is "in the first"—perhaps meaning that both rains will be poured out in the first month, guaranteeing an abundant harvest.

31. Edgar, "The Cessation of the Sign Gifts," 375.

32. Sherrill, *They Speak with Other Tongues*, 83.

33. Ibid.

34. Some Charismatics *do* claim they can speak human languages (or that they know others who can), but these claims are nearly always based on little more than hearsay or speculation. Pat Boone, for example, says his wife, Shirley, spoke in Latin when she first received the gift. [Pat Boone, "Baptized in the Holy Spirit," *Charisma* (August 1988), 58.] No tape or independent corroboration of this claim is offered, however, nor have Mrs. Boone's more recent "tongues" been in Latin. It would be helpful if tongues-speakers who believe their languages are

translatable human dialects would allow those claims to be tested under controlled conditions.

35. Samarin, *Tongues of Men and Angels*, 112–13.

36. Edgar, "The Cessation of the Sign Gifts," 372.

37. Ben Byrd, *One Pastor's Journey Into and Out of the Charismatic and Faith Movements*, (Columbus, Ga.: Brentwood, 1987), 45 (emphasis in original).

38. Samarin, *Tongues of Men and Angels*, 254–55. See also Joseph Dillow, *Speaking in Tongues* (Grand Rapids: Zondervan, 1975), 172–75.

39. Hunter, "Receiving the Baptism," 54.

40. John Kildahl, *The Psychology of Speaking in Tongues* (New York: Harper and Row, 1972), 74.

41. Ibid.

42. Nicholas P. Spanos, Wendy P. Cross, Mark Lepage, and Marjorie Coristine, "Glossolalia as Learned Behavior: An Experimental Demonstration," *Journal of Abnormal Psychology* 95:1 (1987), 21–23.

43. Kildahl, *The Psychology of Speaking in Tongues*, 55.

44. Ibid., 54.

45. Ibid., 38–56.

46. Samarin, *Tongues of Men and Angels*, 228.

47. E. Mansell Pattison, "Speaking in Tongues and About Tongues," *Christian Standard* (February 15, 1964), 2.

48. Charles R. Smith, *Tongues in Biblical Perspective* (Winona Lake, Ind.: BMH, 1972), chap. 5.

11. What Is True Spirituality?

1. Linda Fehl, "A Personal Letter from Linda Fehl" (advertisement) *Charisma* (December 1990), 87.

2. Ibid. (emphasis in original).

3. "Subliminal Deliverance" (advertisement) *Charisma* (November 1990), 145.

4. Ibid.

5. Ibid. (emphasis in original).

6. Walter L. Walker, "What About Subliminal Tapes?" *Charisma* (October 1990), 128.

7. Ibid., 132.

8. Ibid.

9. Norvel Hayes, "From Heaven Come God's Weapons for the Church" (Tulsa: Harrison, 1979), 15–16.

10. Melvin L. Hodges, *Spiritual Gifts* (Springfield, Mo.: Gospel Publishing House, 1964), 16.

11. In Romans 8, Paul makes a clear differentiation: to be natural (carnal) is to be unregenerate, unsaved, to not know God. To be spiritual means to possess the Holy Spirit through belief in Jesus Christ as Lord and Savior.

12. Charles R. Smith points out that "The doctrines of free love and 'spiritual marriages' have too often appeared in association with tongues. Perversion of the Biblical teaching relating to sex and marriage can be seen in the Mormons and the Shakers. Aimee Semple McPherson was not the only tongues leader to receive a 'revelation' that her marriage was 'not in the Lord' and that she should enter another union. One of the serious problems of the Pentecostal movement has been the fact that many of its leaders have fallen into immorality. One well-known Pentecostal preacher, a woman widowed for three years, professed to be 'with child of the Holy Ghost.' Parham, 'father of the modern Pentecostal movement,' was arrested for the grossest of immoralities." [Charles R. Smith, *Tongues in Biblical Perspective* (Winona Lake, Ind.: BMH, 1972), 23.]

13. Walter J. Chantry, *Signs of the Apostles* (Edinburgh: Banner of Truth, 1973), 99–101.

14. Ibid., 100.

12. Does God Promise Health and Wealth?

1. Kenneth E. Hagin, "How to Write Your Own Ticket with God" (Tulsa: Faith Library, 1979).

2. Kenneth E. Hagin, "Godliness Is Profitable" (Tulsa: Faith Library, 1982).

3. Kenneth Copeland, *The Laws of Prosperity* (Fort Worth: Kenneth Copeland, 1974).

4. Charles Capps, "God's Creative Power Will Work for You" (Tulsa: Harrison, 1976).

5. Charles Capps, *Releasing the Ability of God Through Prayer* (Tulsa: Harrison, 1978).

6. Oral Roberts, *God's Formula for Success and Prosperity* (Tulsa: Healing Waters, 1955).

7. Gordon Lindsay, *God's Master Key to Prosperity* (Dallas: Christ for the Nations, 1960).

8. Jerry Savelle, *Living in Divine Prosperity* (Tulsa: Harrison, 1982).

9. Most Word Faith advocates would affirm the personality of the Holy Spirit. In effect, however, their teachings depersonalize him by consistently speaking of him as a power to be drawn upon rather than understanding the biblical truth that it is *we* who are to be *his* instruments.

10. Cf. Hagin, "How to Write Your Own Ticket," 3, where Hagin sees a vision of Jesus, and says to him, "Dear Lord, I have two sermons I preach concerning the woman who touched Your clothes and was healed when You were on earth. *I received both of these sermons by inspiration*" (emphasis added). Later, Hagin quotes what Jesus told him in reply: "You are correct. My Spirit, the Holy Spirit, has endeavored to get another sermon into your spirit, but you have failed to pick it up. While I am here, I will do what you ask. I will give you that sermon outline. Now get your pencil and paper and write it down." [Ibid., 4.] Hagin claims to have received numerous visions, as well as eight personal visitations from Jesus. Hagin has written, "The Lord Himself taught me about prosperity. I never read about it in a book. I got it directly from heaven." [Kenneth E. Hagin, "How God Taught Me About Prosperity" (Tulsa: Faith Library, 1985), 1.] That claim, as we shall see, is a lie (see footnote 81 of this chapter).

11. Kenneth E. Hagin develops this point in his book *The Authority of the Believer* (Tulsa: Faith Library, 1979), long sections of which were taken verbatim from others' writings (see footnote 81 of this chapter).

12. Robert Tilton, *God's Miracle Plan for Man* (Dallas: Robert Tilton, 1987), 36.

13. Charles Capps, *The Tongue: A Creative Force* (Tulsa: Harrison, 1976), 78.

14. Ibid., 79.

15. Ibid., 79–80 (emphasis in original).

16. Ibid., 136–137 (emphasis in original).

17. Norvel Hayes, "Prostitute Faith" (Tulsa: Harrison, 1988), 22–23.

18. Norvel Hayes, *Putting Your Angels to Work* (Tulsa: Harrison, 1989), 8.

19. Ibid.

20. Kenneth Copeland, "The Force of Love" (Fort Worth: Kenneth Copeland Ministries, n.d.), cassette tape #02-0028.

21. Ibid.

22. Ibid.

23. Kenneth Copeland, "The Believer's Voice of Victory" broadcast July 9, 1987.

24. Ibid.

25. "Praise the Lord" broadcast on the Trinity Broadcasting Network (July 7, 1986).

26. "Praise the Lord" broadcast on the Trinity Broadcasting Network (November 15, 1990).

27. Charles Capps, "Seedtime and Harvest" (Tulsa: Harrison, 1986), 7 (emphasis in original).

28. Earl Paulk, *Satan Unmasked* (Atlanta: Kingdom, 1985), 97.

29. Robert Tilton, *God's Laws of Success* (Dallas: Word of Faith, 1983), 170.

30. "Praise the Lord" broadcast on the Trinity Broadcasting Network (January 6, 1988).

31. "Praise-a-thon" broadcast on the Trinity Broadcasting Network (November 12, 1990).

32. Benny Hinn, "Our Position in Christ" (Orlando: Orlando Christian Center, 1990), cassette tape #A031190.

33. Kenneth E. Hagin, "As Christ Is—So are We" (Tulsa: Rhema), cassette tape #44H06.

34. Walter Martin, "Ye Shall Be As Gods," Michael A. Horton, ed. *The Agony of Deceit* (Chicago: Moody, 1990), 97.

35. Kenneth Copeland, *Believer's Voice of Victory* Magazine (August 8, 1988), 8.

36. Ibid. The idea that Jesus emptied himself of his deity during his incarnation (known as kenotic theology) is a heretical teaching promoted by nineteenth-century liberal theology. Conservative theology has always maintained that Christ's self-emptying (cf. Phil. 2:7) means that he laid aside the independent use of his divine attributes, not that he ceased to be God. His immutability makes that impossible: "Jesus Christ is the same

yesterday and today, yes and forever" (Heb. 13:8; cf. Mal. 3:6; James 1:17).

37. Kenneth Copeland, "Substitution and Identification" (Fort Worth: Kenneth Copeland Ministries, n.d.), cassette tape #00-0202.

38. Christ alone could atone for our sins (1 Peter 1:18–19). He is the *only* begotten Son of God (John 1:14; 3:16). One of the key messages of the New Testament book of Hebrews is the utter supremacy of Christ and the uniqueness of his priesthood (7:22–28; 9:11–15, 26–28; 12:2).

39. Kenneth Copeland, "What Happened from the Cross to the Throne?" (Fort Worth: Kenneth Copeland Ministries, n.d.), cassette tape #02-0017.

40. Ibid.

41. Frederick K. C. Price, *The Ever Increasing Faith Messenger* (June 1980), 7.

42. Kenneth Copeland, "What Satan Saw on the Day of Pentecost" (Fort Worth: Kenneth Copeland Ministries, n.d.), cassette tape #02-0022.

43. Kenneth Copeland, *Voice of Victory* (September 1991), 3.

44. Ibid.

45. Kenneth E. Hagin, "How Jesus Obtained His Name" (Tulsa: Rhema), cassette tape #44H01.

46. Pat Robertson, *Answers to 200 of Life's Most Probing Questions* (Nashville: Nelson, 1984), 271.

47. Capps, *The Tongue*, 8–9.

48. Hagin, "How to Write Your Own Ticket," 8 (emphasis in original). Hagin's supposedly inspired four-point sermon is: Say it, do it, receive it, and tell it. Hagin claims Jesus told him, "If anybody, anywhere, will take these four steps or put these four principles into operation, he will always have whatever he wants from Me or God the Father." [Ibid., 5.]

49. Ibid., 10. Hagin evidently misses a key passage in Mark 9, where Jesus healed a boy whose father had prayed, "I do believe; help me overcome my unbelief" (v. 24). Hagin and other Word Faith teachers would no doubt label such a prayer "negative confession." But Jesus honored it as the honest expression of that man's heart.

50. Capps, *The Tongue*, 91 (emphasis in original).

51. This is a clearly superstitious fear, closely akin to the Hindu idea of "karma" or the pagan view of "bad luck."

52. Kenneth E. Hagin, "Words" (Tulsa: Faith Library, 1979), 20–21 (emphasis added).

53. Bruce Barron, *The Health and Wealth Gospel* (Downers Grove: InterVarsity, 1987), 128.

54. Ibid., 131.

55. Kenneth E. Hagin, "Praying to Get Results" (Tulsa: Faith Library, 1983), 5–6.

56. Ibid., 5. Hagin claims the woman had begun to rise supernaturally out of the wheel chair and into the air. Fearful, she pulled herself back into the chair. That was when Hagin castigated her.

57. Kenneth E. Hagin, "Having Faith in Your Faith" (Tulsa: Faith Library, 1980), 4.

58. Ibid., 4–5 (emphasis added).

59. In a chapter titled "Pleading the Blood," Hagin tells of how he once overheard a missionary rebuke a scorpion bite with the words, "In the Name of Jesus, I plead the blood against this!" He writes, "So I picked up that phrase, 'In the Name of Jesus, I plead the blood'. . . and all through these years I've always pled the blood in the Name of Jesus. *There's power in the blood*, glory to God! It's worked for me, and it'll work for you, too." [Kenneth E. Hagin, "The Precious Blood of Jesus" (Tulsa: Faith Library, 1984), 30–31.] The notion that repeating a phrase can work miracles is pure superstition (cf. Matt. 6:7).

60. Kenneth E. Hagin, "You Can Have What You Say" (Tulsa: Faith Library, 1979), 14 (emphasis in original).

61. "Praise the Lord" broadcast on the Trinity Broadcasting Network (September 15, 1988).

62. Ibid.

63. "Believer's Voice of Victory" broadcast on the Trinity Broadcasting Network (January 20, 1991).

64. "Success in Life" broadcast on the Trinity Broadcasting Network (December 2, 1990).

65. "Success in Life" broadcast on the Trinity Broadcasting Network (December 5, 1990).

66. Ibid.

67. Ibid.

68. "Success in Life" broadcast on the Trinity Broadcasting Network (February 14, 1991).

69. Kenneth L. Woodward and Frank Gibney, Jr., "Saving Souls—Or a Ministry?" *Newsweek* (July 13, 1987), 53.

70. Ibid.

71. Tilton berates listeners who do not pay their vows to his ministry. One of the biggest problems his ministry faces is how to deal with people who make vows, then cannot pay when the promised results fail to materialize. [Cf. "Success in Life" (April 5, 1991).]

72. "Praise the Lord" broadcast on the Trinity Broadcasting Network (September 21, 1990).

73. Kenneth E. Hagin, "How Jesus Obtained His Name" (Tulsa: Rhema), cassette tape #44H01.

74. Kenneth E. Hagin, *Exceedingly Growing Faith* (Tulsa: Faith Library, 1983), 10.

75. God allegedly once told Charles Capps that "you are under an attack of the evil one and I can't do anything about it. You have bound me by the words of your own mouth" (Capps, *The Tongue*, 67).

76. It would appear that many of the heroes of faith named in Hebrews 11 did not really have strong faith after all—if the Word Faith definition of faith is valid. Certainly those who experienced scourgings, chains, and imprisonment (v. 36); who went about in shabby clothes, destitute, afflicted and ill-treated (v. 37); who lived in the deserts, mountains, caves and holes in the ground (v. 38) must not have been very adept at creating their own reality. Yet they gained approval from God for their faith (v. 39). That is because Hebrews 11 teaches that real faith has to do with our obeying God, not his giving us material things.

77. Capps, *The Tongue*, 27 (emphasis in original).

78. Ibid., 43.

79. D. R. McConnell, *A Different Gospel* (Peabody, Mass.: Hendrickson, 1988).

80. Ibid., 3–14.

81. Ibid., 8–12. McConnell also states that Hagin plagiarized the writings of a Christian and Missionary Alliance minister named John A. MacMillan. W. R. Scott gives solid evidence

that these accusations are true as well. Specifically, it seems incontrovertible that Hagin lifted at least three-quarters of his book *The Authority of the Believer* verbatim from MacMillan's magazine article of the same title. [W. R. Scott, "What's Wrong with the Faith Movement?" (unpublished paper, n. d.), Appendix B, 2–10.] Scott also documents Hagin's plagiarism of Finis Jennings Dake, *God's Plan for Man* (Lawrenceville, Ga.: Dake Bible Sales, 1949). [Ibid., Appendix A, 1–2.] Dake was a well-known Assembly of God pastor and author of a Pentecostal study Bible.

Hagin's pattern of plagiarism would seem to cast doubt on his credibility. It certainly invalidates his many claims that he received these teachings by divine inspiration.

82. McConnell, *A Different Gospel*, 15–56.
83. Ibid., 57–76.

Epilogue

1. These include D. R. McConnell, *A Different Gospel* (Peabody, Mass.: Hendrickson, 1988), which I recommended in chapter 12; Bruce Barron, *The Health and Wealth Gospel* (Downers Grove: InterVarsity, 1987); and Gordon Fee, "The Disease of the Health and Wealth Gospels" (Costa Mesa: Word for Today, 1979). Raul Ries's charismatic ministry magazine has also published an excellent and very thorough article exposing the errors of the Word Faith movement [Tom Fontanes, "Positive Confession," *Passport* (January–February 1988), 11–17]. Albert James Dager's "Media Spotlight" newsletter often contains excellent analyses of charismatic tangents, though Dager is sympathetic to basic charismatic teaching. Information about many of the tapes I quoted from in chapter 12 was supplied by the Christian Research Institute (CRI), San Juan Capistrano, an organization that is also predominately charismatic. CRI has produced reams of material and numerous tapes exposing the Word Faith movement. Their biblical discernment and careful scholarship have been superb.

2. Chuck Smith, *Charisma vs. Charismania* (Eugene, Ore.: Harvest House, 1983).

3. John Goodwin, "Testing the Fruit of the Vineyard," *Media Spotlight, Special Report: Latter-Day Prophets* (Redmond,

Wash.: Media Spotlight, 1990), 24–30. Goodwin and his staff were extremely helpful in locating primary sources for some of the tapes I quoted in chapter 6.

4. In some cases, however, the trend toward ecumenism is not unwitting, but carefully calculated. David du Plessis, for example, was quite candid about his enthusiasm for the ecumenical movement. Many other charismatic leaders, including John Wimber, have taken up the mantle of ecumenical advocacy. I agree with the assessment of Masters and Whitcomb:

> The overwhelming majority of charismatic leaders still hope for a world-wide ecumenical church under the leadership of the Pope. The charismatic movement has certainly spread extensively within the Roman Catholic Church. However, while vast numbers of priests now employ charismatic jargon and methods of worship, their Catholic doctrines remain totally unchanged. [Peter Masters and John C. Whitcomb, *The Charismatic Phenomenon* (London: The Wakeman Trust, 1988), 9–10.]

5. Thomas R. Edgar, "The Cessation of the Sign Gifts," *Bibliotheca Sacra* (October–December 1988), 385.

6. Edward D. O'Connor, "Gentle Revolution: The Catholic Pentecostal Movement in Retrospect," *Voice* (September 1971).

7. Gordon H. Clark, *First Corinthians: A Contemporary Commentary* (Nutley, N.J.: Presbyterian & Reformed, 1975), 225.

8. One extreme charismatic group in Taiwan, The New Testament Church, headed by self-styled prophet Elijah Hong, have cleared a jungle on Shuang Lien Mountain in central Taiwan, renamed it Mt. Zion, and are looking for the Lord to reappear there soon. The group's adherents, numbering in the thousands, proselytize all over Asia, and the sect's influence is swelling. ["Alleluia!," *Asiaweek* (October 6, 1989), 46–51.]

Subject Index

Scripture Index